PRAISE FOR
*A LAND AS GOD MADE IT:*
*JAMESTOWN AND THE BIRTH OF AMERICA*

"Horn, who heads the library at the Colonial Williamsburg Foundation, offers a history that will put Plymouth in its place."
—*Publishers Weekly*

"[*A Land As God Made It* features] lots of dirt on the struggles of the Jamestown settlers to milk the New World for gold that wasn't there, plus some interesting what-ifs about the Spanish attack that almost was."
—Mark St. John Erickson, *Daily Press*

"A meticulous history. . . . Possessing Jamestown's inherent drama."
—*Booklist*

"Horn's writing is accessible and often dramatic. He adds new twists and depths to familiar stories, such as the fate of the Lost Colony or the relationship between John Smith and Pocahontas."
—*Virginia Gazette*

"Horn demonstrates that the Jamestown experience, for good and ill, played a formative role in defining America."        —*Library Journal*

"[Horn] presents the story of early Virginia almost as though it were the plot of a colorful novel. . . . Horn's astute history is a story of courage and cowardice, wisdom and stupidity, cross-cultural friendship and racist brutality, religious greatness and religious hypocrisy, and all the qualities that make America what it is today."
—*Virginian-Pilot*

"[A] splendid and skillful reconsideration of Jamestown's role in American history."        —*The Oklahoman*

# A Land As God Made It

POWHATAN

...eld this state & fashion when Capt. Smith
was delivered to him prisoner
1605

POWHATAN

MAR
GOAGS

CHE

WONS

Cape Henry

Cape Charles

Smyths Ile

Washeborne
C.

THE

VIRGINIAN SEA

34

38

# A Land As God Made It

---

## Jamestown and the Birth of America

*James Horn*

BASIC
BOOKS

A Member of the Perseus Books Group
New York

*For Sally, Ben, and Lizzie*
*with love*

Hardcover edition first published in 2005 by Basic Books
A Member of the Perseus Books Group
Paperback edition first published in 2006 by Basic Books

Books published by Basic Books are available at special discounts for bulk purchases in the
United States by corporations, institutions, and other organizations. For more information,
please contact the Special Markets Department at the Perseus Books Group, 11 Cambridge
Center, Cambridge, MA 02142, or special.markets@perseusbooks.com.

The Library of Congress has catalogued the hardcover as follows:

Horn, James P. P.
   A land as God made it : Jamestown and the birth of America / James Horn.
      p. cm.
   Includes bibliographical references and index.
   ISBN-13: 978-0-465-03094-1 (hc : alk. paper)
   ISBN-10: 0-465-03094-7 (hc : alk. paper)  1. Jamestown (Va.)—History.  2. Virginia—
History—Colonial period, ca. 1600–1775.  I. Title.

F234.J3H66 2005
975.5'4251—dc22

                                                                              2005013054

Paperback: ISBN-13: 978-0-465-03095-8; ISBN-10: 0-465-03095-5

10 9 8 7

Reveal to us the courts of China and the unknown straits which still lie hid: throw back the portals which have been closed since the world's beginning at the dawn of time. There yet remain for you new lands, ample realms, unknown peoples; they wait yet, I say, to be discovered.

— *Richard Hakluyt, the younger 1587*


After good deliberation, hee [Wahunsonacock] began to describe mee the Countreys beyonde the Falles, with many of the rest. . . Nations upon the toppe of the heade of the Bay. . . the Southerly Countries also. . . [and] a countrie called Anone, where they have an abundance of Brasse, and houses walled as ours. I requited his discourse, seeing what pride hee had in his great and spacious Dominions, seeing that all hee knewe were under his Territories.

— *Captain John Smith, 1608*

# Contents

*Acknowledgments*  XI

Prologue: Before Jamestown  I

1  Two Worlds  II

2  The "Pearl and the Gold"  39

3  Smith's Epic  73

4  Innocence Lost  99

5  Virginea Britannia  131

6  War and Retribution  157

7  Redeeming Pocahontas  193

8  For "The Good of the Plantation"  225

9  "Fatall Possession"  249

Epilogue: After the Fall  279

*Illustration Credits*  291
*Notes*  293
*Index*  323

# Acknowledgments

I should like to thank all the friends and colleagues who have helped me with this book over the years. Early versions of the argument were presented at the University of Sussex, the Henry E. Huntington Library, and Jamestown, and I am grateful for comments by participants. Thanks to Warren M. Billings, Karen Kupperman, Timothy Breen, Alan Taylor, Peter Onuf, and Martha McCartney, among others, for many stimulating discussions. I have also benefited enormously from conversations with William M. Kelso and Beverly Straube of the Jamestown Rediscovery project, who have generously shared their expert knowledge. Thanks to all those colleagues on several 2007 committees (on which I have the privilege to serve) for stimulating my thinking about why Jamestown matters.

At the Colonial Williamsburg Foundation, I am most grateful to Colin Campbell and Cary Carson for their support and encouragement. Thanks to my colleagues at the John D. Rockefeller, Jr. Library for all the many ways they have helped, especially Inge Flester, Gail Greve, George Yetter, and Don Stueland. I should like to thank also the staffs of the British Library, the Alderman Library at the University of Virginia, and the Swem Library at the College of William and Mary. I am grateful to Marianne Martin for providing expert help tracking down illustrations, and to Rebecca L. Wrenn, of the Omohundro Institute of Early American History and Culture, for drawing the maps.

Don Lamm provided excellent advice at an early stage of the manuscript and helped me sharpen the writing. Lara Heimert, Executive Editor at Basic Books, has done a wonderful job of editing. I am especially grateful for her tireless efforts to encourage me to shorten unwieldy paragraphs and sentences (those that remain are wholly my responsibility). I am grateful also to David Shoemaker, Kay Mariea, Jennifer Blakebrough-Raeburn, and other staff at Basic who have brought the book to completion.

I cannot adequately express my gratitude to my family for their patience during the long process of research and writing, and particularly the last few months when all too often I disappeared into my study. The book is dedicated to them: my wife, Sally, and Ben and Lizzie, with all my love.

# Prologue

## *Before Jamestown*

*L*ONG BEFORE JAMESTOWN, in the summer of 1561, a Spanish caravel buffeted by storms somewhere off the coast of present day South Carolina was driven several hundred miles to the north. As the winds dropped and the rain cleared, the crew saw an immense bay; so wide that had it not been for a faint trace of land on the horizon they might have been forgiven for thinking they had been blown back out to sea.

Crossing the bay's gray-green waters to the southern shore, the ship proceeded cautiously inland, where the Spaniards found "many fine harbors," fertile meadows, fresh running springs, and everywhere an abundance of trees—pines, hickories, oaks, cedars, cypresses, poplars, black walnuts, and maples—growing in wild profusion to the water's edge. They anchored in a large river, possibly the Chickahominy, to replenish supplies and make repairs and there encountered a small group of Indians, two of whom (a "principal person among them" and his servant) agreed to accompany them on their voyage. Whether the ship's commander, Antonio Velazquez, realized that he had found the Bahia Santa Maria (Chesapeake Bay), first sighted by Pedro de Quejo thirty-six years earlier, he knew he had made an important discovery. With the two Indians on board, he decided to return to Spain.[1]

Reaching Lagos, Portugal, in late August, Velazquez left his ship and traveled overland to Seville to sort out some business affairs. He then made his way some three hundred miles to Madrid to report his voyage and present the young Indian, Paquiquineo (named Don Luís de Velasco in honor of the viceroy of Mexico), to the king, Philip II. On the journey, he and Don Luís took the road through the beautiful river valley of the Guadalquivir, a checkerboard of wheat fields, vineyards, olive groves, and citrus orchards, to the Moorish city of Córdoba with its great mosque, before turning north into the high, austere tableland of the *Mesta,* given over to vast sheep walks and scattered rural industries. Arriving in Madrid, little more than a large village when Philip II established his court there earlier in the year, they would have found a bustling town packed with courtiers, royal officials and their staffs, high-ranking churchmen, retailers, and merchants, all having flocked to the new capital of Spain.

Exactly when Don Luís was presented to the king is unknown. To those who witnessed it, however, the meeting must have appeared a study in stark contrasts: on the one hand Don Luís, an *indio* from a remote part of the North American littoral, who knew nothing of European civilization or Christianity; and on the other Philip II— ruler of an empire embracing the Americas and large parts of western Europe, the greatest the world had ever seen—believed by his subjects to be God's shepherd on Earth and herald of a universal Catholic monarchy that would reunite Christendom and eventually all peoples under "one monarch, one empire, and one sword." Perhaps because of the king's curiosity about the Indian's land and the possibility of converting the people there to Catholicism, or perhaps because he was intrigued by the Indian's evident intelligence, Don Luís soon became one of Philip's favorites.[2]

At first, Don Luís may have enjoyed the life at court and in Madrid, but during the winter his thoughts turned homeward; after speaking of his desire to return to his own land, the king granted him permission to go back in the spring. Arrangements were made for Don Luís, accompanied by Valezquez, to travel first to New Spain (Mexico), and then the Indian and a small group of Dominican missionaries would continue on to the Bahia Santa Maria. Accordingly, Don Luís joined the convoy that sailed from Cádiz at the end of May and arrived at San Juan de Ulua, roadstead of Vera Cruz on the Gulf Coast of Mexico, ten weeks later.

Don Luís together with several companions first went to Mexico City to meet the viceroy, Velasco, who wished to oversee the mission to the Indian's homeland. Forty years after the collapse of the Aztec Empire, most of the old city of Tenochtitlán had been demolished and replaced with a great public square around which were located the new city's principal buildings, constructed in Spanish baroque style out of the stone and rubble of Aztec pyramids and temples. The Indian had little opportunity to acquaint himself with the city, however. Shortly after arriving, he became seriously ill (possibly smallpox or dysentery) and was thought lost. Gradually nursed back to health at a Dominican convent, he and his servant were baptized and chose to remain with the friars to learn the Catholic faith and Spanish ways.[3]

Several years passed, but Don Luís remained determined to return to his own people and began pressing once again for an opportunity to establish a mission among them. Fortunately, his idea of planting a colony to the north of previous settlements along the Atlantic seaboard coincided with the rising fortunes of an extraordinary man who was to have enormous influence on Spanish North America. Pedro Menéndez de Avilés, captain-general of the Indies convoys, had recently been appointed *adelantado* (governor) of "La Florida" and ordered by the king to take charge of Spain's interests in the north, specifically to move decisively against recent French efforts to establish colonies that might threaten the safety of the Spanish treasure fleets. It was to Menéndez that Don Luís directed his appeal to return to his own land (which the Spanish called Ajacán) and bring about the conversion of his "parents, relatives, and countrymen to the Faith of Jesus Christ, and baptizing them and making them Christians as he was."[4]

Menéndez needed little persuasion. Following his ruthless destruction of a French colony at Fort Caroline (near modern-day Jacksonville, Florida) in late summer 1565, he launched a plan to establish a string of fortified settlements along the mainland coast from the Gulf of Mexico to the Bahia Santa Maria that would permanently secure North America for Spain. The Chesapeake Bay, he believed, was the "key to all the fortifications in this land since, beyond here, as far as Tierra Nova [Canada], there is no place to settle in." According to Menéndez's understanding of the geography of North America, the Chesapeake Bay led to two great stretches of water, one running five or six hundred leagues northeast to Newfoundland, the other flowing to a huge inland lake that, at its western edge, lay only a few miles from an arm of the South Sea.[5]

Using the Chesapeake as a base, Menéndez wrote enthusiastically to Philip II, fleets of Spanish galleys would gain control of northern waters, ousting other nations from the valuable fisheries of Newfoundland and preventing further efforts by the French to find a northwest passage to Cathay. The king would become lord of all the Indies, north and south. A navigable route to the South Seas would establish a vital link with Spanish possessions in the East, stimulate trade with Spanish North America, and promote the further integration of a worldwide empire. He characterized the mid-Atlantic region as a new Andalucia, it having a similar climate and being on the same latitude as the province in southern Spain. The region would be well suited to colonization by Spanish plants, animals, and people, and had many natural resources ripe for development. There were reports, too, of traces of silver and gold as well as turquoises and emeralds, the latter being common "near the mountains." Even unicorns had "been seen in this land."[6]

Don Luís's wish to return to his own land and convert his people to the Catholic faith thus accorded perfectly with Menéndez's ambitions. Like his master, Philip II, Menéndez was a man of deep religious convictions; integral to his plans to secure Florida was the role he assigned to religious orders, Dominicans and Jesuits, to convert the Indians as a necessary preliminary for civilian settlement. In 1566, he dispatched a ship carrying Don Luís, his servant, and two Dominicans to the Bahia Santa Maria, but unaccountably they failed to find the entrance of the Bay. After first making landfall on the Atlantic shore of Maryland and then sailing too far south to the Outer Banks of North Carolina, their ship was driven out to sea by strong winds. Worse was to come. Despite vigorous protests by the friars, instead of returning to Florida, the ship's captain set sail for Spain. As the American coast slipped away, Don Luís must have wondered whether he would ever see his land again.[7]

## Don Luís and the Fathers

Upon returning to Spain, Don Luís lived with a group of Jesuits in Seville, where he came to hear about the Jesuits' lack of success in converting the Indians of the northern American mainland. Seizing the opening, he offered to lead an expedition to Ajacán, once again assuring the fathers of his devout wish to bring over his people to the Catholic faith. Sent to Havana in 1570, he quickly became involved in discussions with Menéndez and the vice-provincial of the Jesuit order in Florida, Father Juan de Segura, about an expedition. By way of further encouragement, Don Luís told them of a passage that would lead to "the discovery of great kingdoms such as Tartary," as well as others adjoining it. Father Segura was convinced that God, through the instrument of Don Luís, had granted him a magnificent opportunity to bring about the conversion of the Indians. After careful preparations, the small group of Jesuits, made up of Fathers Segura and Luís de Quirós, six others, and a boy, Alonso de Olmos, sailed from Cuba.

Arriving in the Bahia Santa Maria in September 1570, the expedition probably landed first near modern-day Newport News to give thanks for their safe arrival before moving about twenty miles up the James River. Directed by Don Luís, they disembarked at present-day College Creek (not far from where the English would later establish Jamestown) and, following a small stream, made their way across the peninsula to a Kiskiack village on the York (Pamunkey) River, whose people were "subjects" of Don Luís's family. There they began constructing a small wooden house that would serve as their living quarters and chapel. Eager to send their ship away as quickly as possible so that it would return the sooner with provisions, Father Quirós gave a brief description of their surroundings the day after landing, which he dispatched with the ship: "We find the land of Don Luís in quite another condition than we expected, not because he was at fault in his description of it, but because Our Lord has chastised it with six years famine and death, which has brought it about that there is much less population than usual."

The Jesuits had landed during a severe drought; but if they were worried about food shortages, they were at least comforted by the Indians' friendliness. Great joy was expressed at the return of Don Luís, whom the Indians believed had died long ago. They seemed to think he "had risen from the dead and come down from heaven," wrote Quirós, "and since all who remained are his relatives, they are greatly consoled in him. They have recovered their courage and hope that God may seek to favor them, saying that they want to be like Don Luís, begging us to remain in this land with them." It was clear, however, that the Indians were in no position to support the mission as the fathers had anticipated. Instead of the Indians supplying the Spanish through the good offices of Don Luís, the Spanish would have to support the Indians by importing "a generous quantity of corn" to sustain the mission "and to let all this tribe take some for sowing."

By cultivating the land, Father Quirós believed, putting a brave face on the situation, it would be possible to cultivate the Indians' souls. If planting could begin in March or April, "many of the tribes will come here after being scattered over the region in search of food and there will be a good opportunity for the Holy Gospel." He added, "The chief has sought this very thing especially." The situation as Father Quirós sat down to pen his letter was grave but not disastrous. Don Luís remained loyal, the Spaniards had the goodwill of the local people, and they had obtained information from the Indians about the presence of a sea across some mountains three or four days journey inland, which might turn out to be a passage to the Pacific. The priest expressed "great hope" for the conversion of the Indians and their "service to Our Lord and His Majesty" in helping the fathers find "an entrance into the mountains and to China."[8]

Quirós's optimism proved ill founded, however. Don Luís soon abandoned the mission and went to live in the village of a relative about thirty or forty miles upriver. Why did he leave them? One account, written by Brother Juan de la Carrera some years later, described the "wretched native" (Don Luís) as a "second Judas," who, having nothing to fear from the Spanish after Father Segura dispatched their ship back to Havana for supplies, soon "began to indulge in vices and sins publicly without fear of God or man." Acting "more like a pagan than a Christian in his manners, dress, and habits," Carrera continued, Don Luís "went off and lived with his uncle, a chief, in a country far distant from ours. There he allowed himself free rein in his sins, marrying many women in a pagan way."[9] Perhaps Carrera was right: Don Luís had fooled them all with his profession of faith and talk of helping to convert his people. Perhaps his life with the Dominicans and then Jesuits was a pretense sustained over nine long years to orchestrate his eventual return to Ajacán.

The winter months were desperate: The famished missionaries lived as best they could by rationing their dwindling supplies, gathering roots and berries from the forest, and bartering metal goods for corn in neighboring villages. Father Segura tried to persuade Don Luís to return to them, reminding him they had come to the country at his invitation and under his protection, and arguing that they could not carry out their work of conversion without him. The father admonished him severely for the immoral and "shameful" life he led, saying that if he set such a bad example it would be impossible to "implant the Gospel" and redeem his people.

Segura's criticism may have been the final straw for Don Luís. Having been adopted as one of his people's chief men, he would not have expected to be spoken to in such a manner, especially considering the Jesuits' own perilous situation. In early February, in a final plea for help, Segura sent three of his companions to where the Indian was living; but Don Luís took the opportunity to launch an attack, killing two of the three himself. Then, accompanied by a small war party, he moved on to the mission, where he and his men killed Father Segura and the others with the priests' own axes, leaving only the boy, Alonso, alive.

Alonso's survival was vital because it was he who eventually provided definitive news of the fate of the mission to the Spaniards. By the summer of 1571, authorities in Havana were seriously concerned about the fathers. A supply ship sent to the Bahia Santa Maria in the spring could find no trace of them, although some Indians wearing "cassocks and religious robes" who tried to lure the Spanish ashore were spotted at a village not far from the mission. Two Indians captured by the Spanish crew during an attack on their ship refused to provide information about the whereabouts of the Jesuits, but they did indicate that Alonso still lived.

An expedition under the personal command of Menéndez, consisting of four ships and 150 soldiers, was organized the following year and arrived in the Bay in August. The governor dispatched a small frigate with thirty soldiers upriver to search for Alonso and take hostages. Following a skirmish at College Creek, the soldiers killed about twenty Indians and captured thirteen, including "a principal chief," possibly Don Luís's uncle. Using a combination of bribes and threats, the Spanish recovered Alonso from his captors and learned from him the full story of the killing of the fathers.

Menéndez told the Indians with whom he was bargaining that he would hang his captives if they did not deliver Don Luís to him. When after a few days it became clear that Don Luís was not going to appear, the governor ordered that eight or nine of the hostages be hanged from the ship's rigging in clear view of any Indians looking on from the riverside. An eyewitness reported that the "country remains very frightened from the chastisement the Governor inflicted, for previously they were free to kill any Spaniard who made no resistance. After seeing the opposite of what the Fathers were, they tremble. This chastisement has become famous throughout the land." As a literal parting shot, the pilot of one of the ships steered towards land as if intending to speak to a crowd of Indians gathered on the shore, but instead the soldiers opened fire, killing "many."[10]

What became of Don Luís is a mystery. No further reports of his whereabouts came to the ears of Spanish officials. He had vanished into the interior without trace.

## The Spanish Legacy

Don Luís's decision to destroy the Jesuit settlement had far-reaching consequences. Menéndez's attack was probably the first time Indian peoples of the region had experienced the destructive power of European weaponry, and it made a lasting impression on those who witnessed or suffered by it. For their part, although the Spanish did not lose interest in the Chesapeake after the failure of the mission, they made no further attempts to settle the area. Developments elsewhere in the Americas and Europe kept Philip II fully occupied and his resources stretched for years to come. After 1572, his interest lay not in colonizing the region but in ensuring that the northern coast neither became a haven for pirates nor fell into the hands of foreign rivals.

Stories of gold and silver in the interior persisted, however. In 1588, Vicente Gonzáles, who had previously visited the region in 1570 and 1572, entered the Bahia Santa Maria and explored both shores of the Bay, during which he met "a certain chief" wearing many gold rings and a golden crown who told him of a mountain within three days travel that had "nothing else [but gold] in it." Bartolomé Martinez, a Spanish official living in Santa Elena during the early 1570s, recalled for many years after the event the conversations he had with Alonso de Olmos, who described the region as "a very fertile land, with gold, and silver and pearls." The Indians, Alonso assured Martinez, wear "golden circlets on their brows and bracelets on their wrists and ear rings."[11]

Pedro Menéndez established the reality of a Spanish presence in North America. Henceforth, foreign nations with ambitions to plant a colony in the mid-Atlantic region had to reckon with Spanish warships patrolling coastal waters from their bases in Florida as well as from the West Indies. More important, Menéndez's dreams about the region's potential would inspire fantasies of untold riches in the minds of European colonizers for a century to come. Hopes of finding a passage to the Orient figure prominently in English accounts of early Virginia from the 1580s until the 1650s alongside stories of gold and silver mines located somewhere in the mountains inland. Finally, descriptions of fertility and natural abundance, first expressed by Spanish chroniclers and explorers in the early sixteenth century, would later become crucial to English propagandists in their efforts to justify the establishment of colonies populated by farmers and artisans as well as by traders and soldiers.[12]

# 1

# Two Worlds

AHUNSONACOCK AND HIS BROTHER Opechancanough, the two great Powhatan chiefs of the Jamestown era, were in their twenties or early thirties when the Spanish arrived. They would have known about the Jesuit mission at Kiskiack and what happened there, and may have witnessed Menéndez's subsequent "chastisement." Possibly, the threat of further Spanish attacks encouraged alliances between James River and York (Pamunkey) River peoples that led to the rapid expansion of the Powhatan chiefdom across the region after 1572. But if so, the threat never materialized. Aside from occasional exploratory voyages, a full generation was to pass before another European power, the English, sought to establish a colony in the Chesapeake Bay. By that time, the Powhatans had grown into a formidable political and military force.[1]

## The Rise of the Powhatans

The rise of the Powhatan chiefdom was the central political development of the late sixteenth and early seventeenth centuries, shaping the

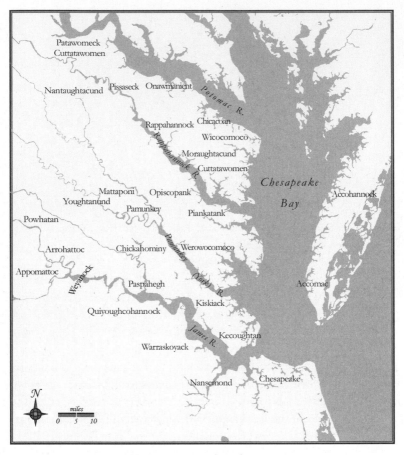

*The Powhatans. (Drawn by Rebecca L. Wrenn)*

lives of Indian peoples living throughout the coastal plain (tidewater) of Virginia, as well as those of the strangers who arrived from across the ocean. Six regions located between the upper James and York Rivers—"the Countreys [of] *Powhatan, Arrohateck, Appamatuck, Pamunky, Youghtamond,* and *Mattapanient*"—were inherited by Wahunsonacock sometime after 1570 and, together with lands along the lower York River, comprised the historic core of his empire. Three decades later, Wahunsonacock ruled over thirty or so tribes, spread across Tsenacommacah (the Powhatan name for their lands), from south of the James River to the Potomac and from the coast to the falls.[2]

As described by William Strachey (a prominent settler who arrived in Virginia in 1610), Wahunsonacock was a man of "goodly" looks, "well beaten with many cold and stormy wynters," yet "of a tall stature, and cleane lymbes." In earlier years, Strachey wrote, the great chief was a "strong and able salvadge [savage], synowie, active, and of a daring spiritt, vigilant, ambitious, subtile to enlarge his dominions." In addition to the lands he had inherited, the rest of his territories had been "either by force subdued unto him, or through feare yeilded." At about the time the English arrived, the Chesapeakes, who lived at the entrance of the Bay and had resisted absorption into Tsenacommacah, were destroyed in an attack that resulted in the slaughter of men, women, and children. In other attacks, such as that suffered by the Kecoughtans, who lived at the mouth of the James River, entire peoples were uprooted and moved to different locations to strengthen the Powhatans' control of newly conquered territories.[3]

A vivid example of the methods used by the great chief to assert his authority is recounted by Captain John Smith. For reasons that are unclear, in 1608, Wahunsonacock mounted a surprise attack on neighboring Piankatanks, who lived along the north bank of the river of the same name. First, he sent some of his men to lodge among them, then he surrounded their village and, at an appointed time, launched a swift and deadly attack. Two dozen men were slain. The women and children, along with the chief, were captured and presented to Wahunsonacock so that they could "doe him service"; and to intimidate visitors, the scalps of warriors were hung between two trees at Wahunsonacock's residence at Werowocomoco.[4]

The Powhatans were surrounded by numerous Indian peoples who were highly influential in shaping Tsenacommacah. Southward were the Algonquians of the Roanoke region who inhabited the coastal areas of Pamlico, Albemarle, and Currituck Sounds. Inland were the Iroquoian

Tuscarora, whose territories stretched a hundred miles along the North Carolina coastal plain and fall line from the Neuse River to the lands of the Meherrins and Nottoways (also Iroquoian), situated on the tributaries of the Chowan. Indians known to the English as the Mangoags lived in the Carolina piedmont and enjoyed a reputation for aggressiveness in their attacks on peoples of the coastal region. Siouan-speaking Monacans and Mannahoacs, who inhabited the fertile river valleys along the upper reaches of the James and Rappahannock Rivers, were ancient enemies of the Powhatans and carried out frequent raids along their western border. To the north were the Susquehannocks, who lived at the head of the Chesapeake Bay; and the Massawomecks (Iroquoians), who periodically journeyed from the Great Lakes by way of the Appalachians and the Shenandoah Valley to plunder settlements in the piedmont and the tidewater.[5]

Iroquoian and Siouan peoples in the piedmont and mountains effectively confined the Powhatans to the coastal plain. Aside from periodic raids, Wahunsonacock seems to have been reluctant to engage in protracted hostilities against neighboring enemies. He may have been more concerned about consolidating his authority over the peoples within his own territories than in conducting attacks on powerful nations in far-off lands.[6]

As Wahunsonacock's chiefdom grew throughout the tidewater so did his wealth and influence. His people were required to pay tribute in the form of skins, beads, pearls, food, and tobacco, all collected annually and stored in temples such as those at Orapaks (one of his capitals) and Uttamussak. He claimed a monopoly of prestige goods that were traded in his lands, including copper, iron wares, and other items acquired from Europeans. Copper was traded beyond his dominions with other peoples and used also when necessary to hire mercenary warriors. More generally, gifts of tribute goods to lesser chiefs (weroances), warriors, and priests throughout his lands provided him with an effective means of rewarding those he favored.[7]

Although Wahunsonacock was often described by English observers as a despot or tyrant, his power was not boundless and varied considerably from one area to another. Peoples of outlying regions, such as north of the Rappahannock River or the Eastern Shore, as well as the Chickahominies, who lived on the river that bears their name, behaved far more independently than those of the core area between the upper James and York Rivers. They might recognize his authority, provide support in times of war or when called upon, but they also pursued their own policies and occasionally disobeyed (or ignored) his orders altogether. Wahunsonacock was not an absolute ruler; rather, he was a chief of chiefs.[8]

Wahunsonacock governed his territories through regional or district chiefs, some of whom were close relatives: His brothers Opechancanough, Opitchapam, and Kekataugh maintained tight control over the Pamunkeys; his "sons" Parahunt and Pochins ruled the important districts of Powhatan and Kecoughtan at the falls and mouth of the James River respectively.

Opechancanough was the most powerful of Wahunsonacock's relatives. Like his brother, he was a vigorous and potent leader at the time the English arrived. Perfectly "skill'd in the Art of Governing," it was said he "caused all the Indians far and near to dread his Name, and had them all entirely in his Subjection." Other than his kinship to Wahunsonacock, his influence stemmed from his role as chief of the best-disciplined warriors in all of Tsenacommacah. The Pamunkeys had "neere 300 able men" of their own but could mobilize twice as many allies within a few days. Backed by his warriors, Opechancanough would prove a formidable enemy.[9]

Little is known about Opechancanough's origins, but a few intriguing references suggest that he may have been none other than Paquiquineo (Don Luís). A settler, Ralph Hamor, wrote in 1615 that the Chickahominies were hostile to the Spanish because "*Powhatans* father was driven by them from the *west-Indies* into those parts." A much later account by Robert Beverly related that the Powhatans did not recognize Opechancanough as Wahunsonacock's brother but rather as "a Prince of a Foreign Nation, [who] came to them a great Way from the South-West: And by their Accounts, we suppose him to have come from the *Spanish Indians*, some-where near *Mexico*." Both could be garbled stories of Paquiquineo's stay in Mexico City and travels in the West Indies before returning to the Ajacán with the Jesuit fathers. But whether or not Opechancanough and Paquiquineo were the same person, there is little doubt they were contemporaries, possibly kin, and surely would have known one another.[10]

## Peoples of the Great River

Tsenacommacah was well populated at the beginning of the seventeenth century. Perhaps 15,000 people, dispersed in several hundred villages and hamlets, lived in territories belonging to the Powhatan chiefdom. The most populous areas were inland, away from exposed areas of the coast or Bayside, and corresponded to the upper branches of the major rivers and their tributaries, lands along the fall line, and the river valleys of the piedmont. Powhatan settlements, like those of peoples to the north and south, were usually situated near rivers on sheltered necks or along the smaller estuaries and tributaries. High ground close to the water was preferred because it protected against possible flooding and provided a vantage point for keeping an eye on the comings and goings along the river and on the approaches to the village from inland.[11]

Rivers and coastal waters provided a superb means of travel and were commonly used for transporting men and goods over long distances. In the piedmont and coastal plain, rivers were used to travel east and west; in the Valley of Virginia, the main directions were north and south, some movement going west into the Ohio River basin. Footpaths and trails supplemented the waterways and formed an intricate network across the entire eastern seaboard. The most important was the Great Indian Warpath, which ran the length of the northern continent from Canada to Florida, and which in the Chesapeake region followed the western edge of the Blue Ridge Mountains for much of the way before turning inland into the Valley of Virginia at Tutelo. This major trail sent off numerous branches that crisscrossed the piedmont and coastal plain or led westwards across the mountains to the Mississippi Valley. Far from being cut off from one another, settlements and regions were linked by extensive and ancient routes along which people, goods, and news moved easily.[12]

Most Powhatan settlements were small by European standards, usually consisting of fewer than a hundred people "of kindred & alliance." As William Strachey observed: "Their howses are not manie in one towne, and those that are stand [set apart] and scattered, without forme of a street, far and wyde asunder." Even the largest towns rarely contained more than twenty or thirty houses, these dotted in small groups over tens of acres. Houses throughout Tsenacommacah were of a similar design. Built like "Arbors of small young springs [saplings] bowed and tyed," covered tightly "with mats, or the barkes of trees very handsomely, that notwithstanding either winde, raine or weather, they are as warme as stooves, but very smoaky."[13]

An illustration of Secota (Secotan, near the Pamlico River in North Carolina) provides an impression of such a settlement. At one end of the village is a river—"from whence they fetch their water"—that provided fish, crabs, and oysters. In the top left of the drawing, a couple of men are shown hunting deer that have strayed into the village. The layout reflects the mix of agriculture, fishing, hunting, and foraging that characterized seasonal changes in diet and the variety of local resources. Some of the larger villages, notably those inhabited by local chiefs, were more elaborately designed and included the chief's longhouse, mortuary temple, and storehouse, as well as areas set aside for important ceremonial functions.[14]

—·—

POWHATAN SOCIETY was organized for war, a response to the threat posed by powerful enemies to the north and west—the Monacans, Mannahoacs, Susquehannocks, and Massawomecks—and Wahunsonacock's territorial ambitions. Warfare involved a variety of tactics, such as frontal assaults, hit-and-run sorties by small raiding parties, ambush, and deception. Most attacks took the form of raiding parties involving no more than a two dozen or so warriors. In these circumstances, the object was to shoot to kill or maim the enemy from the

*John White/Theodor De Bry, Secota, 1585.*

safety of cover or to ensure weight of numbers if attacking at close range. Pitched battles between opposing armies were less common.

Indians frequently used "Stratagems, surprizes and Treacherys" to best their enemies. In a mock battle witnessed by John Smith, the Indians divided themselves into two companies of about a hundred men, one called "Monacans," the other "Powhatans," each company ordered into ranks of fifteen men abreast. After agreeing to terms that the women and children of the vanquished would be the prize of the victors, the two armies approached each other, the men "leaping and singing after their accustomed tune which they use only in warres." Each side then shot at the other; when they had discharged all their arrows, they joined in hand-to-hand fighting: "As they got advantage they catched their enimies by the haire of the head" and acted the beating out of losers' brains with wooden swords. When Monacan numbers decreased, the Powhatans charged in a half-moon formation in an effort to surround them, at which the Monacans fled "all in a troope" to the cover of nearby woods. This, however, was a ploy to lure the Powhatans into an ambush, where fresh warriors were hiding. The Powhatans, perceiving the danger, withdrew to an area of the field where they had arranged their own ambush, but the Monacans declined to pursue them and instead disappeared into the forest.[15]

War was the ultimate test for every male, a searching examination where only the strong, intelligent, or lucky would survive. Men were expected to display strength and courage in hand-to-hand combat, fortitude if captured and tortured (while they were slowly put to death in excruciating pain, they would throw insults at their enemies), and wisdom in council. A set of values that highlighted individual battle skills was vital to maintaining an effective fighting force and applied to all the peoples who made up Tsenacommacah, but there were important distinctions also between warrior groups. Pamunkey and Powhatans made up the core of Wahunsonacock's fighting forces and combined may have numbered five or six hundred men. They were considered the most dependable and loyal of his warriors. In addition, the great chief and Opechancanough were able to call upon allies from neighboring peoples (some paid for their services), troops who fought alongside the elite forces. A combined warrior strength of from 1,200 to 1,500 was easily large enough to overwhelm local resistance to Wahunsonacock's will.[16]

When important decisions, such as whether to go to war, were made, custom demanded that chiefs take advice from their counselors and priests. Counselors ("cawcawwasoughs" or "cockerouses") were usually drawn from village elders, warriors, and priests, and at a district level might include some town weroances. Priests were the principal buttress of the chief's authority, their avowed ability to foresee the future making them indispensable in providing political decisions. "When they intend any warres," Smith noted, "the Werowances usually have the advice of their Priests and Conjurers, and their Allies and ancient friends, but chiefly the Priests determine their resolution." Strachey put it more forcefully, remarking that priests "at all tymes" governed "and direct[ed] the Weroances . . . in all their accions."

More generally, priests were vital intermediaries between the people and spiritual forces that infused earthly society. They read the omens and advised accordingly on preparations for a hunt or a fishing expedition; they sought to influence the weather, bringing rain or quelling storms; and they fulfilled the role of healers through their knowledge of herbs and certain curative techniques. On occasion, priests would seek a secluded place deep in the woods or on "some desolate promontory Toppe" where they called upon Okeus and other deities for guidance. William Strachey observed that the Indians were much given to "straunge whispers" which "run among . . . [them] and possesse them with amazement [about] what maie be the yssue of these straunge preparations, landed on their Coasts." According to the Powhatan Uttamatomakkin, Okeus had forewarned the great chief's priests about the arrival of the English sometime before they appeared in the Chesapeake Bay.[17]

Religion and spirituality were of fundamental importance to Indian peoples and were expressed in a rich variety of beliefs about powerful deities, local spirits, myths, and prophecies. The Powhatans revered a "great good God," Ahone, who lived in the heavens above and whose

*The Powhatan god, Okeus.*

perfection was boundless. Ahone had created the cosmos, the Earth, and lesser gods; had taught the Indians how to plant corn; he was the "author of their good." He made "the Sun to shine"; through his "vertues and Influences the under earth is tempered, and brings forth her fruictes according to her seasons."

Ahone was a remote god, unconcerned with the affairs of men. In everyday affairs, the most important deity in the Indians' pantheon was Okeus, who, unlike the peace-loving Ahone, looked "into all mens accions" and judged them according to a "severe scale of Justice." The vengeful god punished the people with sicknesses, struck down their ripe corn with "blastings, stormes, and thunderclappes," and stirred up wars. As the "malitious enemy of mankind," Okeus was the origin of all harm and misfortune; to appease him, the Powhatans dedicated their temples to him, offered him sacrifices, and worshipped him. But Okeus was also the god the priests would consult and ask to intercede in times of war and crisis.[18]

FROM THE OAK AND CONIFER FORESTS of the Blue Ridge Mountains to the fertile lowlands bordering the rivers and Bay, Indian peoples—Iroquoian, Siouan, and Algonquian—had evolved highly successful methods of harvesting the natural resources of the land and rivers. Early European observers were unanimous in their admiration for Indians' adaptation to their environments and were aware of the subtle as well as more obvious distinctions between the various peoples who inhabited the land. Throughout the region, different tribes might enjoy a good deal of autonomy, but everywhere the sharp edges of conflict were evident, resulting from the expansion of the Powhatan chiefdom and longstanding hostility between Algonquians and neighboring Siouan and Iroquoian peoples.

When the English arrived in Virginia early in the new century, they would encounter a powerful and complex chiefdom. It was therefore portentous that when Wahunsonacock first came face-to-face with Captain John Smith, the great chief took the opportunity to describe to him "his great and spacious Dominions" and impressed upon the Englishman, in case he missed the point, that "all hee knew were under his Territories." Tsenacommacah was his.[19]

## The Coming of the English

For much of the sixteenth century, England played only a minor role in western voyaging, which was confined largely to the seasonal flow of shipping to the Newfoundland fishing banks and occasional (illegal) trading ventures to Brazil and the Caribbean. Little attention was given initially to the discoveries of the Portuguese, Spanish, and French, or to the increasing amount of information about America available in Europe. Even the famed exploits of conquistadors in Mexico and Peru and the overthrow of the Aztec and Inca empires made seemingly little impact in England. Few before midcentury lamented, as did John Rastell, lawyer and publisher, the backwardness of English ventures in the New World or shared his vision of English settlements in North America:

> O what a thynge had been than
> Yf they that be Englyshe men
> Myght have ben the furst of all
> That there shulde have take possession
> And made furst buyldynge and habytacion
> A memory perpetuall . . . [20]

During Queen Elizabeth I's reign, however, a remarkable awakening of interest in the possibility of establishing English colonies in America occurred. Colonization was viewed as a project that would be of great benefit not only to individuals and their financial backers but also to the nation as a whole. In 1583, Sir George Peckham, a prominent Catholic supporter of colonial ventures, wrote a lengthy treatise that set out the "Law of Nations" sanctioning trade between Christians and "Infidels or Savages"; the "Law of Armes," which allowed the taking of foreign lands by force; and the "Law of God," which enjoined Christian rulers to settle those lands "for the establishment of God's worde." From ancient times and "since the nativitie of Christ," he exclaimed, "mightie and puissant Emperours and Kings have performed the like, I say to plant, possesse, and subdue." John Dee—astrologer to the queen, alchemist, and mathematician—advocated building a strong navy that would be the foundation of an "Incomparable Brytish Empire." He laid out the basis of Elizabeth I's right to take possession of "foreyn Regions," following the same principles by which "other Christian Princes do now adayes make Conquests uppon the heathen people."[21]

But it was left to Richard Hakluyt the younger, the foremost proponent of colonization of his age, to give fullest expression to England's ambitions and provide a rationale for colonization that would guide overseas expansion for generations to come. Hakluyt was convinced that founding colonies would be a clear signal of England's intent to stake a claim to American lands and seas as the Spanish and other nations had done. The "plantinge of twoo or three strong fortes upon some goodd havens" on the mainland between Florida and Cape Breton would provide convenient bases for fleets of privateers operating in American waters, eventually weakening Spanish power in the Old World as well as the New. Cut off the king of Spain's treasure from the New World, Hakluyt argued, and "his purpose [would soon be] defeated, his powers and strengthe diminished, his pride abated, and his tyranie utterly suppressed."

Planting English colonies in America, Hakluyt believed, would be a "moste godly and Christian work" that would ultimately lead to "gayninge . . . the soules of millions of those wretched people [Indians]," bringing "them from darknes to lighte." Conversion would be achieved not by the brutal methods employed by the Spanish but by way of "a gentle course without crueltie and tyrannie [such as] best answereth the profession of a Christian." Once Indians realized they would be treated well by the English, they would "revolte cleane from the Spaniarde" and "yelde themselves" to English rule. The exploited peoples of Spain's empire in the New World, Indians and enslaved Africans, could be turned against the Spanish if English colonizers could win them over with plain dealing. By these means, the English would establish a universal Anglican church in America that would serve as a counterbalance to the expansion of Catholicism in Spanish possessions.

Hakluyt was sincere in his advocacy of "inlarging the glorious gospell of Christ," but he was sufficiently realistic to understand that colonization would not go very far if it was based on evangelical arguments alone. More important to encouraging investment in western ventures was the likelihood of profits. English settlements in America, he confidently asserted, would promote commerce and prosperity, as well as social benefits at home. In time, he wrote, the colonies would "yelde unto us all the commodities of Europe, Affrica, and Asia, as far as wee were wonte to travell, and supply the wantes of all our decayed trades." The northern parts would supply timber, masts, clapboard, pitch, tar, cordage, and naval supplies; the southern parts wine, silk, fruits, oil, sugar, and salt.

Trade with the Indians would bring a valuable return, but to produce the goods England needed, large numbers of people would have to colonize America. This would be doubly advantageous: Not only would an expansive new market for English goods be created, thereby stimulating production and providing relief for poor workers in depressed English manufactures, but also the country would profit from the growing volume of colonial goods that could be sold at home and in Europe. In the colonies, the able-bodied poor, unemployed, and idle, an "altogether unprofitable" drain on the country, could be found work to their own and the nation's advantage. If England, as Hakluyt thought, was "swarminge at this day w[i]th valient youthes rusting and hurtfull by lacke of employement," the solution was to transport them overseas. Petty thieves, vagabonds, and criminals who "for trifles may otherwise be devoured by the gallowes" could redeem themselves by laboring in America.

Hakluyt proposed the creation of permanent English societies in America, where "new" lands lying on latitudes stretching from North Africa to Scandinavia could be developed to produce commodities traditionally imported from Europe and the Levant. English settlements and a flourishing transatlantic trade would bring "inlarged domynions, power, Revenewes, and honnour" to the nation as well as a means "to cutt the combe of the frenche, of the spanishe, of the portingale," and other enemies. Colonies might be established as bases for piracy and plunder, but their long-term survival depended on the production of goods in demand in England and Europe.[22]

Hakluyt's arguments found a receptive ear in the queen. Against the background of the growing power of Spain during the middle decades of the century, Elizabeth was acutely aware that the threat posed by the Spanish to her kingdom was incomparably greater than it was in her father's time fifty years earlier. The annexation of Portugal by Philip II in 1580, and with it Portuguese possessions in Africa, the Far East, and

Brazil, had translated Spain's already vast empire into truly global proportions, the first empire in history "on which the sun never set." Philip believed that his divinely appointed duty was not only to spread the Catholic faith to the millions of his new subjects in distant lands but also to defend the faith against heretics closer to home. As the queen watched Spain's empire reach its zenith, she knew that sooner or later the full force of Spanish arms would be turned against her own realm.[23]

Initial English efforts to establish New World colonies were a complete failure.[24] Martin Frobisher's three voyages between 1576 and 1578 to Meta Incognita, the southern shore of Baffin Island, in search of gold and a northwest passage around the top of the American continent to the Orient, ended in bankruptcy and ruin. A few years later, Sir Humphrey Gilbert's scheme to establish plantations in Newfoundland and along the North American seaboard was also a disaster and resulted in a total financial loss and Gilbert's death at sea.[25]

To the south, in the warm, tropical waters of the Caribbean, English privateers enjoyed better fortune. John Hawkins and Francis Drake, among a host of others, plundered gold, silver, pearls, and precious commodities carried by Spanish treasure fleets and pillaged Spain's possessions in the West Indies and along the Spanish Main. Even so, despite notable achievements such as Drake's daring raid on a mule train taking a fortune in Peruvian silver to Nombre de Dios on the coast of Panama in 1573, and his voyage around the world between 1577 and 1580, the English had still not succeeded in establishing a single New World colony.[26]

ROANOKE, OFF THE COAST of North Carolina, was England's most important attempt at establishing a permanent settlement in the New World before Jamestown. When news reached London that Gilbert had perished at sea, the queen's new favorite, Walter Ralegh, wasted little time in petitioning her for exclusive rights to explore and colonize North America. His palatial residence in London, Durham House, became the cockpit of his colonization plans for the next twenty years:

There he gathered a remarkable group of men who brought together scientific knowledge and practical experience. John Dee, assisted by the young polymath, Thomas Hariot, schooled mariners on navigation and astronomy and prepared the maps and charts that would guide them through American waters; Simon Fernandes, an Azorean pilot who had made many Atlantic crossings, knew the most convenient sea routes and, familiar with the North American coast, would pilot voyages; and John White, an artist who had been with Martin Frobisher on his second voyage, was given the task of making accurate drawings of the land, its peoples, and flora and fauna.[27]

Why Ralegh chose to plant a colony along the mid-Atlantic coast is unclear. The decision may have been influenced by his reluctance to risk the same fate as his half brother, Gilbert, who in far northern waters searched for a northwest passage; but, more likely, he saw opportunities to check the advance of the Spanish in North America from a fortification well to the north of earlier French settlements in Florida (and therefore less open to attack), yet still within easy reach of the important sea lanes of the Caribbean and western Atlantic. A colony that would lay claim to North America for England and serve also as a base from which to launch raids on Spanish silver fleets would have had obvious appeal to him as well as to potential investors.

Following a successful reconnaissance voyage in 1584 that brought back glowing reports of the Outer Banks (as well as two Indians, Manteo and Wanchese), a small garrison of a little more than a hundred men was established on Roanoke Island the following year under the command of Ralph Lane, an experienced soldier and a veteran of Irish campaigns.[28] When Lane wrote back to England from "the new Fort in Virginia" in September 1585, he expressed high hopes for the colony: "It is the goodliest and most pleasing territorie of the world" he reported, "(for the soile [continent] is of an huge unknowen greatnesse, and very wel peopled and towned, though savagelie) and the climate so wholesome, that we have not had one sicke, since we touched land here." If the country could be settled by the English and stocked with horses and cattle, he concluded, "no realme in Christendome" would be comparable to it. All sorts of commodities produced in Spain,

*John White/Theodor De Bry, Roanoke, 1590*

C H A W A
N O
R G I
O K
I A
Ramushouuog
Ohaunoock
Catokinge
Waratan
Mascoming
Skicoak
W E A P E
M E O C
Chepanuu
Chesepiooc
Chesepiooc sinus
Apasus
Comokee
Pasquenoke
Trinety harbor
Americæ
pars, Nunc Virginia
dicta primum ab Anglis
inuenta sumtibus Dn Walteri
Raleigh, Equestris ordinis Viri
Anno Dñi M D LXXXV regni vero
Serenis: nostræ Reginæ Elisabethæ
XXVII
Hujus vero Historia peculiari
Libro descripta est, additis
etiam Indigenarum
Iconibus
OCCIDENS
MERIDIES
SEPTENTRIO
ORIENS

France, Italy, and "the East parts" were to be found in great abundance in Virginia—wines, oils, flax, resins, pitch, currants, sugars—and required only labor to cultivate them.[29]

Explorations during the summer revealed a low, flat country, heavily wooded—except for marshlands and occasional Indian clearings—and drained by many rivers that flowed into an inner "Sea" (modern day Currituck, Albemarle, and Pamlico Sounds). The one major disadvantage of the region was the shallowness of the waters in the Sounds, which were unsuitable for large vessels. Consequently, as winter approached, Lane decided to send out an exploratory party in search of a deep-water harbor where the colony could be relocated the following year.

An expedition that included Thomas Hariot and John White traveled northward through Currituck Sound, along the coast, and into the Chesapeake Bay. The party first explored the area around Lynnhaven Bay and then proceeded along the shore to the Elizabeth River, which they followed inland for about fifteen miles to Skicoac, the principal town of the Chesapeake people. The explorers were impressed by what they saw. The area was well wooded and fertile, and there could be no doubt of suitable anchorages for ocean-going vessels in the many large rivers. During the winter, the expedition moved farther inland to the Nansemond River; they might also have made a brief exploration of the tip of the James-York peninsula before returning the way they came to Roanoke in late February or early March 1586.[30]

Soon after Hariot and White returned, Lane mounted an expedition westwards into the interior. Following the waters of Albemarle Sound to their head, Lane then sailed up the Chowan River where he encountered the aged chief of the Chowanoc people, Menatonon, at his capital. There, Lane received unexpected good news. From the chief and his son, Skiko, Lane learned of a land to the west; this territory was inhabited by the Mangoags, who traded for a "marveilous and most strange Minerall" known as *"Wassador,"* brought from mines in a distant country called Chaunis Temoatan. As Menatonon had probably guessed, here was a story to whet the appetites of the English: Not only was there the possibility of discovering gold mines, or, at the very least, large quantities of copper, but near the mountains where the mines were said to be located was a great sea that could be the Pacific.

Menatonon also told Lane about a province bordering the sea, three days farther upriver and four days overland to the northeast, ruled by a powerful king whose seat was on an island in a bay. Menatonon reported that the king had such great quantities of pearls that not only was he adorned with them, but also his chief men and followers, and his "beds, and houses [were] garnished with them . . . that it [was] a wonder to see." He traded with white men, but Menatonon advised Lane to go only with a strong force and plenty of provisions, for "that king would be loth to suffer any strangers to enter into his Countrey, and especially to meddle with the fishing of any Pearle there, and that hee was able to make a great many of men into the fielde, which he sayd would fight very well." Although Lane could not have possibly foreseen its significance, this was the first time the English had heard of Wahunsonacock.[31]

As it turned out, Lane would have no opportunity to pursue further explorations into the interior or to the Chesapeake Bay. When he returned to Roanoke Island, hostilities with local peoples, notably the neighboring Secotans, intensified. Over the next few months there were several pitched battles, and the Secotan chief, Wingina, was killed. Without the support of local Indians, Lane could not see how the colony could survive. He decided to abandon the colony as soon as possible. He got his chance in June, when a large fleet commanded by Sir Francis Drake, which had been asked by Ralegh to call in at the colony after cruising in the West Indies, arrived off the Outer Banks and offered to take the men back to England.[32]

The collapse of Lane's colony might have been the end of the matter, but one more dramatic scene was to be played out. Roanoke had proved unsuitable because its shallow waters could not accommodate ocean-going vessels, but the discovery of fertile lands farther north on the Chesapeake Bay seemed to hold greater potential. Perhaps a settlement could be established there that would serve as a harbor for English ships and provide a base from which to organize expeditions into the interior and attacks on the Spanish. The new colony, sponsored by Ralegh under the leadership of John White, was therefore to be established on the Chesapeake Bay. Conceived differently from the first expedition, White's would be made up of civilians (including families as well as single men) instead of soldiers, who would not antagonize local peoples as Lane's men had done, and would be largely self-sufficient, developing the sorts of commodities promoted enthusiastically by Hakluyt.[33]

Departing from Plymouth in early May, three ships carrying 117 colonists—including seventeen women and nine children—arrived off the Outer Banks in mid-July, where White intended to inquire about the fate of a small garrison of fifteen men left on Roanoke Island the previous year shortly after Lane's departure. What followed was a fiasco. The pilot, Fernandes, refused to take the colonists any farther, claiming it was already late in the season for privateering ventures and that his men wanted to get back to the Caribbean as soon as possible. Whether this was really the reason is uncertain, but in any event, after six weeks on the island it had become clear following attacks on the settlers that the Secotans and other neighboring Indians were as hostile to the new colony as they had been to Lane's.

The colonists decided that White should return to England with Fernandes, alert their backers to the unlikely turn of events, and raise fresh supplies. In the meantime, they would move about fifty miles inland; there, they might find Indians less hostile and so be able to support themselves through the fall and winter until White got back. White left at the end of August but for various reasons was unable to return for three years. By this time, the colonists had disappeared, leaving only an indication that they (or some of them) had moved to the nearby island of Croatoan. Nothing more was heard of them for the next twenty years.[34]

The failure of Roanoke stemmed from many causes. Politically, the times were not auspicious. In the spring and summer of 1588, England faced the threat of losing control of the English Channel to a great Spanish Armada and invasion by the armies of Philip II. At the critical moment when a relief expedition mounted by Ralegh was ready to sail for Roanoke, it was prevented from leaving by the invasion scare. More generally, the sea war against Spain that had steadily escalated in the 1580s—during which scores of privateers set out to plunder Spanish treasure fleets and New World settlements—had a mixed influence on colonizing schemes in this period. A garrison at Roanoke might be effective as a privateering base because English mariners could thus replenish supplies and repair their ships without having to return home; but the attraction of cruising the Caribbean for rich prizes undermined attempts to establish permanent settlements.

The simple fact was that privateering offered better and quicker returns than colonizing schemes. Masters and their crews were far more interested in the prospect of taking richly laden Spanish galleons than in seeing to the needs of a fledgling colony that held little likelihood of showing financial return in the short-term. A single prize, such as the *Santa Maria de San Vincente,* captured by Grenville on his return from Roanoke in 1585, was worth at least £12,000 or £15,000, possibly two or three times more. By comparison, the value of salable products brought back from Virginia was insignificant. With open war against Spain after 1585, profits from raiding Spanish possessions in the West Indies and the Spanish Main, as well as from the capture of treasure and merchant ships, were potentially enormous.[35]

Despite its failure, Roanoke had a continuing influence on future colonizing efforts. Richard Hakluyt and other writers such as Thomas Hariot, whose *Brief and True Report of the New Found Land of Virginia* was published in 1588, had crafted a coherent argument in favor of colonization and described the means by which colonies would benefit their sponsors, settlers, and the nation. England had staked a claim to the mid-Atlantic seaboard and maintained colonies there for several years. The possibility that Ralegh's settlers had survived somewhere along the coast became an important argument in favor of English claims to the region and provided a direct link to the colony founded later on the Chesapeake Bay.

## Virginia Venture

By the time the English once again attempted to establish permanent settlements in North America in the early years of the seventeenth century, the entire complexion of western planting had changed. Queen Elizabeth I died in March 1603 and was succeeded by King James I in a smooth transition of government that was achieved with little political disruption. Because the king did not wish to continue the sea war against Spain, he quickly negotiated a peace treaty ending the plunder of Spanish shipping and possessions; yet he had no intention of renouncing English claims to the American mainland north of Florida.

Outspoken in his condemnation of piracy in the Atlantic and Caribbean, James nevertheless gave tacit support to some influential public men and merchants from Plymouth, Bristol, and London who sought to establish colonies along the northeastern seaboard. Men such as Sir Thomas Smythe, head of the East India Company; Sir John Popham, Lord Chief Justice of the King's Bench; and Sir Ferdinando Gorges, governor of the fort at Plymouth, involved as they were in numerous public and private enterprises, advocated creating a chartered company, with state backing, which would advance settlements in North America while spreading the considerable costs (and risks) among investors.[36]

Precisely how the early Jamestown venture originated is unclear. Captain John Smith credits Bartholomew Gosnold the role of "one of the first movers" of the plantation, "having many years solicited many of his friends, but found small assistants [assistance]." Gosnold came from a well-connected Suffolk family, was known to Richard Hakluyt, and had married a cousin of Sir Thomas Smythe's. He had gone to sea, initially as a privateer and then as an explorer. In 1602, he made a highly successful voyage to the coast of New England, where he traded with Indians for furs and gathered sassafras roots and cedarwood. It was he who likely involved his cousin, Edward Maria Wingfield, also from a distinguished family, who had served in Ireland and the Netherlands and knew Sir Ferdinando Gorges, a fellow prisoner of war in Flanders in 1588. Wingfield was sufficiently important to be named as one of the patentees in the first charter, the legal instrument that gave royal permission for the settlement of Virginia.

The third of the "first movers" was from a very different social background. John Smith was born in 1580 in the village of Willoughby, Lincolnshire, the son of a middling yeoman farmer. He was not cut out for the life of a farmer, however, and fixed his gaze on distant horizons. Like many footloose young men of his generation, he chose a military career, fighting first in northern France and the Netherlands and then with the imperial army of Archduke Ferdinand of Austria against the Turks in central and eastern Europe. After five years of many "brave adventures," among which was the extraordinary feat of killing three Turkish champions one after the other in hand-to-hand combat, he returned to England in 1604 a worldly and battle-hardened gentleman-knight. Weary of war but casting about for new adventure, he heard of Gosnold's efforts to raise support for a colony in America. With money in his purse left over from his travels, he chose to join the venture.[37]

Between them, Gosnold, Wingfield, and Smith managed to attract the backing of several other gentleman but, as Smith later recalled, "nothing could be effected" until "certaine of the Nobilitie, Gentry, and Marchants" became involved in the summer of 1605, notably Popham and the king's first minister, Robert Cecil (the Earl of Salisbury), who brought a coalition of West Country and London merchants together under the aegis of the crown. Merchants in Plymouth and Bristol were anxious to exploit the fish, oil, furs, and timber of New England, and their London counterparts, with their connections to the Mediterranean and the Levant, were keen to promote colonies that would produce commodities traditionally imported from southern Europe, as well as the kinds of industrial crops—tobacco, hops, hemp, flax, rape, and woad—that were being intensively cultivated on marginal lands near London and elsewhere in southern and central England.[38]

Pushed through by Lord Chief Justice Popham, the royal charter of April 10, 1606, divided the North American coast into two distinct spheres of interest. The Plymouth Company (including merchants and financiers from Bristol, Exeter, and smaller West Country outports) was granted the right to settle an area not then "actuallie possessed by

THE PORTRAICTVER OF CAPTAYNE IOHN SMITH ADMIRALL OF NEW ENGLAND.

Ætat: 37.
A° 1616.

These are the Lines that shew thy Face; but those
That shew thy Grace and Glory, brighter bee:
Thy Faire-Discoueries and Fowle-Overthrowes
Of Salvages, much Civilliz'd by thee
Best shew thy Spirit; and to it Glory Wyn;
So, thou art Brasse without, but Golde within.

*John Smith.*

anie Christian Prince or people" between latitudes 38 degrees and 45 degrees, stretching from the Chesapeake Bay to just above present-day Bangor, Maine. A second company, representing London merchants, was allowed to establish a colony to the south somewhere between Cape Fear, North Carolina, and New York (latitudes 34 degrees and 41 degrees). Neither company was granted exclusive rights to all the territory within the regions specified, but each was permitted to establish a settlement within those bounds and given jurisdiction over lands fifty miles north and south, a hundred inland, and a hundred out to sea.

To govern the enterprise and to ensure that national interests did not become subordinated to those of the two companies, a royal council made up of thirteen members appointed by the king and called the "Counsell of Virginia" was created. The Virginia Council oversaw the affairs of both companies and was made up of men divided between the two groups, all of whom were prominent investors actively involved in sponsoring the ventures. Government in the colonies would be undertaken by local councils that would carry out the instructions of the Virginia Council in London.

Two separate colonies were to go forward simultaneously under the same terms as set out in the charter; they would be sponsored by two separate companies whose leading members sat on the royal council. Seemingly a clumsy arrangement, it was in fact a pragmatic expression of the different priorities of West Country and London merchants. It also had the merit of uniting national and private interests to create a common approach to the founding of the colonies.

The geographic bounds set out in the charter were also pragmatic. By the opening of the seventeenth century it was becoming clear that if Spanish warships remained a threat along much of the coast from Florida to South Carolina, and the French were moving into the Gulf of St. Lawrence and Canada, to have any real chance of success English colonizing projects would necessarily have to be located somewhere along the nine hundred miles from Cape Fear to Nova Scotia. New England presented one possibility; the other was the Chesapeake.[39]

ON THE EVE OF THE JAMESTOWN expedition, only a handful of Englishmen had ever seen the Chesapeake Bay. Thomas Hariot and John White had led an exploratory party to the Elizabeth River area and wintered there in 1585–1586, and a mariner sent by Ralegh, Samuel Mace, may have reconnoitered the larger rivers of the Bay in 1603. Relatively little was known about the region, especially in comparison to what was known about New England, which had recently seen at least three successful expeditions, including that of Gosnold, in as many years. Few could have foreseen in 1606 that Virginia, not New England, would become the first major site of English colonization in America or that the price paid would be so bloody.

The Indians of Tsenacommacah knew even less about the far-away lands of the strangers who periodically visited their shores. Aside from Don Luís, Wanchese, Manteo, and a few unnamed others, none had traveled to the distant nations across the sea and returned to tell the tale. Europeans had first arrived in the Chesapeake or coasted its waters some eighty years before, but, with the important exception of the Spanish attack instigated by Pedro Menéndez, they had posed little discernible threat. Every fifteen to twenty years, one or two ships entered the Bay; but they soon disappeared over the horizon, leaving little or no trace of their fleeting visits. In the light of previous experience, the Powhatans could not possibly have imagined the numbers of English settlers who would arrive during the next few years or understood their purpose. The two worlds of the English and Powhatan were rapidly converging and would soon collide in a series of violent encounters along the James River, changing both forever.

# 2

## The "Pearl and the Gold"

*O*N A RAW DECEMBER DAY, three small ships slipped quietly down the Thames on the ebb tide, their departure unnoticed except perhaps by a few friends, relatives, and curious onlookers who gathered along the riverside to watch the little fleet pass by. The largest of the three, the heavily armed merchantman *Susan Constant* (120 tons), was packed to the gunnels with supplies and carried seventy-one passengers and crew, including the expedition's most experienced mariner, Captain Christopher Newport. A highly successful privateer, he had made many voyages to the Caribbean and had taken part in the sacking of numerous Spanish towns and capture of prize ships. He knew as much about American waters as any Englishman alive and was given sole command of the fleet until the expedition reached Virginia.[1]

Following closely behind the admiral, as the lead ship was known, was the *Godspeed,* commanded by Bartholomew Gosnold, which, although less than half the size of her companion, nevertheless carried fifty-two men. At the rear was the tiny pinnace *Discovery,* of just 20 tons, captained by John Ratcliffe (alias Sicklemore), a mysterious character whose background is unknown. She carried twenty-one men crowded together on her decks wherever they could find space in between the clutter of provisions and equipment. Altogether, 144 mariners and adventurers set out from Blackwall docks to the east of London in the last days of 1606 to found an English colony somewhere on the Chesapeake Bay.[2]

Who were these "first Planters" and what led them to embark for Virginia? Leaving aside the crew, between a third and a half were described as gentlemen. Many had been recruited by Gosnold, Wingfield, and the wealthy London merchant, Sir Thomas Smythe, one of the expedition's principal financial backers. Like Captain John Smith, Wingfield, and Newport, several were ex-soldiers and privateers who had fought against the Spanish or in the Irish wars. The two Anthony Gosnolds (father and son) and John and George Martin either were relatives of leading members of the expedition or had served with them elsewhere. Captain Gabriel Archer had been with Bartholomew Gosnold on his voyage to New England, and Richard Crofts may have known Wingfield in Ireland. At least two of the party, Captain George Kendall and William Brewster, were in the pay of Lord Salisbury, and it is likely that someone (possibly Kendall) was a Spanish spy. Most of the gentry were in their twenties and thirties, and some of them, such as George Percy, brother of Henry, the 9th Earl of Northumberland, were younger sons seeking their fortunes in a venture that offered the prospect of soldiering and plunder.

Among the nongentry were a dozen skilled craftsmen and artisans— a blacksmith, a mason, two bricklayers, four carpenters, a tailor, two barbers, and a surgeon; the rest of the company was made up of unskilled workers of various kinds: common seamen, laborers, and boys. The majority of men whose origins have been traced were from the southern and eastern regions of England, especially from London and its surrounding counties. Suffolk, Lincolnshire, and Huntingdonshire, the home counties of Gosnold, Smith, and Wingfield, contributed at least twenty-three settlers (slightly more than a third of those whose home parishes are known). London and Essex contributed a similar number. It is possible that many of the poorer men whose home parishes have not been located were also from the capital, probably from the docklands and riverside parishes east of the city where they may have been picked up during final preparations for the voyage in the fall and early winter. Other counties, from Yorkshire and Lancashire in northern England to Cornwall in the far southwest, contributed one or two settlers each.[3]

"We finde it in daily experience," Ralegh observed, "that all discourse of magnamitie, of Nationall Vertue, of Religion, of Libertie, and whatsoever else hath bene wont to move and incourage virtuous men, hath no force at all with the common-Souldier, in comparison of [with] spoile and riches."[4] Ralegh was referring to the wars against the Spanish but his remarks apply equally to colonizing projects, allowing that the desire for riches was hardly confined to the rank-and-file. From the king and his ministers, the merchants, financiers, and investors who put up the money, to the laborers who ventured themselves on the voyage, all must have hoped that Virginia would return the kinds of profits that had eluded previous efforts in Roanoke and the far north.

Richard Hakluyt and Thomas Hariot's vision of the Atlantic becoming a great highway for English commerce, which necessarily implied a long-term commitment, was a view beyond the grasp of most investors who looked forward to more immediate returns. To maintain public interest and attract settlers, there would have to be a spectacular discovery of some sort or a certain promise of riches to come to warrant continued investment in the venture. For if the Chesapeake turned out to be worthless, as the Spanish judged it, why should the English persist there?

Neither did the majority of first planters have long-term plans to settle in Virginia. Most went to explore the land and, with luck, find gold or silver mines ("To get the pearl and gold"), and discover a river passage to the South Sea. They signed on with the expectation of returning home within a year or two, preferably rich. Like John Smith, they went to seek their fortune in America just as they had previously sought adventure and plunder in campaigns against the Spanish on land and sea. Although the Virginia adventurers were instructed to sow wheat and other crops "for Victual" to promote self-sufficiency, the colony was not intended to be primarily an agricultural settlement. Women and children were not taken along to create the conditions for family life; they would come later once the colony was secured. In the meantime, the task of the first expedition was to rediscover the Chesapeake and take possession for the English.[5]

## Storms and Portents

The voyage did not begin well. The fleet was held up for six weeks off the north coast of Kent by stormy weather within sight of the twin towers of St. Mary's, the Anglo-Saxon church high on the cliffs of Reculver, where the Reverend Robert Hunt, one of Richard Hakluyt's protégés, had preached for many years. No seaman, as the *Susan Constant* wallowed in heavy seas, Hunt became so sick that "few expected his recoverie," leading some of the company ("little better than Atheists," Smith commented) to interpret his presence as an ill omen. In the cramped and unwholesome conditions on board the over-crowded ships, the "flames of envie, and dissention" flared up. Hunt tried to dampen the discontent with "godly exhortations"; but for his pains earned the hostility of some of the gentry, who wanted him put ashore. Even before they had lost sight of England, the men had fallen into factions and infighting.

Eventually, the three ships managed to beat their way out of the Downs and, with Hunt still on board, left the English coast behind them. They took the southerly route, well known to Newport and other privateers, which would bring them to the Canaries and across the Atlantic to the West Indies. But the bickering soon started again. On February 12, George Percy reported seeing "a blazing Starre" in the night sky, another ominous portent. The next day, John Smith, who was on board the *Susan Constant* along with many of the gentry, was arrested for mutiny and "restrained as a prisoner." He was accused by several of the expedition's leaders of plotting to "usurpe the governement, murder the Councell, and make himselfe kinge," aided by his "confederates," who were dispersed in all three of the ships.

What led to the accusation? Mutiny probably implied insubordination. Smith may have been too insistent in his advice to Newport and Wingfield and too liberal in his criticisms of their decisions. Opinionated and vocal, Smith chafed under the command of men he considered incompetent, and he found it difficult to restrain himself in talk with the crew and other gentry on board. During his years fighting in Europe he had become used to an easy-going familiarity with his fellow soldiers, who judged a man's worth more by ability than by rank. In the pompous figure of Wingfield, Smith saw precious little ability and only unwarranted arrogance. Wingfield and Newport, for their part, viewed Smith as nothing more than a young upstart and braggart, a man who spent too much time questioning and not enough following orders. Smith's claim to gentleman status, earned on the battlefields of eastern Europe, did not impress Wingfield. To him, Smith was merely a vulgar commoner who had pretensions above his station.[6]

Contributing to bad blood among the men was the curious arrangement whereby the leadership of the colony was kept secret. The Virginia Council had sealed the names of the leaders in a box and expressly commanded that it was not to be opened until they reached their destination. Presumably, the device was intended to keep members of the gentry who had signed up for the voyage committed to the venture. If they had known the membership of the colony's ruling council before leaving England, some not included might have decided not to go. In practice, however, the measure created unnecessary uncertainty in the men's minds about who would be in charge in Virginia (apart from Newport and the other ships' captains, who, it was assumed, would continue to play a leading role), and increased rather than reduced the likelihood of shipboard disputes.[7]

Toward the end of March, the fleet sighted Martinique and soon after dropped anchor at Dominica, described by George Percy as a "very faire Iland," where they traded for provisions with "Savage Indians" who, Percy wrote, would "eate their enemies when they kill[ed] them" and who "worship[ed] the Devill for their God." Newport knew the islands well and guided the three ships to Guadaloupe, then past

Montserrat and St. Christopher to Nevis, where the men were sent ashore for several days to recover from the long voyage. There, they bathed in natural springs of hot and cold water, hunted, fished, and took their ease.

Despite the beautiful surroundings and welcome respite from the tedium of being at sea, another argument broke out between the gentry that resulted in the building of a "paire of gallowes" for the hapless Smith, who was still under arrest for insubordination. Again, it is not clear what Smith's offense was. Possibly, the gallows were built on the orders of Newport in an effort to reestablish discipline by making an example of Smith. As commander of the fleet, Newport had the authority to exact summary justice, especially if it was deemed necessary to quell a mutiny. To emphasize his contempt for Smith, Newport would have had him hanged like a common criminal rather than shot as befitted a gentleman. But he did not get the opportunity. Gosnold, who was on better terms with Smith than any of the other leaders, together with the Reverend Hunt, interceded to save him. Dissent ran deep among the colony's leaders well before they reached Virginia, and Newport and Wingfield had already come to detest Smith.

Leaving the West Indies on April 10, the ships headed northwards. After eleven days at sea, they ran into "a vehement tempest" somewhere off Virginia, which lasted all night "with winds, raine, and thunders in a terrible manner." The squall was so violent that the mariners lost their bearings and for several days were unsure of where they were or the how to gain entrance to the Bay. Smith, perhaps in a sideswipe at Newport, interpreted the tempest as divine intervention. "But God, the guider of all good actions," he wrote, "forcing them by an extream storme to hul all night, did drive them by his providence to their desired port, beyond all their expectations, for never any of them had seene that coast." For good measure, he claimed also that Captain Ratcliffe had been ready to abandon further attempts to reach the Bay and return to England forthwith. God, not Newport, according to Smith, had ensured the safe arrival of the English in America, and if that were so, there must be a purpose.[8]

## Trouble in Eden

Storm-tossed and weary, a vigilant lookout sighted "the Land of Virginia" at dawn on April 26. The same day, the fleet passed between the capes and "entred into the Bay of Chesupioc directly, without any let or hindrance." It was a moment of joy and relief. A little more than four months after leaving the cold damp of an English winter they would soon experience the warmth of their first Virginia spring. They had avoided capture by Spanish warships, weathered violent storms, escaped shipwreck, and lost only one member of the company. Although they had arrived somewhat later than anticipated, they had at least been able to replenish their supplies and get some rest in the West Indies, and they still had time to plant crops for an autumn harvest.

So it was in an optimistic mood that Newport ordered the fleet to drop anchor on the southern shore of the Chesapeake Bay. He, Wingfield, and Gosnold went ashore with twenty or thirty men (probably not far from where John White and Thomas Hariot's exploratory party from Roanoke spent the winter in 1585–1586) to view the country. First impressions were highly favorable. Here were "faire meddowes and goodly tall Trees, with such Fresh-waters running through the woods," George Percy exclaimed, "as I was almost ravished at the sight thereof."

Having spent most of the day ashore, exploring along the waterside and a little way inland, the men returned to their ships as darkness fell. A group of Indians were waiting for them. Percy described the scene: "At night, when we were going aboard, there came the Savages creeping upon all foure, from the Hills like Beares, with their Bowes in their mouthes, charged us very desperately in the faces, hurt Captaine Gabrill Archer in both his hands, and a sayler in two places of the body very dangerous. After they had spent their Arrowes, and felt the sharpnesse of our shot, they retired into the Woods with a great noise, and so left us."

The Indians had probably been watching the Englishmen for a while and had carefully planned their attack by taking advantage of nightfall and the cover of the trees into which they made their raucous retreat. Percy made no further reference to the incident, and Smith was similarly reticent about the subject. But it was an inauspicious beginning to the colony, and more particularly to relations with local peoples.[9]

Safely back on board, Newport that same night ordered the opening of the box containing the names of the council appointed to govern affairs in Virginia. Seven men were listed. Newport, Wingfield, Gosnold, and John Ratcliffe were the recognized leaders of the expedition. Captain John Martin was the son of the goldsmith Sir Richard Martin, Master of the Royal Mint and three times Lord Mayor of London. As a young man, he had sailed with Sir Francis Drake and was with the fleet that picked up Lane's colony when Roanoke was abandoned twenty years before. He was the only member of the Jamestown expedition who had a direct connection with the earlier colony. In his middle-to-late forties, he was one of the senior members of the party and was accompanied by his son, John, and possibly another relative, George Martin.

Captain George Kendall was a cousin of Sir Edwin Sandys, the distinguished parliamentarian and supporter of the colony. Kendall owed his nomination not so much to Sandys, however, as to his connections with Lord Salisbury, who wanted someone in Virginia to provide regular and accurate reports about what was going on in the colony. The final name on the list was John Smith, who was the youngest of the councilors. Most likely, Gosnold recommended him in recognition of his early involvement in the venture.[10]

According to the instructions from London, a president was to be elected from the seven men named who would serve for one year unless removed by a majority of the council. It was expected that the president and council would reach agreement by discussion; but if it came to a vote, a simple majority would decide an issue, in which the president was granted two votes. The arrangement had some advantages. A small council avoided unwieldy meetings and too many discordant voices in government. The election of the president by the council in Virginia left the decision to the leaders on the spot, and therefore encouraged support for the man they chose to be in charge.

But there were serious drawbacks, all too evident even on that first day. The council would not permit Smith to take up his place, a decision that further damaged relations between him, Wingfield, and Newport, and immediately called into question the authority of the Virginia Council's orders. And what of those not named who might reasonably have expected to be appointed, for example, George Percy and Gabriel Archer? Limiting the size of the council was no guarantee against factionalism and positively encouraged resentment by men excluded from taking part in running the colony's affairs. As it turned out, command remained split between the elected president, Wingfield, and Newport, who had the task of exploring the country for two months before returning to England with ships laden with "Goods and Marchandizes."

The next couple of weeks were spent surveying the James, called the Powhatan or King's River, and making contact with local peoples. In a shallop (a small boat with sails and oars) transported from England for use on the rivers and shallow waters of the Bay, the men continued along the southern shore, taking soundings as they went. Entering a river (probably the Lynnhaven), they came to a plot of cleared ground five miles "in compass" without "either Bush or Tree," where they found a large dugout canoe and "good store of Mussels and Oysters" left by Indians, "which lay on the ground as thicke as stones."

Leaving their boat well guarded, they went on foot several miles into the woods and saw a great deal of smoke from burning grass, where Indians were either clearing the land or, as Percy thought, giving a signal to bring warriors together for an attack on the intruders. In fact, they saw neither an Indian nor a town, only a great abundance of flowers and trees as well as "fine and beautifull Strawberries, foure times bigger and better than ours in England." The men did, however, make a significant discovery: On their way back to the ships they found a deepwater channel across the James near a point of land they called "Cape Comfort," sufficiently large to allow the passage of ocean-going vessels. This was good news, especially for Newport and the mariners because they now had the happy prospect of taking the ships upriver as soon as they wished rather than spending weeks reconnoitering the lower reaches of the Bay searching for a suitable harbor.

Before heading into the interior, Newport had one more important task to perform: On "the nine and twentieth day," Percy reported, "we set up a Crosse at Chesupioc Bay, and named that place Cape Henry." Percy's terse description does little justice to the event. The planting of the cross at the entrance of the Bay signified that they had taken possession of the region in the name of James I; henceforth the land (to their minds) was English. We have little idea about what actually took place during the ceremony. The cross was either put together from trees cut down nearby or brought from England for the purpose, but of its size and form there is no word. Newport and Wingfield likely gathered the company together so that the Reverend Hunt could give thanks for their safe arrival; then one or both of them would have made a formal declaration claiming Virginia for the crown and naming the cape for the king's eldest son, Prince Henry.[11]

Compared to other European ceremonies of possession, the event was probably a modest affair. There were no elaborate rituals, speeches, or processions, nor were the local peoples involved. It was enacted for the symbolic purpose of announcing to other nations, notably the Spanish, that Virginia was now English. As far as they were concerned, the "natural people" who inhabited the region had no say in the matter. Unlike Spanish conquistadors, Newport was not required to proclaim to local peoples that they should now subject themselves to their new rulers and conform to the Christian religion, and neither was he to reveal why the English had come to Virginia.

Following the ceremony, Newport moved the three ships to Cape Comfort, anchored, and prepared the shallop to explore farther up the James River. During the next two weeks, they made contact with the Kecoughtans, who "entertained them very kindly," then proceeded upriver, where they met the Paspaheghs near the mouth of the Chickahominy River, and the Quiyoughcohannocks, who lived on the opposite bank. They received a warm welcome from the Paspaheghs and were treated to a long oration from "an old Savage," incomprehensible to English ears.

The English were impressed by the weroance of the Quiyoughco-hannocks, Choapock, who cut a striking figure as he came down to the water's edge at the head of a group of warriors to greet the new arrivals. The chief wore a headdress of "Deares haire colloured red," two long feathers sticking up like a pair of horns and great plates of copper on either side of his head. Pearls and bird claws set in fine copper hung from his ears and a chain of beads from his neck. His face was painted blue and silver and his body was covered in a crimson dye. But what struck the Englishmen most was the chief's demeanor. He "entertained us in so modest a proud fashion," Percy observed, "as though he had beene a Prince of a civil government, holding his countenance without laughter or any such ill behaviour." Visiting his "Palace" atop a steep hill, they passed through "Woods along fine paths, having most pleasant Springs" and went through "the goodliest Corne fields that ever was seene in any Countrey."

After a couple of days, they continued on and reached the land of the Appomattocs, at the confluence of the Appomattox and the upper James Rivers, where initially the Indians were reluctant to allow them to land. Eventually, they were permitted to spent a day or two looking around before heading back to their ships.[12]

By the end of the second week, Newport had learnt it was possible to navigate the James in ocean-going vessels as far as the Appomattox and that most of the Indians along the river were (or appeared to be) friendly. With things seemingly going their way, the men could now look for a convenient place to establish a settlement. Gosnold favored a point of land named by the English "Archers Hope" near the creek where, years earlier, the Spanish Jesuits' mission had arrived with Don Luís, but Wingfield objected because they could not bring the ships close to the shore. The eventual site chosen, two miles upriver "in Paspihas Countrey," was a marshy peninsula they called Jamestown Island.

The island seemingly had a number of natural advantages. A settlement on the island would be far enough from the coast (about fifty miles) to avoid being surprised by Spanish warships, a major concern of the Virginia Council. And the site, surrounded by water except for a narrow land bridge at the western end, could be easily defended against local Indians should they prove hostile. There was plenty of game for food and timber for building and exporting back to London. Most important, a deepwater channel ran close enough to the land for their ships to be moored near the site; thus, the laborious task of transporting provisions and equipment ashore would be eased and the settlement could be defended from the river by the ships' cannon.[13]

On May 14, the men disembarked and started to unload their stores and set up camp. "Now falleth every man to worke," John Smith remarked, as the task of building a settlement began. Some of the men constructed a rudimentary fortification from brush in the shape of a half moon, some cleared the undergrowth so they could pitch tents, some cut down trees for clapboard, and the remainder prepared the ground for tillage or made fishing nets.[14]

Having established a beachhead, Newport was anxious to explore upriver. The Virginia Council's instructions required that he look for mountains where he might find valuable minerals and ascertain whether the rivers led to a great lake that might be a passage to "the East India Sea." Accordingly, a week after their arrival, he led a party of twenty-three men (including Smith, Percy, and Gabriel Archer) on a voyage of discovery up the James, determined, as Archer put it, not to return before finding the "head of this Ryver, the Laake mentyoned by others heretofore, the Sea againe, the Mountaynes Apalatsi, or some issue."[15] From a broad perspective, the voyage represented a belated continuation of the exploration of the Bay begun more than twenty years earlier by White and Hariot's expedition from Roanoke. They had scouted the lower reaches of the James along its southern shore to the Nansemond, and now Newport intended to carry the exploration of the river to its conclusion in the interior.

All along the river during the next few days, the company was met by friendly peoples apparently eager to trade. Newport learned much from them, notably the existence of a great king, Powhatan (Wahunsonacock), who ruled over "at least 20ty severall kingdoms," and that in lands to the west his enemies, the powerful Monacans, lived in the mountains of "Quirank." Newport was heartened by the mention of mountains that might contain copper (or even gold), but the James River did not lead to a great lake, as the explorers soon discovered when they reached the rocks and shoals of the falls a little way above the palisaded town of Powhatan (present-day Richmond).

Nevertheless, having explored the river as far as possible, he was keen to mark the achievement with another monument. On May 24, he ordered the men to erect a cross carrying the inscription "Jacobus Rex," which was intended to serve notice to other Europeans (if not the locals) that the English now claimed ownership of all the lands along the James River. At the end of the ceremony, the men raised a "greate showte" proclaiming James I sovereign, which caused some uneasiness in their Indian guide; but Newport reasured him "that the two Armes of the Crosse signifyed kyng Powatah and himselfe, the fastening of it in the myddest was their united Leaug [league], and the shoute the reverence he dyd to Pawatah."

The Englishmen considered the voyage a great success. They had enjoyed the hospitality of the Indians at the falls and of a chief they thought was Wahunsonacock himself. They had a good idea of the extent of the river and had learnt much about the peoples who lived along it. Described by Percy as "one of the famousest Rivers that ever was found by any Christian," the James ran about 160 miles inland and was between a quarter and two miles wide. On each side, the country abounded with fair meadows, trees, wild fruits, and game, and its waters teemed with sturgeon, "very large and excellent good," a rich variety of fish, banks of oysters, and many great crabs.

On the return journey, they discovered the lands of the "Pamaunche" (Pamunkey), rich in "Copper and pearle," where the people wore copper ornaments in their ears, around their necks, "and in broad plates on their heades," and where the king (Opechancanough) had a "Chaine of pearle" worth from at least £300 to £400. During the many feasts and entertainments with their Indian hosts, they had established cordial relations with the many peoples who lived along the river, including a firm bond of friendship with the "greate kyng Pawatah" himself.[16]

But appearances were not what they seemed. Newport had no compunction about misleading the Indians about his true intentions and the meaning of the cross at the falls. Following instructions from the Virginian Council not to offend "the naturals," he deliberately encouraged the impression that his men were more interested in trade than in occupying the land. Perhaps with the experience of Roanoke in mind, the Company's leaders accepted that the colony might well be dependent on the goodwill of local peoples initially, not only for food supplies but also for information about the region and trade.

For their part, the Powhatans had misled Newport about the identity of "Pawatah," who was in fact one of Wahunsonacock's sons, Parahunt (tanx or "little" Powhatan), not the great chief himself. They also deceived Newport by blaming the Chesapeakes for the attack on the English at Cape Henry a month before; in fact, peoples loyal to the Powhatans were responsible. Most important, the lavish hospitality extended to the English at the falls and elsewhere was merely a subterfuge to keep them upriver.

While Newport's men were feasting and enjoying the company of the Indians, an alliance of five tribes—Quiyoughcohannocks, Weyanocks, Appomattocs, Paspaheghs, and Kiskiacks, about two hundred warriors in all—launched "a very furious Assault" on the unsuspecting colonists at Jamestown and threatened to overwhelm the settlement.[17] The Indians came right up to the camp and shot their arrows through the tents, wounding twelve of the English, two of whom later died. After an hour of intense fighting, the attack was beaten off, largely thanks to the murderous effect of small shot from the ships' cannons.

It is unclear who ordered the attack. Newport, who returned to the island the following day, hoped that only the Indians of the vicinity were hostile and that the peoples upriver remained friendly. The alliance, however, was made up not only of local Indians who lived near Jamestown, such as the Paspaheghs and Quiyoughcohannocks, but also included peoples from the Appomattox and Pamunkey (York) Rivers. More likely, Wahunsonacock wanted to test the newcomers' strength. If so, the outcome must have been disturbing. In spite of their pitifully small numbers, the colonists had held off a couple hundred of his warriors and had demonstrated, as had the Spanish earlier, the destructive power of firearms and cannon. He must have realized that frontal assaults would be bloody and fruitless and might have determined that the safest course was to watch, wait, and gather more information about the settlers' intentions. He might have realized also that if the newcomers had come to stay, in the long run his military superiority and the security of his lands could be guaranteed only by the acquisition of English weapons.

As far as the English were concerned, the immediate outcome of the attack was to convince the colony's leaders of the need for much stronger fortifications than the brushwood fence they had initially constructed. Accordingly, the men were put to work building a fort "triangle wise" with "three Bulwarkes at every corner like a halfe Moone" where cannon were placed. Two of the bulwarks fronted the James River, where the greatest threat to the English in the form of a Spanish assault lay, and one faced inland. After a couple of weeks hard labor, the air ringing with the sounds of the felling of trees, sawing of timbers, hammering of clapboards, and curses of men suffering from blistered and bloody hands, the fort was completed.

It was not exactly what the Virginia Council had in mind. In their instructions to the colony's leaders, they had recommended a town with a central market square (fortified if need be) with streets of "a Good breadth" running off it in straight lines. In this way, the streets could be commanded by field pieces placed in the square, which would be the natural focus of the settlement where the storehouse, church, and other public buildings would be located. The council's instructions suggest that the colony's principal settlement would be a long-term development, that it would grow as more settlers arrived and perhaps even rival the cities of New Spain in time; a fitting ambition for a colony that was England's answer to Spain's rapidly expanding American empire.[18]

But the colony's leaders in Virginia were not thinking about long-term developments or Spanish cities when they began constructing their fort. For them, it was imperative to build adequate fortifications as soon as possible because no one knew when the next attack would come or whether it would be a much sterner test of their defenses. A triangular design based on models in Ireland, or possibly forts on the Florida coast erected by the Spanish and French, offered suitable examples and would be relatively quick and easy to construct.[19] A stout palisade, or curtain, about eight feet high provided sufficient protection from Indian arrows; loopholes cut in the timbers and cannon mounted on the three bulwarks allowed the Englishmen to fire back safely. The fort commanded a clear view of the river, built as it was on one of the island's ridges. Although a navigable channel ran close to the shore at the western end of the ridge, where the colony was planted, to the east the channel was farther off from the land. If Spanish warships did enter the James, they could get close to the island only as they approached the settlement itself, by which time they would be directly under the fort's guns.

ON THE EVE OF HIS DEPARTURE for England on Sunday, June 21, Newport invited the colony's council to dine with him by way of "a farewell." Seated on tree stumps and sea chests around a table made of rough planks and barrels set up near Wingfield's tent—smoky torches providing a flickering light and perhaps a modicum of relief from biting insects—the men had much to celebrate. We can guess something of the conversation that warm summer evening. Within just six weeks of disembarking at Jamestown, they had fortified themselves against the Indians, sown a good crop of wheat, and produced samples of clapboard and sassafras for export. As the evening drew on and the wine flowed freely, talk turned more and more to the rich promise of the lands they had discovered along the river. There was an abundance of trees fit for many purposes—oaks, ash, walnut, poplar, pine, cedar, and "sweete woodes"—and there were gums "pleasant as Franckumcense" of "great vertewe in healing greene woundes and Aches." Most intriguing of all, in the mountains there might be gold or other precious minerals.

In a letter of June 22, the colony's leaders entreated the London Company to organize a second expedition as soon as possible lest "that all devouringe Spaniard lay his ravenous hands uppon theas gold

# BOSTON TEA PARTY SHIPS & MUSEUM EXPERIENCE

Name: _____

Address: _____

E
M
A
I
L

| | | | | | | | | | |
|---|---|---|---|---|---|---|---|---|---|

| | | | | | | | | | |
|---|---|---|---|---|---|---|---|---|---|

Did you have a good time?          ○ **YES**    ○ **NO**

Was it worth what you paid?        ○ **YES**    ○ **NO**

Will you recommend us?             ○ **YES**    ○ **NO**

What was your favorite part of the experience?_____

_____

Actor's Name(s) _____

**Please rate us**

| | Excellent | Good | Fair | Poor | N/A |
|---|:---:|:---:|:---:|:---:|:---:|
| Actors | ○ | ○ | ○ | ○ | ○ |
| Ships | ○ | ○ | ○ | ○ | ○ |
| Town Meeting | ○ | ○ | ○ | ○ | ○ |
| Tory Patriot Hologram | ○ | ○ | ○ | ○ | ○ |
| Robinson Tea Chest Exhibit | ○ | ○ | ○ | ○ | ○ |
| Talking Portraits | ○ | ○ | ○ | ○ | ○ |
| Movie, *Let it Begin Here* | ○ | ○ | ○ | ○ | ○ |
| Abigail's Tea Room | ○ | ○ | ○ | ○ | ○ |
| Griffin's Wharf Retail Emporium | ○ | ○ | ○ | ○ | ○ |

Please share your comments, impressions and suggestions on how we may improve:_____

_____

_____

_____

_____

_____

_____

**For Tour and Attraction discounts in 22 states
go to www.trustedtours.com**

*MONTHLY COMMENT CARD DRAWINGS
WIN A FREE VACATION*

showing mountains." Knowing Newport would provide a full report as soon as he reached London, the council gave little more than a hint of future profits, but William Brewster could hardly contain himself. Virginia, he believed, was "the moste Statlye, Riche kingdome in the world," and, writing to Lord Salisbury, he predicted that his patron yet might "lyve to see Ingland, moore Riche, & Renowned, then anye kingdon, in all Ewroopa [Europe]."

Gabriel Archer calculated the likely returns of the colony in a manner that would have been music to the ears of Hakluyt, Hariot, and the wider merchant community: Not only could Virginia provide all the crops "the North Tropick of the world affordes," but the settlers could "by [their] industry . . . make oyles wynes soape ashes . . . Iron [and] copper." With enough laborers, it would be possible to supply all the clapboard, wainscot, and sassafras England wanted, together with 5,000 lbs. of tobacco a year, dyestuffs, and medicinal drugs. The great sturgeon to be found in the rivers would be worth at least £1,000 annually and there was also plenty of cod and herring off the capes. He concluded, "I know not what can be expected from a common wealth that either this land affordes not or may soone yeeld." As supper broke up and the men went back to their quarters, the colony's potential must have seemed boundless.[20]

It was the possibility of gold mines in the interior near the falls rather than colonists' enthusiastic reports of timber and other commodities that excited attention in London, however. Sir Walter Cope, a confidant of Salisbury's and a leading member of the London Company, was brimming with an excitement reminiscent of the gold fever that had swept the city thirty years earlier following Martin Frobisher's discovery of Meta Incognita. Shortly after Newport's return on August 12, Cope wrote about the "barrel full of earth" brought back from Virginia, which, he had been told by "an excellent tryer of myneralls," might yield 1,200 or as much as 2,000 lbs. of gold per ton. Unfortunately, the next day his hopes were dashed. After four trials, it was determined beyond all doubt that the ore was worthless. "Oure newe dyscoverye ys more Lyke to prove the Land of Canaan then the land of ophir," he wrote, a land of milk and honey rather than a land of gold. Newport had been duped, possibly deliberately by one or more of the colony's leaders, because even the suggestion of gold would bring about a stampede of investors eager to put their money into the venture.[21]

When news about the worthless ore got around the city there was much speculation about the colony's prospects. Dudley Carlton told John Chamberlain that although Virginia had much to recommend it, "silver and golde they have none"; and Don Pedro de Zúñiga, the Spanish ambassador in London, bluntly informed Philip III the country was "sterile." The only possible explanation for the Company's continued interest in it, he warned the king, was as a base for piracy. At least a few merchants, including Sir Thomas Smythe, thought there might have been a mix up in the samples of ore and reported that Newport, realizing his mistake, was eager to return to the colony to bring back the true gold-laden deposits as soon as possible. Whether or not the Company believed this story, there was certainly enough good news from the colony to justify sending more settlers and supplies, and preparations got underway for another voyage.[22]

It was fortunate the Company did not know what had been going on in the colony since Newport's departure; if they had, they might have reconsidered. In the first flush of optimism after landing, John Smith described Jamestown as "a verie fit place for the erecting of a great cittie," but, aside from considerations of defense, the choice did not turn out to be a wise one.[23] The site they had chanced upon was waste ground used by the Paspaheghs for hunting, the best lands along the river having been occupied for centuries by local peoples. Large areas of swamp and marshland (natural breeding grounds for swarms of mosquitoes) rendered half the island uninhabitable and unsuitable for tillage. The absence of freshwater springs meant that drinking water had to be drawn either from brackish wells dug by the settlers or from the river, which in the summer became increasingly saline and polluted. And, unknown to the colonists, fresh water would be all the more difficult to find because the land was suffering from a severe drought.

Six weeks after Newport sailed for England, the terrible roll call began: "The sixt of August there died John Asbie of the bloudie Flixe

[flux]. The ninth day died George Flowre of the swelling. The tenth day died William Bruster Gentleman, of a wound given by the Savages, and was buried the eleventh day. The fourteenth day, Jerome Alikock Ancient, died of a wound, the same day Francis Midwinter, Edward Moris Corporall died suddenly." On August 22, the colony suffered its greatest loss with the death of Bartholomew Gosnold, perhaps the only man who could have held the fractious leaders together.[24]

And so through the end of August into September, George Percy wrote, "Our men were destroyed with cruell diseases as Swellings, Flixes, Burning Fevers, and by warres, . . . but for the most part they died of meere famile." There "were never Englishmen left in a forreigne Countrey in such miserie," he continued, "as wee were in this new discovered Virginia. . . . Thus we lived for the space of five moneths in this miserable distresse, not having five able men to man our Bulwarkes upon any occasion."

Percy was mistaken in his assumption that "meere famine" was the principal cause of the settlers' sickness and death. The departure of the ships had removed the floating taverns and beer houses and forced the men to rely on "the common kettell" of a pint of wheat and barley boiled in water per man a day, but from May to September they were able to live on sturgeon and sea-crabs, a vital and nutritious supplement to their meager diet. Instead of starvation, the major killer was polluted river water, "full of slime and filth," which led variously to salt poisoning, dysentery, and typhoid. An epidemic swept the settlement and left half the 104 men and boys dead before the end of September. By the onset of winter, fewer than forty survived.[25]

The colony was on the brink of collapse. With Newport gone and Gosnold dead, the leadership disintegrated. On September 10, John Ratcliffe, Smith, and Martin confronted Wingfield and removed him from office, declaring he was "very unworthy to be eyther President or of the Council." The following day, in what passed as a court hearing, it was alleged that Wingfield had hoarded food and drink for his own use while the colony starved, and that he had maliciously accused Smith of mutiny and Jehu Robinson and others of planning to steal the shallop and sail away to Newfoundland. It was said that he had plotted with the Spanish to destroy the colony, that he was an atheist, and that he "affected a Kin[g]dome."

Wingfield's spirited response, delivered in person to the London Company in England the next year, paints a bleak picture of the poisonous relations between the remaining members of the council and sheds further light on events during that terrible summer. He charged the principal ringleaders with forsaking "his Majesties government," as set down by the Virginia Council, and of erecting "a Triumvirate" for their own greed. Smith, he considered, was unworthy of the title of gentleman and unfit to be in his company. "It was proved to his face," he claimed, "that he [Smith] begged in Ireland like a rogue, without lycence." As for Martin, he had never ventured more than a couple of hundred yards beyond the fort and his slackness during his watches and in carrying out his duties was "too well known."

Ratcliffe (the new president) and his confederates had overthrown the lawful government and imposed a regime of arbitrary rule, Wingfield warned. By way of examples of the chaos in Jamestown, he related that a blacksmith, one James Read, was condemned to be hanged for striking Ratcliffe. Standing unsteadily on a ladder serving as makeshift gallows, Read saved himself by revealing a plot he said had been fomented by George Kendall (also recently deposed from the council) to raise a rebellion. A few days later, Kendall, convicted and condemned, was executed, "being shott to death." Were "this whipping, lawing, beating, and hanging in Virginia knowne in England," Wingfield remarked, "I feare it would drive many well affected myndes from this honorable action of Virginia."[26]

Were the accusations against Wingfield justified? Was he guilty of ineptitude and misconduct that led to the unnecessary deaths and sickness of many of his men? Percy, one of Wingfield's supporters, described his valor during the Indian attack on the settlement in late May and later warned him that witnesses were being bribed to testify against him; nevertheless, he had little to say about his (Wingfield's) ousting from the presidency. The London Company chose not to pursue either Wingfield's or the council's allegations and quietly dropped the whole matter; hardly surprising given how damaging the news would have been if it had become common knowledge. It is clear, however, that Wingfield could not command the respect of the men under his charge. Disgraced and abandoned by his friends, he was left with little choice but to leave the colony at the first opportunity.

Had the Powhatans decided to launch a large-scale attack during the summer, it is unlikely the depleted and sickly encampment would have survived. In a seemingly providential turn of events, however, neighboring peoples chose not to resume hostilities and in fact saved the ragged and disease-ridden Englishmen from further suffering by bringing food to the fort. "God the patron of all good endeavours," Smith wrote, "in that desperate extreamity so changed the harts of the Salvages, that they brought such plenty of their fruits, and provision as no man wanted [i.e., went hungry]."

One reason for the Indians' change in attitude may have been the departure of the *Susan Constant* and *Godspeed*. Both Opechancanough and the chief of the Quiyoughcohannocks, Choapock, inquired about the ships in early July. With the ships gone, the English were seen as less of a threat now that they were unable to range freely up and down the James River in their floating fortresses. The turnabout in relations was confirmed in September when the Paspaheghs and other local peoples returned runaways from the colony as a token of friendship, proving also that they were "no Canyballs," as the English had feared. Yet why had Wahunsonacock decided to allow the Englishmen to remain on Jamestown Island, at least for the time being? What purpose did he have in mind for the "tassantasses" (strangers)? Because the English did not have to look beyond divine intervention for an answer, it was not an issue they troubled themselves with. Only in the next few months, as summer turned to fall and then winter, would Wahunsonacock's intentions become clear.[27]

## The Temptation of Captain John Smith

Although the worst of the sickness had now passed, the new regime proved no more popular than the old. Smith described Ratcliffe and John Martin as "little loved, of weake judgement in dangers, and lesse industry in peace." According to his account, Smith took on the effective day-to-day management of the colony, putting men to work building houses to replace their tattered tents and "Cabbins worse than nought" and preparing the ground for crops. "At this time," he wrote, "were most of our chiefest men either sicke or discontented, the rest being in such dispaire, as they would rather starve and rot with idleness, then be perswaded to do anything for their own reliefe."

When provisions brought by the Indians began to run low, Smith and half a dozen men were sent downriver to trade with the Kecoughtans at the mouth of the James River, where the Indians "at first scorned him, as a famished man" and offered only a handful of beans and a little bread for his hatchets and copper. In a deadly show of force, Smith demonstrated that his men were quite capable of taking anything they wanted, but made it plain following his attack that he preferred to trade on fair terms. The Kecoughtans apparently conceded and freighted the Englishmen's boat in return for what Smith offered. They then brought the men "Venison, Turkies, wild foule, bread, and what they had, singing and dauncing in sign of friendship till they departed." A combination of firmness and fairness was how Smith characterized his dealings with the Indians during the next two years.[28]

Successful though his trip had been, the corn he brought back to the fort would not last long. Failing to find sufficient provisions locally, the colony's leaders decided to mount a voyage upriver to the falls. They drew lots and it fell to Smith once again to lead the expedition, much to the relief of Ratcliffe and Archer, who were glad to be getting rid of their arrogant rival. Smith set off in early November "for the discovery of the country of Chikhamania [Chickahominy]," and, finding the people friendly and eager to trade, was able to fill his barge with corn and return to the fort without delay.

After two more trips in which Smith was able to bring back sufficient food to ensure the colony was provisioned for the next few months, he returned to the Chickahominy to complete his exploration of the river. Smith proceeded upriver as far as possible, but upon reaching shallow waters he decided not to risk the barge any farther.

*John Smith is captured by the Pamunkeys.*

Finding a couple of Indians with a canoe who were willing to row them to the river's source, he set out with two companions, John (Jehu) Robinson and Thomas Emry.

About twenty miles above Appocant, the last Chickahominy town they had visited, in a "vast and wilde wilderness," the Englishmen went ashore with the Indians. Taking one of the Indians as a guide, Smith decided to explore and left the other Indian with Robinson and Emry by the canoe. Within a quarter of an hour, Smith heard a loud cry and "hallowing of Indians" and, fearing an attack, quickly bound his Indian guide to his arm as a human shield. Suddenly, he found himself surrounded by two hundred warriors. Defending himself with his pistol, Smith held off the warriors as best he could, but was eventually overwhelmed and brought into the presence of the Indians' leader, Opechancanough. Robinson and Emry were not so fortunate; both were killed.

In fear of his life, Smith played for time and took from his pocket "a round Ivory double compass Dyall," which he presented to the chief. Speaking through his guide (and former shield), who understood some words of English, he described "the use therof." As he later recalled:

Much they marvailed at the playing of the Fly and Needle, which they could see so plainely, and yet not touch it, because of the glasse that covered them. But when he demonstrated by that Globe-like Jewell, the roundnesse of the earth, and skies, the spheare of the Sunne, Moone, and Starres, and how the Sunne did chase the night round about the world continually; the greatnesse of the Land and Sea, the diversitie of Nations, varietie of complexions, and how we were to them the Antipodes, and many other such like matters, they all stood amazed with admiration.

Despite being "amazed," however, the Indians tied Smith to a tree and were about to shoot him when Opechancanough intervened: "Holding up the Compass in his hand, they all laid downe their Bowes and Arrowes." Then, with a shout of triumph, after passing by the body of Robinson ("who had 20 or 30. arrowes in him"), they marched Smith off to the nearby town of Rasawek, about six miles away.[29]

What had led to the unprovoked attack? Apart from the incident at Kecoughtan, the English had been at peace with the Indians for five months, and the peoples Smith had met along the Chickahominy River had seemed especially friendly. He had not anticipated trouble. The populous areas downriver made a striking contrast to the "desolatenes" of the place in which he found himself, and he must have therefore been astonished to be suddenly confronted by hostile Indian warriors and their king. Why were they there? Possibly, Smith and his two companions had simply stumbled across a large Pamunkey hunting expedition. But another possibility is that Opechancanough and Wahunsonacock wanted to learn more about English intentions and, hearing of Smith's visits to the Chickahominies, had decided to capture him for questioning.

At Rasawek, all the women and children turned out to see Smith. The men formed a ring and danced around him in "severall Postures," singing and "yelling out such hellish notes and screeches." Following three dances celebrating the slaying of the Englishmen and capture of the captain, Smith was taken to a house and given more bread and venison "then would have served twentie men" for his supper and as

*The "triumph" of the Pamunkeys over John Smith.*

much again in the morning; this "made him thinke," he wrote, "they would fat him to eat him."

In fact, Smith was well treated. His cloak, compass, and pocketbook were given back to him, and he enjoyed occasional conversations with Opechancanough himself, who, Smith remarked, "took great delight in understanding the manner of our ships, and sayling the seas, the earth and skies and of our God." For his part, the Pamunkey chief informed Smith of what he knew about Tsenacommacah and the lands beyond. He told him of "certaine men cloathed at a place called Ocanahonan, cloathed like me," Smith noted, "and that within 4 or 5 daies journey of the falles was a great turning of salt water." The references were the first mention of the possible survival of the lost colonists of Roanoke and proximity of the South Sea. Smith knew immediately he had stumbled across potentially sensational news.

Within a few days it became clear why his life had been spared. Encouraged by Wowinchopunck, weroance of the Paspaheghs, the Indians were preparing another general assault on Jamestown and Opechancanough wanted Smith to advise them on how best to go about it. In return for betraying his countrymen, he would be granted "life, libertie, land, and women." Calculating that a refusal would lead to his execution, he devised a stratagem by which he could alert the settlers to the Indians' plans while seemingly going along with his captors.

On the pretext of sending a letter to the fort to let his compatriots know he was alive and well, Smith wrote a message detailing the Indians' intent. He instructed the settlers to "send him such things as he writ for," possibly trade goods that he may have had in mind to appease the warriors, and to make as impressive a show of their weaponry as possible, he having emphasized to the Indians the danger of "the Mines, great gunnes, and other Engins" in and around the fort. Three warriors went off to Jamestown—"in as bitter weather as could be of frost and snow"—and returned in a few days with the goods Smith had promised. Because the Indians had no knowledge of written language (according to Smith), they could only explain Smith's apparent ability to communicate over long distances by the use of magic, or because "the paper could speake." And so Smith was able simultaneously to claim magical powers, and thus enhance his prestige with the Indians, and at the same time warn the settlers to prepare themselves for an attack.

To Smith's mind, the ploy worked in both respects: There was no attack on the fort and he had managed to stay alive. But he had probably entirely misconstrued the Indians' intentions. It is more likely that the Indians wanted to substantiate his claim that he was a leader of the Englishmen at the fort and so acquire some valuable trade items from the English as a form of ransom. If Opechancanough and Don Luís were the same person, the Indian would have been quite familiar with writing. Even if this was not so, it is unlikely that the Powhatans had never before encountered European books or would have thought that writing was some form of sorcery. The return of the messengers perhaps confirmed that Smith was someone of influence, worth keeping alive and presenting to the great chief, Wahunsonacock, himself.

Over the next several weeks, Smith was conducted on a series of marches and countermarches back and forth across the frozen landscape between the Chickahominy and Potomac Rivers. First they visited the Youghtanund and Pamunkey peoples, and then the Toppahannocks, at a place where a few years before a ship had entered the river and carried off some of the people. Having determined that the English prisoner was not the culprit, the Indians were friendly and Smith was even able to learn something from them about the peoples who inhabited the north side of the Rappahannock as far west as the Mannahoacs. Passing through a fertile country of hills and dales on the return journey, Smith and his escort eventually arrived at the chief's house in Pamunkey, where he was to experience a final ordeal before meeting the great "Emperour," Wahunsonacock.[30]

Smith described the ritual in some detail. Early in the morning,

> a great fire was made in a long house, and a mat spread on the one side, as on the other, on the one they caused him to sit, and all the guard went out of the house, and presently came skipping in a great grim fellow, all painted over with coale, mingled with oyle; and many Snakes and Wesels skins stuffed with mosse . . . the skins hanging round about his head, backe, and shoulders, and in a manner covered his face; with a hellish voice and a rattle in his hand.

With "most strange gestures," the priest placed a circle of cornmeal around the fire; at this point, Smith wrote, "three more such like devils came rushing in with the like antique [antic] tricks, painted halfe blacke, halfe red: but all their eyes were painted white, and some red stroakes like Muchato's [moustaches], along their cheeks." They danced around Smith, and then three more priests arrived, "as ugly as the rest." At last, they all sat down and the chief priest put five wheat corns on the floor. He began a short oration at the end of which all the priests gave a "short groane" and laid down three more grains. They continued until they had circled the fire twice. Then they took "a bunch of little stickes" that they laid down between the circles of corn. "Till night," Smith wrote, "neither he nor they did eate or drinke, and then they feasted merrily, with the best provisions they could make."

The ceremony lasted for three days, after which he was told the meaning "was to know if he intended them well or no. The circle of meale signified their Country, the circles of corne the bounds of the Sea, and the stickes his Country. They imagined the world to be flat and round like a trencher [platter], and they in the middest." Having satisfied the priests, Smith was feasted by Opitchapam, the great chief's brother and heir, and shortly after taken to Werowocomoco to meet Wahunsonacock himself.[31]

———

WEROWOCOMOCO WAS SITUATED at Purtan Bay on the north side of the York River about fifteen miles as the crow flies from Jamestown.[32] The scene that met Smith's eyes as he was brought into the presence of Wahunsonacock was meant to impress him and had all the studied theatricality of a courtly spectacle. Outside the house to which Smith was guided, two hundred "of those grim Courtiers" (warriors) watched him carefully "as if he had beene a monster." At his entrance, "all the people gave a great shout," the queen of Appomattoc brought him water to wash his hands, and another woman brought him a bunch of feathers as a towel to dry them. In front of a fire, "proudly lying upon a Bedstead," was Wahunsonacock. He wore a great cloak made of raccoon skins, the tails hanging down, and wore chains of large pearls around his neck. A young woman sat at his head and another at his feet, and several rows of men and women stood along each side of the house, their heads and shoulders painted red, wearing "the white downe of Birds" in their hair (or some other ornament), and great necklaces of white beads.

Smith was the first Englishman to meet the chief. He was impressed by the old man's "grave and Majesticall countenance," which, he freely admitted, "drave me into admiration to see such a state in a naked Salvage." Communicating as best he could, the "great king" welcomed Smith, assured him of his friendship, and told him that he would be freed within four days. Wahunsonacock had taken much pleasure in hearing Opechancanough's relation of their earlier conversations, and then the king quizzed Smith on why the Englishmen had come to his lands.

Smith replied they had been in a fight "with the Spaniards our enemie," and that they had retreated to the Chesapeake Bay where they had been forced to put in by bad weather and the need to find fresh water. They were directed upriver, but their pinnace had sprung a leak; they had then encamped at Jamestown to make repairs and wait for the return of Captain Newport, whom Smith described as his father. The chief demanded why they went farther up the James River in their boat; Smith replied: "On the other side the maine, where was salt water, my father had a childe slaine, whiche wee supposed Monocan his enemie had done whose death we intended to revenge." The story was not especially convincing, but Wahunsonacock chose not to press him on it.

The great chief then told him of the many peoples of the region and beyond, including "a fierce Nation that did eate men," the Pocoughtronack, and nations to the north where, a year before, the Powhatans had slain a hundred warriors in battle. "Many Kingdomes hee described mee to the heade of the Bay," Smith continued, beyond which were to be found men "that passed that way in Shippes like ours." Wahunsonacock confirmed also what the Pamunkey chief had said about the people at Ocanahowan and described the "Southerly Countries," including a land called "Anone, where they have abundance of Brasse, and houses walled as ours." "I requited his discourse," Smith noted, "seeing what pride hee had in his great and spacious Dominions."

Wahunsonacock invited Smith to "forsake Paspahegh [Jamestown]" and to live in a "Countrie called Capahowasicke," downriver from Werowocomoco. The offer was not intended to apply to Smith alone. Knowing that the English could not feed themselves, the great chief promised to provide the captain and his men with corn, meat, and other provisions in return for copper and iron goods. Smith and the settlers would be guaranteed food and safety if they acknowledged the great chief as their lord and became a subordinate people within his chiefdom.

Writing in the third person, Smith described the dramatic ceremony that followed:

> two great stones were brought before Powhatan: then as many as could lay hands on him [Smith] dragged him to them, and thereon laid his head, and being ready with their clubs to beate out his braines, Pocahontas the Kings dearest daughter, when no intreaty could prevaile, got his head in her armes, and laid her owne upon his to save him from death.[33]

The event would in time assume mythic importance as a symbol of the transcendent power of love over racial hatred. But did it take place? Smith was the only one present to record what had happened, and even he did not write about it until years later. What we can say with some certainty is that the ritual did not happen as he described it. Pocahontas would not have acted on her own initiative to save the Englishman. As far as we know, she had never met Smith before the ceremony. Since she was just eleven years old, such a public display of disobedience to her father in the presence of his great men would have been unthinkable.

What occurred was probably a ceremony of adoption, in which Smith was symbolically killed and then reborn, marking a passage from his old existence as an Englishman to his new life as an Anglo-Powhatan. Pocahontas merely played her role as she was instructed, very likely a far less dramatic part than Smith describes. It is possible, however, that the ritual took on greater significance for her as she got

King Powhatan comands C:Smith to be slaine, his
daughter Pokahontas beggs his life his thankfullness
and how he subiected 39 of their kings. reade history.

printed by James Reeve

*John Smith saved by Pocahontas.*

to know Smith better during her visits to the fort over the next year. Exactly what that significance might have been is uncertain. Given her age and background, it was not romantic love; but she may have seen him as a father figure or special friend (he once called her his "dearest jewel and daughter"), and he may have viewed her as an exceptionally bright young girl who had the ear of Wahunsonacock.

The list of Algonquian words that Smith learned appears in his *A Map of Virginia* (1612) and provides a clue to how their relationship might have developed. Among the 137 words are a few sentences: "*Utteke, e peya weyack wighwhip*. Get you gone, and come againe quickly"; and "*Kekaten pokahontas patiaquagh ningh tanks manotyens neer mowchick rawrenock audowgh*. Bid Pokahontas bring hither two little Baskets, and I wil give her white beads to make her a chaine." Smith knew that understanding the Powhatans' language would be vital for negotiations, and he may well have sought out Pocahontas's company when the opportunity arose so that he could learn from her. In these conversations, a bond may have developed between them, at least in her mind, which she would not forget.[34]

Whatever the basis of Smith's relationship to Pocahontas, it is clear that Wahunsonacock had decided to spare the lives of Smith and the settlers by absorbing them into his dominions. As the colonists' numbers rapidly dwindled during the summer, his view of them had changed. Instead of seeing them as a threat, he decided they might be useful in providing English copper and other trade goods brought from across the ocean. By incorporating them, he would control access to highly prized European commodities to underline further his status among his own peoples and neighbors.

But there was another motive for Smith's reprieve. Two days after being saved by Pocahontas, the Englishman was taken to a great house in the woods, where Wahunsonacock met him. Dressed "more like a devil then a man with some two hundred more as blacke as himselfe," the great chief told Smith they were now friends and that he would be released shortly and allowed to return to Jamestown. He was instructed to send Wahunsonacock "two great gunnes, and a grindstone" (for sharpening knives and swords) to seal their accord. The chief repeated his offer of giving Smith "Capahowasicke," with the significant addition of making him a son and weroance, to be known henceforth as Nantaquoud.[35]

The Powhatans wanted guns as well as copper and truck. They had witnessed the firepower of ships and knew the settlers had many cannons within the fort. If they possessed two of the "great gunnes," they could easily breech the palisade and overrun the Englishmen's defenses. And in the long run, if they could secure a regular supply of weapons and gunpowder, they would not only prove a match for further new arrivals but also be able to take on their enemies to the west and north, the Monacans and Mannahoacs in the piedmont and the Susquehannocks and Massawomecks beyond the Bay. Combining European weapons with their own battle tactics, the Powhatans could expand their territories far beyond their current borders.

Smith never recorded his answer, but it is more than likely that he agreed to the chief's terms. He was in no position to bargain. But contrary to the suspicions of some of the colony's leaders who would later accuse him of treachery, Smith had not been the least tempted by Wahunsonacock's offer of a chiefdom in return for guns. His self-image as an English captain and Christian knight would have made it impossible for him to contemplate joining what he perceived as a barbarous, or "savage," nation. Although offered a rank among the Powhatans that would elude him among his own countrymen, there was never a moment he seriously considered throwing off his Englishness and becoming an Indian king.

Smith's month of captivity was undoubtedly a turning point in his life. He had traveled more extensively than any other Englishman throughout the region, knew more about the different peoples and Powhatans' way of life, and apparently commanded the respect of their two greatest chiefs. Never one to be modest about his accomplishments, Smith claimed to have saved the fort from destruction, established good relations with the Indians, found evidence of the survival of at least some of the Roanoke colonists, and discovered the existence of the South Sea beyond the western mountains. Henceforth, Smith would be a force to be reckoned with, especially in future relations with the Powhatans.

# 3

## SMITH'S EPIC

*A*S HE RECOUNTS IT, Smith had the last laugh on Wahunsonacock. He knew full well that the Indian guides sent to escort him back to Jamestown after his release from captivity could not possibly drag two demiculverins weighing one and a half tons each to Werowocomoco; and sure enough, when he presented the cannons, "they found them somewhat too heavie." To underline the great guns' destructive power and give a tacit warning to the Powhatans, he had the cannons loaded with stones and fired into nearby trees, bringing down branches and limbs in a cascade of splintered wood and ice. The "poor Salvages," Smith wrote, "ran away halfe dead with feare." Considering it unwise to antagonize their neighbors too much, and wishing to maintain good relations, the English provided various gifts for Wahunsonacock, his women and children, and sent the Indians on their way apparently well contented.

Smith's safe return to the fort must have been viewed as little short of miraculous to most of the settlers, and yet he received a mixed welcome. According to him, the men were overjoyed to see him back, probably because they hoped he might bring news of gold mines or an alliance with the Indians that might guarantee them sufficient food to survive until the return of Newport. But Gabriel Archer, who had been sworn to the council in Smith's absence, was not so happy and charged him with being directly responsible for the deaths of Emry and Robinson, killed by Opechancanough's warriors at the head of the Chickahominy River.

Citing chapter twenty-four of the Book of Leviticus, Archer argued that Smith should pay for the dead men's lives with his own. So "speedie is our lawe thear [Virginia]," Wingfield commented drily, the unfortunate Smith was tried, found guilty, and sentenced by the president, Ratcliffe, to hang the following day. The draconian measure reflected the continuing bitter infighting between the colony's leaders. But more immediately, it represented an effort to silence Smith, who was opposed to a plan by the colony's leaders to abandon the settlement once and for all. Arrangements were already well advanced for Ratcliffe, Archer, and most of the "better sort" to sail for England in the pinnace, leaving the preacher, Robert Hunt, and the surgeon, Thomas Wotton, together with the remaining men to their fate; or, as Smith put it, to leave them "to the fury of the Salvages, famine, and all manner of mischiefes, and inconveniences, (for they were but fortie in all to keepe possession of this large Country)."

There had been talk of abandoning the colony before. Wingfield and Smith had been accused of plotting to escape, and, as provisions ran low during the early winter, some of the gentry, including Archer, had tried to persuade the council to leave. Had Smith returned a week or two later, he might well have found the leaders and the pinnace gone. In any event, because the Indians had not killed him (and one can only guess at Ratcliffe and Archer's frustration), Archer must have reasoned that he would have to do the job himself—employing whatever specious legal arguments to rid himself of the insufferable captain. With Smith out of the way, they could put their plan into effect, leaving the godforsaken colony to its fate.[1]

Smith was saved once again by pure luck. In the evening of January 2, the same day Smith returned from captivity, Newport arrived with "neare a hundred men well furnished with all things [that] could be imagined necessary," and in the celebrations that followed, the charges against Smith were dropped. We do not know what Newport's reactions were upon his return to Jamestown. When he left in the summer, only a couple of men had been lost and the settlement appeared to be in relatively good shape. Six months later, nearly two-thirds of the men were dead, the deposed president of the council was under close arrest, one member of the council had been shot, and another was about to be hanged. The leading gentry had decided to desert the colony, and nothing of value had been discovered or produced.

In the face of almost a total loss, Newport may have believed that only a spectacular discovery would save the colony, and he therefore began planning an expedition in search of gold in the mountains. The discovery of mines would fulfill promises to investors in London and justify continuing expenditure; it would also guarantee his own fortune and that of everyone involved in the venture. Given Smith's standing with the Powhatans, Newport must have thought it likely that the Indians would cooperate in helping them find gold. Perhaps they knew of mines or where rich deposits could be found in the interior. A meeting with Wahunsonacock as soon as possible was imperative.

## The First Supply

The 100 (or 120) men of the "first supply" who arrived with Newport in the *John and Francis,* and with Francis Nelson in the *Phoenix* several months later, were little different in character from those of the first expedition. Seventy-three individuals are listed, of whom thirty-three were described as gentlemen, twenty-one as laborers, and the remainder as artisans of one kind or another. Among the latter were two refiners and two goldsmiths who would help in the search for gold-bearing ore, six tailors to make clothes for the men, a gunsmith, two apothecaries to advise on medicinal products, a perfumer, a blacksmith, and a tobacco-pipe maker.

Jamestown's new arrivals brought the total number of settlers to around 140 and underlined the urgent need to build adequate housing and repair the fort. In bitterly cold weather, Newport put the men to work, "some of them about a faire stoare house, others about a stove [common kitchen], and his Maryners aboute a Church." After the lethargy of previous months, survivors of the original expedition must have welcomed the activity and renewed purpose that Newport's colonists brought with them. After the dismal quiet that had settled over Jamestown during the summer and fall, the fort was once again filled with the sounds of saws and hammers and calls of men unloading the ship.[2]

Then disaster struck. In early January, a few days after the men had disembarked, a stray spark set fire to one of the houses. Flames spread quickly throughout the fort destroying everything in their path, including the church, kitchen, storehouse, houses, and most of the supplies. The heat was so intense that, apart from three dwellings, the entire settlement was burnt to the ground. The men were left to face the icy conditions with nothing but the clothes on their backs and the provisions still aboard the ship. It was a crippling blow and immediately reduced the English once again to dependence on the Indians for food. Newport's impending visit to Werowocomoco suddenly took on added urgency.[3]

The destruction of the settlers' supplies had another important consequence, at least for John Smith. Without question, he was the key to negotiations with the Powhatans and to continuing gifts of provisions. Once or twice a week, he wrote, Wahunsonacock sent "many presents of Deare, bread, *Raugroughcuns*" (raccoons) to him and his "father" (Newport). "Such acquaintance I had amongst the Indians, and such confidence they had in me," boasted Smith, that they would not come near the fort until he came to them, and would not sell anything until he had first received their presents. Apart from Smith, the only other leader they recognized was Newport, and only because Smith had described his "greatnesse" did they consider "him [Newport] the chiefe, the rest his children, Officers, and servants."

By creating a role for himself as the son of the English great chief (just as Wahunsonacock had tried to persuade him to be one of his adopted sons) Smith had made himself indispensable to the English and Powhatans alike. From the Indians' point of view, with the exception of Newport and Smith, Jamestown's leaders were ciphers. For this reason, events during the next year and a half were largely shaped by negotiations between Wahunsonacock, Smith, and Newport in a number of highly significant meetings that together represent one of the most remarkable series of encounters between Englishmen and Indians in the New World.[4]

Shortly after the fire, Smith and Newport left Jamestown in the hands of Ratcliffe and Martin and set off for Werowocomoco accompanied by a guard of thirty or forty men. Perhaps in the hope of loading up with provisions, they chose to take the pinnace and a barge and sailed down the James, rounded Point Comfort, and proceeded about twelve miles up the Pamunkey River to Wahunsonacock's residence. Wary of being ambushed, Newport sent Smith on ahead with half the men. He arrived without incident and was conducted by several hundred warriors into the presence of the king, where he was warmly received. Wahunsonacock had gone to some trouble to impress his visitors; he was attended by his "chiefest men," his wives, and hundreds of his people, all dressed in their finest attire. Smith presented the great chief with a suit of red cloth, a white greyhound, and a hat, to which the Indian signified his pleasure by declaring "a perpetuall league and friendship" with the English.

The initial courtesies over, Wahunsonacock inquired after Newport, whom he wished to see. Smith told him he would arrive the following day. Despite the chief's obvious disappointment at Newport's absence, the conversation was relaxed. "With a merrie countenance he asked me for certaine peeces which I promised him, when I went to Paspahegh [Jamestown]," Smith recounted. "I told [him] according to my promise, that I proffered the man that went with me foure Demy Culverins, in that he so desired a great Gunne, but they refused to take them; whereat with a lowde laughter, he desired [me] to give him some of lesse burthen, as for the other I gave him, being sure that none could carrie them."

Wahunsonacock then invited Smith and his men into his house, acknowledging each in turn and giving them each four or five pounds of bread. Referring to the offer to make him a chief, Smith requested the provisions and land (Capahowasicke) he had been promised at their earlier meeting. The great chief replied that he should have them, but first his men should lay down their arms at his feet, "as did his subjects." Smith told him that it was "a ceremonie our enemies desired, but never our friends," but if he should doubt their friendship, Newport would give the chief one of his men "in full assurance of our loves." Furthermore, the captain said, the English would conquer the "Country of Manacam [Monacan] and Pocoughtaonack his enemies" and render them subjects of the Powhatans. According to Smith, his response so pleased Wahunsonacock that with "a lowd oration" he proclaimed the captain a Powhatan chief: "All his subjects should so esteem us, and no man account us strangers nor Paspaheghans, but Powhatans, and that the Corne, weomen, and Country, should be to us as his owne people." Smith had been confirmed an Indian weroance, and his men and all the settlers at Jamestown declared Powhatans.

Here was a strange reversal. The previous year in ceremonies at Cape Henry and the falls, Newport had claimed Virginia and its peoples for the English; but at Werowocomoco, Wahunsonacock pronounced the English his people. Moreover, the distinction the great chief made between Paspaheghs and Powhatans was significant. The English were not to be accounted as a separate people, such as "Paspaheghans," but were to be absorbed into the Powhatans. English guns and copper were far too valuable to circulate outside Wahunsonacock's direct control, and as a separate people the English might eventually threaten the Powhatans themselves or be a rallying point for disaffected peoples. Either way, Wahunsonacock calculated the English were both sufficiently dangerous and valuable to warrant immediate inclusion with his own people. What Newport made of this, or whether he understood what had transpired, is unclear, but Smith's candid description of his negotiations gave his critics plenty of opportunity subsequently to accuse him of plotting to play the king and rule Virginia with his newfound Powhatan ally.[5]

The following day, Newport arrived and the English marched in file with a trumpeter at their head to Wahunsonacock's house, where they were greeted in a friendly manner. Thirteen-year-old Thomas Savage was presented to the chief (who received him "as his Sonne"), and in return Wahunsonacock gave the English his trusty servant, Namontack, "one of a shrewd, subtill capacity." Go-betweens (often children or adolescents) who understood the language and culture of both groups would be vital in negotiations over the next few years and would help Indians and Englishmen understand one another better; or, at least, that was the hope. Trading was reserved for the next day when once again the English marched from their pinnace to meet the chief. This time, however, relations appear to have been less relaxed.

Wahunsonacock again inquired why the English came into his presence armed, at which Newport, perhaps conceding that the chief might justly feel threatened, withdrew his men back to the river half a mile from the village. Then, terms of trade were discussed. Wahunsonacock wanted to see all the hatchets and copper the English had brought before deciding how much corn he would give. Smith advised strongly against it, arguing that it was an "auncient tricke" to greatly lower the price the Indians would pay. Nevertheless, Newport agreed. Smith remarked, in criticism of Newport, that the great chief "having his desire, valued his corne at such a rate, that I thinke it better cheape in Spaine: for wee had not foure bushells for that we expected to have twentie hogsheads."[6]

Smith was angry with Newport for ignoring his advice. He was, after all, by far the most experienced of the English traders; he had illustrated this by bargaining for hundreds of bushels of corn in return for a couple of pounds of blue beads, which he made out to be "composed of a most rare substance of the colour of the skyes and not to be worne but by the greatest kings in the world." Newport had cheapened the value of English copper by his liberality, and Smith knew that if the settlers continued to be dependent on the Indians for food in the months to come, such rashness would cause needless hardship. But worse, he knew Wahunsonacock had duped Newport and consequently the English had temporarily lost any advantage Smith had gained over the Powhatans. The great chief might well believe he had the measure of Newport; if he could trick him in trade he could fool him in war. Trade, like diplomacy, was a game of bluff, stratagem, and maneuver designed to best the opponent, and Wahunsonacock had effortlessly outwitted the English leader in his dealings at Werowocomoco.

Newport's behavior makes sense, however, in the context of his objectives. Smith was concerned about long-term trade and the delicate balance of power between the English and the Indians; Newport, on the other hand, was interested primarily in finding gold, and to have any chance of success he needed the support and advice of the Powhatans. He certainly did not want to jeopardize the fragile peace by haggling over a few barrels of corn, and was therefore content to buy their goodwill with copper pots in return for information and possibly an alliance against the Monacans. He would continue to placate the Indians and hope they would help him find the mines he believed lay somewhere in the western mountains.

Returning to the fort in early March with 250 bushels of corn, the English seemingly had enough supplies to see them through the remainder of the winter and into early spring. Nonetheless, conditions in Jamestown remained miserable. Part of the problem was that the ship's crew consumed much of the food brought from England for the settlers' use and then sold the remaining provisions at extortionate prices. Reduced to a diet of "meale and water," and exposed to bitterly cold weather without adequate clothing or shelter, many of the weaker settlers died. But the "worst mischiefe," according to Smith, was the gold fever that swept through the camp. Instead of employing themselves in producing useful commodities that could be sent back to England, sowing crops, and rebuilding the fort, everything was abandoned in the frenetic search for gold.

Smith was sent to "digge a rocke" at Cinquoteck, about twelve miles upstream from the Wahunsonacock's residence, where the Pamunkey chiefs lived, which was "supposed a Mine." Then, following the discovery of what some settlers believed were traces of gold in the mud along the northern bank of the James River, suddenly "there was no talke, no hope, no worke, but dig gold, wash gold, refine gold, [and] loade gold." Egged on by "golden promises," Smith grumbled, the men were made the "slaves" of Ratcliffe, Martin, and the "gilded refiners" who had arrived with Newport. Smith's complaints were disingenuous, however. He may have been skeptical about finding gold along the banks of the James River, and probably believed that at least some of the men could be put to more productive work, but he was just as interested in discovering gold mines as Newport or Ratcliffe.[7]

―――――

ON APRIL 10, Newport's ship left Jamestown loaded with "ore." On board were Gabriel Archer, Edward Maria Wingfield, and the Indian Namontack, dispatched to England to discover as much as possible about the distant land across the ocean. Smith accompanied Newport in the pinnace as far as the capes. On the way back, he explored the Nansemond River, where he and his men encountered a populous "warlike Nation" who lived along the river and its tributaries. Sailing as far inland as possible, he discovered a fertile country "so sweete, so pleasant, so beautifull, and so strong a prospect, for an invincible strong Citty, with so many commodities, that I know as yet I have not seene." He reckoned he was within a day's journey of the Chowan River, which would lead a search party quickly down to Roanoke "where beginneth the first settlers."[8]

Back at the fort, Smith and a new member of the council who had arrived with the first supply, Matthew Scrivener, put the men to work cutting down trees, rebuilding the fort, church, and storehouse, and preparing the ground for planting corn and other crops. All seemed to be going well apart from a growing problem of "theeverie" by local Indians of the settlers' tools and weapons. The thefts had become so brazen that Smith decided to put a stop to them. One Indian caught in the act was put "in the bilboes" (iron shackles secured to the ground) for a few hours; but, undeterred, he returned the next day with three others armed with wooden clubs and attempted to carry away what he could. Smith challenged the intruders, a fight ensued, and the four men were chased out of the settlement.

It was not an end to the trouble. A few days later, while Smith and Scrivener were at work in the cornfields outside the fort, two Indians confronted them and threatened to give them a beating. The Indians followed the Englishmen into the fort and were taken prisoner, along with eight others found within the walls. In the negotiations that followed, the English demanded the return of all tools and weapons stolen by the Indians or else the men would hang. Smith was instructed by the council to question the Indians closely, using torture if necessary, to find out whether the thefts were part of a plot to destroy the settlement.

Pretending to execute the captives one by one, Smith forced Macanoe, a counselor of the Paspaheghs, to confess: The Paspaheghs and Chickahominies, according to the Indian, hated the English and planned to surprise the colonists in the fields "to have had our tools." Wahunsonacock had persuaded the Indians to take the Englishmen's tools and weapons by stealth rather than by ambush. He was also plotting to lure Newport into a trap when he returned, the signal for a general attack on the settlement.

Whether or not Macanoe's story was true is unclear, but if it was then the great chief's offer to absorb the English into his dominions as Powhatans, made only a few weeks earlier, was subterfuge. Smith was convinced that the love the Indians feigned towards him was "not without a deadly hatred," and, if Macanoe was to be believed, the same could be said of their attitude towards the English as a whole. The discovery of a plot emphasized the importance of maintaining their defenses at Jamestown, becoming self-sufficient in food, and exercising extreme caution beyond the fort. Survival depended on a deadly game of keeping one step ahead of their adversaries.[9]

The arrival of Captain Francis Nelson in the *Phoenix* brought a welcome respite from worries about relations with local Indians. Nelson had left London with Newport in the fall of the previous year, but lost his bearings off the Virginia coast in bad weather and made his way back to the West Indies, where he wintered. Putting their enforced leisure on the islands to good use, the men gathered plenty of provisions before setting off once again for the colony in the spring; there they arrived to the "exceeding joy" of the settlers, who had believed them long lost. Smith was as complimentary about Nelson's crew as he was critical of Newport's. What they had they freely shared, and Nelson himself was warmly regarded for his honest dealing. As one settler put it: "[W]ee would not have wished so much as he did for us." Together with existing supplies, the settlers now had enough food to last another six months, and in addition had planted crops to get them through the winter.

With about 150 settlers now at the fort, Ratcliffe considered it timely to mount an expedition to "search [for] the commodities of [the] Monacans countrie beyond the Falles" in the hope of sending the *Phoenix* back to England with news of gold mines or a passage to the South Sea. Smith was opposed to the plan, or so he claimed, preferring to load the ship with cedar, readily available nearby, rather than with "gilded durt." The disagreement once again illustrates Smith's efforts prevent others, this time Ratcliffe, from making the kind of breakthrough discovery he hoped to achieve himself.

In any event, the plan came to nothing because Nelson was reluctant to involve his men without guarantee of payment for wages and the hire of his ship. Expeditions into the interior were no part of his commission. Interestingly, another argument against the plan was "the wrong" that would be done to Captain Newport, then absent from the colony, "to whom only all discoveries did belong, and to no other." Nelson's ship was loaded with cedar and set sail at the beginning of June with the sickly John Martin on board, keen to return to London to hear news of the Virginia ore he had sent back with Newport in April.[10]

## Voyages of Discovery

Smith paid scant regard to the notion that Newport had a monopoly on discoveries, and had already made up his mind to attempt his own exploration of the Chesapeake Bay. With Newport and Nelson gone, and no ships expected before the fall, there was little to be done at the fort; and if he remained at Jamestown, he might well get into trouble with the feckless Ratcliffe. During his last visit to Werowocomoco, he had gone down to the Pamunkey River with Wahunsonacock, where the king had shown him the great canoes in which his men crossed over the Bay to the Eastern Shore. Smith's interest in the region may have been sparked by the chief's description of its peoples and his boast of how they were forced to pay him "tribute Beades." As with the Monacans, he might have speculated about the possibility of winning over allies against their common Indian foes, the Powhatans.

Yet the main reason for Smith's decision was the hope of finding gold or silver and a navigable route to the East, following up on the information he had learned from Opechancanough and Wahunsonacock. He was well aware that when Newport returned to Virginia he would continue his search for the elusive gold mines in the interior, but here was a chance to upstage the veteran mariner by carrying out his own exploration first. If successful, he would become the most powerful man in North America; if not, he might be able to bring back valuable information about the Bay, its inhabitants, and possibilities for trade. Moreover, he did not require a large force.

Smith recruited fourteen men for the venture, six gentlemen, four soldiers, and a "Doctour of Physicke." In an open barge of two or three tons, the men accompanied the *Phoenix* to Cape Henry and then sailed to the tip of the Eastern Shore, where they discovered several small islands, which they named Smith's Isles. Rounding Cape Charles, they encountered a group of "grimme and stout Salvages . . . with long poles like Javelings" who, Smith noted, "boldly demanded what we were, and what we would." After reassurances, the Indians eventually directed the Englishmen to "Acawmacke," a few miles away, where the local ruler, Esmy Shichans, lived. He was described as a "proper civill Salvage," and his country as having "a pleasant fertile clay soyle" and "good Harbours for small Barks, but not for Ships." The Indians spoke the language of the Powhatans and described the Bay, islands, and rivers in such a way that the explorers were greatly encouraged.[11]

Following the coast in search of fresh water, they discovered many small islands and inlets before arriving at the Wighcocomoco River (Pocomoke), where the people at first greeted them "with great furie," yet later, "with songs, daunces, and much mirth, became very

*John Smith, Map of Virginia, 1624 (originally published in 1612). Detail.*

tractable." Shortly after, caught in a sudden squall off the main, the barge was nearly sunk by enormous waves that shattered the mast and swamped the boat. For two days, the men took shelter among some small, uninhabited isles, "which (for the extremitie of gusts, thunder, raine, stormes, and il weather) we called Limbo," marked on Smith's map by an angry fish in the middle of the Bay.

Having ridden out the storm, and using their shirts to repair the sail, they continued their voyage and discovered several villages along the Kuskarawaocke River (possibly the modern Nanticoke). When they learned about the presence of Massawomecks from inhabitants, Smith was determined to find them. He knew from conversations with Wahunsonacock and Opechancanough that they were enemies of the Powhatans, and therefore possible allies, and he believed they might have information about lands beyond the head of the Bay. Returning back down the coast, they found no trace of the Massawomecks, however, and so crossed over to the Western Shore and sailed northwards for thirty leagues. Finding few inhabitants, "the mountains very barren, the vallies very fertile, but the woods extreame thicke, full of Woolves, Beares, Deare, and other wild beasts," the men tired of the voyage and pressed to return to Jamestown.

As the strength and spirits of his fellow adventurers failed, Smith took it upon himself to deliver a speech comparing their exploits to those of the first English explorers in the region. He recalled the brave words of Ralph Lane, who had persuaded his men not to abandon the search for the mines of "Chaunis Temotoan" while "they yet had a dog, that being boyled with Saxafras leaves, would richly feed them in their returnes." Why, then, should they go back to Jamestown when they still had a month's supply of provisions, and the worst was already behind them? Assuming a suitably heroic pose, Smith declared, "Regaine therefore your old spirits; for return I wil not, (if God assist me) til I have seene the Massawomekes, found Patawomeck, or the head of this great water you conceit to be endlesse." The speech was only partially successful. After a couple of days of bad weather, they decided to turn back, but Smith managed to persuade the company not to pass by the "Patawomeck."

Entering the river in mid-June, they sailed thirty miles before seeing any inhabitants; then, finding a couple of local Indians, they followed them up a creek to a small bay. Near the village of Onawmanient, they saw about three or four hundred "Salvages, so strangely paynted, grimed and disguised, shouting, yelling, and crying as so many spirits from hell could not have shewed more terrible." Smith and his men prepared to encounter them and fired several shot, grazing the musket balls off the water. The thunderclap of muskets echoing around the bay had the desired effect and the Indians dropped their weapons. From them, Smith discovered that they had been commanded to attack by Wahunsonacock: "He so directed from the discontents at James towne, because our Captaine [Smith] did cause them [to] stay in their country against their wills." In other words, Wahunsonacock knew of the bitter disputes among the settlers and had been encouraged by Ratcliffe's faction to ambush Smith if they could.

Continuing upriver, they went as far as possible in the barge and found "mighty Rocks" and waterfalls from the high mountains, which had left behind a "tinctured spangled skurfe [residue]" so that the bare rocks appeared "guilded." Smith directed some of the men to dig along the cliffs and found the soil to be clayey sand speckled with what appeared to be "pin-dust," or fine golden flecks. Smith was not certain what he had found, and certainly did not want to jump to the conclusion that it was gold; but on returning downriver, he mentioned his discovery to the weroance of the Patawomecks, who called the mineral "Matchqueon" and told the Englishman of a mine nearby. Smith marched off with six armed men and a group of Indian guides to find it, whom he chained together as hostages to protect against treachery. After seven or eight miles, they found "a great Rocky mountaine like Antimony; wherein they [had] digged a great hole with shells and hatchets." The Indians washed the mineral to clean off the dirt and put the remaining silvery powder in small bags, which they would "sell all over the country to paint there bodyes, faces, or Idols."

They had spent the best part of a month searching for the "glistering mettal" that turned out to be worthless, but in the course of their exploration they had found some furs and an abundance of fish, fruits, and other natural produce. They had encountered numerous peoples, friendly and hostile, and were now aware of how populous the region was and the extent of Wahunsonacock's dominions. With supplies running low, the expedition returned to Jamestown, stopping en route at Kecoughtan and Warreskoyack. They arrived at the fort on July 21 with the happy news of their discoveries and "the good hope we had by the Salvages relation that our Bay had stretched into the South Sea, or somewhat neare it."

———

THE NEWS WAS WELCOME. Conditions had gone from bad to worse during Smith's absence. The colonists were so aggrieved by "the pride and needlesse cruelty of their silly President" that they were on the verge of mutiny. Ratcliffe had squandered the stores and forced the men to hard labor building a "pallace in the woods" for his own use. Sick and battered, the men begged Smith to depose Ratcliffe and take over the presidency himself as the next in line. What happened next is not clear; but it appears that Smith agreed and, as his first act, placed his friend Matthew Scrivener in charge, assisted by some honest officers, whilst he decided to take the barge once again and "finish his discovery."[12]

Setting off a few days later with twelve men (eight of whom accompanied him on his first voyage), the company quickly made their way to Stingray Island—so named because Smith had been badly stung there by a ray a week earlier—past the mouth of the Potomac, and on to the headwaters of the Bay. Here they encountered seven or eight canoes full of Indians speaking a strange language who, they later learned, were Massawomecks. The Indians prepared to attack. With only five men able to fight, Smith decided that desperate measures were called for to save themselves. He placed their hats on sticks along the sides of the barge and gave each man two muskets, so that five men looked like twenty. The ruse succeeded; seemingly overmatched, the Indians returned to shore. The Englishmen followed, still eager to make contact and to trade. Initially wary, eventually two unarmed Indians approached and, satisfied that there was no danger, urged the remainder to join them. Smith traded for supplies, bows, arrows, targets (wooden shields), clubs, and "beares-skins," and learnt by sign language that the Indians had been at war with the Tockwoughs. Parting for the night, Smith expected to meet again in the morning, but to his surprise found they had gone.

Smith set course for the Eastern Shore and entered the Tockwough River, where they were immediately surrounded by a fleet of canoes and once again seemed about to come under attack. Fortunately, Smith was able to convey their friendly intentions because one of the Indians spoke Algonquian. Smith related how they had beaten the Massawomecks in a recent battle and had taken their enemy's weapons as a token of their victory. The Tockwoughs were impressed and led them to their "pallizadoed towne," where the entire population came out to welcome them with dances, songs, and feasting, "stretching their best abilities to expresse their loves." They possessed many hatchets, knives, and pieces of iron and brass, which they told him came from the "Sasquesahanocks," who lived on a principal river at the head of the Bay, two days farther than the barge could pass because rocks blocked their way.

This was the kind of information Smith had been waiting for. If the Indians' report was reliable, it was possible the Bay did in fact lead to a great river, or rivers; and if so, the Susquehannocks would surely know whether it would lead them to the South Sea. To be sure, the news that their barge would not be able to travel far before reaching the falls was disappointing, but on the other hand the existence of metal goods was strong evidence of contact with Europeans or perhaps Asians. The question in Smith's mind was where contact had taken place.

In conversations with Wahunsonacock, the great chief had informed Smith of a "mightie River, issuing from mightie Mountaines betwixt the two Seas" at the head of the Bay, and of a people beyond "with short Coates, and Sleeves to the Elbowes, that passed that way in Shippes like ours [those of the English]." Smith not only had located the whereabouts of one of the powerful nations who lived on the far northern borders of the Powhatans' territories but also had the means of communicating with them (unlike with the Massawomecks) through a Tockwough interpreter. Little wonder he impressed upon his hosts the urgency of inviting a group of the Susquehannocks to meet him as soon as possible.

The Tockwoughs agreed. A few days later, the Englishmen were visited by sixty of the "gyant-like people," who arrived with gifts of venison, tobacco pipes three feet long, targets, bows, and arrows. According to Anthony Bagnall, Nathaniel Powell, and Anas Todkill, who were credited with writing the account of the expedition (given the style and content, Smith must have contributed a good deal also), the Susquehannocks pleaded with the English captain to become "their Governour and Protector, promising their aydes, victualls, or what they had to be his, if he would stay with them, to defend and revenge them of the Massawomeks." They worshipped him like a god, the Englishmen reported; they held their hands up to the sun, and then, with a "fearefull song," embraced him, "which done with a most strange furious action, and a hellish voice, began an Oration of their loves; that ended, with a great painted Beares skin they covered him: then one ready with a great chayne of white Beads, weighing at least six or seaven pound, hung it about his necke, the others had 18 mantels, made of divers sorts of skinnes sowed together; all these and many other toyes they layd at his feete."[13]

This was the second time Smith had been offered the opportunity to govern an Indian people. But Smith wanted nothing to do with them and their wars unless there were clear advantages for the English; and as it turned out, there were not. Much to his disappointment, he learned that the Susquehannocks knew nothing of the South Sea but rather traded with nations who inhabited lands "upon a great water beyond the mountains." This, they realized, was some "great lake, or the river of Canada." The hatchets and other metal goods were bartered from the French: They were the people "with short Coates, and Sleeves to the Elbowes" mentioned by the Powhatan king. Smith was now certain that a direct water passage to the Orient from the Chesapeake Bay did not exist, although it was possible one might be found issuing out of the Great Lakes. The information would have given him little comfort because, if he was right, it would be French traders and explorers in the St. Lawrence who were most likely to find a passage and reap the rewards.

Leaving the Susquehannocks "sorrowing for [their] departure," the company explored some of the larger inlets and rivers of the upper Bay, including the Susquehanna River. Continuing where they had left off on the first voyage, Smith and his men were determined to ensure their own immortality by naming (or renaming) the lands and rivers they found after themselves: "The Sasquesahanocks river we called Smiths falles; the next poynt to Tockwhogh, Pisings poynt; the next it poynt Bourne. Powells Isles and Smals poynt is by the river Bolus; and the little Bay at the head Profits poole; Watkins, Reads, and Momfords poynts are on each side of Limbo; Ward, Cantrell, and Sicklemore, betwixt Patawomek and Pamaunkee, after the names of the discoverers."

The highest mountain they could see to the north, "Peregrines mount," and "Willowbyes river" were named for Smith's erstwhile friends and patrons, the Berties of Lincolnshire. Whenever they went inland, they left messages placed in holes in trees, cut crosses into the trunks, and occasionally left behind brass crosses "to signifie to any, Englishmen had beene there."[14] Whereas Newport and his company had earlier given names to prominent features and the peoples along the James River, Smith and his men wrote their names across much of the Chesapeake region.

Having surveyed the head of the Bay and assured themselves that the information from the Susquehannocks was essentially accurate, they turned southwards and explored the smaller rivers along the Western Shore. They first entered the Patuxent River, about which Smith had little to say other than noting the people very friendly ("more civill then any"), and then moved on to the Tappahannock (Rappahannock River), where they halted about twenty-five miles upstream at the village of the Moraughtacunds and were "kindly entertained."

There they encountered an old friend from the first expedition—whom they had last seen far up the Potomac River—a Wicocomoco called Mosco who had proved himself a most valuable guide and advisor. He warned the Englishmen not to visit the Rappahannocks, Smith wrote, "for they would kill us for being friends with the Moraughtacunds" (who had lately abducted three of the king's women). Ignoring the advice, they crossed the river and made their way to a small creek where they found four of the Rappahannock canoes laden with goods. Smith sent one of his men, Anas Todkill, ashore to check for an ambush and see what the Indians had to trade.

Making his way a few hundred yards from the creek and over a rise, Todkill spotted two or three hundred warriors hiding behind trees; they immediately attempted to grab the Englishman and carry him off. He managed to yell out a warning, at which point the English fired their muskets into the trees, scattering the attackers and giving Todkill the chance to run for his life. (Mosco had advised them to set up the Massawomeck shields along the bows of the barge "like a forecastle," so the English were able to fire at the Rappahan-nocks without risk.) They then rescued Todkill, who had been gingerly inching his way towards the creek, miraculously unscathed though covered in the blood of Rappahannock dead and wounded. They then took the canoes and made their way back to the Moraughtacunds, where they celebrated their victory.

The next morning, they sailed farther upriver, passing by the villages of Pissacoack, Matchopick, and Wecuppom, situated "upon high white clay clifts," before finding themselves under fire at a narrow point of the river by thirty or forty Rappahannocks who had disguised themselves among the trees. The previous day, the Englishmen had fixed more of the Massawomeck shields along the gunnels of their barge, so the attack did no damage; but the Indians seemed pleased by the outcome, "dauncing and singing very merrily" to show their contempt as the Englishmen continued on their way. Unlike the Rappahannocks, the Pissasecks, Nantaughtacunds, and Cuttata-women, whom they next encountered, were very friendly and the company enjoyed their hospitality. Just beyond Cuttatawomen, the expedition suffered its only fatality with the death of Richard Fetherstone, who "all the time he had beene in this Country, had behaved himselfe, honestly, valiantly, and industriously." Fetherstone was buried in "a little bay" the Englishmen named "Fetherstons bay" and was honored by a volley of shot.

The following day, the group sailed as far into the freshes as possible—about eighty miles from the mouth of the river. Here they were suddenly attacked by about a hundred "nimble" Indians "skipping from tree to tree." After half an hour, the attack abruptly ended and the Indians disappeared as quickly as they had come; but on their way back to the barge, the Englishmen discovered a wounded Indian who had been shot in the knee. Smith had Anthony Bagnall, the surgeon, dress his wound. After some food the Indian was well enough to speak.

With Mosco interpreting, Smith first asked what countries lay beyond the mountains, to which he replied that "he and all with him were of the [land of] Hasinninga," where there were three kings more, namely, of Stegora, Tauxuntania, and Shakahonea. Asked why they had attacked the English, who came in peace "to seeke their loves," the Indian, who was called Amoroleck, said that "they heard [the English] were a people come from under the world, to take their world from them." Queried on how many worlds he knew, he answered that he knew "no more than that which was under the skie that covered him, which were the Powhatans, with the Monacans, and the Massawomeks, that were higher up in the mountains." He had little information about what lay beyond the mountains, but told them the Monacans were their neighbors and friends and inhabited "the hilly Countries by small rivers, living upon roots and fruits, but chiefly by hunting." The Massawomecks, by contrast, "did dwell upon a great water, and had many boats, and so many men that they made warre with all the world."

Smith rewarded the Indian with "many toyes" and tried to persuade him to stay with the company on their journey; Amoroleck in turn tried to persuade the Englishmen to wait for his hunting party to arrive, saying he was brother of the king of the "Hasinninga" and would speak on their behalf and they would be friends. Deciding not to risk ambush, however, the company pushed off downriver under the cover of darkness. Sure enough, they found themselves under attack from an unseen enemy following along the riverbank, arrows whistling around them and falling into the water on both sides of the barge.

After about twelve miles they reached a broad bay and dropped anchor out of range of the enemy's arrows to rest and wait for daybreak. As the sun rose, Amoroleck called to his companions gathered along the shore and told them how the English had saved his life and would set him free if they would agree to peace, saying it was impossible to "doe [the English] any hurt." Following a "long discourse," the Indians, who, it transpired, were Mannahoacs, hung their weapons from the trees. Two warriors then swam out to the barge and delivered a bow and a quiver of arrows as a gift and token of friendship. Smith "used them so kindly as he could, told them the other three Kings should doe the like, and then the great King of our world [James I] should be their friend, whose men we were." They agreed upon terms, and the English met the four kings of Hasinninga, Tauxuntania,

Stegora, and Shakahonea on a marshy point nearby. There they traded what little they had and then left the four or five hundred "merry Mannahocks" singing and dancing in celebration and set sail down-river for Moraughtacund.

Along the way, Smith and his men stopped at the villages of their friends, who (according to the English) were overjoyed to learn of their "Victory" against the Mannahoacs, who had long been at war with them. The bellicose Rappahannocks also sought peace; Smith ordered them to deliver their king's bow and arrows to him and told them they were not to come into his presence armed. In the presence of the kings of Nantaughtacund and Pissaseck, the Rappahannocks duly bound themselves friends of "King James" and all his men, and pledged peace with the Moraughtacunds.

Smith demanded the king's son as a hostage, but instead the king offered the three women stolen by the Moraughtacunds earlier, the theft that had sparked hostilities between the two peoples. This was agreed, and as many of the English and Indians who could cram them-selves into four canoes went down to Moraughtacund to conclude the peace brokered by Smith. Mosco served as the intermediary and per-suaded the Moraughtacunds to comply. When the three women were brought to the English captain, he gave to each a chain of beads and then handed over one to the Rappahannocks, one to the Moraughta-cunds, and the third to Mosco. With the conclusion of peace, the next day was spent in feasting, dancing, and singing, "all promising to be our friends," Smith wrote, "and to plant Corne purposely for us; and we to provide hatchets, beads, and copper for them."

On the final stage of the journey, the company reconnoitered the Piankatank River and then sailed to the southern bank of the James where the Chesapeakes and Nansemonds lived, thinking it "fit to know all [their] neighbours neare home, as so many Nations abroad." They first sailed into "the country of the Chisapeack," where the shores were "overgrowne with the greatest Pyne and Firre trees [they] ever saw"; but, finding little evidence of the inhabitants, they returned to the main river. Entering the Nansemond, they spotted six or seven Indians fishing. The Indians immediately fled, but the Englishmen found them again a little farther on. This time, one of the Indians swam out and guided the barge several miles inland while the others ran along the shore. Coming to a small island, the Englishmen saw large fields of ripe corn and met their guide's family, who treated them with "much kindnesse." Other villagers invited them to continue farther upriver to see their houses, and so they sailed on until they found themselves in a narrow passage.

The men quickly began to sense that something was wrong. Their suspicions were confirmed when eight canoes full of armed Indians suddenly appeared in the river to cut off their retreat. Meanwhile, along the riverbanks, two or three hundred warriors had appeared and began shooting so rapidly that soon arrows were flying thick and fast. Firing at the canoes, Smith's men first routed their attackers on the river and then concentrated their fire onshore. The exchange was intense but brief. The Nansemonds retired into the trees and Smith was left to ponder his next move. In keeping with his practice on the voyage, he chose to offer peace terms and demanded the king's bow and arrows, a chain of pearl, and four hundred baskets of corn. If they did not agree, he would destroy their village, crops, and canoes. The Indians agreed and Smith took as much corn as he could carry, apparently departing "good friends." The next day, September 7, they returned to Jamestown in triumph, thereby completing in six weeks a journey that had taken them to the farthest reaches of the Bay.[15]

SMITH AND HIS MEN were acutely aware of the epic proportions of their two voyages, which were subsequently likened in their writings to famous Spanish discoveries and feats by great explorers in times past. How "many ever with such small meanes as a Barge of 2 tuns, sometimes with seaven, eight, or nine, or but at most, twelve or sixteene men," Smith asked, "did ever discover so many fayre and navigable Rivers, subject so many severall Kings, people, and Nations, to obedience, and contribution, with so little bloudshed"?[16]

Smith exaggerated when he claimed to have conquered thirty-five Indian kings during the voyages, but there is little doubt that he increasingly saw himself in the role of King James' plenipotentiary. In his writings, his encounters take on a strikingly similar pattern. Time and time again, Smith and his men forced initially hostile peoples to obey them and sue for peace. On the first expedition, for example, "Our Captaine ever observed this order to demand their bowes and arrowes, swordes, mantells and furrs, with some childe or two for hostage, whereby we could quickly perceive, when they intended any villany."

At the Tockwough village on the Eastern Shore, the Susquehannocks worshipped Smith as a god and begged him to be their governor and protector. On the Rappahannock River, he made the four chiefs of the Mannahoacs surrender their bows and arrows and agree to peace. Downriver, the Rappahannocks were also assured of the friendship of the English king in return for abandoning hostilities against neighboring peoples. As the expedition progressed, the company seemingly took on superhuman powers as they fought off hundreds of warriors with little or no injury. Amoroleck, the captive Mannahoac, told his compatriots that to do the English "any hurt it was impossible."[17] Smith and his men—protected by their sturdy barge and Indian shields—had apparently become invincible.

That Smith should talk up the exploration of the Bay in such grandiose terms is hardly surprising. But there is plenty of evidence to suggest that the Indians had an entirely different view of their encounters with the English. Smith's own account reveals how dependent the expedition was on local peoples for provisions and information. Smith and his men were not looking for war and conquest; they were far more interested in finding out whether a water passage existed westwards, whether gold mines existed in the interior, and whether there was the potential for trade. The peoples they met usually quite reasonably assumed the Englishmen were trading partners, as when at Moraughtacund the Indians promised to provide corn in exchange for English hatchets and copper (a somewhat similar arrangement to the one offered by Wahunsonacock to Smith the previous December). Weapons given to Smith were tokens of friendship, not trophies of battle signaling defeat and submission. It is inconceivable that with a dozen men he had conquered the entire region. Even Smith, the supreme self-propagandist, is hardly convincing as a Chesapeake Cortes or Pizarro.

Self-memorializing became something of a specialty for John Smith. His *A Map of Virginia* and *The Proceedings of the English Colonie in Virginia* (both published in 1612) were testaments to his exploits during the two voyages of discovery and confirmed his role (at least to his own satisfaction) as the central presence in the narrative of the founding of Virginia: a heroic figure towering above his ineffectual counterparts, struggling manfully against impossible odds to save the colony from collapse.

Critics, however, took a less elevated view. If the English now had a good idea of the extensiveness of the Chesapeake region, unlike the Spanish in Central and South America, they had discovered little of real worth in their new world: no gold, silver, or precious minerals, no convenient access to the Pacific, and no advanced Indian civilizations that could be readily plundered. In telling language, the unfavorable comparison with Spanish exploits was underlined by the adventurers themselves:

> It was the Spanyards good hap to happen in those parts where were in-finite numbers of people, who had manured the ground with that providence, it affoorded victualls at all times. And time had brought them to that perfection, they had the use of gold and silver, and the most of such commodities as those Countries affoorded: so that what the Spanyard got was chiefly the spoyle and pillage of those Countrey people, and not the labours of their own hands. . . . But we chanced in a Land even as God made it, where we found onely an idle, improvi-dent, scattered people, ignorant of the knowledge of gold or silver, or any commodities, and carelesse of any thing but from hand to mouth, except ba[u]bles of no worth; nothing to incourage us, but what acci-dentally we found Nature affoorded.[18]

Expeditions were judged by results and, like many a hapless con-quistador before him, Smith had been unable to bring back positive news about the likelihood of riches to be found inland. In fact, what he had learnt was almost wholly discouraging: Mention by the Powhatans of a sea somewhere far beyond the mountains was probably a reference to the Canadian Great Lakes, not the Pacific, and Smith's exploration of the Potomac and head of the Bay confirmed that no large river would carry the English through the mountains to the other side of the landmass. As prospects of riches faded, it would be Hakluyt's vision of sustainable agriculture, not the example of the Spanish conquistadors, that would eventually guide the colonists' efforts. And for this, as Smith was well aware, they needed to possess the land.

# 4

## INNOCENCE LOST

*A*T THE FORT, conditions were not quite as bad as they had been six weeks earlier when Smith returned from his first voyage; but even so, the colony once again teetered on the brink of collapse. Another hot, humid summer had taken its toll in the camp and many of the men had died or were chronically sick. Ratcliffe had been imprisoned for mismanagement by the council, provisions spoiled by rain, and nothing done in preparation for the new arrivals expected any day. Elected president on September 10, Smith immediately began putting the settlement in order. The fort was recast into a "five-square form" by dismantling part of the eastern palisade (probably in a bad state of disrepair) and building new curtain walls at an angle from the northern and southeastern bulwarks, which nearly doubled its size. The church and storehouse were repaired, and houses made ready. Military discipline was restored and the men trained daily in "a fielde prepared for that purpose" called "Smithfield," in honor of their captain and a reminder of the ancient market district in London just outside the walls, familiar to anyone from the city.

Smith must have enjoyed being in charge at last. Death, disease, or disgrace had seen off his rivals on the council; and at the same time, his own knack for survival and undoubted achievements gave substance to his role as leader. Some might have questioned his methods in dealing with the Indians, but no one could deny his ability in a crisis or challenge his right to the presidency, his due as the only surviving member of the original council who had not yet served.[1]

## The "Map of Virginia"

About the same time Smith took over the presidency, the Spanish ambassador in London, Don Pedro de Zúñiga, wrote a letter to King Philip III informing him about a "map of Virginia" he was about to dispatch. How the map came into his hands is a mystery, yet there can be no doubt that it was a copy of a drawing Smith had sent to a friend, possibly Henry Hudson, with a long letter (published as *A True Relation*) earlier in the year. The sketch, which represented Smith's knowledge of the region down to early summer 1608, is an enigma. It consists of a line drawing of the major rivers and shows in some detail the James, Chickahominy, Pamunkey, and Mattaponi. Marked along their upper courses are the Indian villages visited by Smith either during his captivity or on trading expeditions from Jamestown.

The trail Smith was forced to take when captured the winter before is indicated by a dotted line and illustrates clearly the extent of his travels into the interior. Information picked up from Indian sources is reflected in the general (almost schematic) rendering of the Toppahannock (Rappahannock) and Patawomeck (Potomac) Rivers. Smith's imperfect understanding of the geography of the Chesapeake Bay is obvious. At the very top of the map is a roughly drawn coastline with the note, "Hear the salt water beatethe into the river amongst theis rocks being the south sea," and slightly to the right is another note describing the "Pocoughtawonauck. A Salvag people Dwelling upon this seay beyond this mayne that eate the men & women."

Yet the most intriguing feature of the map lay not in the depiction of a direct passage to the Pacific via the James, which Smith would rule

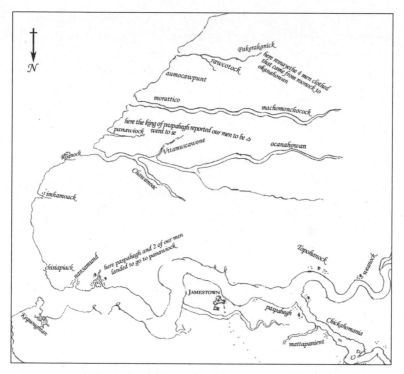

*Detail from John Smith's sketch map of 1608 (Zúñiga map).*
*(Drawn by Rebecca L. Wrenn)*

out soon after his second voyage around the Bay, but in the information it contained about possible survivors of Sir Walter Ralegh's lost colony. Three notations appear on the lower left-hand side: On the southern bank of the James River, "here paspahegh and 2 of our men landed to go to panawiock"; near the Roanoke River, "here the king of paspahegh reported our men to be and went to se[e]"; and at Pakerakanick, "here remay[n]e the 4 men clothed that came from roonock to okanahowan." Also included are various place names: "chisiapiack," "imhamoack," "Roanock," "Chawanoac," "Uttamuscawone," "panawiock," "ocanahowan," and so on.

What did these cryptic captions mean and how did Smith obtain the information? He had first heard of "Ocanahowan" in two separate conversations with Opechancanough and Wahunsonacock in the winter. The Powhatan chief mentioned that besides the men at Ocanahowan, others were to be found "within a day and a halfe of Mangoge, two dayes of Chawwonock, [and] 6. from Roanoke." The lack of reluctance to tell Smith what he knew of the whereabouts of survivors, if that is who they were, suggests their fate may have been common knowledge among local peoples. However, the specific notations on the map came not from Wahunsonacock but from another source: an expedition led by the Paspahegh chief, Wowinchopunck, which included two Englishmen, that set off from Warraskoyack (probably the Pagan River) in January 1608, to look for a "place called Panawicke, beyond Roanoke" where, it was reported, many "apparelled" men lived.

Although Smith later recorded that Wowinchopunck played the villain and "deluding us for rewards" returned within three or four days, notes on the map indicate that the small search party traveled a good way south, possibly as far as the Neuse River, and had some success in finding out where a few surviving lost colonists might be found. The search party was unable to make contact with the survivors themselves, but Smith may have wondered whether a future expedition led by a more reliable guide would fare better. In any event, he thought the information sufficiently important to include on his sketch.[2]

The map, along with a cargo of cedar wood, arrived back in England in early July 1608 and must have caused a sensation among leaders of the London Company. Rumors of the survival of the Lost Colony had been circulating in the capital for some time. During the peace treaty negotiations between England and Spain in 1604, James I had refused to recognize Spanish claims to the whole of America and asserted that English settlers had been in peaceful possession of Virginia "for more than thirty years." London theatre goers the following year heard the character "Seagull" in *Eastward Hoe* declare that "A whole Country of English is there man, bred of those that were left there in 79 [1587]; They have married with the Indians, and make 'hem bring forth as beautifull faces as any we have in England: and therefore the Indians are so in love with 'hem, that all the treasure they have they lay at their feete."[3]

The play offered a satirical account of Ralegh's abandoned colony and inflated stories of Indian gold, but may have reflected also popular hearsay about what had happened to the settlers and the continuing hope of finding riches in the American interior. Smith's map, on the other hand, was the first reliable news to emerge since John White's final voyage nearly two decades before and if, as now seemed likely, at least some of the settlers had survived, then the Company's (and England's) claim to Virginia from the Roanoke region to the James River by right of occupation would be considerably strengthened.

Smith's information, though vague, was sufficient to persuade the Company to order further efforts to find the colonists and if possible bring a survivor back to England. Finding the lost colonists would be a tremendous propaganda coup for the Company: It would redeem Ralegh's failure and open the possibility of bringing together the Roanoke and James River regions under a single English colony. If some English men and women still lived, they would have invaluable information about the region because their survival would have depended on the cooperation of friendly local peoples. They might know about sources of gold and copper in the interior or whether a passage to the South Sea truly existed, which is why the Company explicitly issued Newport with instructions to continue the search for the lost colonists when he set out for Virginia with the second supply later in the summer.[4]

Newport's arrival in mid-October was especially galling to Smith. He had been president for little more than a month and was now placed in a position where he would have to share command with Newport, the direct representative of Company interests in the colony. Equally infuriating, the instructions Newport carried from London appeared to the president to be the usual mishmash of hopelessly unrealistic schemes he associated with the colony's leaders. "How or why," Smith remarked, "Captaine Newport obtained such a private commission as not to re-turne [to England] without a lumpe of gold, a certainty of the south sea or one of the lost company of Sir Walter Rawley" he could not say. Yet why was Smith, who had been chiefly responsible for stimulating the Company's renewed interest in finding survivors, so critical of Company plans?

One possibility lies in timing. Smith sent the sketch map to England at the beginning of June. By the time Newport arrived back at Jamestown in October, Smith may have doubted that a direct route to the Indies or gold mines existed. Given what he had learned from Wowinchopunck, Smith may have no longer believed anyone from the Lost Colony would be found, though such a view would seem to contradict the inclusion of information about survivors on his sketch map and his willingness some months later to send out two more expeditions.

A more likely explanation for Smith's criticism of the Company's instructions lies in his hostility to Newport. By the fall, Smith considered himself indispensable to Jamestown's survival; he had saved the colony from self-destruction and from the Powhatans and was determined to maintain his grip on the colony's affairs. A sensational discovery such as finding survivors of the Lost Colony might propel Newport to national fame while casting Smith into the shadows. He was probably relieved therefore that Newport opted to take an expedition westwards into the lands of the Monacans to look for mines rather than south to Roanoke. He may have been confident Newport would fail to find what he was searching for upriver, but who knows what he might have found if he had turned southwards?

## The Coronation

An especially sharp exchange between Smith and Newport in front of the council shortly after Newport's arrival brought out into the open Smith's frustrations not only with Newport but also with the London Company. It was bad enough the Company had sent seventy settlers to Virginia without adequate provisions, Smith thought, but instead of building up food supplies for the winter and producing useful commodities for export to England (clapboard, pitch, tar, soap ashes, and glass) that at least had some value, Newport convinced the council to agree to support his expedition into the interior. Even worse, Newport also persuaded the colony's leaders to agree to Company proposals to stage a "coronation" of Wahunsonacock, which they believed was an essential preliminary to win over the Powhatans to the English.

When Smith objected to the plan, Newport countered by arguing that the president was trying to hinder him only because he (Smith) wanted to carry out the expedition himself, but could not because of his "crueltie" towards the Indians; a clear suggestion of unease among the council about Smith's aggressiveness towards local peoples during the summer while on his voyages of discovery. To this Smith had no reply. Few doubted he had undertaken his two voyages in the hope of preempting Newport, and it now appeared that he was trying to prevent Newport from succeeding where he had failed. As for the Indians, Smith believed he had used force only when necessary. Nevertheless, persuaded by Newport's arguments and wishing to comply with Company instructions, the council overruled Smith's double vote and adopted Newport's proposals.[5]

Smith had lost control of the council, but had no intention of being relegated to the sidelines. To prove that Newport's allegations about his mistreatment of the Indians were false and to demonstrate that he would go along with the coronation idea even though he strongly disagreed with it, Smith undertook to go to Werowocomoco to inform Wahunsonacock of the gifts awaiting him at Jamestown supposedly sent by the English king. Accompanied by Captain Richard Waldo, who had recently been appointed to the council, together with Master Andrew Buckler, Edward Brinton, Samuel Collier, and Namontack, just returned from England, Smith left the fort and traveled northwards along the Indian trail to the Pamunkey River.

On reaching the Indian capital and learning the great chief was elsewhere, the Englishmen were entertained by an unusual spectacle while they awaited his return. In a clearing surrounded by trees, the Indians prepared a fire and instructed Smith to sit on a mat in front of it. Suddenly, from the woods, a "hideous noise and shriking [shrieking]" was heard. Smith and his men were so alarmed that they rushed to take up their arms, but upon finding a large crowd of men, women, and children, Smith was reassured that no mischief was afoot and resumed his place in front of the fire.

Thirty young women, naked apart from a few green leaves that covered "behind and before," emerged from the woods, their bodies painted, "some white, some red, some black, some partie colour, but every one different." The leader of the women wore a pair of stag's antlers on her head, an otter skin at her girdle, and carried a bow and quiver of arrows in her hand. Others carried a sword, a club—or "potstick"—and also wore horns as well as other objects. "These feindes with most hellish cries, and shouts rushing from amongst the trees," recounted Smith, "cast themselves in a ring about the fire, singing, and dauncing with excellent ill varietie, oft falling into their infernall passions, and then solemnely againe to sing and daunce."

After more than an hour "in this maskarado," the women invited Smith to their lodging, "but no sooner was hee within the house, but all these Nimphes more tormented him than ever, with crowding, and pressing, and hanging upon him, most tediously crying, love you not mee?" Then there followed a great feast of fruits, fish, roast pig, beans, and peas in which all the Indians celebrated the young women's ritual and the bounty of the harvest. The singing and dancing continued until nightfall, when they all retired to their lodgings.[6]

The next day, Smith returned Namontack to Wahunsonacock and invited the great chief to visit Jamestown to receive his gifts. The visit would be the occasion on which an alliance against the Monacans would be formed. Wahunsonacock's reply put the Englishman in his place. "If your king have sent me presents, I also am a king, and this my land, 8 daies I will stay [at Werowocomoco] to receave them. Your father [Newport] is to come to me, not I to him, nor yet to your fort, neither will I bite at such a baite: as for the Monacans, I can revenge my own injuries." Surmising why the English were so anxious to attack the Monacans, he added, "But for any salt water beyond the mountains, the relations you have had from my people are false." Following further discussions and courtesies, Smith returned to Jamestown with the message. Newport's reaction to the chief's demands is not recorded, but he had little choice but to agree.

Accordingly, he and Smith, accompanied by fifty well-armed men, made their way twelve miles overland to Werowocomoco, where the gifts—some pieces of copper, a basin, pitcher, bed and bedclothes—which were transported by boat, were put on display. The coronation itself proved a farce. Wahunsonacock would consent to wear the "scarlet cloake and apparel" brought by the English for the purpose only after being assured by Namontack that they would do him no harm. Even worse, he steadfastly refused to kneel, "neither knowing the majestie, nor meaning of a Crowne, nor bending of the knee," Smith wrote. Eventually, after "many perswasions, examples, and instructions, as tired them all, . . . by leaning hard" on the king's shoulders, the Englishmen managed to get him to stoop low enough for Newport to place the crown on his head. In his honor, the English fired a volley, which caused "the king [to] start up in a horrible feare," but seeing that all was well he thanked the English and "gave his old shoes and his mantle [cloak] to Captain Newport" as a token of his favor. He would not, however, agree to help the English explore the lands of the Monacans, refusing to commit men or guides other than Namontack.[7]

Smith had been critical of the "strange coronation" because the colonists in his opinion had the chief's favor "much better, onlie for a poore peece of Copper"; whereas "this stately kind of soliciting made him so much overvalue himselfe, that he respected us as much as nothing at all." The ritual was intended by the English to confirm their recognition of Wahunsonacock's status among his own peoples and, at the same time, to symbolize his submission and allegiance to James I. The great chief was called upon to play the part of a local lord under the authority of the English king and his envoys in Virginia.[8]

But Wahunsonacock was far more astute than either Smith or Newport realized. The coronation had cost him nothing. He had made the English come to him, he had accepted their gifts, and in return he had given them nothing, merely a pair of his old shoes and a cloak (their value presumably residing in the fact they had been close to his royal body). And he had confirmed his prestige in the eyes of his own people by inverting the meaning of the ritual: It was he who received the tribute of the English, not the other way round. The crown, the bed, and the other presents were stored in the "god's house" at Orapaks and kept as symbols of his influence over the English. Every year at the sowing of the corn, Wahunsonacock would parade among his people, the crown upon his head, and dispense gifts of beads.[9]

Smith was correct in his assessment that the Powhatan chief did not understand the symbolism of the crown, nor the act of receiving it. But more accurately, Wahunsonacock did not accept the *English* meaning of the ritual, just as the English completely missed the significance the Indians attached to the event. The great chief was no vassal of the English. Even as he took part in the elaborate charade, he was already devising plans to rid himself of the troublesome intruders for good.

## "Faction and Idle Conceits"

Doubly frustrated by Wahunsonacock's refusal to assist his expedition into the interior and by Smith having been proven right about the coronation, Newport returned to Jamestown with little to show for his efforts. Yet he remained determined to carry out his plans. He put together a force of 120 chosen men, including all of the council apart from Smith, and set out for "the discovery of the Monacan," leaving the president at the fort with the remaining eighty settlers to lade the ship. Smith was outraged. He was by far the most experienced explorer of the company and knew more about the region than any other Englishman, yet he had been deliberately excluded. That said, he must have realized that this was very much Newport's expedition; and he could blame only himself for being given the task of producing commodities to be sent back to England because he had spoken so forcefully in favor of it earlier when objecting to Newport's plans. Moreover, he had had his chance in the summer and had found neither gold nor a passage to the Pacific. Now it was Newport's turn to make the attempt.

In hindsight it is easy to condemn the hope of finding gold mines or a route to the Indies expressed in the London Company's instructions and Smith's and Newport's various expeditions. But Company plans would hardly have surprised contemporaries, especially those sufficiently well connected to be privy to court gossip. Early in 1608, rumors began circulating in embassies and foreign capitals of a possible Spanish attack on Virginia. Sir Charles Cornwallis reported from Madrid in February that a great fleet was being prepared, ostensibly to protect Spanish shipping from Barbary pirates, but in reality to go to Virginia. Several months later, he sent a letter to the Privy Council giving details of an armada, made up of twenty-three or twenty-four galleons as well as smaller ships, that was on its way to New Spain to protect the treasure fleet. Yet the armada might also be deployed in Virginia to destroy the colony, as the Spanish did to the French in Florida (that is, without quarter).[10]

Known to London Company leaders, as surely it would have been, the news would only have spurred on efforts to find something of value in Virginia that might persuade James I to send English warships to protect the colony, or at the very least to provide some kind of return on monies already invested. With the threat of an imminent Spanish attack, there was no time to develop the natural resources of the land as advocated by Thomas Hariot, Richard Hakluyt, and latterly John Smith. English investors' demand for quick profits and the uncertain future of the colony pointed in the same direction: the urgent need to achieve a significant discovery before the settlement was either abandoned or destroyed. And for this, the Company pinned their hopes on Newport, not Smith.

But as Smith had predicted, Newport's expedition proved a waste of time and effort. The men marched about forty or fifty miles beyond the falls and passed through a couple of Monacan towns and a "faire, fertill, well watred countrie," which must have taken them to within view of the Blue Ridge Mountains, but they found no signs of precious minerals other than a "small quantitie of silver" discovered by their refiner, William Calicut. Neither could they obtain corn from the Powhatans and so returned to Jamestown tired, hungry, and dispirited.[11]

After the men got back, Smith wasted little time in organizing them into work gangs: some to begin trials of glass at the recently built "Glasse House" about a mile from the fort, which included eight

"Dutchmen" (Germans) and Poles recruited specifically for the purpose; others to produce pitch, tar, and soap ashes; and thirty men under Smith's direct supervision who were taken a few miles off to produce clapboard and wainscot and learn how to survive in the forest. On his return to the fort, finding provisions running low, Smith decided to take the "discovery barge" once again to the land of the Chickahominies and trade for corn.

Ordering George Percy to follow, he set off with twenty men and a second barge for transporting provisions on a journey he had last taken shortly before Christmas the previous year. Reaching the Chickahominy River in a few hours, Smith found the Indians in no mood to bargain, "refusing to trade, with as much scorne and insolencie as they could expresse." Rather than negotiate for food, the captain landed his men and threatened to attack, declaring he had come not to trade but to avenge his imprisonment and the murder of his two men last year. From Smith's point of view, his threats had the desired effect: The Indians loaded his two barges with a hundred bushels of corn, and Percy's in same measure when it arrived. In return, the president delivered to the Indians some of his trade goods, and after four or five days, apparently parting "good friends," Smith and his men left the Chickahominies and made their way back to Jamestown.

Although most of the men at the fort welcomed his return with several barges full of provisions, according to Smith, "some so envied his good successe, that they rather desired to starve, then his paines should prove so much more effectuall then theirs." A couple of the gentry (Smith blamed Ratcliffe and Newport) even proposed to have him banished from the fort for leaving his post without their consent. The precise basis for the accusations are difficult to unravel, but again there were complaints that Smith had been too aggressive in his dealings with the Indians. Nevertheless, the small band of malcontents were in no position to threaten his position. As long as he was able to keep the men fed, he remained popular with them, many of whom probably shared his views about how best to deal with the Powhatans.[12]

More of a threat to the well-being of the settlement was what was taking place on Newport's ship, the *Mary and Margaret*, anchored just off the island. The ship had become a floating tavern and marketplace where sailors, settlers, and visiting Indians alike bartered for food, drink, hatchets, and all sorts of goods brought from England. Within a couple of months, Smith complained, "of two or three hundred Axes, Chissels, Hows, and Pick-axes, scarce twentie could be found." Worse yet, the sailors sold to the Indians anything they could get their hands on, even pike heads, knives, powder, and shot, in return for furs, baskets, and provisions. "Tenne times more care [was taken] to maintain their damnable and private trade," he fulminated, "then to provide for the Colony things that were necessary." While the sailors feasted on provisions supplied by the London Company, the colonists existed on short rations of corn meal and water. All of Smith's outrage about the corruption of Newport and his crew, thieving sailors, idleness, wasted effort, and disaffected settlers boiled over in a lengthy letter written in response to the Company's instructions sent with Newport.

He began by addressing concerns raised by the Company: The colony's leaders were "set upon faction," they planned to divide the country without permission, and they provided little information about their progress. Investors in London were reaching the end of their tether. The cost of Newport's latest voyage alone was "neare two thousand pounds." If the settlers could not produce commodities of sufficient value to meet the expense by the ship's return, they were "like to remain [in Virginia] as banished men."

Smith asked the Company what he should do: He could not prevent dissension other than by ordering the men to abandon the colony because he made "many stay that would els[e] fly." Ratcliffe, "a poore counterfeited Imposture," and Gabriel Archer had been chiefly responsible for sowing dissension among the men and keeping the leaders "always in factions." As for a plan to divide the country, Smith disclaimed any knowledge, although he was aware that the accusation had been made by Ratcliffe and his "confederats" in an "idle Letter" sent to Lord Salisbury. "What it was I know not, for you saw no hand of mine to it; nor ever dream't I of any such matter."

Nevertheless, the reference is puzzling. Was it simply pure fabrication on Ratcliffe's part to discredit him? The Company's knowledge of the plan suggests that Salisbury received the letter shortly after Newport's return from Virginia early in the summer of 1608, possibly via Archer, who went back on the same ship. This timing corresponds with Newport's stay in the colony from January to April, when Smith had only recently returned from captivity. Did Ratcliffe, and possibly Archer, deliberately garble Smith's description of his encounter with Wahunsonacock and the offer of the "Countrie called Capahowasicke" to suggest that the captain had conspired with the Indians to carve out a land of his own? If so, Smith's encounter with the Powhatans in December 1607 was more significant than even he might have realized. The length of his captivity and his return unscathed evidently led some of the colony's leaders to think his release was not the outcome of his quick-wittedness and instinct for survival (as Smith portrayed it) but rather had a more sinister explanation. No matter how vigorously Smith denied being tempted by the promise of an Indian chiefdom or of collaborating with the Powhatans, he never entirely shook off the suspicion that he must have struck some kind of deal with the great chief to save his own life; indeed, he was never wholly trusted by the colony's leaders again.

So Smith could do little more than repeat that he knew nothing about plans to divide the colony and move on to other issues raised by the Company that he could more easily deal with. The first, predictably enough, was Newport and his crew. If the Company had expended two or three thousand pounds on commodities for the voyage, the settlers themselves had not seen a hundred pounds worth. Most of the supplies and goods had been siphoned off by Newport (who had "an hundred pounds a yeare for carrying newes") and his cronies; or they were bartered by sailors to the colonists, who were forced to buy their victuals at exhorbitant prices. Smith urged the Company to "let us know what we should receive, and not stand to the Saylers courtesie to leave us what they please."

He complained bitterly about Newport's fruitless expedition into the interior. It had proved impossible to transport the "5 pieced barge," which had been purposefully built in London and sent over with Newport to aid exploration of the James beyond the falls. Designed "to be bourne by the Souldiers" over the rocks and shoals that marked the limits of the navigable river, it was so heavy that five hundred could not have managed it unless they "had burnt her to ashes" and "carried her in a bag." At the council meeting when Smith criticized the Company's instructions, he had told them that to find "the South Sea, a Mine of gold; or any of them sent by Sir Walter Raleigh . . . was as likely as the rest" (that is, a delusion). As for the "great discovery of thirty miles" to the mountains, he sneered, far from bringing back news of a passage to the East or gold mines, Newport's men had not been able to find even enough corn to feed themselves and had returned "sicke and neare famished" to Jamestown.

Smith reserved much of his contempt for Newport, but he also had plenty to say about the Company's schemes. Despite the recent emphasis given to making spectacular discoveries, the Company had not jettisoned ideas to set up industries or harvest the natural bounty of the land. But Smith cautioned investors not to demand quick or substantial profits from the newly established glassworks or efforts to produce pitch, tar, soap ashes, and clapboard. Consider, he went on, "what an infinite toyle it is in Russia and Swethland, where the woods are proper for naught els, and though there be the helpe both of man and beast in those ancient Common-wealths . . . yet thousands of those poore people can get necessaries to live, but from hand to mouth."

Raising a question in the minds of Company adventurers whether such projects in Virginia were worth the money expended, he continued: "And though your Factors there [Russia] can buy as much in a week as will fraught you a ship, or as much as you please; you must not expect from us any such matter, which are but a many of ignorant miserable soules, that are scarce able to get wherewith to live, and defend our selves against the inconstant Salvages: finding but here and there a tree fit for the purpose, and want all things els the Russians have." It was a question that would haunt not only the Company until its demise but also colonial projectors for decades beyond.

Would the production of industrial goods in America be profitable given the huge distances to be traveled in bringing them to market? Why promote manufacturing on the other side of the Atlantic at all when it could be developed at far less cost at home? If Spain brought back unimaginable riches in gold and silver from the Indies in her great treasure ships, could anyone truly believe that England would reap similar wealth in a few years from iron, timber, and glass manufactured in the forests of Virginia by a couple of hundred half-starved, disease-ridden settlers? Rather than dreaming up hopelessly unrealistic schemes for making money, Smith argued, the Company should first invest in building up the colony; it should send carpenters, husbandmen, gardeners, blacksmiths, and masons to cultivate the land and construct towns, not transport useless wastrels who were good for nothing but cursing and consuming the meager provisions the few hardworking sort produced.

From the letter's contents and tone it might be thought that Smith had given up on the colony, but this was by no means true. The letter was not meant to be read alone, but rather served as a context for a manuscript he had been preparing whenever the opportunity had presented itself during the previous couple of months. The "Mappe of the Bay and Rivers, with an annexed Relation of the Countries and Nations that inhabit them" was to his mind the real treasure sent back to London with Newport in early December 1608. The manuscript was a good deal briefer than the published version of 1612 (modeled on Thomas Hariot's account of Roanoke) and focused on the country and its peoples.

Smith's description offered no quick and easy route to riches, but it served to emphasize the extensiveness and natural abundance of the region. Virginia "may have the prerogative," he wrote enthusiastically, "over the most pleasant places of Europe, Asia, Africa, or America, for large and pleasant navigable rivers[;] heaven and earth never agreed better to frame a place for mans habitation being of our constitutions, were it fully manured and inhabited by an industrious people."

The map, along with the description, incorporated Smith's most recent findings from the two voyages of discovery of the previous summer. Presenting to the eye the "way of the mountaines and current of the rivers, with their severall turnings, bayes, shoules, Isles, Inlets, and creekes, the breadth of the waters, the distances of places and such like," it was a remarkable achievement, surpassing in detail and practical significance, if not aesthetic quality, even the wonderful watercolor maps of Roanoke and the mid-Atlantic coast drawn by John White. Smith gave expression to the sheer expanse of the Chesapeake (approaching a third of the land area of England), the magisterial Bay and its broad waterways, myriad creeks and islands, and diversity of native peoples. No small island, cramped strip of coast, or minor river valley, Virginia was a country of "Counties," the bounds of which even Smith had been unable to encompass. Although at the time of his voyages around the Bay the English occupied only tiny Jamestown Island, Smith's map effectively staked England's claim to the whole region by right of discovery and by virtue of an English presence in name if not in person. Jamestown was the English capital of a vast province.[13]

Smith tried to avoid exaggeration and falsehoods. Virginia was not a land of milk and honey, fantastic creatures, gold and silver mines, and opulent Indian civilizations. He could not say how far beyond the western mountains lay the Pacific or whether a convenient passage existed that would carry his countrymen to Cathay. His posture was that of the pragmatist. He reported what he had seen himself and sought to provide an accurate description of the region's resources.

But for all the understatement, his account was carefully crafted to have widespread appeal in England. Many of the trees, fruits, vegetables, medicinal plants, animals, fishes, and birds were the same or similar to those found in Europe, but they existed in super abundance; and although his descriptions of native peoples were remarkably balanced, no one could overlook his emphasis on their small numbers. In short, here was a vast new land: fertile, well watered with abundant natural resources, and inhabited by only a few thousand Indians; all that was required to reap its bounty was "the industry of men," that is, English settlers.[14]

## Survival and Betrayal

Smith must have been greatly pleased to see Newport's ships, laden with clapboard, wainscot, and "the trials of pitch, tarre, glasse, frankincense,

*John Smith, Map of Virginia, 1624 (originally published in 1612).*

and sope ashes," finally disappear from view down the James River on their way back to England. Once again, he was in charge, and, as the weather turned bitterly cold in December, he first concerned himself with securing sufficient provisions to keep the two hundred settlers alive during the winter. To that end, he set off with a couple of boats for the Nansemond River. Much to his annoyance (and as Matthew Scrivener had found on a similar expedition a week or two earlier to Werowoco-moco), the Indians refused to trade because, they said, they were "so commanded by Powhatan."

Threatening to take their corn by force if they refused to bargain, Smith persuaded the Nansemonds to part with a hundred bushels and returned to Jamestown just in time for festivities celebrating the "first marriage we had in Virginia," that between John Laydon and Anna Burrowes, maidservant of one Mistress Forrest, who had arrived with the second supply; possibly the one bright spot in what must have been an increasingly worrying time. Trying his luck upriver, Smith could find "neither corne nor Savage, but all fled"; and exploring as far as the Appomattox River, he found the people there had little to trade. Smith realized now that Wahunsonacock had ordered an embargo on trade with the English and concluded that the Powhatan chief must be confronted or else the colony would starve.

In fact, Smith had been invited to meet the chief at Werowocomoco, where Wahunsonacock promised he would load the Englishman's ship with corn if in return he would send men to build him a house, provide a grindstone, fifty swords, "some peeces [cannon]," and copper and beads. Smith was aware he might be walking into a trap but had little choice but to agree; sending Richard Savage and four of the Germans ahead to build the house, he set off in the pinnace and two barges with forty-six men in the final days of the year.

They headed first for Warraskoyack, where the chief warned them that Wahunsonacock had sent for them "only to cut your throats." Smith thanked him for his advice and "the better to try his love" asked for guides to lead Michael Sicklemore, "a very honest, valiant, and painefull [thorough] souldier," to Chowanoc "to search for the lost company of Sir Walter Rawley, and silk grass." Leaving Samuel Collier with the Warraskoyacks to learn their language, Smith and his men moved on to Kecoughtan, where the worsening weather forced them to remain for a week. Driving rain turned to sleet and then snow, but the Englishmen "were never more merrie," better fed, or warm than when they stayed in the smoky houses of the Kecoughtans, feasting on oysters, fish, venison, and wild fowl. It must have seemed a strange way to pass the Christmas season and a strange beginning to their journey, yet doubtless a welcome delay to the confrontation with the Powhatans shortly to come. So it was probably with some reluctance that they left behind Kecoughtan, rounded the peninsula, and sailed up the Pamunkey River to Werowocomoco.[15]

Finally arriving at the Indian capital on January 12, 1609, two weeks after setting out, they found the river frozen nearly half a mile from the shore. Smith and his men were obliged to wade through icy water and ooze to reach the river bank. The next day, Smith met Wahunsonacock. The great chief said he had not sent for them and asked him when they planned to leave; he assured Smith that he had no corn to trade, although he would spare forty bushels for the like number of swords. Looking over the goods the English had brought, he repeated that he was interested in trading for guns and swords only. He said that he valued a basket of corn more highly than a basket of copper because he "could eate his corne, but not his copper."

The dialogue between Smith and Wahunsonacock that followed is the most extensive verbatim exchange between the two men, and although we cannot possibly know for sure whether the voice of the Powhatan chief is authentic, it is nevertheless the closest we can come to hearing the chief's words from his own lips. The war of words is significant, too, in content. The gloves were off, there was to be no more dissembling, no more charades. Smith wanted corn, Wahunsonacock wanted English weapons, and neither was prepared to compromise. Moreover, as both of them realized, much more was at stake than either corn or weapons. Smith began by emphasizing his friendship and ended with a thinly veiled threat:

Powhatan, though I had many courses to have made my provision, yet
believing your promises to supply my wants, I neglected all, to satisfie
your desire, and to testifie my love, I sent you my men for your building, neglecting my owne: what your people had you have engrossed,
forbidding them our trade, and nowe you thinke by consuming the
time, wee shall consume for want, not having to fulfill your strange de-
mandes. As for swords, and gunnes, I told you long agoe, I had none to
spare. And you shall knowe, those I have, can keepe me from want, yet
steale, or wrong you I will not, nor dissolve that friendship, wee have
mutually promised, except you constraine mee by your bad usage.

Wahunsonacock promised that he would supply them with what they
could spare within two days, but he made his doubts of the Englishman's intentions clear:

Yet Captaine Smith . . . some doubt I have of your comming hither,
that makes me not so kindly seeke to relieve you as I would; for many
do informe me, your comming is not for trade, but to invade my
people and possesse my Country, who dare not come to bring you
corne, seeing you thus armed with your men. To cleere us of this feare,
leave abord your weapons, for here they are needlesse we being all
friends and forever Powhatans.

The rest of the day was spent in further discussions and continued
into the next, when the chief talked at length of war and peace and his
fears about why the English had come into his country:

Captaine Smith you may understand, that I, having seene the death of
all my people thrice, and not one living of those 3 generations, but my
selfe, I knowe the difference of peace and warre, better then any in my
Countrie. But . . . this brute [rumor] from Nansamund that you are
come to destroy my Countrie, so much affrighteth all my people, as
they dare not visit you: what will it availe you, to take that perforce,
you may quietly have with love, or to destroy them that provide you
food? What can you get by war, when we can hide our provision and

flie to the woodes, whereby you must famish by wronging us your friends; and whie are you thus jealous of our loves, seeing us unarmed, and both doe, and are willing still to feed you with that you cannot get but by our labours?

Smith, like his adversary, sought to pose as the wronged party and responded by stressing again his love for the Powhatans despite their failure to supply the colony with food as promised. He ignored the chief's view of the English as adopted Powhatans, and he rejected the suggestion the English could survive only if they remained on friendly terms. They could take what they wanted by force if they chose, but they preferred to live in peace. Knowing the colony was once again on the brink of starvation, Wahunsonacock was hardly persuaded by Smith's assertions and must have wondered at the Englishman's brazenness in standing before him and making such claims.

Seeing that the English persisted in refusing to lay down their arms, the chief spoke of his disappointment in Smith:

I never used anie of [my] Werowances, so kindlie as youre selfe; yet from you I receave the least kindnesse of anie. Captaine Newport gave me swords, copper, cloths, a bed, tooles, or what I desired, ever taking what I offered him, and would send awaie his gunnes when I intreated him: none doth denie to laie at my feet (or do) what I desire, but onlie you, of whom I have nothing, but what you regard not, and yet you have whatsoever you demand. Captain Newport you call father, and so you call me, but I see for all us both, you will do what you list, and wee must both seeke to content you: but if you intend so friendlie as you saie, send hence your armes that I may believe you, for you see the love I beare you, doth cause mee thus nakedlie [to] forget my selfe.

Smith refused to acknowledge Wahunsonacock's authority and, as the chief had suggested, did not even follow the orders of his English "father," Newport. But by this time Smith was convinced that the Powhatans were merely waiting for an opportunity to "cut his throat." He therefore decided to surprise the chief, take him hostage, and make his escape with as much corn as he could carry. To "keepe him from suspition" and "trifle the time" until his men landed, he replied:

> Powhatan, you must knowe as I have but one God, I honour but one king; and I live not here as your subject, but as your friend, to pleasure you with what I can: by the gifts you bestowe on me, you gain more then by trade; yet would you visite mee as I doe you, you should knowe it is not our customes to sell curtesie as a vendible commoditie. Bring all your Country with you for your gard, I will not dislike of it as being over jealous. But to content you, to morrow I will leave my armes, and trust to your promise. I call you father indeed, and as a father you shall see I will love you, but the small care you had of such a child, caused my men [to] perswade me to shift for my selfe.

These were the last words the two men exchanged.

Shortly after, Wahunsonacock having departed with his wives, children, and baggage, warriors surrounded the great chief's house. Seeing the danger, Smith took up his pistol, sword, and shield and "made such a passage" among the chief's men that they fell back, tumbling over one another to get out of his way. Unwilling to confront the English in a pitched battle, the Powhatans chose further delaying tactics. An "ancient Oratour" explained that Wahunsonacock had left only because he feared that more of Smith's men would soon be arriving from the pinnace; the old man assured the captain that Wahunsonacock was his friend "and so [would] be for ever." As a token of the great chief's love for him, Smith was given a bracelet and chain of pearl and the Indians agreed to load corn onto his barge. But in fact, Wahunsonacock had ordered that Smith be murdered later that evening. The English could not leave before the tide turned, and in the meantime the Indians entertained them "with all the merry sports they could devise," all the while planning to ambush them at supper when their guard was down.

Smith was rescued once again by young Pocahontas, who had got wind of the plot and "came through the irksome woods" in the night to urge him to be gone as soon as possible. He gave earnest thanks for her news and offered such gifts as she would take; but "with the teares runninge downe her cheeks, shee said shee durst not be seene to have any: for if Powhatan should know it, she were but dead," and so slipped away into the darkness. Smith chose not to flee, however, and when "eight or ten lusty fellowes" arrived at the house with great plates of meat and other provisions, he made them sit down and taste every dish. All the while, the soldiers kept their matches alight and their muskets at the ready. Smith informed the warriors that he knew why they had come and that he would confound their plans and all their other "intended villanies"; and so they spent the next several hours watching one another until the Englishmen were able to escape safely on the midnight tide, having passed the time "with such mirth, as though [they] never had suspected or intended any thing."[16]

RATHER THAN RETURN TO JAMESTOWN, Smith opted to head upriver and bargain for corn with the Pamunkeys. He understood full well the risk. It was possible that Opechancanough might be more determined than his brother to rid himself of the tiresome captain, but Smith knew they did not have sufficient food to get them through the winter and had little chance of finding enough elsewhere. Yet if he had known about another group that left Werowocomoco that night, he might have reconsidered his plans. Wahunsonacock was ready to dispense with Smith because he had succeeded in winning over to his side the Germans sent to build his house. He had made them substantially the same offer that he had made Smith a little more than year before, with the exception that he did not intend to raise any of them to the status of a chief. He would free them from "those miseries that would happen [to] the Colony," and provide food, shelter, and protection; in return, the men would bring him English weapons and tools and anything else he required.

Two of the Germans, Adam and Franz, were dispatched by the Wahunsonacock to Jamestown with a cock-and-bull story about needing tools, clothing, and weapons, and in this manner they made off with "a great many swords, pike-heads, peeces, shot, powder, and such like."[17] They also persuaded six or seven others of the colony to join them; these, in turn, managed to get away with as much as they could transport, so that Wahunsonacock quickly amassed some three hundred hatchets, fifty swords, eight cannon, and eight pikes. Smith would not learn of the German's treachery for another two weeks, and by then the damage had been done.

Arriving at the Pamunkey town of Cinquoteck, the president and his men spent a couple of days resting until the appointed day for trade. Then the president, George Percy, Francis West, brother of Lord De La Warr, and twelve others made their way up to Opechancanough's house, set a quarter of mile from the river, where soon after the chief arrived with many men but few provisions. Smith did not mince his words:

> Opechancanough, the great love you professe with your tongue, seemes meere deceit by your actions. Last yeere you kindly fraughted our ship: but now you have invited mee to starve with hunger: you know my want, and I your plenty; of which by some meanes I must have part.

The chief readily agreed to trade and promised to be better provided the next day.

When the Englishmen returned the following morning, they found four or five Indians with great baskets of food. Soon after, Opechancanough arrived and discoursed at length about the trouble he had gone through to keep his promise; but as he spoke, John Russell informed Smith that they were betrayed because six or seven hundred warriors had surrounded them. Time "not permitting any argument" about the best course of action, the captain approached the Pamunkey chief and in plain words challenged him to single combat, adding a wager:

> Opechancanough you plot to murder me, but I feare it not, as yet your men and mine, have done no harme, but by our directions. Take therefore your arms; you see mine; my body shalbe as naked as yours; the Ile in your river is a fit place, if you be contented: and the conquerour (of

us two) shalbe Lord and Master over all our men; otherwise drawe all your men into the field; if you have not enough, take time to fetch more, and bring what number you will, so everie one bring a basket of corne, against all which I will stake the value in copper; you see I have but 15 men, and our game shalbe, the conquerer take all.

If Opechancanough comprehended the challenge, he could hardly be blamed for ignoring it. He had nothing to gain and everything to lose by accepting. He chose, therefore, to try to draw Smith out of the house and make him an easy target for his bowmen positioned outside. In the heat of the moment, the Englishman may not have thought too much about his reaction, but what happened next sealed his own fate among the Powhatans and cast a bloody shadow over the colony for years to come.

Commanding Percy and West to make the house safe and two men to guard the door, Smith grabbed Opechancanough by his long scalp lock, aimed a pistol at his breast, and led him "neare dead with feare" (more likely shock) among his people, forced him to surrender his weapons, and made him order his men to do the same. Then he addressed the astonished throng with his usual mixture of threats and fair promises:

I see you Pamaunkies the great desire you have to cut my throat; and my long suffering your injuries, have inboldened you to this presumption. The cause I have forborne your insolencies, is the promise I made you (before the God I serve) to be your friend, till you give me just cause to bee your enimie. If I keepe this vow, my God will keepe me, you cannot hurt me; if I breake it he will destroie me. But if you shoot one arrow, to shed one drop of blood of any of my men, or steale the least of these beades, or copper . . . you shall see, I will not cease revenge, (if once I begin) so long as I can heare where to find one of your nation that will not deny the name of Pamaunke.

Referring to his capture and "good usage" by Opechancanough in the winter of 1607, Smith offered in return to overlook the Indians'

C.Smith taketh the King of Pamavnkee prifoner 1608

The Countrey wee now call **Virginia** beginneth at Cape Henry diftant from Roanoack 60 miles, where was S.r Walter Raleigh's plantation: and becaufe the people differ very little from them of Powhatan in any thing, I have inferted thofe figures in this place becaufe of the conveniency.

*John Smith in combat with Opechancanough.*

treachery: "[I]f as friends you wil come and trade, I once more promise not to trouble you, except you give me the first occasion."

Incredibly, even after the attempts on his life and the terrible personal insult he had dealt Opechancanough, he still tried to persuade the Indians to remain on friendly terms. The contortions he went through to avoid facing the reality that the English and Powhatans were at each others' throats illustrate the extent of his dilemma. He had told his men his concern about being seen as a "peace-breaker" in England and the likely consequences for him: "I could wish those [to be] here," he exclaimed in frustration, "that make these [the Indians] seeme Saints, and me an oppressor."

And yet the root of Smith's problem ran deeper. He had lost his influence with Wahunsonacock and Opechancanough and with it the prime advantage he had held over other leaders of the colony since his miraculous return from captivity early in 1608. Nor could he hope any longer for the Indians' help in supplying the colonists with food. Smith understood, just as Wahunsonacock did, the Englishmen's dependence on the Powhatans for provisions. If they sought to destroy the Indians, they would starve: "[T]hen by their losse" Smith wrote, "we should have lost our selvs." Hence his desperate efforts to avoid conflict. And yet the Powhatan chief no longer needed Smith; now that he could depend on the Germans, he could get what he wanted by treachery rather than trade. Though Smith did not yet know the cause, the balance of power had shifted decisively towards the Powhatans.[18] He returned to Jamestown in early February with 279 bushels of corn and other provisions, but the cost had been enormous.

———

MORE BAD NEWS awaited him back at the fort. A couple of weeks before, Matthew Scrivener, Captain Richard Waldo (both of the council), Anthony Gosnold, and eight others were drowned during "that extreame frozen time" when their boat sank crossing to Hog Island. The loss further depressed morale, but Smith would not tolerate idleness and, gathering the men together, proclaimed starkly that henceforth "he that will not worke shall not eate." The president's

inability to supply the colony had lost him their support and the settlers were on the verge of mutiny.

Meanwhile, as Smith strove to find a means of forcing the men to
work, two of the Germans still with Wahunsonacock sent a compatriot
back to the fort to find out why they had not been joined by more of
the colonists. News of the German's errand came to the ears of Smith,
who sent out a party of twenty men to bring the traitor back to the
fort. Smith joined in the search and, passing by the newly constructed
glasshouse alone, was suddenly attacked by Wowinchopunck, chief of
the Paspaheghs, who hoped to gain favor with Wahunsonacock by
killing the Englishman. Locked in hand-to-hand combat, the two men
fell into the river nearby, where the Indian tried to drag Smith under
the water, only to be thwarted when a couple of colonists came to
Smith's rescue.

Wowinchopunck's attack persuaded Smith to inflict immediate
reprisals against the Paspaheghs and, with a small force, he carried out
a quick and brutal raid on their village. Smith and his men killed six or
seven warriors, took as many prisoners, burned the Indians' houses,
and made off with their canoes. Wowinchopunck offered peace and
once again reminded the English that they could not survive long
without Indian help. Through one of his men, he gave Smith an ultimatum: "[Y]ou will have the worst by our absence, for we can plant
any where, though with more labour, and we know you cannot live if
you want our harvest, and that reliefe wee bring you; if you promise us
peace we will believe you, if you proceed in reveng, we will abandon
the Countrie." It was an arrangement that suited the Englishman: He
promised to leave the Indians alone if they provided food, this being
the kind of agreement he had hoped to work out with the Powhatans.
But whereas he could overawe the Paspaheghs, the same was not true
of the powerful peoples farther upriver who formed the core of the
Powhatan chiefdom.[19]

During the next few months, Smith kept the men busy repairing
the fort and producing pitch, tar, soap ashes, and glass. They also constructed a blockhouse on the narrow neck of land at the western end of
the island that led to the mainland, where they could keep a check on

who entered and left the island. With the advice of two Paspaheghs, Kemps and Tassore, they planted thirty to forty acres of corn near the fort. The hogs continued to thrive on Hog Island, where a blockhouse was built to alert the settlement to the arrival of shipping. Construction of another fort was begun across the river, "upon a high commanding hill, very hard to be assaulted," in case they were forced to abandon Jamestown.

Scarcity of food continued to be a major concern. Because the corn they had taken from the Indians had rotted in the casks or been devoured by rats ("from the ships"), leaving them with nothing "but what nature afforded," Smith was left with little choice but to disperse his men. In May, about a third of the two hundred English were sent twenty miles downriver with Ensign William Laxon, one of the original settlers, "to live upon oysters"; twenty went with George Percy to Point Comfort to try their hand at fishing; and a similar number were dispatched upriver under the command of Francis West to live off the land at the falls. The rest stayed at Jamestown.

Despite the settlers' desperate situation, however, the majority were still reluctant to work. They had signed up as soldiers, not as fisherman and farmers, and rather than find their own provisions preferred to trade anything and everything to the Indians: "[N]ot only our kettles, hows, tooles, and Iron," Smith wrote, but also "swords, pieces, and the very Ordnance and howses." For food, "they would have had imparted all to the Salvages . . . [and] would have sould their soules." Once again he addressed the company and declared that anyone who did not daily produce as much food as he did himself would be banished from the fort "till he amend his conditions or starve." All talk of abandoning the colony was to cease, and anyone who attempted to take the pinnace "for Newfoundland" would find himself bound for the gallows instead.[20]

Time was running out for John Smith. Many of the men were ready to revolt, and the Indians were openly hostile. Somehow picking up rumors that a Spanish assault might be imminent, the renegade Germans planned to join an invading force to drive the English out. Learning of the disarray at Jamestown, they informed Wahunsonacock that the moment to attack had now come. The plan came to nothing, probably because the Powhatans remained wary of a frontal assault on the fort; yet the situation revealed the extent of discontent among the Englishmen as well as the continuing threat posed by settlers who ran away to the Indians.

Yet, for all the challenges Smith faced in the colony, ultimately it was neither his own men nor the Powhatans who would cause his downfall but (as he might well have foreseen) the changing tide of events in London. As far as the Company's sponsors were concerned, the colony had failed to fulfill their expectations and required immediate and thorough reorganization. A new beginning was called for, one that placed the colony on a very different footing.

# 5

# VIRGINEA BRITANNIA

WINTER WAS AS UNFORGIVING to the people of London as it was to the small group of Englishmen huddled by the frozen banks of the James River. Snow blanketed the capital, covering small side streets and squares, drifting into narrow alleys, and piling up in doorways and yards. Thoroughfares, bustling with traffic, turned into quagmires of slush under the steady tramp of passersby and the coming and going of carts and carriages. Taverns filled with the stink of damp clothes, unwashed bodies, smoke, and ale as men and women took refuge from the cold outside to dry off and take a drink in front of a good fire. Seen from the hills a few miles to the north, the city presented a wondrous panorama of frost-whitened roofs pierced by ancient church spires sparkling in the bright morning sun. But for all its frigid beauty, the intensely cold weather exacted a terrible price. Within weeks of the first snowfall the cost of food, coal, and firewood rocketed, bringing misery to the poor, crowded in squalid slums and poorer quarters ringing the city walls, who had little enough to subsist on even in the best times. To the old and sick the bitter cold proved just as deadly as the plague that had stalked the streets the previous summer, and they perished in their thousands. The winter of 1608–1609 was one of the hardest in living memory.[1]

———

IT IS UNLIKELY THAT Sir Thomas Smythe gave much thought to the plight of the poor as he left his house in Philpot Lane, in the heart of London's commercial district, and walked over to the old Royal Exchange, although he might very well have been pondering the fate of the colonists in Virginia. The leading merchant of his day, at fifty he was still a man of prodigious energy and influence and was connected to many of the major mercantile ventures of the period. In his youth, he had been fascinated by Sir Humphrey Gilbert's schemes to found an English empire in the North Atlantic; but luckily for him, he did not take part in Gilbert's disastrous last voyage. He had been governor of the East India Company since its founding, had helped set up the Turkey and Russia companies, and was involved in many others. A man of action as well as the counting house, he had been knighted for gallantry at Cadiz by the Earl of Essex, an honor later confirmed by James I, and was appointed ambassador to Russia in 1604. He was a member of Parliament, served as one of the four principals of the navy, and knew personally the king's most important ministers and courtiers. In Smythe, the Virginia Company could not have found a more powerful advocate or anyone better suited to harness the support of nobles, merchants, and the church to transform a private colony into a national undertaking.[2]

## New Beginnings

Initial steps to reform the colony had begun nearly a year earlier. In the spring of 1608, Henry Clinton, Earl of Lincoln, who had recently been added to the Virginia Council, urged that several thousand men be sent to Jamestown as soon as possible to populate the colony. Meanwhile, Sir Thomas Gates, captain of an English company in the Netherlands, was commissioned to lead a large-scale expedition to the "land of Virginia." Gates was an enthusiastic supporter of colonies and a seasoned military campaigner. As a young lieutenant, he had taken part in the raid on Santo Domingo and Cartagena led by Sir Francis Drake in 1585, and had been present when Ralph Lane's men were taken off Roanoke Island on the return leg of the voyage. A decade later, he distinguished himself during the attack on Cadiz and (like Smythe) was knighted for his services by Essex. He had been foremost in petitioning the king for a charter to colonize America and was the first-named grantee in the letters patent issued to the London Company by James I. Rather than accompany the first voyage to Virginia, however, he returned to the Netherlands, where he served with Sir Thomas Dale at the garrison of Oudewater in South Holland. It was from there that Gates made his way to England in May 1608.[3]

It was while Gates was settling into his new quarters that Christopher Newport had arrived from Virginia bringing details of the colony's near collapse and Wingfield's overthrow. As usual, Don Pedro de Zúñiga, the Spanish ambassador in London, was in touch with events. Said to have four English earls in the king of Spain's pay, including Sir Robert Cecil, the Earl of Salisbury (James I's first minister), Zúñiga was well placed to keep a close eye on developments as they unfolded. Writing to Philip III in late June, Zúñiga noted that, despite being almost bankrupt, the Company was preparing to send out another expedition. He repeated his opinion that as there was little in Virginia of any value, the English must be planning to establish a fortified base in Virginia for the purpose of "carry[ing] on piracy from there." Only the prospect of plunder could explain why the colony continued to attract settlers.[4]

Piracy was not on the minds of the Company's leaders, but as Sir Thomas Smythe strode out purposefully from his house on that crisp, sunny morning in late January 1609, he was already aware that the colony "went rather backwards than forwards." Having read John Smith's long letter criticizing the Company's policies, which had arrived with Newport from Virginia a few days before, and having had discussions with John Ratcliffe (also recently returned) and others, it was clear to Sir Thomas that the Company and colony needed to be reorganized as soon as possible. With his characteristic thoroughness, he convened a series of meetings with the Company's governing members and invited those knowledgeable about Virginia, such as Richard Hakluyt and Thomas Hariot, to attend.

What emerged was an unusually candid appraisal of the problems that had beset the colony from its beginning, which served as a response to Smith's criticism and to the rumors of "errors and discouragements" already circulating in London. Although the first expedition had given "no hope of any extraordinary consequence," it had confirmed "the *Navigablenesse* of the [James] *River, pleasure, fertility* and *scituation* of the land," which had justified sending out further men and supplies. Now, however, "experience of error in the equality of Governors, and some out-rages, and follies committed by them had a little shaken so tender a body [the colony]."

All "the inconveniences of these three supplies" (the expeditions of 1606, 1607, and 1608) could be reduced to two main problems: "the form of government, and length and danger of the passage by the southerly course of the Indyes." To counter the first, it was agreed that the king should be petitioned "for a special charter with such ample and large privileges and powers as would enable them to reform and correct those errors already discovered, and to prevent such as in the future might threaten them." To deal with the second problem, the Company decided to employ Captain Samuel Argall, "an ingenious, active, and forward young gentleman," to find a shorter passage to the Chesapeake by sailing directly from the Canaries "in a straight western course," avoiding Spanish possessions and keeping clear of "the roade of Pyrates."[5]

The task of drafting a new charter was given to Sir Edwin Sandys. The son of a prominent Elizabethan cleric who had become archbishop of York, he had been born into the highest rank of society and enjoyed a privileged upbringing. In contrast to his father, a staunch Calvinist and vigorous persecutor of dissent, the young Sandys took a pragmatic view of religion; he wrote a wide-ranging appraisal of different religions in Europe titled "A Relation of the State of Religion," a work that assessed not only the possibility of unifying various rival branches of Protestantism but also the Christian religion itself. Well-educated and traveled, he aligned himself with King James VI of Scotland a year before the king ascended the English throne (to become James I of England) and was "employed by his majesty in several affairs of great trust and importance."

From 1604, he fell out of the king's favor, however, after gaining prominence as a leading opponent of government policies in the House of Commons in defense of the rights and privileges of Parliament against royal encroachment. He was connected to leading London merchants, including his distant relative, Sir Thomas Smythe; and having served as a member of the Virginia Council in London since 1607, he was well informed about the colony. A man of exceptional intelligence, organizational ability, and political experience, Sandys was destined to play a leading though controversial role in the Company until its eventual demise.[6]

The charter proposed important changes to the way the Company and colony had been administered during the previous three years. A new corporation, "The Tresorer and Companie of Adventurers and Planters of the Citty of London for the Firste Collonie in Virginia," was created, made up of a treasurer (the principal officer) and a governing council that served as the permanent administrative body of the Company and was directly answerable to it by way of weekly and quarterly meetings. Although continuing to reflect the interest of the Crown, a new Virginia Council was created, made up of men drawn from adventurers nominated by the Company rather than by the king and his ministers (the royal council established in 1606 formally relinquished its powers). Granted authority to establish "all manner of laws, directions, instructions, forms and ceremonies of government and magistracy, fit and necessary, for and concerning the government of the said colony and plantation," the council's jurisdiction was limited only by the restriction that such ordinances were not contrary to the "laws, statutes, government and policy in England."[7]

All aspects of policy and administration of the colony were firmly located in the Company's hands in London, but to buttress the authority of the "principall officer" in Virginia, a new position was created. The "governour" was given extensive powers, including the right to enforce martial law if necessary, to ensure the "most dispatch and terror . . . fittest for this governement." He would be assisted in Virginia by an advisory council, but could not be overruled or ousted by them. To leave no doubt about their determination to overhaul the leadership of the colony and enforce strict discipline, the Company appointed Sir Thomas West, twelfth Baron De La Warr, a high-ranking nobleman and soldier, the colony's first lord governor and captain general. Sir Thomas would be supported by Gates as lieutenant governor.[8]

Significant proposals were made also to greatly expand the colony's territory. Henceforth, not only were the bounds north and south of the original settlement increased from fifty to two hundred miles, inland the colony was extended from "sea to sea, west and northwest," that is, from the Atlantic Ocean to the Pacific Ocean. The choice of two hundred miles north and south of Cape Comfort, at the mouth of the James River, was not arbitrary: It was based upon information from John Smith's explorations and claims to a greater Virginia that included Roanoke Island to the south and lands as far as the head of the Chesapeake Bay to the north, just as the extension of territories from "sea to sea" reflected the continuing hope of finding a river passage somewhere near the head of the Bay that would ultimately lead to the Pacific and beyond to the Far East. If the Company was critical of Captain Smith's vigorous style of leadership they clearly recognized the potential value of his recent discoveries and were determined to protect them from interlopers.[9]

At the same time Sandys was drafting the charter, Sir Thomas Smythe threw himself into raising the money to outfit a large-scale expedition and recruiting settlers. Organized as a joint-stock venture, individual subscribers, companies, and corporations who purchased shares would be the major source of capital for the Company and in return would share the land, minerals, and other profits according to the size of their investment seven years following the adoption of the new charter. "Bills of adventure" (shares) could be purchased for £12 10s. each, or an individual could volunteer to join the expedition for an equivalent according to his or her rank, skill, or particular responsibilities: a single share for the humblest, multiple shares for artisans, military officers, ministers, and the colony's leaders.

Efforts were made to sign up more skilled artisans from abroad: glassmakers from Italy, millwrights from Hamburg to establish sawmills, Polish workers to oversee the production of pitch, tar, potash, and soap ashes, and French vignerons and salt workers. A "broadside" (news sheet) that was published in February 1609 and distributed throughout London and neighboring counties encouraged "all workmen of whatever craft they may be, blacksmiths, carpenters, coopers, shipwrights, turners, and such as know how to plant vineyards, hunters, fishermen, and all who work in any kind of metal, men who make bricks, architects, bakers, weavers, shoemakers, sawyers and those who spin wool and all others, men as well as women who have any occupation, who wish to go out in this voyage for colonizing the country with people" to come to Sir Thomas Smythe's house, where they would be registered as "Adventurers" of the Company and allocated "houses to live in, vegetable-gardens and orchards, and also food and clothing" in the colony at the Company's expense, as well as shares in the division of land.

The following month, the Company sent a letter to Hugh Weld, the Lord Mayor of London; the city's aldermen (governing body of the city); and London companies (guilds) inviting them to invest in the Company and requesting that they make a voluntary contribution to "ease the city and suburbs of a swarme of unnecessary inmates, as a continual cause of dearth and famine, and the very originall cause of all the Plagues that happen in this Kingdome" by assisting the Company in removing vagrants to Virginia. Settlers, Smith and his advisors had determined, were to be drawn from all sections of English society: "noble persons, Counts, Barons, [and] Knights"; middle ranks of craftsmen, artisans, and working men and women in general; and the homeless poor plucked off the streets of London. By the time the charter received royal approval on May 23, fifty-five London companies and 619 individuals had invested in the Company, and hundreds of colonists had signed up for the voyage. A month later, another broadside was sent to cities and towns throughout "the Land" encouraging merchants and gentleman to join the venture "in all equall priviledges and profites."[10]

If the appeal to potential investors and colonists was broad-based, so was the vision of the colony's future. In an ambitious piece of propaganda titled *Nova Britannia,* also intended to attract investors and settlers, Robert Johnson, merchant and deputy treasurer of the Company, described the natural resources of Virginia. The air and climate, he exclaimed, were "most sweete and wholesome, much warmer then England, and very agreeable to our Natures," and the country itself "large and great" with excellent harbors of which the "world affords no better for Shippes of all burdens." Here was a pleasant land of "valleys and plaines streaming with sweete Springs," of hills and mountains containing "hidden treasure, never yet searched," of "strong and lustie" soils and many sorts of "mineralles," of an "infinite store" of fish, fowls, and game, all kinds of trees, as well as "fruits and rootes good for meate [nourishment]."

With such abundance, "what may we hope, when Arte and Nature shall joyne, and strive together, to give best content to man and beast," Johnson asked. The colony would supply the kingdom's timber, copper, iron, and, in time, there would be vines to produce wine as good as any "from the Canaries," silkworms and mulberry trees for silk manufacture, hemp and flax for cordage and linen, pitch, tar, turpentine, and soap ashes, all of which "may set many thousands [of settlers] a worke, in these such like services." Establishing industries in Virginia would enable England to become self-sufficient in raw materials and manufactured goods, encourage the growth of a powerful mercantile marine, and employ the poor and idle, who "swarme[d] in lewd and naughtie practices" across the land.[11]

## "Get Thee Out of Thy Countrey"

Much of the argument advanced by Johnson was conventional and echoed the writings of the two Richard Hakluyts and descriptions sent back from Jamestown. But in addition to familiar mercantile arguments, a new emphasis was placed by Johnson and the Company's leadership on advancing "the kingdome of God" by bringing the Protestant faith to the Indians. The brilliance of Sir Thomas Smythe and his associates in the spring of 1609 was to harness the idea of a Protestant crusade in Virginia to a sense of national honor and virtue, thereby associating the Company's venture with a religious undertaking of incalculable significance for their own generation and generations to come. In the writings of propagandists and clerics, Virginia was a place where the forces of Satan and Jesus Christ would contest the hearts and souls of millions who lived in blindness without the knowledge of "Scripture, or Christ, or Moses, or any God."[12]

Taking as his text Genesis 12, verses 1 to 3, the Reverend William Symonds expanded on the destiny of the English as soldiers of Christ: "For the Lord had said unto Abram, Get thee out of thy countrey, and from thy kindred, and from thy fathers house, unto the land that I will shew thee, and I will make thee a great nation." The "Lord that called Abraham into another Countrey," Symonds continued, "doeth also . . . call you [the English] to goe and carry the Gospell to a nation that never heard of Christ." This was the great work that had fallen to the English as the chosen people of God.[13]

George Benson, Fellow of Queen's College, Oxford, saw the settlement in Virginia as clear evidence of the fulfillment of biblical prophecy whereby the true faith would be spread to the far corners of the world. Just as England "was one of the first parts of the Christendom that received the Gospel, so now, it is the first part that ever planted and watered the Gospel in so great, fair fruitful a Country." By following God's injunction and overthrowing Satan's throne in America, the preacher William Crashaw gave assurance to his listeners: "[W]e shall honour our God, our religion, our Nation, and leave that honour on our names, which shall make them flourish till the worlds end." What "comfort to those subjects who shall be a means of furthering of so happy a work," the Reverend Richard Crakanthorpe exclaimed, "not only to see a New Britain in another world, but to have also those as yet heathen barbarians and brutish people, together with our English, to learn the speech and language of Canaan."

Redeeming the Indians fully justified English settlement and colonists' actions. As Robert Johnson argued: Our intrusion into their possession [land] shall tend to their great good . . . yet not to supplant and root them out, but to bring them from their base condition to farre better: First, in regard of God the creator, and of Jesus Christ their Redeemer, if they will believe in him. And secondly, in respect of earthly blessings, whereof they have now no comfortable use." Should the Indians resist, then the colonists could lawfully make war on them providing the ultimate objective was to reclaim them from their barbarous and sinful ways. Conversion must follow conquest, or, as Robert Gray put it in a memorable turn of phrase: "Those people are vanquished, to their unspeakable profite and gaine."[14]

The outpouring of sermons from the pulpit and press during 1609 offered a providential history of the English people that connected the nation's emergence as a Protestant bulwark against Catholic Spain to events unfolding in Virginia. How else could the marvelous salvation of the English people themselves be explained other than by the direct intervention of God? Had not the English been saved from a return to popish superstition and idolatry by the early death of the Catholic Mary Tudor and succession of the young Queen Elizabeth? Had not God intervened in the nation's gravest crisis when Philip of Spain had dispatched a vast host in 1588 to invade England and occupy the land? And had not in recent times the godly King James, England's "Constantine, the pacifier of the World and planter of the Gospell in places most remote," been miraculously saved by the last-minute detection of a foul Catholic plot to blow up the Houses of Parliament while he was sitting in session? Who could seriously doubt, as the cleric John Aylmer had boldly asserted half a century before, that "God is English," or that the English occupied a special place in the affections of the Lord?

Converting the Indians would ultimately lead to the flowering of the English church and nation in North America and the establishment of a Protestant empire in the New World that would counterbalance Catholic Spain's. William Symonds confidently predicted that, "keeping the feare of God, the Planters in shorte time, by the blessing of God, may grow into a Nation formidable to all the enemies of Christ, and be the praise of all that part of the world." He did not doubt that God would provide for them and "shew [them] to possesse in peace and plenty, a Land more like the Garden of Eden: which the Lord planted, than any part else of all the earth." It was a story brimming with biblical precedents. The colonists' leaders were compared to Abraham, Moses, and David: warriors, heroes, and holy men of the Old Testament who, befriended by God, had led their peoples to the chosen land. They had not shirked their duty, but through unquestioning faith had overcome great adversity in fulfilling their commission from the Lord to their everlasting glory. Such was the promise held out to those who heeded God's call in their own days and ventured their purses or persons to settle Virginia, the new Canaan.[15]

## The Lost Colony

As preparations for the expedition to Jamestown went ahead through the spring and early summer of 1609, Don Pedro de Zúñiga became increasingly alarmed. Lord De La Warr was about to leave with six or seven hundred men, "a great part of them 'principals' [gentry], and some women," he reported to Philip III, to be followed soon after by Sir Thomas Gates with another four or five hundred men and one hundred women. The Spanish ambassador remained convinced that the colony was to serve primarily as a base for "piratical excursions" on a scale that would effectively cut off the flow of silver from the Indies and ruin trade; but he also worried about the growing involvement of James I who, he claimed, openly took "a hand in this business." The publication of a book (Robert Johnson's *Nova Britannia*), "for the exaltation of their religion and its extension throughout the world," Zúñiga wrote, encouraged all "to support [the colony]."

The ambassador described how "the King of that region [Wahunsonacock]" had been deceived by the English, and expressed his concern that once the settlers had fortified themselves they would destroy the Powhatans "so as to take possession of everything." Six weeks later, Zúñiga was even more worried. "For all the information I have sent Your Majesty about the determination of these [people] to go to Virginia," he wrote, "it seems I always fall short, for the preparations they are making here are the most urgent they know how to make, for they have seen to it that the ministers, in their sermons, stress the importance of filling the world with their religion, and of everyone exerting themselves to give what they have to so great an undertaking."

Large sums of money were being raised, and skilled artisans recruited to build ships and new settlements in the colony. Lord Ellesmere, the Lord Chancellor, told an informant of the Spaniard's that at first the Company had chosen to send the colonists "little by little." "[B]ut now," he continued, "we see that what we should do is establish ourselves [on a large scale] all at once, because when they open their eyes in Spain they will not be able to do anything about it, and although they learn about it they are so poor these days they cannot be strong enough to stand in the way of our project." The story may have been apocryphal, but it fully justified Zúñiga's stern advice to the king, namely, that he should "quickly command the extirpation of these insolents" before it was too late.[16]

In fact, secret plans for the colony drawn up by Sir Thomas Smythe and his advisors were far more ambitious than either Zúñiga or Philip III could have imagined. The Company issued Gates with confidential instructions shortly before the expedition was about to leave London in May, itemizing "foure principall waies of enricheing the colonies and providinge return of commodity.

> The first is the discovery either of the southe seas or royall mines . . . the second is trade whereby you recover all the commodities of those countreys that ly far of[f] and yet are accessable by water; the third is tribute . . . [and] the fourth is labour of your owne men in makinge wines, pitche, tarre, sope ashes, steele, iron, pipestaves, in sowing of hempe and flaxe, in gatheringe silke of the grasse, and providinge the [silk]worme and in fishinge for pearle, codd, sturgion, and such like.

Jamestown was to be reduced to a small garrison because the place was "unwholesome" and vulnerable to enemy shipping. The governor was advised to select a site for the colony's new chief seat away from major rivers, accessible only by small boats or from overland; for example, above the falls of the James River "whither no enemy with ease [could] approache nor with ordnance [cannon] at all but by land."

But the Company had another proposal for the site of a new capital, one that conjured up a radically different vision of the colony to that projected by John Smith's voyages of discovery around the Chesapeake Bay the year before. "Foure dayes journey from your forte southewards," Gates was informed, "is a towne called Ohonahorn seated where the River of Choanocki devideth itself into three braunches and falleth into the Sea of Rawnocke." Farther inland, at "Oconahoen" (Ocanahowan), was "a brave and fruiteful" country, well watered and "every way unaccessable by a straunger enemy." Nearby were the rich copper mines of "Ritanoc," and at "Peccarecamicke" lived four "of the Englishe" left by "Sir Walter Rawely, *which escaped from the slaughter of Powhaton of Roanocke, upon the first arrivall of our Colonie*" (my italics).[17]

Without doubt, the passage in Gates's instructions detailing lands to the south of Jamestown was derived in part from John Smith's sketch map and description of 1608. "Peccarecamicke" is clearly the "Pakerakanick" of Smith's map and "Oconahoen" had been mentioned by Smith in conversations with Opechancanough and Wahunsonacock. But the instructions also included new information. Smith makes no reference to "Manqueocke" and "Caththega" en route to "Ohonahorn." From some source or sources the Company had discovered further information about lands to the south as well as intelligence relating to the lost colonists' slaughter.

Thomas Hariot, one of the few Englishmen alive who had explored the North Carolina region, was one source. In the winter of 1608–1609, Sir Thomas Smythe had involved him in discussions about the future of the colony, and it might have been Hariot who provided details of the area from Roanoke Island to the southern bank of the James River. He had been told many times by Indians that southwest of the "old fort in Virginia" there were great deposits of "red metal"; more recently, Indians encountered by Jamestown settlers had informed them of a "rich mine of copper or gold" at a "towne called

Ritanoe, neere certaine mountains lying West of Roanoac." Hariot and another of Sir Thomas's advisors, Richard Hakluyt the younger, probably provided the impetus for a new vision of Virginia that linked North Carolina ("ould Virginia") to the James River valley.[18]

But who informed the London Company about the killing of the lost colonists? The most likely candidate is a shadowy Indian called Machumps, who may have learned of the slaughter from his sister, Winganuske, one of Wahunsonacock's favorite wives, or from other relatives close to the great chief. Machumps had been sent to England by Wahunsonacock late in 1608 with Newport to see the country, and remained there (probably in London) until returning with the Gates fleet the following summer. Little is known about what he did while in the capital, how he met William Strachey, or why the Indian told him about the killing. When Machumps arrived in London in January 1609, Strachey had probably already decided to join Gates's expedition. He had no better prospects at home, and as a man of literary pretensions he might have decided to write a description of Virginia. Hearing of the arrival of Machumps, he may have wondered whether the Indian could provide him with the information about the Powhatans and the country that he would include in the first part of his book. What he learnt from the Indian was a great deal more than he had bargained for.[19]

Strachey quickly passed on the information to the Company who, in turn, relayed it in the form of a report (now lost) to the king. The "men women, and Children of the first plantation at Roanoak," Strachey wrote, "(who 20. and od yeeres had peacably lyved and intermixed with those Savadges, and were out of his Territory)," were "by practize and Commaundement of Powhatan" (Wahunsonacock) "miserably slaughtered without any offence given him." Machumps also provided a description of the "high-land," the piedmont of North Carolina: "At *Peccarecanick*, and *Ochanahoen*, . . . the People have howses built with stone walls, and one story above another, so taught them by those English who escaped the slaughter at *Roanoak*." In this same region, at "Ritanoe, the Weroance *Eyanoco* preserved 7. of the English alive, fower men, twoo Boyes, and one young Maid, (who escaped and fled up the River of *Chaonoke*) to beat his Copper, of which he hath certayn Mynes."[20]

What had happened to the lost colonists and why was the new information so important to the Virginia Company? The conventional explanation is that after John White left them in August 1587, the colonists split into two groups. A small group of women, children, and those unable to travel were transported to Croatoan, where they would be safe with the friendly Indian Manteo's people, and the main body moved northwards to the territory of the Chesapeakes, near the entrance to the Chesapeake Bay, where they settled down with the Indians. Soon after the arrival of the English at Jamestown, Wahunsonacock sent his men to destroy the Chesapeakes and the colonists still living with them. The chief was acting on the advice of his priests, who had warned him "that from the *Chesapeack* Bay a Nation should [would] arise, which should dissolve and give end to his Empier." Not one to take any chances, the great chief ordered the killing of "all such who might lye under any doubtfull construccion of the said prophesie." In one swift and decisive action, Wahunsonacock ended the first English colony in America as the second began.[21]

An alternative explanation, however, makes better sense of what little certain evidence exists. The main group of colonists, consisting of about ninety to a hundred men, women, and children, moved westward into the Carolina interior, *not* northwards to the territory of the Chesapeakes. Setting out in a pinnace left behind by White, they followed Albemarle Sound—the route taken by Ralph Lane two years earlier—to the Chowan River where they planned to winter with the friendly Chowanocs.[22] Moving "50. miles further up into the maine" to the fertile lands along the Chowan would put them out of immediate danger of attack by the Secotans, Weapemeocs, and other hostile peoples near Roanoke Island. The colonists remained there for the next few years awaiting White's return, either living with the Chowanocs or in a small settlement nearby; but, as time passed and it became less and less likely that White's or any other ships were coming back, they gradually realized that they would never again see England or their countrymen and so settled down and intermarried with neighboring friendly Indians. Here, in villages along the Chowan and Roanoke Rivers nearly two decades later, the lost colonists, their children, and Indian allies were tracked down and slaughtered by Wahunsonacock's warriors.[23]

But why did the Powhatans attack them? What possible threat did the colonists pose after settling with the Chowanocs in "South Virginia"? Wahunsonacock may have believed that survivors would serve as go-betweens in forging alliances between the new English arrivals and the Indian peoples that they (the lost colonists) lived with and so could pose a threat to the chief's influence in the region. There was also the possibility that peoples to the south and west of Wahunsonacock's territories would ally themselves with the English newcomers. Strachey noted that the Powhatan chief had taken great care "to keepe us by all meanes from the acquaintaunce of those nations that bordure and Confront him, for besydes his knowledge how easely and willingly his enemyes wilbe drawne upon him by the least Countenance and encouragement from us, he doth by keeping us from trading with them monopolize all the Copper brought into *Virginia* by the English."[24]

Because Wahunsonacock's authority over the majority of the thirty or so peoples that made up his chiefdom was based primarily on military threats and his control of "prestige goods" such as copper and highly prized European commodities, he could not allow the English to establish themselves in (or adjacent to) his dominions where they might act as protector and benefactor of his as well as neighboring peoples. In this line of reasoning, he was remarkably shrewd, for the English did try to forge alliances with peoples of the Powhatan chiefdom and those beyond. As the instructions to Gates bear out, Sir Thomas Smythe and the Company were planning to create an English Virginia that embraced peoples to the south of the Powhatan's core territories, an area where English survivors from Roanoke Island might still be found. Despite the Powhatans' efforts, however, a few of the colonists either escaped or were beyond the warriors' reach. Four remained at Pakerakanick, where they lived under the rule of a weroance named "Gepanocon, enemy to Powhatan," and seven more lived at Ritanoe protected by the Mangoag chief, "Eyanoco."[25]

Wahunsonacock's killing of the lost colonists and their offspring was not merely a fiction dreamt up by the English to justify making war on the Powhatans—they hardly needed justifications beyond those already rehearsed at length in their propaganda, and news of the chief's action did not automatically lead to hostilities—but it did force Sir Thomas Smythe and his advisors to rethink the colony's future relations with the Indians. According to Strachey, although horrified by news of the slaughter, King James, because he was a "most just and most mercifull Prynce," had "given order that Powhatan [Wahunsonacock] himself with his Weroances, and all his people . . . be spared, and revenge only taken upon his *Quiyoughquisocks* [priests], by whose advise and perswasions was exercised that bloudy Cruelty." True to the words of sermons that rang out from countless English pulpits during the spring and summer 1609, the Powhatans could yet be saved if removed from the baleful influence of their priests, "being the ministers of Sathan."[26]

Wahunsonacock was to be spared but not trusted: "[I]t is clere even to reason beside our experience that he love[s] not our neighbourhood," the Company believed. Gates, therefore, was to take the chief prisoner or force him to be a "tributary" (subordinate). Lesser chiefs would be required to acknowledge no other lord but James I: "[A]nd so we shall free them all from the tirrany of Powhatan." Each weroance, "lord of a province," would provide corn at every harvest, baskets of dye, skins, and laborers "to worke weekley" for the English, according "to his proporcion in greatnes of territory and men." This tribute would be much less onerous than under Wahunsonacock, and in return the Indians would be protected from their enemies and enjoy many "commodities and blessings" from the English, "of which they [were] yet insensible." Priests would be imprisoned or executed. To better effect conversion of the Indians, the Company recommended the colony take into custody those "which [were] younge and to succeede in the[ir] governmente" to be educated in the colonists' "manners and religion." In this way, it was anticipated that the "people will easily obey . . . and become in time civill and Christian."

The Company's Indian policy, premised on the treachery of Wahunsonacock and his priests, was at the heart of the colony's new beginning. Subject directly to James I, represented in Virginia by his appointed governor, lesser Powhatan weroances would henceforth be released from the "bloudy Cruelty" of Wahunsonacock and be freed also from the exorbitant payments in food, skins, and other goods they were forced to give him in tribute. The English saw themselves as the liberators of Indian peoples who had been conquered by the Powhatan chief, and they were confident that oppressed peoples would willingly submit to English rule because they would be treated much better by the English than by the Powhatans, enjoying "freely the fruictes of their owne Territoryes" and partaking in "a peaceable and franck trade with the English." Indians would become "Citizens with the English," protected from their enemies and allowed to live in freedom and safety.

In return, the Indians would pay the English a tribute "to be agreed upon" that would assure the Company's garrisons were adequately provisioned. The people "who are now for the most parte of the yeare idle," wrote Strachey, "and doe little ells then sharpen their arrowes against the English, shall fynd by the geathering . . . of Tribute somwhat els to entertaine themselves withall." The Company would profit from Indian tribute and the Indians would become better off from working the land and from participating in English trade. Replacing Wahunsonacock with English overlords would unlock the natural bounty of Virginia, break the dominance of the Powhatans, turn Indian warriors into farmers, and bring about the conversion of native peoples to Christianity. Peace would bring prosperity to English and Indians alike.

Until such time as Wahunsonacock and his priests could be removed, the English were advised by the Company to proceed cautiously. Alliances were to be made only with peoples outside the region that were hostile to the Powhatans, such as the Monacans and Massawomecks. Establishing a settlement at "Oconahoen" (Ocanahowan), several days journey to the south of Jamestown, would situate the English among peoples unfriendly towards Wahunsonacock and open up a new front against the Powhatans, just as locating a garrison above the falls of the James River would strengthen relations with the Monacans and Mannahoacs and allow easy access into the interior where gold mines might be found. Mindful of John Smith's lengthy criticisms of the colony's mismanagement, the Company instructed Gates to ensure that trade with the Indians was conducted only by those specifically authorized. Bartering English weapons "or of anything iron" that could be turned against the English was strictly prohibited; even the practice of metalworking or carpentry in the presence of Indians was forbidden in case they learned how to make weapons themselves.[27]

Thus Company plans for Virginia, as relayed to Gates, rested on two basic assumptions: First, once Wahunsonacock and his priests were dealt with, the people would embrace English rule and would willingly render tribute to the English; and second, if some of the lost colonists who had survived the Powhatans' slaughter in the piedmont to the west of Roanoke Island could be found, they might provide invaluable information about the interior. Having lived in the country for twenty years, Roanoke colonists must have established extensive contacts with local peoples who had sheltered and traded with them. Company officials were understandably eager therefore to make contact not only with English survivors but also with the Indian communities in which they had lived for so long.

In the "warme Vallyes" near "*Peccarecanick*" it might be possible to grow sugar canes, oranges, lemons, and "all sortes of Southren fruites" as cultivated in Mediterranean latitudes, William Strachey believed. Friendly peoples of "South Virginia" might know of mines in the mountains and even have heard of a river passage to the great sea in the west. Because of their intimate knowledge of the region, the Indians might be able to "open the womb and bowels of this country" to the inestimable benefit of the Company, its financial backers, and the nation. The new colony was to be located deeper in the interior near the falls of the James River and on the rapids of the Roanoke River where colonists would be safe from attack by the Spanish, live close to Indian peoples hostile to the Powhatans, and be well placed for further expeditions inland, where perhaps great wealth yet remained to be discovered.[28]

---

WE CAN ONLY SPECULATE about what John Smith would have thought of Sir Thomas's plans if he had been privy to the Company's discussions in the spring of 1609. He might have found much to agree with, particularly in regard to organizing the settlers into work gangs to produce the kinds of commodities—wine, pitch, tar, soap ashes, iron, hemp, and flax—that he believed would ultimately provide a sound return to investors, and in enforcing discipline among the men to keep them busy. He would have certainly agreed with the necessity to prevent unregulated trade with the Indians that had debased the value of English goods and seriously compromised his own efforts to acquire food from neighboring peoples for the starving garrison, and he might possibly have concurred with the idea of Indians supplying the English with goods as a form of tribute.

But from his own experience of dealing with the Powhatans, he would have known that proposals to capture Wahunsonacock and his priests were completely unrealistic and that the very attempt could only lead to war. As he struggled to hold the colony together in the face of mounting Powhatan hostility he probably already knew that war was inevitable, but his reasons for confronting the Indians had little or nothing to do with weaning them away from their chief and religious leaders. Smith would have found the soaring Old Testament rhetoric of Anglican ministers incomprehensible in relation to the Virginia and Indians he knew. The Powhatans would have to be confronted because they threatened English possession of the land and therefore the production of useful commodities.

Likewise, the Company's decision to remove the capital from Jamestown to a new site upriver beyond the falls or inland at "Ocanahowan" in the North Carolina piedmont would have been equally incomprehensible to Smith. It had taken the settlers nearly two years to establish themselves at Jamestown, and only now were they beginning to produce modest quantities of goods for export. Abandoning the fort would necessitate a further period of building at new sites during which little of value would be produced. Even when construction was completed, he might have asked, how would the colony's commodities be transported over the falls and from interior locations for shipment to England, and how would the Company's ships provision such remote outposts?

The Company was rightly concerned about Jamestown's vulnerability from Spanish attack, but removing settlements far inland might make trade so difficult as to be prohibitively expensive. By 1609, Smith was skeptical, too, of the likelihood of finding survivors from the lost colony. Michael Sicklemore had returned from the Chowanocs in January or February with "little hope and lesse certaintie of them [that] were left by Sir Walter Rawley," and Nathaniel Powell and Anas Todkill, sent by Smith to search in the lands of the Mangoags, learnt nothing of the lost colonists apart from "they were all dead."[29] Smith was a pragmatist. What was needed were not elaborate schemes to create another colony to the south or pious projects to convert the Indians to Christianity but rather sufficient men and resources to meet the military threat posed by the Powhatans. Once they had secured the settlement, they needed to build upon efforts to produce goods for export, already beginning to bear fruit at Jamestown.

In the early summer, however, Smith had more immediate concerns on his mind than wondering about the Company's future plans. Christopher Newport had not returned to Virginia in the spring with fresh supplies as he had expected, and the colony was again on the brink of collapse. Smith had managed to foil several plots to destroy the colony hatched by the four "irreclamable" Germans who had joined the Powhatans, but many of the settlers remained rebellious, waiting for an opportunity to strike against him or to join neighboring Indians in the hope of living "idly amongst the Salvages." Meanwhile, Wahunsonacock was biding his time and was content to watch and wait for the colony to disintegrate and for John Smith to be overthrown. The chief had been told by the Germans that Smith was out of favor with the English king, James I, because of his harsh treatment of the Powhatans and that he would be executed for his crimes when a new expedition arrived. For very different reasons, therefore, Smith and Wahunsonacock must have greeted news of the sighting of a ship in the James River in mid-July with keen anticipation.[30]

## Two Ships

The *Mary and John,* commanded by Samuel Argall, had been dispatched by the Company in early May to find a more direct route to Virginia than the "southern passage" and thereby substantially reduce the cost of future voyages to the colony. Argall was also to find out whether the waters off Virginia's coast were of value for fishing, and, on reaching Jamestown, was to give Captain Smith advance notice of the fleet on its way from England and the change of leadership that would occur as soon as the new deputy governor, Sir Thomas Gates, arrived. Following instructions, Argall left Portsmouth and set his course southwest until he reached 30 degrees north, then headed due west until he was within a few hundred miles of Bermuda before turning northwards to the Chesapeake Bay, where he made landfall on July 13 after a crossing of nine weeks.

What he found upon arriving at Jamestown confirmed the Company's fears. The colony, he reported, was in "great confusion," partly owing to discord among its leaders, "each striving to rule over the other," but principally because of the "idleness and bestial sloth of the common sort, who were active in nothing but adhering to factions and parts, even to their own ruin." Although they were starving, many of the men continued to refuse to sow their own crops and had been "dispersed in the Savages townes, living upon their almes for an ounce of Copper a day." Understandably, the famished colonists were overjoyed to find Argall's ship well provisioned with fish he had taken on the voyage, wine, and biscuit, which "though it was not sent us," John Smith confessed, "our necessities was such as inforced us to take it."

Delighted by Argall's arrival and news of Gates's fleet, Smith could have only been exasperated by the Virginia Company's criticism of his "heard [hard] dealing with the Salvages," especially now that it was be-coming increasingly evident that the Powhatans were determined "to starve them [the English] and drive them out," and must have bridled at complaints of his failure to freight ships returning to England with commodities.[31] But these were relatively minor irritants in comparison to the great fortune of Argall's arrival.

At the same time the *Mary and John* was making its way steadily across the Atlantic towards Virginia, another ship, *La Asunsión de Cristo,* commanded by Captain Francisco Fernández de Écija, slipped away from San Augustín at midday on June 11, bearing north. Écija, a man of great experience who had lived in Florida ever since the days of Pedro Menéndez de Avilés, commanded one of the two companies of soldiers stationed at the garrison.

Because Écija knew the Indians and the coastal waters of the region intimately, it was no surprise that when General Pedro de Ibarra, gov-ernor of Florida, was ordered by Philip III to send out a reconnaissance expedition to find Jamestown, he should turn to Écija. His ship was a small vessel similar to a brigantine (called a *zabra*) of a type frequently used to explore inshore waters and rivers. Besides the crew, on board were twenty-five officers and soldiers, a Guale Indian woman ("a na-tive of Santa Elena and interpreter for that country"), and two pieces of artillery. It was hardly a massive show of force; rather, the emphasis was on gathering information in preparation for the possibility of a larger expedition should the king decide to follow the advice of his ambassador in London, and his Council of State in Madrid, and con-front the English interlopers. The council had earlier expressed the opinion that the "matter of Virginia [was] not to be remedied by any negotiation, but by force, punishing those who [had] gone there," and recommended that an armada "be assembled, with all possible speed, to go hunt them and drive them out from wherever they may [be], punishing them exemplarily." Before taking action, however, Philip III demanded further details about the English colony, the settlers' inten-tions, and what they had accomplished.

Fortunately for the English, as it later transpired, Écija adopted a leisurely pace as he proceeded up the coast. Nearly three weeks passed before they reached the Rio Jordán (Santee River), three hundred miles from San Augustín and less than half way to their destination. The captain sent a small party ashore with an Indian interpreter, Alonso, a Christian convert they had picked up along the coast, and learned from local peoples that thirteen days prior a ship had anchored two leagues (seven to eight miles) to the south, which they understood "had been to the village or fort of the English." Possibly, this was Argall's ship, not coming from but going to Jamestown.

Écija learned also that four or five days journey away, the English had settled on an island in a river that ran to the sea and, apart from a narrow strip that connected the island to the mainland, they were surrounded by water. At this place, he was told, the English had built a fort made of wood and had made alliances with "neighboring caciques [chiefs]," who provided them with food in return for clothes and tools because the colonists "did not bother with sowing but with fortifying." Ships reportedly "came and went every day," and three months before seven had sailed from the settlement, six to the north and one south, the latter flying colors and beating a "war-drum." The information must have made Captain Écija uneasy. He may have been skeptical about the numbers of ships mentioned and the frequency of their comings and goings, but there could be no doubt that the English were busily establishing themselves in the region, confirming what had been told to him by Governor Ibarra. How many men and ships the settlement had, what type of fortifications, and whether alliances with the Indians had been struck, it was up to Écija to find out.[32]

Rounding Cape Fear and proceeding cautiously along the Outer Banks, they saw "great smoke-signals along the coast at two or three leagues from one another" made by the Indians, but could detect no signs of English activity and so continued northwards skirting the North Carolina shore. Finally, at five o'clock in the afternoon on July 14, they arrived off Cape Henry, where they spotted a ship "in the bay." Opting not to risk an engagement late in the day, they dropped anchored and posted a guard for the night.

At dawn, the lookout reported that the ship had not moved and appeared to be guarding the entrance to a large river. After waiting for a favorable wind, the Spanish hoisted sail and set a course directly towards the ship. As they approached, clouds of smoke rose up from both banks of the river, clearly intended as signals to alert the English and Indians alike to their presence. Any prospect of surprising the English was lost. At the same time, Écija became aware that the ship he faced was much larger than his own and he began to have second thoughts about an engagement. If his vessel was badly damaged in action, he might not be able to get back to Florida and therefore would be unable to report the valuable information he had learned from Indians en route to the "Bay of Jacán [Chesapeake Bay]."

After several hours' standoff, the English ship headed into the interior, showing the way up the river, where Écija surmised Jamestown was located. When the Spanish did not follow, the ship returned and began bearing down on them, her captain having realized that the new arrival was probably hostile. Consulting with his officers, Écija decided not to fight or attempt to slip past (for fear of becoming trapped), and ordered a hasty retreat on a southerly course with as much sail as possible. The English ship gave chase the rest of the day, but under cover of darkness the Spanish succeeded in getting away and headed back along the coast to San Augustín.[33]

The ship that had blocked Écija's way was Argall's, which had arrived the day before and was taking soundings at the entrance to the James River before going up to Jamestown. But what would have happened if Écija had arrived a week earlier? At the very least the Spanish would have seen for themselves the colony's disarray, which might have encouraged Écija to test the fort's defenses, either by land or with his two cannon from the river. Even a relatively small-scale Spanish attack might have resulted in mayhem. Mutinous Englishmen may have rebelled and joined forces with Écija, or the Germans might have brought Powhatan warriors into the fray on the side of the Spanish to overwhelm John Smith and those still loyal to him. With the English dispersed up and down the river, the fort might have been destroyed before the colonists could rally.

Curiously, however, Smith made no comment about the settlement's salvation in his writings. Only an oblique reference to the traitorous Germans who, he wrote, with "much devotion . . . expected the Spanyard, to whom they intended to have done good service," suggests that he was even aware of the danger.[34] Purely by chance, Argall had arrived in the Bay in the nick of time to prevent Écija from finding and destroying Jamestown. For their part, the Spanish came closer to eradicating the colony than they could have possibly imagined.

Unaware at how perilously near the colony had been to destruction, Smith and his men gathered at Jamestown on a hot summer's day to enjoy the luxury of a small measure of wine, beer, fish, and English biscuit brought by Argall. Given the circumstances of the previous six months, the president must have felt heartened by how things had turned out. Argall's arrival had cheered the men, they had survived the winter with few losses, and a great fleet was bringing hundreds of new settlers and fresh supplies to the colony. For once, prospects looked bright.

# 6

## WAR AND RETRIBUTION

*T*HE FLEET THAT LEFT Plymouth Sound in early June 1609 was one of the largest expeditions yet to sail to the North American mainland and represented a personal triumph for Sir Thomas Smythe who had organized the voyage in less than a hundred days. Leading in the van was the 250-ton *Sea Venture,* her admiral's (flagship) colors flying proudly in the evening breeze; then came the vice-admiral, *Diamond,* four smaller ships (the *Blessing, Unity, Lion,* and *Swallow*), a pinnace, *Virginia,* and the *Falcon* bringing up the rear.[1] They carried approximately five hundred settlers "of all sortes" and the hopes of the nation. The ships "beginne ther viage toward Virginia," Sir Stephen Powle, a senior court official, wrote in his diary, "god . . . guide them to his glory and our goode."[2]

On board the *Sea Venture* was Sir Thomas Gates, the colony's interim governor until Lord De La Warr arrived later in the year, Christopher Newport (the vice admiral), responsible for taking the fleet safely to Virginia, and Sir George Somers, appointed admiral of Virginia, effectively the second in command. A "Gentleman of approved assurednesse, and ready knowledge of Sea-faring actions,"

Somers (like Newport) had taken part in several privateering voyages to the West Indies and Azores in the 1590s and had led an attack on a Spanish fleet in Kinsale harbor during an abortive invasion attempt on Ireland. Well known for his vigorous anti-Spanish beliefs, he was an enthusiastic advocate of English colonization and a founding member of the Virginia Company who had been involved in initial discussions about the colony with Edward Maria Wingfield, Bartholomew Gosnold, and John Smith. Besides the expedition's leaders, on the *Sea Venture* also were William Strachey, the Reverend Richard Buck (Jamestown's minister), and several gentlemen, including John Rolfe, destined to play a leading role in the colony during the next decade.[3]

## The Tempest

Leaving the Devon coast behind them, Newport and Somers set their course southwards; but strong onshore winds forced the fleet to put in at Falmouth, Cornwall, where it remained for nearly a week, a delay that would prove costly. When they set out again, they sailed southwest to latitude 26 degrees before turning westwards to head for Virginia, a course that would keep them well to the north of the Spanish West Indies. The ships stayed together throughout June and much of July, "not a whole watch at any time loosing the sight of each other," the winds fair and friendly but the heat "fervent," which caused many to fall sick "of the Calenture" (a shipboard fever experienced in hot climates). Gabriel Archer on the *Blessing* witnessed thirty-two dead cast into the sea from two ships and was told the *Diamond* had the "plague in her."

Then on St. James' Day (July 24), little more than a week from Cape Henry by Newport's estimation, the clouds thickened in dark masses and winds whistled in the rigging. The fleet found itself engulfed by a huge storm that "swelling, and roaring as if it were by fits, some houres with more violence then others, at length did beate all light from heaven; which like an hell of darknesse turned blacke . . . , so much the more fuller of horror." For an entire day and night the tempest raged; but far from losing energy, Strachey wrote, fury was "added to fury" and an even more powerful storm followed the first, causing the sea to rise into the sky where it "gave battell unto Heaven." Water filled the air and was hurled against the ships in great gluts by howling winds that "(as having gotten their mouthes now free, and at liberty) spake more loud, and grew more tumultuous and malignant." Screaming winds, sheeting rain, and torrents of spume hammered crew and passengers alike, rendering them deaf to all but the thunderous cacophony of the elements. The terrified colonists clung to whatever they could find to secure themselves, but not a moment went by, Strachey recalled, when the sudden "splitting, or instant oversetting of the Shippe was not expected."[4]

Nor was the "Horacano" the worst of the perils that beset the *Sea Venture*. Shortly after the storm struck, in mountainous seas the ship's seams worked loose, causing her to leak so heavily that she quickly took five feet of water into her hold. News that the ship was sinking turned even the hardiest mariner's blood cold so that most of the company, including Strachey, gave themselves up for lost. Gates organized the men into three gangs and put them to work on pumps and buckets in regular shifts around the clock, and so they labored for their lives for three days and four nights without rest or sleep, stripped naked "as men in the Gallies, . . . destitute of outward comfort, and desperate of any deliverance," to keep each other from drowning.

During this "Egyptian night of three daies perpetuall horror," the sky remained as black as pitch so that neither the stars by night nor the sun by day could be seen. The ship was driven before the storm in whatever direction the winds took her, sometimes north, sometimes northeast, sometimes south. To keep her afloat, they threw overboard their cannon, luggage, and stores, but, despite their desperate efforts, the *Sea Venture* continued to take in water. When the hold had nine feet of water, the exhausted company began to make plans for the end, committing the ship to the sea and their "sinfull soules to God." But at that moment, with all hope gone, "when no man dreamed of such happinesse," the skies brightened a little and Sir George Somers, who had lashed himself to the deck to keep watch, with a shout of joy as loud as his weary body could muster, cried "Land."

There, through the rain, was a shoreline so close that they could see the trees along the beach bent over in gale force winds. Miraculously, the storm had driven them far off course to the Bermudas, a crescent-shaped archipelago of small uninhabited islands lying about six hundred miles off the coast of North America. With all her canvas spread, Somers ordered the *Sea Venture* directed towards the largest of the islands; but before reaching it, she struck first one reef, then another, and was violently thrust between two rocks. There she "stuck fast . . . lieing upright as if she had bin on the stocks." At about the same time, the wind dropped and gave way to a calm that allowed the crew and 150 passengers to get ashore safely in their boats with as much of the remaining provisions and equipment as they could manage.[5]

Feared by "all sea travellers alive, beyond any other place in the world," the Bermudas were known to mariners as "The Devils Ilands" and were said to be "terrible to all that ever touched on them." But such was God's beneficence, Strachey observed, that "even this hideous and hated place," became "both the place of our saftie, and meanes of our deliverance." The island, which they named St. George's, was covered with great stands of palmetto trees (the heart of which tasted like melon when roasted and cabbage when boiled) and luscious berries that looked like damsons. Wild hogs, introduced by Spanish mariners many years before, roamed in "sweet smelling" woods of cedars and palms. During the fall and winter, the skies filled with birds, some of which, such as the nocturnal cohow, having no fear of humans were taken by the hundred. Fish too numerous to name and sea turtles so large that they supplied more meat than three hogs and could easily feed half the company were found in abundance in coastal waters teeming with life. The island of their deliverance, it turned out, was no barren speck of rock in the midst of a vast and furious ocean, no enchanted isle of devils and evil spirits, but a "Country so abundantly fruitful of all fit necessaries" for life that the castaways soon realized what they had first thought was the most "forlorne place in the world" was "in truth the richest, heathfullest, and pleasing land . . . as ever man set foote upon."

The crew set to work salvaging as much of the ship's timbers, rigging, and iron as possible, leaving only her bare ribs. Meanwhile, Gates and Somers had divided the company into several groups, some to build "cabbins" from saplings and palmetto leaves on the large bay named for Gates where they had come ashore, others to catch fish and birds or search for fresh water. Around campfires that first evening, as they cooked their food and enjoyed fresh provisions and water, exhausted but grateful to be alive, they must have uttered many a prayer for their unexpected salvation. During the night, there was more good news when wild pigs, attracted by domestic swine rescued from the shipwreck, visited the camp.

During the next few weeks, hunting parties were dispatched regularly into the woods and soon a large stock of boars, sows, and pigs were penned for future consumption. With their immediate wants satisfied, the company's commanders turned to the problem of how to get off the island and continue on to Virginia. Fitting hatches from the *Sea Venture* to their longboat to create a small deck, and adding a mast and oars, the ship's carpenters fashioned a "Barke of Aviso" (messenger boat) to make the voyage to Jamestown and bring help. Eight men carrying instructions to return with the colony's pinnace as soon as possible set out at the beginning of September.[6]

Gates was eager to learn what was happening in Virginia and impatient to be off the island, but he faced growing opposition to his plans. At the same time the newly converted longboat departed, a conspiracy was discovered: Six "principals" were plotting against efforts to contact Jamestown. John Want, "an Essex man," described by Strachey as "both seditious, and a sectary in points of Religion," was the ringleader who, along with his fellow conspirators, had tried to persuade the carpenters and blacksmith to stop work on the longboat. The reasons emerged several months later during a second conspiracy. God had placed them on the island and provided them with all manner of sustenance, so why leave this earthly paradise when conditions in Virginia would surely be worse? The conspirators claimed that the governor's authority had ceased when their ship was wrecked and that they were now "freed from the government of any man." God's providence not only had saved their lives but had removed all requirements of service and obedience to their superiors. In effect, a state of nature had been created where all were equal and where it was "no breach of honesty and conscience, nor Religion" for each man to look after his own welfare and provide for himself. If they went to Virginia, on the other hand, they might be forced to stay "in that Countrie by the authority of the Commander thereof, and their whole life to serve the turnes of the Adventurers, with their travailes and labours."

This was the kind of leveling talk propagated by religious sects that ruling classes in England and throughout Europe dreaded. As Gates confronted the conspirators, he knew that not only his plans but also the very basis of his authority was being questioned, and, in the view of those contending against him, replaced by that of a higher power. John Want and the leader of the second conspiracy, Stephen Hopkins, were devout men, knowledgeable in the scriptures and, according to Strachey, able to "reason well therein." If the governor did not act decisively, he risked losing control of the company and possibly would never get off the island. Gates, however, was an experienced commander; there was no doubt in his mind that such challenges to his authority constituted mutiny and were, by express instruction in the terms of his commission, to be dealt with severely, by martial law if necessary. He banished the leaders of the first conspiracy to a nearby island and, in a court martial, condemned Hopkins to death, later pardoning him following the entreaties of many of the "better sort" on his behalf for mercy.

Strachey characterized the deputy governor as having saved the colonists from their own self-destruction by his resolute action, but, despite Strachey's gloss, it is clear that serious divisions had arisen.

When there was no sign of rescue by November, Gates instructed his carpenters to take timber from the woods and tackle from the wreck and build a pinnace from scratch. By the end of the month, Somers, who had been fishing and drawing a map of the islands while coasting the shoreline in a small flat-bottomed boat, concluded that the boat they had sent out must have been lost, and ordered a couple of carpenters with twenty men to construct a second "little Barke" on a bay some way from the main encampment.

As the months passed by and work on the two vessels continued slowly, relations between the two commanders soured. A later report commented "that the sea and land-commandours [Somers and Gates], being alienated one from another (a qualetye over common to the English)" there was "produced, not only a separation of the company (even in this extremitie, even in this straight place), but an affection of disgraceinge one another, and crossinge their designes." Possibly the two men had never been able to get along, or perhaps the strain of shipwreck and being stranded on the island had tainted their opinion of one another. Whatever the cause, within four months of being cast up on the Bermudas, the company had split into opposing camps and their commanders were at loggerheads. Even on an island paradise the English could not escape the bitterness of factionalism.

The folly of permitting Somers and Newport to sail with him in the *Sea Venture* must have weighed heavily on Gates in the months after the shipwreck. Concerned about "the younger and ambitious spirits" among the fleet, who by now would have arrived at Jamestown, he had sent orders with the longboat dispatched in September naming Peter Wynne lieutenant governor (unaware that Wynne had died several months earlier), charging him to govern the colony according to the tenor of Gates's instructions from London and with the assistance of six gentlemen councilors "of qualitie and knowledge of vertue." Wynne was to resist any attempts to make changes to the form of government, an oblique reference either to certain leaders (such as Gabriel Archer and John Ratcliffe) who had scores to settle with John Smith, or to Smith himself who, in the absence of Gates and Somers, might assume rule of the colony alone. Gates had no way of knowing how many of the fleet had survived the passage, whether any members of the new council appointed to assist him (which included Ratcliffe and Martin) yet lived, and what conditions were like at the fort. Had he known, he would not have been reassured.[7]

## The Fall of John Smith

Instead of a great fleet, pennants flying, making its way proudly up the James River to reestablish the colony, four bedraggled ships, the *Unity, Lion, Blessing,* and *Falcon,* reached Jamestown on August 11, joined a week later by the *Diamond* and the *Swallow.* William Box, "an honest Gentleman," described the dismal scene: "Some [had] lost their Masts, some their Sayles blowne from their Yards; the Seas so over-raking our Ships, much of our provision was spoyled, the Fleet separated, and our men sicke, and many dyed, and in this miserable estate [they] arrived in Virginia."

Relief at having made landfall was tempered by the continuing non-appearance of the *Sea Venture* and the continuous bickering between the newly arrived leaders and John Smith. The president claimed that his enemies had poisoned the minds of passengers and crew against him on the voyage and sought to overthrow him, and would have done if "those lewd Captains" and "unruly Gallants" had been able to agree among themselves. But they were hopelessly divided, putting forward first one then another to replace Smith and reaching no agreement about how they would govern: "[T]o day the old Commission [charter] must rule, to morrow the new, the next day neither, in fine they would rule all, or ruine all," Richard Potts, clerk of the colony's council, remarked.

The endless rows and arguments so exhausted the patience of Smith and his supporters that they would have been better off, Potts concluded wearily, if the fleet had never arrived and "we for ever abandoned . . . for on earth for the number was never more confusion, or misery, then their factions occasioned." On their side, Gabriel Archer and other gentry leaders maintained they had not plotted to turn Smith out of the presidency but had merely nominated Francis West, Lord De La Warr's younger brother, to govern them when Smith's term was over. This was no mutiny, Archer argued, for "the Kings Patent we ratified." Both Archer and George Percy alleged that Smith consorted with the mariners to gain their favor while failing to show "any due respect" to "many worthy Gentlemen." Smith, said

John Ratcliffe, desired to be "sole governer without assistants and would at first admit of no councell but himselfe."[8]

Having asserted his right to continue as president until his term expired in the next few weeks, Smith avoided further disputes by sending Francis West with 120 men to the falls and John Martin accompanied by George Percy downriver to Nansemond with 60 men. New arrivals (the third supply) had quadrupled the colony's population to more than four hundred. Quartered in open fields around the fort, they fell upon the small quantity of corn growing there "and in three days at the most wholly devoured it," convincing Smith of the imperative to disperse the men as soon as possible to avoid completely running out of supplies and to prevent sickness from spreading through the settlement. Moving nearly 200 men off the island reduced those remaining at Jamestown to about 250, a significant but manageable number, and created two new settlements under Martin and West.[9]

Martin set out in early September, sending most of the men overland with his lieutenant, Michael Sicklemore, and following on himself with George Percy and the rest of the expedition by boat. After a stormy and wet night, they rendezvoused on the west bank of the Nansemond River and sent messengers to bargain with the "kinge" of the Nansemonds (possibly Weyhohomo) for the purchase of a small island "opposite againste the mayne" where the Englishmen had chosen to establish themselves. The "great Weroance" had no intention of trading the island, however, which was a sacred place, and wanted nothing to do with the English. Learning from a couple of Indians that the two messengers had been "sacrifysed" (their "Braynes . . . cutt and skraped outt of their heades w[i]th mussell shelles"), Martin ordered the island to be taken by force. Percy reported: "[W]e Beate the Salvages outt of the Island," burned their houses, ransacked their temples, pillaged the corpses of their dead kings in their tombs, "And caryed away their pearles, Copper and braceletts, wherew[i]th they doe decore [adorn] their kings funeralles."

Meanwhile on the mainland nearby, Martin's soldiers captured one of the king's sons and another Indian. After being accidentally shot in the chest, the chief's son, in "his passyon and feare," managed to break

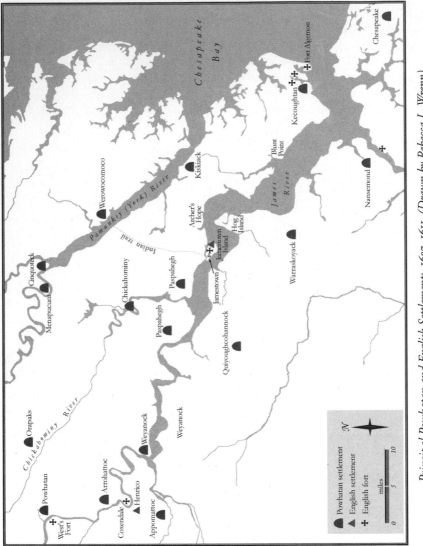

*Principal Powhatan and English Settlements, 1607–1611. (Drawn by Rebecca L. Wrenn)*

his bonds and escape (with "his wound bleedinge"). Having lost his most valuable hostage and fearing retaliation, Martin decided not to risk further attacks but to retreat to the island and abandon efforts to plunder the "greate store of maize" ripening in the Indians' fields. The expedition was transformed from a self-sustaining settlement that might have lived in peace with the Indians to a beleaguered garrison surrounded by hostile Nansemonds enraged by the violent seizure of their island and desecration of their kings' tombs.[10]

At the falls, Francis West's colony did not fare much better. Well supplied with six months of provisions, West began laying out his settlement and constructing a fort near the James River. It was situated much too close to the river according to Smith, who visited the site a week or so later and reckoned it liable to flood. He also ordered the men to move to the palisaded Indian village of Powhatan onto higher ground nearby, recently acquired from Parahunt, Wahunsonacock's son, in return for protection against the Monacans and some copper. In Smith's version of events, his orders to resituate the settlement to the village of Powhatan were met with outright hostility by West's men and he was obliged to withdraw from the fort to save his own skin. Supported by the ship's captains, whom he described as "faithfull friends," Smith returned soon after and made another effort to persuade the mutinous company to shift to the "Salvage fort," but the men refused.

If Smith could not persuade them, a war party of Powhatans had more success. Finding some of West's men foraging in the woods, they killed as many as they were able, then attacked the settlement and freed Indian prisoners held there before retiring with cloaks and swords belonging to the slain Englishmen. Consequently, when the president made his third visit to the settlement shortly after the assault, he found most of the men more than willing to move to the village of Powhatan, which Smith described as so well fortified as "to have defended them from all the Salvages in Virginia." All the while, for reasons that are unclear, West had gone to Jamestown and, on returning to the falls, was incensed to find that Smith had relocated the men in his absence. Another round of bitter arguments followed that resulted in West's men going back to their original settlement and a disgruntled Smith leaving them to their fate.[11]

Two other accounts provide a more sinister interpretation of Smith's actions, however. Henry Spelman, a youth of fourteen who accompanied Smith to the falls, alleged that the president "conspired with the Powhatan to kill Captain Weste; which plot took but small effect." George Percy claimed the Powhatans began attacking West's men not long after they began building their fort and, following a "greate devisyon" [quarrel] between Smith and West, the president "Animated the Salvages agenste Capte West and his company, Reporteing unto them thatt [the] men had noe more powder lefte them then wolde serve for one volley of shott."

Would Smith have betrayed his countrymen and conspired with the Powhatans to destroy West's settlement? Taking Spelman and Percy's allegations of the president's animosity to West and Martin more or less at face value, Smith knew full well that the establishment of English settlements at Nansemond and the village of Powhatan would trigger full-scale Indian resistance to the intrusion into their lands. Because neither the warlike Nansemonds nor Powhatans would suffer permanent garrisons in their territories, he sent out Martin and West knowing that both would be thoroughly discredited by defeat and the loss of their men.[12]

But another possibility fits more closely with Smith's method of dealing with troublesome political rivals. He had risen to prominence in the colony because of the key role he played in brokering relations between the English and Powhatans. He had been the vital go-between in negotiations with the Indians for much-needed provisions that had kept the colonists alive and saved the settlement from collapse on many occasions. With his enemies back in Jamestown in strength and lacking a restraining hand from Gates (who by September 1609 was presumed lost), Smith must have reasoned that his only chance of maintaining his position was once again to demonstrate that only he could rescue the colony from potential disaster.

From this perspective, he did not buy the village of Powhatan from Parahunt as he claimed in his writings—it is inconceivable that Wahunsonacock's son would have sold his father's birthplace to the English for a few pieces of copper and the promise of protection from the Monacans—but rather Smith offered to provide Parahunt with copper in return for allowing West's men to lodge in the village and share some of their food with the settlers. (He did much the same during the previous spring and early summer when he had distributed his men among neighboring Indians' villages as supplies at Jamestown ran low). Smith gambled that his negotiations with Parahunt would give a clear signal to West and his men that he still enjoyed influence with the Powhatans. No matter how much his rivals detested him, if Smith could make himself indispensable by ensuring good relations with the Indians (or at least averting hostilities), he might yet continue to play a leading role in the colony.

In the circumstances, the gamble was probably his only hope of maintaining his authority in the colony, but it failed for reasons largely beyond his control. He had already lost much of his credibility with the Powhatans at the beginning of the year when Wahunsonacock had grown tired of him and the Englishman had committed a cardinal blunder by humiliating Opechancanough in front of his warriors. But even if relations with the Powhatans had been better, it is unlikely that Smith could have maintained his position for long. Antagonisms among the English leaders ran too deep. Percy spoke for many when he described Smith as an "Ambityous[,] unworthy and vayneglorious fellowe" who sought "to take all Mens Authoreties from them" and who aimed at "A soveraigne Rule." Smith could not overcome the leaders' hatred of him, and ultimately it was they—Martin, Ratcliffe, Archer, and West—who brought about his downfall.

As Smith slept in his boat on the way back from the falls, a lighted match "accidentallie" fell into his lap and ignited his powder bag, which exploded and burnt "his flesh from his bodie and thighs, 9. or 10. inches square in a most pitifull manner." His clothes on fire and in excruciating pain, he leaped into the river and was more dead than alive by the time he was pulled out. The terrible injury was no accident but a deliberate attempt to kill him, this time by the English. When Smith was brought back to Jamestown, "neare bereft of his senses by reason of his torment," his enemies quickly closed in to finish him off. Martin, Ratcliffe, and Archer plotted to murder him "in his bed," but thinking better of it deposed him instead and placed him under guard on one of the ships returning to England.

To make certain that Smith was ruined in the eyes of Company officials (should he survive the voyage), the three leaders spent the next few weeks drawing up a comprehensive list of his abuses in office, including his determination to rule alone without the aid of a council, compelling the colonists to work against their wills by starving them, and plotting to "have made himselfe a [Indian] king, by marrying Pocahontas." John Ratcliffe wrote to the Earl of Salisbury that Smith "is sent home to answere some misdeamenors whereof I perswade me he can scarc[e]ly clear him selfe from great imputation of blame." Smith departed the colony in much the same condition as he had arrived two and a half years before—in disgrace and at loggerheads with the colony's leading gentry—but on this occasion there would be no comeback.[13]

THE FLEET CARRYING the ex-president and about two dozen other passengers arrived in the Thames at the end of November 1609. Smith had somehow survived the voyage, but it turned out to be a frustrating winter. Gradually recovering from his injury, he was doubtless relieved to learn the Company had no immediate intention of abandoning Virginia and may have been gratified also by the Company's decision not to follow up on charges made about his conduct. Yet, although he had avoided being called to account, he must have been bitterly disappointed by the Company's reluctance to employ him further. He may have been questioned about the state of the settlement when he left, but there is no evidence that the Virginia Company had any intention of stirring up more trouble in Jamestown by sending him back with Lord De La Warr. Ironically, if he had been concerned earlier about the possibility of being abandoned in Virginia, he now found himself abandoned in London, cut off from any realistic prospect of returning to the colony. Smith's Virginia adventure had come to an abrupt and inglorious end.

## "A worlde of miseries"

Not long after the wounded and dispirited Smith arrived back in London, the Spanish ambassador, Zúñiga, wrote with relish to Philip III about the disappearance of Gates and the *Sea Venture* and deteriorating conditions in the colony. The "captain's ship was lost, along with the most illustrious people and the instructions for governing that region," the ambassador reported. "They tell me that the sailors do not come very happy because [people] are suffering great hunger there," he continued, "and they bring nothing of consequence in the ships."

John Beaulieu, a court official, reported another tidbit of gossip about divisions that had broken out at Jamestown following the arrival of a new minister (the Reverend William Mease). Mease was "somewhat a puritane" who was so unpopular with most of the settlers that they refused to hear his sermons; but he was "supported & favored" by another faction. "This is an unluckie beginning," Beaulieu confided to his friend William Trumbull in Brussels, "I pray God the successe and the end may prove happier." A week later, he passed on more bad news. For "want of some man of authoritie [in the colony]" he wrote, "there fell such a dissension among that companie about the distributing of the Vittles [provisions] . . . as that nowe the report is that being fallen together by the eares, diverse [many] of them have been slayne." With thousands of pounds of investors' money lost, up to two hundred settlers missing (more than a third of the entire expedition), including the governor, and the colony in disarray, it is hard to see how the news that reached the Company in the fall could have been worse.[14]

Sir Thomas Smythe responded with his usual vigor. Following a series of meetings with Argall, officers of the three ships who had just arrived, and former settlers, Smythe set out to gather as much accurate information about what had happened as possible. By mid-December 1609, the Company drew up *A True and Sincere Declaration* that avowed their

determination to persist with their plans for the colony despite the grievous setback. It was a carefully reasoned and bold defense that combined
a restatement of the colony's purpose, religious arguments, comparisons
with Spanish colonizing efforts, a description of what had happened to
Gates's fleet, and an explanation of how the Company would ultimately
make Virginia profitable. As had been stated repeatedly in the propaganda blitz of the previous year, the "principal and main ends" of the
colony were to bring the Christian religion to the Indians, to take possession of a new land for the English, and to produce all kinds of
commodities that would be of value in England.

If these were the right and proper goals for the colony when Gates's
expedition set out, the Company asserted, why should they be abandoned now? The disaster of the hurricane could not have been
foreseen: "Who can avoid the hand of God, or dispute with Him?
Who knows whether He that disposed our hearts to so good begin-
nings be now pleased to try our constancy and perseverance, and to
discern between the ends of our desires whether piety or covetousness
carries us swifter?" The history of the Spanish conquest of the Indies
provided many examples of "fleets, battles, and armies lost . . . and yet
with how indefatigable industry and prosperous fate" they had overcome all obstacles and created populous and wealthy colonies. Why
should this "great action" of the English, therefore, be "shaken and dis-
solved by one storm?"

The Company was forthright in its assessment that the colony required the firm hand of a resolute governor; but once that had been
remedied by the early dispatch of Lord De La Warr, there was nothing to hinder the development of Virginia as the Company had
anticipated. All kinds of valuable commodities could be produced,
such as wines, pitch, timber, iron, steel, soap-ashes, dyes, and cordage. But more than this, the Company revealed in a brief but
sensational passage, they had recently learned that "some of our nation planted by Sir Walter Raleigh [are] yet alive within fifty mile of
our fort" (Jamestown), "as is testified by two of our colony sent out
to seek them, who, though denied by the savages speech with them,

found crosses and letters, the characters and assured testimonies of Christians, newly cut in the barks of trees."

The reference is mystifying. "Two of our colony" could only refer to Nathaniel Powell and Anas Todkill, who had been escorted by the Quiyoughcohannocks to Mangoag territory in the North Carolina interior, but John Smith reported they had learned nothing about the lost colonists save that they were dead. Had the Company picked up fresh intelligence or was it trying artfully to maintain interest in Virginia when fortunes were at low ebb? Although the information was quite specific, "crosses and letters . . . newly cut in the barks of trees," there was no follow-up by the Company and little apparent effort to make contact with survivors beyond the instructions issued to Gates eight months before. And, of course, the Company was aware of the role Wahunsonacock had played in ordering the slaughter of the lost colonists and their descendants about the time the English first arrived in the James River. Perhaps the survival of some of the lost colonists and their future benefit to the colony was viewed by the Company's sponsors in much the same light as the commodities they were confident the settlers would one day produce, potentially valuable assets that needed only investment and time to bring them to fruition.

Despite the Company's best efforts to reassure the public, however, news of the disaster that had befallen the *Sea Venture,* fueled by "ignorant rumor," spread like wildfire through the city, not only seriously compromising efforts to recruit settlers for the expedition Lord De La Warr planned for the spring but also leading investors to withdraw from the venture in droves. So serious was the hemorrhage of financial support that the Company's leaders were compelled to remind all those who had promised "to adventure and had not performed it" that their actions exposed "600 . . . of our brethren," Christians "of one faith and one baptism, to a miserable and inevitable death" in Virginia. Before the "tribunal of heaven," the Company warned, each man would be called to account for his actions and examined as to what he had done "for the advancement of that Gospel which ha[d] saved him, and for the relief of His maker's image [his fellow man], whom he was bound to save." Sir Thomas Smythe remained determined that Virginia would not become another lost colony.[15]

———

REPORTS ABOUT SHORTAGES of supplies and dissension in the colony that circulated in London were not exaggerated. The departure of the fleet carrying Smith for England in October had been a signal for a general uprising by the Powhatans, who, provoked by English aggression, "all revolted, and did murder and spoile all they could incounter." Virginia continued in the grip of a severe drought that had led to serious food shortages among the Powhatans as well as the English. Attempts by the colonists to pillage the Indians' meager supplies may have been the last straw.

"Feareinge to be surprysed by the Indyans" (but possibly fearing his own men more), John Martin abandoned his post at Nansemond and, leaving Michael Sicklemore in command of the starving and rebellious garrison, returned to Jamestown. Not long after, seventeen men mutinied and stole a boat, claiming they intended to make for Kecoughtan to trade with the Indians for provisions; but the rebels were "served accordinge to their dessertts," according to Percy, "for nott any of them weare heard of after." With supplies running out, Sicklemore and a dozen of his men tried to bargain with the Indians for food and were killed, "their mowthes stopped full of Breade, beinge donn as it seamethe in Contempte and skorne thatt others might expecte the Lyke when they shold come to seeke for breade and releife amongste them." The remainder of the garrison, about half the number that had set out a few weeks before, returned to Jamestown. They were soon joined by West's men, who had suffered heavy losses at the falls. This left only Fort Algernon, recently established at Point Comfort at the mouth of the James River to keep a lookout for ships entering the Chesapeake Bay, as the sole remaining settlement outside of Jamestown Island.[16]

By now, the new president, George Percy (elected president of the council in the absence of Gates), was seriously worried about rapidly diminishing food supplies. With approximately three hundred men and women crowded in the fort, even at the meager ration of half a can of meal a day, Percy calculated that they would be unable to eke out provisions for much longer than three months. They would be entirely out of food by February, in the middle of winter, with little hope of supplies from London. Following a discussion with the colony's leaders, Percy dispatched John Ratcliffe and about thirty men to Orapaks to trade for food with the Powhatans; and Francis West with thirty-six men was sent up the Bay to trade with the friendly Patawomecks.

Both expeditions were a disaster. Following an invitation by Wahunsonacock to send a ship that he would freight with corn, Ratcliffe and his men were lured into an ambush that left most of them dead. Ratcliffe was captured and suffered a horrendous end, his flesh scraped from his bones by Powhatan women and thrown into a fire in front of him. Meanwhile, along the south bank of the Potomac, West had managed to fill his pinnace with corn but had antagonized the Patawomecks by "harshe and Cruell dealinge," cutting off the heads and "other extremetyes" of two Indians. On returning to the James River and being informed by Captain James Davis at Fort Algernon of the "Greate wants" of the settlers at Jamestown, West's men mutinied and forced him to turn around and set a course directly for England. Strachey described West's deserters as traitors and "professed Pirats, with dreams of Mountains of Gold, and happie Robberies," who, at one stroke, had wrecked the hopes of the colonists. West's men had made enemies of the Patawomecks and taken away the colonists' best ship, the *Swallow*, "which should have beene a refuge in extremeities."[17]

Within a couple of months, attacks by the Nansemonds and Powhatans had resulted in the death or desertion of about 130 settlers, nearly a third of the colony. Moreover, the "Greate wants" of the colonists at Jamestown were known to the Indians, who sealed off the island, confined the English to the fort, killed settlers' livestock roaming in the woods nearby, and waited and watched while the settlers starved. The tactics of siege were wholly successful: The Indians avoided casualties from a frontal assault and provided a fitting revenge for English thefts of precious food supplies.

"Now all of us att James Towne," Percy wrote in November 1609, began "to feele that sharpe pricke of hunger w[hi]ch noe man [can] trewly descrybe butt he w[hi]ch hath tasted the bitternesse thereof." To satisfy their "Crewell hunger," some went into the woods in search of "Serpents and snakes, and to digge the earthe for wylde and unknowne Rootes," where they "weare Cutt off and slayne by the Salvages." In desperation, they devoured their horses as well as dogs, cats, rats, and mice, and when these ran out, even their boot leather. But worse was to come as weeks turned into months.

As famine became etched "gastely and pale in every face," Percy recalled, nothing "was spared to mainteyne Lyfe." Starving settlers dug up "dead corpses outt of graves" and ate them. Others "Licked upp the Bloode which ha[d] fallen from their weake fellowes." Some of the colonists, who died in their beds or were killed seeking relief beyond the palisade, were taken up and eaten by those who found their bodies. Neither were the dead the only victims of cannibalism. The famished looked hungrily on those alive who still had some meat on their bones. One of settlers, it was alleged, murdered his pregnant wife "as she slept on his bosom," then "Ripped the childe outt of her woambe and threw itt into the River and after chopped the Mother in pieces and salted her for his foode," for which "barbarous" and unnatural act the president had him tortured to extract his confession before he was executed.[18]

Percy's unwillingness or inability to organize expeditions against the Indians patrolling the island while Jamestown was reduced to a charnel house at first sight appears inexplicable. By the spring, at least 160 men, women, and children (nearly three-quarters of the total in the fort at the beginning of the siege) had perished through disease and starvation or had run away to the Indians.[19] Even when the "starving time" began in the late fall, settlers were suffering from malnutrition and sickness. The *Diamond* brought the plague with her from England, and pestilence spread rapidly through the settlement as sanitary conditions deteriorated. Many of the new arrivals were so weak after their first couple of months in the colony that they were unable to forage in the woods for food let alone take part in punitive expeditions against the Indians, who had shown themselves more than a match for the English at the falls and at Nansemond.

Not until the Indians lifted the siege in early May 1610 to attend to spring planting was Percy able to journey to Fort Algernon to find out how Captain Davis and his men were getting on, and then to his dismay he discovered the garrison so well stocked with fish and crabs (Davis and his men having concealed "their plenty" from the starving settlers at Jamestown so that they could gather enough supplies for a voyage to England) that they were able to fatten their hogs from the surplus. Percy was outraged. If only Davis had made his abundance known earlier, many lives would have been saved. Percy curtly informed Davis that he would transport half of Jamestown's survivors to Point Comfort on the next tide and when they had regained their health would return them and bring down the other half. If that did not prevent further deaths, he would move all the survivors to Fort Algernon, telling Davis that "Another towne or foarte might be erected and buylded butt mens lyves onse Loste co[u]lde never be recovered."

BEFORE PERCY was able to put his plan into action, however, there came news of the sighting of two unidentified ships that had just entered the Chesapeake Bay.[20] The two small vessels belonged to Gates and Somers and brought the shipwrecked settlers from Bermuda. Through the winter and spring, they had labored on constructing their two pinnaces, *Deliverance* and *Patience.* In early May, the boats were ready for the voyage to Virginia, by which time Gates must have been heartily relieved to be leaving the troubled islands. All through their sojourn, a constant refrain of sermons and daily prayers had expressed thankfulness for their salvation and the importance of unity among them; but, despite the homilies, further mutinies had revealed festering resentments. The governor had been compelled to execute Henry Paine, a gentleman, in March for fomenting rebellion; shortly after, he executed several men of Sir George Somers's company because he feared they might be implicated in the plot. Eventually, Gates and Somers managed to gather most of the settlers together and, following a ceremony at which they erected a cross with an inscription (in Latin and English) giving thanks to God for their deliverance from the "mightie storme," they launched their ships and left Bermuda behind them.[21]

As they approached the Virginia capes ten days later, Strachey was struck by the "marvelous sweet smell from the shoare (as from the Coast of Spaine . . . ) strong and pleasant," which, he wrote, "did not a little glad us." Dropping anchor at Fort Algernon, Gates and Somers were relieved to hear of the arrival of the fleet the previous summer, but were then told the "heavie news" of conditions at Jamestown, so awful as to make Gates wonder whether "God had onely preserved them, to communicate . . . an new extremitie."

Making their way upriver to the fort, Gates and Somers found the palisades had been torn down, the church ruined "and unfrequented," and empty houses "rent up and burnt" for firewood. Entering "the town," they saw what appeared "rather as the ruins of some ancient [for]tification than that any people living might . . . now inhabit it." Only sixty or so settlers remained alive and were described as "Lamentable to behowlde." Those able to raise themselves from their beds to meet Gates and his men "Looked Lyke Anotamies" [skeletons], Cryeinge owtt we are starved We are starved." Yet the deputy governor could do little to relieve them. He had brought only sufficient food from Bermuda to feed his own company during the sea voyage, never imagining the colony would be in such a dreadful state of dearth.

And so the death toll continued to rise. Driven out of his wits by despair, one Hugh Price, "In A furious distracted moode did come openly into the markett place Blaspheameinge exclameinge and cryeinge owtt that there was noe god," Percy remarked, "Alledgeinge that if there were A god he wolde nott suffer his creatures whom he had made and framed to indure those miseries." He, like others, met his end in the woods, slain by Indians who "killed as fast" outside the fort "as Famine and Pestilence did within."[22]

The colony had disintegrated, the vital markers of Englishness stripped away. Forsaken by their countrymen and, some thought, even by God, settlers had deserted the settlement and sought refuge with

the Powhatans or had succumbed to the very acts that Europeans stig-
matized as characteristics of "savage" Indians or the monstrous peoples
who lived on the margins of civilization. Extreme deprivation had
brought about a hideous inversion: The English, not the Indians, had
become savages. Far from providing the Indians with "what they most
need: Civilitie for their bodies" and "Christianitie for the soules," as
William Crashaw preached before Lord De La Warr and the Virginia
Council in February 1610, the colonists had forfeited their civility by
preying on one another like wild animals. No story, Strachey commented, "can remember unto us, more woes, anguishes, then these
people [the English], thus governed have both suffered and puld
[pulled down] upon their owne heads."

Appalled by the terrible suffering he witnessed, Gates realized that
he had no choice but to abandon the colony. His provisions were running out and there was no hope of getting food from the Powhatans,
nor was there any means of taking fish from the rivers in sufficient
quantities to keep them alive. Gates knew also, given the unrest he had
faced in Bermuda from men who had had no desire to leave the plenti-
ful islands, that it would be impossible to keep order among his own
company if famine should take hold.

To the great joy of the settlers, and following lengthy discussions
with leaders of the colony, he announced the decision to quit
Jamestown and make for Newfoundland, where they would ren-
dezvous with English ships plying the rich fishing banks and find
passage back to England. Preparations for the voyage were put into effect straight away. Arms, supplies, and goods that could be sold back
in England were loaded aboard the four pinnaces brought together for
the evacuation. The fort's cannon were buried in front of the main gate
that faced the river: a sure sign that in the deputy governor's mind
abandonment was only temporary, but a view not shared by the majority of colonists. Before leaving, he had to plead with his men not to
set the fort on fire: "[M]y Masters lett the towne Stande [for] we
knowe nott butt that as honneste men as our selves may come and in-
habitt here," a point he underlined by having his personal guard go on
board last to ensure that no one was tempted to throw a lighted match

into one of the buildings as they left. Then, discharging a volley of small shot by way of a "woeful farewell," the settlers set off at midday on June 7 and headed downriver for Point Comfort.[23]

## Conflict in Canaan

But "God . . . would not have it [the colony] so abandoned," John Smith wrote years later. The afternoon following their departure, moored off Mulberry Island waiting for the tide to turn, Gates's company spotted a longboat making toward them that proved to be an advance party of Lord De La Warr's expedition, which had recently entered the Bay with three ships and 150 colonists. The lord governor had originally intended to embark for Virginia late in 1609 or early in the new year, but raising the financial backing and recruiting settlers had been more difficult than expected in the wake of the disastrous loss of the *Sea Venture*. The Spanish ambassador, Zúñiga, in one of his last dispatches from London, reported to Philip III in early March 1610 that De La Warr was ready to sail with "a hundred old [veteran] soldiers, good people, and a few knights," to be followed a couple of months later by four more vessels "with a larger number on board."

De La Warr's three ships had left the Isle of Wight, off the south coast of England, on April 11 and made a quick crossing, arriving at Point Comfort in early June. There, "I met with much cold comfort," De La Warr reported of his arrival to Lord Salisbury, "as, if it had not been accompanied with the most happy news of Sir Thomas Gates his arrival, it had been sufficient to have broke my heart and to have made me altogether unable to have done my king or country any service." Gates was ordered to return to Jamestown forthwith and immediately headed back upriver to the utter dismay of his company, who dearly wished they had burnt the place down.

A couple of days later in the afternoon of Sunday, June 10, De La Warr arrived and was met at the fort's main gate with all the pomp and ceremony that Gates could muster from his disheartened men. The lord governor dropped to his knees in front of the assembled settlers and said "a long and silent Prayer to himselfe" before marching briskly past the guard of honor through the town to the "Chappell," where he heard a sermon delivered by the Reverend Richard Bucke. After the service, De La Warr ordered his commission to be read aloud and then, turning to the men, sternly reprimanded them for their "many vanities, and their Idlenesse," but he also sought to encourage them with the good news that he had brought enough food to last a year.[24]

Those who listened to his words must have been bewildered by the rapid change in their fortunes. It was a turnaround of heroic proportions. From being on the brink of collapse, the colony now had a full complement of leaders, some 375 settlers, and for the first time in more than a year, it was well provisioned. De La Warr acted quickly to establish order and discipline. His first priority was to select his council, naming Gates his lieutenant general (effectively deputy governor), Somers, Newport, Sir Ferdinando Wainman (who had accompanied him from England) the master of the ordnance, Strachey the colony's secretary and recorder, and Percy the captain of the fort.

That the colony was to be run along military lines was confirmed by the appointment of George Yeardley, Thomas Holcroft, Samuel Argall, and Thomas Lawson (besides Percy already mentioned) as captains of fifty-man militias, who were to exercise the "landmen" (settlers) "in martiall manner and warlike discipline." Landmen were to be divided into groups of "tennes, twenties, and so upwards," each commanded by "some man of Care and still [skill] in that worke to oversee them and to take dayly accounte of their labours." Gangs were to "mess" [eat] together when convenient and a bell would be rung at intervals throughout the day calling the settlers together for work, meals, and rest.[25]

Order was to be enforced by a strict code of laws that had been introduced a month earlier by Gates, derived from the detailed instructions delivered to him by the Virginia Council shortly before he left England. The "Lawes Divine, Morall and Martiall," as they were later known, set out unambiguously the duties and obligations of settlers (and mariners) as well as penalties for transgressions. Officers were required to ensure that all those under their command attended divine service twice daily, in the morning and evening, and to punish anyone who blasphemed "Gods holy name" or challenged the authority of a preacher or minister. There was to be one church, one God, and one law; no dissension would be tolerated.

Serious crimes such as murder, sodomy, the rape of a "maid or Indian," adultery, treasonous acts and speeches, theft from the common store or from individual settlers, trading with the Indians without permission, and embezzlement of Company goods were all punishable by death. Lesser offences such as slandering the Company or colony's leaders carried the penalty of whippings and galley service (by which was probably meant serving at the oars of longboats). For men from military backgrounds, such as Gates and De La Warr, who had experienced food shortages, desertion, insubordination, and mutiny among their troops in campaigns in Europe, the solution to Virginia's problems required above all a firm hand. Hence, the lord governor made it abundantly clear in his first message to the settlers that he would not hesitate "to draw the sword of Justice to cut off . . . delinquents" if necessary.[26]

Consulting with his council, De La Warr promptly took steps to secure further supplies, rebuild the fort, and fulfill the Company's demands to return saleable merchandize as soon as possible. Although he had plenty of supplies brought from England, the governor realized that to establish the colony on a permanent footing he had to make the settlement self-sufficient. Nothing could be expected from the Powhatans, who had withdrawn from trade or had little to offer, and the settlers' livestock had been either destroyed by the Indians or eaten by the starving English. Most perplexing, the sturgeon that usually began running up the James River in large numbers in April or May had failed to appear.

In these circumstances, the governor was left with little choice but to look elsewhere for supplies. Somers and Argall were dispatched to Bermuda to load the *Patience* and *Discovery* with six months of provisions and to bring back some live hogs to reestablish the colony's store; Robert Tindall (master of the *De La Warr* who had brought the governor to Virginia) was sent to fish at the at the entrance of the Chesapeake Bay between the capes; and at Jamestown some of the men trawled the river with nets, others experimented with planting English vegetables and kitchen herbs in and about the fort.[27]

Meanwhile, the mariners were put to work unloading the ships and "landmen" to cleaning up the town, it being "a very noisome and unwholesome place" in the wake of the siege. Palisades and bulwarks were repaired, and cannon were mounted on the gun platforms and positioned at the gates and in the central "market place" where the guardhouse, store, and "a pretty Chappell" were located. The church (or chapel) was sixty by twenty-four feet, its pulpit and pews made of cedar, the communion table of black walnut, and the font from a hollowed tree trunk "like a Canoa [canoe]." Large windows kept it light and airy and flowers garlanded the interior to ensure that it smelled "passing sweete." Everyday the church's bell rang out at ten and four o'clock to remind the settlers to stop whatever they were doing to say their prayers; and on Sundays and Thursdays, the company was called together for sermons by the colony's preachers.

Around the market place, running parallel to the curtain walls about three yards inside the palisade, houses or barracks-like structures formed rudimentary streets, described as of no "great uniformity" or "beauty." Many of the fort's forty to fifty dwellings would doubtless have seemed curious to the eyes of newcomers. They were framed like traditional "mud and stud" English houses and had wide "Country Chimnies." The walls and roofs were covered with fine woven mats and bark, the latter as good as the best tiles, according to Strachey, in keeping out the rain and "piercing Sunbeames of Summer." If settlers lacked the domestic comforts of home, nevertheless the happy combination of English and Indian building techniques kept their houses cool during the summer, a welcome change from the dwellings they had initially constructed with thatch roofs and mud walls that had been as hot as "Stoves" inside.[28]

---

ALTHOUGH DE LA WARR'S rule quickly gave Jamestown an overtly military character, war was not initially on the governor's mind. His instructions from the Company, like those issued to Gates, urged a conciliatory approach to the Powhatans and reiterated the importance of converting them to Christianity, "the most pious and noble end of this plantacion." De La Warr therefore first attempted negotiation. Messengers were sent to Wahunsonacock demanding that he order his warriors to stop attacking his men and stealing their weapons, but reassuring the chief that the governor did not suppose that "hee (being so great and wise a King)" was responsible for the "outrage," the crimes probably being committed by the Indians' "worst and unruly people."

Specifically, the lord governor requested that those warriors who had attacked and killed four of the settlers at the "Block-house" should be either punished or sent to the English, and that men and arms taken be returned to the fort. The two messengers were to assure Wahunsonacock that the lord governor would "enter friendship with him, as a friend to King James and his Subjects," but if the great chief did not comply, he would use all his means to recover his men and weapons. De La Warr reminded him also that he (Wahunsonacock) "had formerly vowed, not only friendship but homage, receiving from his Majestie . . . many gifts, and upon his knees a Crowne and Scepter with other Ornaments, the Symbols of Civill State and Christian Soveraigntie, thereby obliging himselfe to Offices of dutie to his Majestie." De La Warr accorded Wahunsonacock the courtesy his rank warranted, but there was no question in the governor's mind that the coronation ceremony conducted nearly two years earlier had obliged the chief to render obedience to De La Warr as James I's appointed representative in Virginia.

Wahunsonacock's contempt for the presumptuous English can be gauged from his response: The settlers were to "depart his Country, or confine themselves to James Towne only, without searching further into his Land, or Rivers, or otherwise, hee would give command to his people to kills [the English], and doe . . . all the mischiefe, which they at their pleasure could." To underline that he, not James I or De La Warr, was the ruler of the land, he informed the lord governor not to send his messengers again "unless they brought him a Coach and three Horses, for hee had understood by the Indians which [had been] in England, how such was the state of great Werowances, and Lords in

England, to ride and visit other great men." De La Warr replied in kind. If Wahunsonacock failed to return the settlers he had taken (or who had ran off to join the Powhatans) the English would kill any "Savages" they came into contact with and set fire to neighboring Indian corn fields and towns.[29]

War began, as it would continue over the next four years, with skirmishes and sporadic acts of horrifying violence in which no one was spared. In unseasonable heat during late June and early July, disease once more taking its toll among the new arrivals at Jamestown, De La Warr ordered Gates to lead an expedition to Point Comfort. On the way, the deputy governor witnessed an event that would change his view of the Indians decisively. Approaching Warraskoyack, he sent Humphrey Blunt to recover a longboat that had been blown to the south bank of the James River in a gale. Blunt set off in an old canoe but was driven back to the north shore by the wind; there, he was seized by a group of warriors who were watching him, led into the woods, and "sacrificed."

Gates had seen men picked off by Paspaheghs when they strayed too far from the fort, but witnessing the gruesome murder of one of his own men had a profound effect on him. Since his arrival in Virginia, he had avoided any "violent proceeding" against the Indians despite their provocations, according to William Strachey, "thinking it possible, by a more tractable course, to winne them to a better condition." But now he concluded "how little a faire and noble intreatie workes upon a barbarous disposition" and made up his mind to be revenged upon the Kecoughtans, whom he held responsible for Blunt's death because theirs was the nearest settlement to where the killing took place.

Landing close by their town, about four miles from Fort Algernon, Gates had his drummer "play and dawnse" (a traditional form of Powhatan hospitality) to entice the people to come out to meet him. Waiting for an opportune moment, his men suddenly drew their weapons and fell upon the Indians, putting to the sword five immediately and inflicting "Sutch extreordinary Lardge and mortall wownds" on many others that the soldiers were amazed when some managed to escape. Altogether, between twelve and fourteen were killed and the remainder fled, leaving the town and extensive cornfields to the English.

Why the Kecoughtans had been involved in Blunt's killing is uncertain. They were not reputed to be an aggressive people. John Smith, it will be recalled, spent a "merrie" time with them one Christmas feasting on oysters and fish while sheltering from snow and icy weather, and the deserters from Sicklemore's garrison on the Nansemond River had attempted to reach them to barter for food the previous fall. On the other hand, Gates had no doubt about the Kecoughtans' guilt, an opinion perhaps confirmed by George Percy who, two months before, had planned to mount an expedition against them because they "had trecheously slayne dyvers [many] of our men."

Another compelling reason for the attack on Kecoughtan, from the colonists' point of view, was to possess the Indians' abundant food supplies. Strachey described them as "better husbands [farmers] then in any parte ells" on account of the extensive lands they had cleared and planted. Their territory was "an ample and faire Country . . . comparatively high, wholesome and fruictfull," which could be cultivated to grow vines, corn, and all sorts of fruit, and would be an ideal location for a "Citty, or chief fortefication." Gates was of the same mind; he left George Yeardley (one of his officers in the Netherlands) to hold the area for the English and oversee the harvest of ripening corn while he returned to Jamestown to report to De La Warr. A week later, the lord governor visited the area and ordered two small forts, Charles and Henry, to be built at the entrance to the Southampton River (named in honor of Henry, Earl of Southampton) and garrisoned with companies under Yeardley and Holcroft.[30]

The attack on the Kecoughtans was not to be an isolated incident. Lord De La Warr's ultimatum to Wahunsonacock had warned that his soldiers would kill any Indians they encountered and destroy neighboring towns, villages, and crops; the unfortunate Kecoughtans were merely the first to fall victim to the threat. Following the departure on July 20 of the fleet that carried Gates back to England, the lord governor ordered Percy to take seventy men and attack the villages of the Paspaheghs and Chickahominies.

Percy transported his forces swiftly by boat to the mouth of the Chickahominy. On the night of August 10, he led the soldiers three miles overland to the Paspaheghs' town where they made a surprise attack and killed fifteen or sixteen Indians before putting the rest to flight. The soldiers burned the houses, carried off corn, and decapitated the Indians they had captured. Even the wife of the weroance (Wowinchopunck) and her two children were brutally murdered. Upon returning to their boats, the men threw the children overboard and shot "owtt their Braynes in the water," and would have killed the mother, too, if Percy had not protected her. Her reprieve was short-lived, however. Back in Jamestown, De La Warr ordered her execution, preferably by burning. But at this Percy balked: "[H]aving seene so mutche Blood-shedd thatt day," he confessed he "desyred to see noe more," and instead of having her burned told James Davis to give her a "quicker dispatche." Davis, accompanied by two soldiers, promptly took her into the woods and put her to the sword.

Davis had been a busy man that day. After the attack on the Paspaheghs, Percy's men had sailed a couple of miles up the Chickahominy River where Davis went ashore with the majority of the soldiers. They marched fourteen miles "into the Cowntry" and without opposition cut down the Chickahominies' corn, set fire to their houses, and ransacked their "Temples and Idolles." Having performed "all the spoyle" they could, they returned once again to their boats and headed down-river to Jamestown.[31]

Shortly after, Captain Edward Brewster, commander of Lord De La Warr's company, and Samuel Argall, who had recently returned from fishing off the New England coast after failing to reach Bermuda, led an expedition against the Warraskoyacks. The attack followed the seizure of the "chiefe King," Sasenticum, and his son, Kainta, in July when the fleet was riding off Warraskoyack to take on board a cargo of cedar, black walnut, clapboard, and iron ore before returning to England. Both prisoners and one of the people's chief men were sent with the ships to England to learn English ways, or possibly to help Gates illustrate the difficulties the settlers faced in converting the Indians to Christianity when he returned to report to the Virginia Company about the colony.

Meanwhile, De La Warr had bargained with Tackonekintaco, "an old Weroance" of the Warraskoyacks, and his son, Tangoit, recently captured, to trade five hundred bushels of corn, beans, and peas when the harvest was gathered for copper, beads, and hatchets. In return for his guarantee, the lord governor released the old chief and his son, keeping only a "nephew" as hostage to ensure the agreement was fulfilled. When the Indian hostage escaped and Tackonekintaco failed to keep his bargain, De La Warr decided to send two companies of troops against them. Alerted "by their neighbours harmes," however, the Warraskoyacks had maintained a careful watch on the English and, when the attack was launched, abandoned their villages and took refuge nearby. Brewster and Argall's men devastated their settlements and cut down their corn.[32]

In some respects, the summer offensive against the Kecoughtans, Paspeheghs, Chickahominies, and Warraskoyacks was little more than a continuation of the English practice of seizing corn when the Indians refused to trade. Friend or foe, peaceful or warlike, the colonists made little distinction between the peoples who dwelt near Jamestown, all of whom were to be treated as potential enemies when the settlers' vital interests were threatened.

Nonetheless, the arrival of De La Warr brought about a significant hardening of attitudes. At first committed to ending the war and converting the Indians to Christianity, continuing hostilities persuaded the lord governor that for the time being both objectives were hopelessly unrealistic. The war would have to be prosecuted much more vigorously than hitherto if the colony was to survive. Mobile forces of one or two companies, from fifty to a hundred men, transported by river, would surprise the Indians and kill as many men, women, and children as possible before burning their houses and making off with their corn. Such tactics not only avoided standoffs during which the English could be either starved into submission or picked off at long range by warrior bowmen but also had the effect of destroying Powhatan food supplies while supplementing those of the settlers. Indians, not English colonists, would face starvation during the next winter, and there was little the

Powhatans could do to protect themselves or their villages from the soldiers' lightning raids.

Having dealt with neighboring Indians, De La Warr turned his attention to another priority: the search for "the southe seas or royall mines," as instructed by the Virginia Company. Not having enough healthy men to mount the expedition, the lord governor ordered Yeardley and Holcroft to abandon forts Charles and Henry and transport their men to Jamestown in preparation for a march to the falls to repossess the fort left by his brother, Francis West, a year before.

The first contingent did not get far before disaster struck. While ashore collecting water about thirty-five miles upriver, some of the men were invited to the village where Opossunoquonuske, "Queene" of the Appomattocs lived, to "feast and make merry." Like "greedy fooles," they accepted, "esteameinge of A Little foode [more] then their own lyves and saffety." With the men off guard, the Indians attacked and "Slewe dyvers and wownded all the rest." Only Thomas Dowse, the drummer who had played and danced at Kecoughtan, made it back to the boat and, using the rudder as a shield, managed to escape the hail of arrows that rained down on him. The Appomattocs had cleverly turned the tables on the English, prompting Percy to remark that the "Salvages be nott Soe Simple as many Imagin who be not Acquaynted w[i]th their Subtellties for they had nott forgotten how their neighbours at Kekowhatan wer allured And defeated by Sr. Tho: Gates when he had the same Taborer [drummer] with him."

Among the fourteen killed were all of the "chief men skillful in finding out mines." Following with a second expedition, Edward Brewster took revenge by killing a number of Appomattocs and burning the village; but without the miners, he could do little more than reestablish "Lawares foarte" at the falls. He was joined shortly after by the lord governor, who intended to winter there before exploring the interior.[33]

---

THINGS WERE BEGINNING TO GO wrong for De La Warr. In the six months since his arrival, about a third of the colonists had perished, most of disease, and he himself had been plagued with illnesses that sapped his ability to lead. Despite stern discipline at Jamestown, the first signs of discontent among the men had arisen in the form of a conspiracy by the miners to steal a boat and "Runn away," which led to the hanging of the ringleader. Upriver during the winter, the Powhatans employed the same hit-and-run tactics they had adopted against the previous garrison at the falls, killing Captain William West (De La Warr's nephew) and several others. They taunted the English with songs that celebrated the killing of soldiers and taking of their weapons, and mocked captives—"*Yah, ha, ha, Tewittaw, Tewittawa, Tewittawa*"—who would cry out when sacrificed, unlike Indian warriors who would utter not "so much as a groane for any death" no matter how cruel or "full of Torment."

Doing "little but enduring much," De La Warr's men spent three months upriver before he decided to withdraw and return to Jamestown. The only good news awaiting him when he got back was that Wowinchopunck, chief of the Paspaheghs, had been killed by a small party of soldiers sent by Percy to capture him. There was no respite for De La Warr, however; as his health continued to deteriorate, he was advised to leave the colony temporarily to recuperate on Nevis, "an Island in the West Indies, famous for wholesome Bathes." At the end of March 1611, he put Percy in charge in his absence and set sail, accompanied by fifty-four of his men. Making no headway against adverse currents and winds, the ailing governor found himself bound across the Atlantic to the Azores, where he spent a week recovering before sailing on to England to explain why he had been forced to return so precipitously.[34]

After the high hopes at his departure for Virginia a year before, it was a miserable homecoming. Anxious about his likely reception in London, De La Warr moved quickly to justify his departure and delivered a written statement to the Company in June. Putting a brave face on events, he reported that he had left "upward of two hundred [settlers], the most in health," (the true number was nearer 170) well supplied with food, and confirmed that the country was "wonderfull fertile and very rich": Cattle and swine prospered and they had discovered excellent fishing grounds of cod and ling, "as good as can be eaten, and of a kinde that will keepe a whole yeare, in Shippes hould with little care."

Captain Argall, the lord governor wrote, had "found a trade" with Indians along the "Patomack" [Potomac] River, in whose territories were "the goodliest Trees for masts . . . [and] Hempe better then English, growing wilde in aboundance." North of the Potomac, mines of antimony and lead had been discovered. In short, there was "no want of any thing, if the action [could] be upheld with constancy and resolution." No mention was made of the sickness that had caused the loss of more than a hundred men at Jamestown or the continuing threat posed by the Powhatans who, De La Warr commented laconically, were "not able to do us hurt." Nothing was said either about prospects of finding gold or silver mines or a passage to the south sea.[35]

Fortunately for De La Warr, the survival of the colony did not depend on his testimony alone. Had that been so, it is quite possible the Company would have decided to give up on the venture altogether. Unknown to De La Warr, the triumphant return of Gates to London in the summer of 1610 with news of the miraculous survival of settlers on board the *Sea Venture,* their stay in the Bermudas, and their eventual arrival in Virginia, had reinvigorated support for the colony despite the grim news of the suffering of the colonists during the "starving time." Gates emerged as the colony's key witness and advocate, and it was he who eventually managed to persuade the Company to find the necessary funds to dispatch two more expeditions in 1611.[36]

At the same time, the Company's deliberations led to decisions that would significantly influence the colony's immediate future. Because Jamestown, in "the fennes and marshes," was deemed too sickly a place for the colony's capital, the Company reiterated its earlier instructions to find a new location at the falls and establish secondary settlements along the James River where settlers had a better chance of remaining healthy. Continuing idleness and disputes among the men underlined the importance of maintaining strict discipline, and the manifest enmity of the Powhatans confirmed the imperative of sending forces sufficiently strong to subdue them.[37]

In London, across the fall and winter of 1610–1611, as preparations for successive expeditions to be led by Sir Thomas Dale (recently released from service in the Netherlands) and Gates proceeded, the Company's renewed commitment to Virginia ultimately sealed the fate of Indian peoples and underlined English determination to continue the war and take possession of the Powhatans' land.

# 7

# REDEEMING POCAHONTAS

*I*N MID-MARCH 1611, Sir Thomas Dale, marshal of Virginia, left England with three hundred men, cattle, "and all other provisions necessarie for a yeere." A few weeks before, the Company had written expansively to their financial supporters: "The eyes of all Europe are looking upon our endevors to spread the Gospell among the Heathen people of Virginia, to plant our English nation there, and to settle at in those parts which may be peculiar [particular] to our nation, so that we may thereby be secured from being eaten out of all profits of trade, by our more industrious neighbors," a reference to Spain and possibly also to the French and Dutch.

Dale's departure was a critical moment in the early history of the colony. He would shape the course of Virginia over the next five years, just as Captain John Smith had dominated the first two and a half. Exuding determination, Dale gazes imperiously from his portrait, in which he is presented soberly, almost austerely (no pearls or jewels adorn his doublet), as a man of rank and authority. Probably from yeoman stock, he went as a soldier to the Netherlands in 1588; while there, he was raised to a captaincy and served in Ireland in the

*Sir Thomas Dale.*

mid-1590s and then again during the disastrous Essex expedition of 1599–1601. Returning to the Netherlands, he was stationed with Sir Thomas Gates (whom he had befriended in Ireland) at a garrison in South Holland before becoming involved in the Virginia venture. Able and ambitious, Dale had gained the attention of powerful men during his career, including Sir Robert Cecil and the Earl of Southampton, and had been knighted in 1606 for his loyal service. Several years later, when the Virginia Company decided to appoint a marshal responsible for military discipline in the colony to further buttress the authority of the lord governor and deputy governor, Cecil and Gates recommended him.[1]

Arriving in the James River after a voyage of eight weeks via the West Indies, Dale anchored off Point Comfort and made his way to Fort Algernon to learn about the "Condicon" of the colony from George Percy, who had come down from Jamestown with some others of the council to report. Learning that Lord De La Warr had left for Nevis ten days before and that Somers was in Bermuda, Dale assumed leadership of the colony and quickly took stock of the situation.

Experienced in diplomacy as well as war, he was careful not to over-state his criticisms of what he saw. Shortly after his arrival, he reported to the Company that although he had found "many omissions of nec-essary duties" to support a permanent settlement, he recognized that De La Warr had initially concentrated his efforts on finding "those Mynes w[hi]ch Faldoe the Helvetian had given intelligence of in En-gland" (Faldoe was among those killed by the Appomattocs). He learned from Percy about the attack by several hundred Paspahegh warriors soon after De La Warr's departure that resulted in the loss of the guard (about half a dozen men) at the blockhouse protecting the entrance to Jamestown Island. During that attack, the Indians did so "Showte and hallowe in Tryumphe of their gained victory thatt the Ecchoe thereof made bothe the Ayre and woods to Ringe." Chanting *"Paspahegh! Paspehegh!"* the belligerent warriors made known their in-tent of continuing their attacks before dispersing into the woods. A force of fifty men were sent out of the fort by Percy merely to recover the bodies of the slain Englishmen.[2]

Dale's course of action was clear. With three hundred additional mouths to feed, and knowing that hundreds of settlers would be arriving in a couple of months with Deputy Governor Gates, it was essential to reestablish garrisons at forts Henry and Charles and cultivate the rich corn lands surrounding them. Putting all his men to work, within a few days Dale was able to report that they had cleared more land and set more corn than the Indians the previous year. He appointed Captain James Davis "taskmaster" of the three forts (Henry, Charles, and Algernon) with instructions to report to him directly, and then made his way to Jamestown to take formal charge of the government.

Dale had first to establish his authority over unruly English settlers and to devise a strategy for countering the continuing threat posed by Powhatan warriors. According to one account, "most of the companie were at their daily and usuall workes, bowling in the streets" when Dale first arrived in Jamestown. Neither did the arrival of Dale's fleet signal an improvement in the quality of settlers. Efforts to recruit battle-hardened veterans of the wars in Ireland and the Netherlands had only limited success, and instead of leading an expedition of well-disciplined soldiers, Dale complained to Lord Salisbury in August that of the three hundred men he had brought with him the great majority were "so profane, so riotous, so full of mutinie and treasonable Intendments" that were it not for their names it would be doubted "they [were] Christians." Only about sixty were fit to be put to "any labour or service."

During his first month, therefore, he expanded the "Civill and Politique Laws" enacted by Gates and De La Warr and introduced extensive new provisions appertaining to "Martiall discipline" that set out in detail roles and responsibilities of the settlers as well as severe penalties for noncompliance. Breaches of the "Laws" were punishable by death, prison, service in the "Gallies," or "passing the Pikes," (running the gauntlet along a row of men wielding pikes). The following year, Dale used a variety of harsh punishments to deter settlers from running away to the Indians. Of those he managed to recover from the Powhatans, some were hanged, "Some burned, Some . . . broken upon wheles," others staked and shot. Men who robbed the common store he had "bownd faste unto Trees and so sterved them to deathe."

Later, the "Lawes," compiled by William Strachey in June 1611 and published the following year, would be used by critics of Sir Thomas Smythe to stigmatize Dale and the Virginia Company's actions as cruel and tyrannous, "exceeding the strictest rules of martial discipline," but at the time the laws were welcomed by the venture's leaders as bringing order and stability to the colony. Percy commented they were "well observed" and Robert Johnson remarked that they encouraged "due reverence to the Ministers of the Word, and to all superiors, for peace and love among themselves . . . [G]ood are these lawes, and long may they stand in their due execution." Men of the caliber of Gates, De La Warr, and Dale had been hired by the Company to ensure that the faction and dissent of the colony's early years would not be repeated under the new regime. Strict military discipline, they believed, was necessary to force hard work "and an honest fashion of life" upon disorderly settlers, thereby creating the conditions that would make the colony profitable and turn the tide of the war against the Powhatans.[3]

Rebuilding the fort, an annual event in the early years, was an early priority. Dale divided the men into several gangs to repair the church and storehouse, construct a stable, a new well, powder and munition houses, and a "Sturgion howse" for dressing and curing fish. A blockhouse was to be erected on the north side of the "back River," which separates the island from the mainland, to prevent Indians from killing the settlers' cattle, and a wharf was to be built on the James River by the fort "to lande . . . goods dry and safe upon." Private gardens were allocated to each man to grow his own vegetables and common lands were established for the cultivation of hemp, flax, "and such other seeds" that would be returned to the Company.

Dale planned to introduce a degree of specialization into the colony's food production. Men stationed at the "two Princes ffortes," Henry and Charles, would produce corn to feed the garrisons at Fort Algernon and Jamestown; the latter would raise cattle and hogs as well as produce goods (cured fish, hemp, flax, and timber) for export. He planned also to put into effect the Company's long-delayed instructions "to rayse a principall Towne" upriver at the falls, leaving only a single company of fifty men at Jamestown "for the p[re]servacon of [their] breeders" (cattle). Jamestown was not to be abandoned, but it would no longer be the seat of government or the colony's major settlement.[4]

—●—

DALE'S OBJECTIVE was to control the James and York Rivers, the core of Tsenacommacah, by pacifying its peoples and maintaining fortified settlements at either end of the James as well as at Jamestown and Kiskiack. Following instructions from the Company, a new capital would be laid out at Arrohattoc, about fifty miles from Jamestown, "a convenient, strong, healthie, and sweete Seate to plant a new Towne." Ten miles further upriver, a settlement would be established near the falls, on lands belonging to Parahunt, "to commaund the head of the River, and the many fruitefull Islands in the same." Establishing several new forts and towns would "so over master the subtile, mischevious great Powhatan," Dale argued, "that I should leave him either no roome in his Countrie to harbour in, or drawe him to a firme assotiation w[i]th ourselves." Wahunsonacock would have to abandon his territories and "seeke a straunger Countrie" or come to terms with the English.

Wasting no time to put his plan into action, Dale led an expedition of a hundred men in full armor against the Nansemonds, who posed the only remaining threat to English control of the mouth of the James. Fighting "bothe by Lande and water," the Indians put up fierce resistance; they wounded many of the soldiers, including John Martin and Francis West, and narrowly missed killing Dale, who was hit by an arrow on the brim of his helmet. Never having encountered the English in heavy armor marching in formation, warriors could not understand why they did not inflict heavier casualties.

Perplexed, the Nansemonds resorted to strange "conjuracyons and charmes throweinge fyer upp into the skyes," and running up and down with rattles made "many dyabolicall gestures" and "Spelles and incantacionus Imageinge thereby to cawse Raine to fall from the

Clowdes" to extinguish the soldiers' matches and spoil their powder. But, George Percy commented grimly, "nether the dievall whome they adore nor all their Sorcerres did anytheinge Avayle them for our men Cutt downe their Corne[,] Burned their howses and besydes those w[hi]ch they had slayne browghtt some of them prisoners to our foarte." The Nansemonds were routed—their warriors killed or captured, their villages reduced to smoking ruins, and their fields stripped of ripening corn.[5]

Alexander Whitaker, a minister who had arrived with Dale to undertake missionary work among the Indians, wrote to the Reverend William Crashaw about the Indians' effort to invoke their gods a few weeks later. At a town on the Nansemond River, an Indian priest was seen swinging to and fro "a thinge like a Censer" that emitted smoke and flame. The priest told the English that there "would be very much raine pr[esen]tly"; and, Whitaker reported, "indeed there was forth w[i]th exceedinge Thunder and lightenninge and much raine, w[i]thin 5 miles."

The Nansemond incident was not an isolated occurrence. When Wahunsonacock learned that Dale was preparing an expedition to the falls, he forbade the commander to go or else, he warned, he would destroy the English in "a strange mann[e]r" by making the settlers drunk and killing them all. Dale was "verry merry att this message" and scoffed at the Powhatan chief's threat. Shortly after, according to Whitaker, Dale and his guard went on a reconnaissance mission up the James River to find a suitable site for the new capital and other possible settlements. One night at prayer while encamped at the falls, the men heard a noise coming from the cornfields near their trenches, "like an Indian *huphup* w[i]th an *oho oho*," and some saw "one like an Indian" leap over a fire and run into the corn chanting the same, at which "all [the] men were confusedly amazed." They could say nothing but *"oho oho"* and, picking up the wrong end of their weapons, began to attack one another, "each man Takeinge one another for an Indyan." The "alarum" lasted no more than seven or eight minutes with little harm done apart from a few cracked heads. Then the men awoke as out of a dream and began to search for their enemies, but soon realizing their error, they "remayned ever after verye quiet," shaken by the strange fantasy. "All w[hi]ch things," Whitaker concluded, "make me thinke that there be great witches amonge them [the Indians] and they very familiar w[i]th the divill."

Whitaker's observations bore out the opinions of preachers in England in asserting the real presence of Satan among the Indians and underlined the divinely appointed role of the English in bringing the true faith to a benighted people. For Virginia, according to Whitaker, was like the land of Canaan, flowing with milk and honey, before the Israelites overran it. The Lord, he thought, had "spared this people [the Indians] and inriched the bowels of the Country w[i]th the riches and bewty of nature," so that the English "wantinge [lacking] them might in the search for them Communicate the most excellent merchandize and treasure of the gospell w[i]th them." If there were any young godly and learned ministers whom the Church of England could not or would not put to work, then send them to Virginia, he urged Crashaw, because the "harvest is forward and great here for want of such." As churchmen had intoned over and over again in their sermons, profit and piety went together, but the bounty of the land could not be fully exploited until the Indians were converted to Christianity and saved from the shadow of death. "This is the worke that we first intended," Robert Johnson reminded Company supporters, "and have published to the world to be chiefe in our thoughts."[6]

## Don Molina's Mission

Sometime during the summer of the previous year, a report came into the hands of Philip III from the archbishop of Tuam, near Galway in Ireland. It included a description of Virginia by an Irish sailor named Francis Magnel (Magill or Maguire?), who claimed to have spent eight months in the colony in 1607 and 1608. Magnel's account confirmed that the English had fortified themselves at "James-fort" and described the Indian peoples and natural resources of the region. He claimed that the Indians had told the English that they "could easily take them to the South Sea." On the far side of Virginia, the Indians said, there is a land "where the natives wear long silk robes and red buskins [high boots] and that they have a great deal of gold." The English, Magnel said, "want nothing more than . . . to make themselves lords of the South Sea, so as to have their share of the riches of the Indies, and to be in the way of the traffic of the King of Spain, and to seek other new worlds for themselves." To that end, the Irishman continued, they were sending many of their best carpenters in the kingdom to build ships that would be used in the Indies trade.[7]

A second report, directed to Philip in May 1611 from the Council for War in the Indies, seemingly confirmed Magnel's testimony. Captain Francisco Fernández de Écija's description of his voyage to the James River emphasized English plans to use the Chesapeake Bay as a base for exploring inland waterways to New Spain and the rich silver mines of Zacatecas, as well as finding a river passage to the west coast where they would fortify themselves, build fleets, "and overrun the whole coast of Tierra Firme, Peru, and China, to the great damage of the crown and subjects of Your Majesty." English fleets would eventually become a menace not only in the Caribbean but also in the Pacific, leading to incalculable losses of Spanish shipping and treasure. Given the grave nature of the danger, the council urged Philip to send four or five thousand men to drive the English out of Virginia as soon as possible, "before they take root and possess themselves of more land . . . extend through other regions, as they will go onto do, since none other is their design."

But the king was not prepared to act on second- or third-hand accounts. Instead, he ordered Don Gaspar de Peréda, governor of Cuba, to organize a further reconnaissance expedition, making it clear that, should his men encounter the English, there would be no violence. Philip was determined to wait to hear from Peréda before making a final judgment.

Philip had good reasons for delaying. A long letter from Don Alonso de Velasco that arrived shortly before the report from the Council of War provided a perspective very different from those of Magnel and Écija. The source of Velasco's information was Sir William Monson— admiral of the English Channel (in charge of defenses), who was in the pay of the Spanish—described as "a person of such high authority among sailors" that he was able "in secret and with great skill" to discover news of the colony from those who had recently returned from Virginia with Gates.[8]

According to this intelligence, although the country was fertile and had a good climate, there was no evidence of gold or silver. There was also little risk that English privateers would be able to attack Spanish possessions in the Caribbean because contrary winds and currents effectively blocked their way southerly along the coast. And there was no quick route to the South Sea, which lay "more than 400 leagues" (1,400 miles) away, beyond "high mountains" and "vast deserts which the Indians themselves [had] never . . . explored." Velasco concluded: "[N]o credit can be given to what the Irishman Francisco Manuel [Magnel] says." Furthermore, as the Indians were continually harrying the English, Velasco thought it unlikely that the settlers could long maintain themselves unless reinforced with large numbers of people so that they could "make themselves Lords of the Country," as the Indians now are."[9]

As the king pondered Velasco's letter, broader strategic considerations must have also influenced his thinking. In April 1609, Spain had agreed with the United Provinces on a twelve-year truce, ending the exhausting war that had been going on since the 1560s between the Habsburgs and the Dutch. Following treaties with the French and English in 1598 and 1604, the truce of Antwerp brought peace to Spain's European borders for the first time in more than forty years and ushered in a much-needed respite from the crushing expense of war on several fronts. Was an attack on Virginia worth the risk of provoking hostilities with England?

There can be little doubt that Philip understood the extent of English territorial aspirations in America—a map sent by Velasco in March 1611 revealed that English mariners had detailed the North American coastline all the way from the Outer Banks of North Carolina to Newfoundland. Yet the English had shown themselves incapable of sustaining colonies before and possibly would have no greater success in Virginia. Quite reasonably, given the significance of maintaining his recently concluded peace throughout Europe ("Pax Hispanica"), the king chose a "wait and see" policy. He calculated that even if the English colony did survive, Spain would be in a stronger position to take decisive action after a period of rebuilding her much depleted financial and military resources. Vigilance and more information were required so that, as the king told Velasco, "the most suitable measures [might] be adopted."[10]

A Spanish caravel, commanded by Don Diego de Molina, was dispatched from Lisbon in April 1611 to carry out the reconnaissance mission ordered by King Philip; after putting in at Havana and San Augustín, the caravel reached the Chesapeake Bay by late June, where she anchored off Point Comfort. The subsequent encounter between the Spanish expedition and English soldiers at Fort Algernon, though something of a farce, would have far reaching implications for both nations.

Molina made the first move. Ordering a small sloop to be made ready, he together with the master of the caravel, an English pilot in the service of Spain called Francisco Lembry (or Limbrecke), and ten other men armed with muskets set out towards the fort. As they approached, they spotted some sixty to seventy men; but, despite warnings from the sailors, Molina determined that he would go ashore accompanied by his second in command, Ensign Marco Antonio Perez, and Lembry, leaving the master and remaining men with the sloop hove to in the river. Why he did so is unclear. It was obvious to everyone onboard the sloop that Molina was being lured into a trap. Perhaps he thought the English would be friendly, conforming to the relatively relaxed relations between Spanish settlers and European mariners that existed in parts of the Caribbean where inducements of trade sometimes outweighed politics. He may have hoped to find out what he needed to know, return to his ship, and sail away without trouble.

Whatever his thinking, the play did not pay off. As soon as the three Spaniards reached the shore, they were surrounded by fifty men, relieved of their weapons, and marched off as prisoners. An hour later, a detachment of soldiers returned to the beach and called to the men in the sloop to come ashore. The master refused, saying he would comply only if the English gave them Molina. Shortly after, half a dozen soldiers made their way to the shore asking to speak to the master. One of them, a pilot named John Clark, went out to the Spanish with the intention of bringing their ship alongside the fort. This move also proved a mistake. Clark was promptly seized and taken to the caravel as a bargaining counter for the release of their men. The next day, the Spanish returned in the sloop, "a stone's throw from the land," and offered to exchange Clark for the three prisoners. The English refused, at which the Spanish threatened to fight. Captain James Davis, backed by twenty musketeers, "replied from the shore with great anger, that they might go to the Devil," turned on his heel, and stormed back to the fort. The Spanish were left to return to their ship and push out to sea with the hapless Clark still in their possession.[11]

Dale's anxious postscript to the Earl of Salisbury several weeks later revealed his unease at the escape of the Spanish caravel and loss of Clark. "What may be the daunger of this unto us who are here so few, so weake and unfortified," he wrote, "since they have by this meanes sufficiently instructed themselves concerninge our just height and Seate [location]; and know the readie way unto us both by this discoverer and by the help likewise of our owne Pilott, I refer me to your owne hono[ra]ble knowledg." Molina, Perez, and Lembry had been dispatched to Jamestown soon after their capture to be interrogated by the English, but Dale could expect to learn little about Spanish intentions that would give him any comfort. On the other hand, the Spanish now had reliable information about where the English colony was located, as well as how to reach it, and were poised to learn further details about the placement and strength of fortifications from Clark. Molina could not have predicted how the confrontation at Fort Algernon would turn out, especially after the unpromising beginning. Nevertheless, the mission had been remarkably successful. In capturing the English colonists' chief pilot, John Clark, the Spanish had acquired a valuable and unexpected prize.

Dale did not know whether the caravel had sailed alone or been sent in advance of warships already at sea to scout the Virginia coast and guide a Spanish fleet to the James River. Mindful, however, of the terrible fate that had befallen Jean Ribault's colony at Fort Caroline half a century before—when the entire settlement except for the women and children had been put to the sword—he was not prepared to take chances. Dale pushed ahead with plans to locate a new capital upriver as quickly as possible, which in any event was integral to his broader proposal to establish settlements from Point Comfort to the falls that would serve not only in the war against the Powhatans but also as a defensive tactic to meet the Spanish threat.

## "Lords of the Country"

In early August 1611, as his men were preparing timbers, pales, posts, and rails for the new town to be built upriver, Dale received the news he had been dreading: A fleet of three ships with three caravels had been sighted off the coast. Assuming the worst, he called his captains together to decide whether they should dig in at Jamestown or board their ships and confront the Spanish on the river. Their fortifications too weak to stand a frontal assault, George Percy believed the men would not stand and fight and favored manning the ships where they could not run away. Dale agreed and sought to rouse the men "with the hope of victory" but, he exclaimed, if God "had ordained to set a period to their lives, they could never be sacrificed in a more acceptable service," promising to fire the Spanish ships with his own vessel rather "than basely to yeeld, or to be taken." After more than twenty years of fighting against Spain, the veteran commander was not going to give up the colony without a struggle.[12]

To his great relief, Dale received word shortly before the men embarked that the fleet entering the Bay was not the enemy but Sir Thomas Gates with three hundred colonists, a hundred cattle, munitions, and provisions. After heartfelt greetings, Dale informed the deputy governor (who was now in charge) about what had transpired since his arrival and his plans to found a major settlement upriver. With men daily falling ill in the sickly summer months and 750 settlers now in the colony, Gates needed little persuasion of the imperative to move most of the men off Jamestown Island as soon as possible, spurred on by the prospect of Spanish invasion. In early September, when preparations were complete, Dale dispatched Captain Edward Brewster with 350 handpicked men, mostly artisans who had arrived with Gates, to march overland to the site upriver where the new town was to be built.

Wahunsonacock, who had been closely monitoring activities at Jamestown during these weeks, must have wondered if the English were preparing to abandon the colony when they began loading supplies aboard the two ships and pinnace riding by the fort. But the arrival of Gates with fresh men and supplies dashed any lingering hopes that they intended to leave. Soon after, Brewster's expedition—the largest yet mounted to the upper James into the very heartland of Tsenacommacah—left Wahunsonacock in little doubt about the gravity of the threat. Because the great chief could not afford to miss the opportunity to inflict heavy casualties on the Englishmen, he dispatched his forces.

While Brewster and his men were on the march, some fifty miles along the James River, they were repeatedly attacked by elite warriors commanded by a courageous and charismatic leader, Nemattanew, called by the English "Jack of the Feathers," who went into battle "covered w[i]th feathers and Swans wings fastened unto his showlders as thowghe he meante to flye." Finding their way to a peninsula of high ground jutting into the river a couple of miles below the Indian settlement of Arrohattoc, Brewster and his men rendezvoused with Dale, who had followed by boat with the lumber and supplies. As the men worked to erect a strong palisade across a neck of land and so create a defensible island over the next few weeks, the attacks continued unabated, the Powhatans "shoteing Arrowes into the foarte," where many of the men were wounded and "indangered." Those employed outside the fort's walls were forced back inside or risked being slain, and on at least one occasion a daring group of Powhatans managed to enter the palisade at night and shoot at the sleeping men through the doors of their quarters.

But despite the Indians' determined resistance, the English pressed on with the town—named Henrico in honor of Dale's patron, Henry, Prince of Wales. By Christmas, they had laid out three streets "of well framed houses," built a "handsome Church," erected watchtowers at each corner of the settlement, and storehouses for the Company's provisions and trade goods. In addition, two miles from the fort, they constructed a fence across the peninsula, "from river to river," guarded by sturdy blockhouses, and prepared cornfields sufficient to supply the town and neighboring settlements for several years to come.[13]

Wahunsonacock could do nothing to stop them. A frontal assault would have been disastrous, costly in lives, and would only have underlined the Englishmen's superiority in weaponry and armor. His bowmen's prodigious four-foot arrows, capable of passing straight through an enemy's body, could not penetrate English corselets or shirts of mail, and Indian war clubs were no match for muskets and cannon. A crushing defeat would not only seriously reduce the Powhatans' warrior strength and morale but might also weaken his own authority and encourage those peoples who were allies more through fear than amity to go over to the English. All the great chief could do was to follow the same hit-and-run tactics developed at Jamestown, keeping the English under close surveillance and waiting for a chance to pick off unwary stragglers or deserters who ventured too far from the fort.

Dale's success in establishing a base of operations upriver, in contrast to earlier failures by Francis West and Lord De La Warr, was a turning point in the English struggle to gain control of the James River Valley. From Henrico, Dale led a force late in the year to devastate the villages of the Appomattocs and make off with their corn stocks, to "revenge the treacherous injurie of those people, done unto us." Admiring the fertility of their land, he took possession of it "at that very instant," naming it the "new Bermudas," after the Bermuda Islands, which also enjoyed a reputation for fertility. Over the next couple of years, lands on both sides of the James River from the mouth of the Appomattox to Henrico and beyond were taken up by colonists, making it the most populous area settled by the English.[14]

### "Extremitie and Miserie"

Dale had written to Lord Salisbury in the summer of 1611 in an optimistic frame of mind. With two thousand settlers, he explained, he could take "full possession of Powhatans Countrie," prosecute the war until Wahunsonacock and his chiefs accepted English rule, make the colony self-sufficient, and produce profitable commodities. Yet far from being able to recruit thousands of fresh settlers, the Company could not afford to send even a couple of hundred. The expense of outfitting the expeditions led by Dale and Gates had left the Company on the brink of bankruptcy with little prospect of immediate returns on monies already spent. Not even a revision to the Company's royal charter in the spring of 1612 that transferred more power to rank-and-file Company members, extended the bounds of the colony at sea to include the Bermudas, and instituted a public lottery could attract investment.[15]

Throughout the latter part of 1612 and the first half of 1613, further uncertainty was caused when news of an imminent (or actual) Spanish attack on Virginia swirled around the capitals of Europe. From Madrid came intelligence that the five hundred settlers in Virginia "had . . . suffered great extremitie and miserie"; from Paris and Lisbon came word that a fleet of warships was being prepared to extinguish the colony as they had "the Frenchmen in Florida"; and from the Spanish ambassador in London, Velasco, writing in May 1613 to the king, that nothing had been heard from the colonists for many months, the conjecture being that they had died of famine or had been cut off by the Indians. Ironically, the steady decline of support in England may well have saved the colony by persuading Philip III that the expense of sending a fleet was unjustified because Virginia would "sinke of itselfe" within a year or two.[16]

Dismal news of the death of Henry, the young Prince of Wales, one of Virginia's chief sponsors, and rumors that the colony might either be abandoned by the Company or obliterated by a Spanish force reached Dale in the early summer of 1613. His alarm that the Company was about to dispose of the colony is palpable in his letter to Sir

Thomas Smythe, delivered in a blunt style worthy of Captain John Smith: "Let me tell you all at home this one thing, and I pray remember it; if you give over this country and loose [lose] it, you, with your wisdoms, will leap at a gudgeon [false bait] as our state hath not done the like since they lost the Kingdom of France." He continued, "I have seen the best countries in Europe, but I protest unto you, before the Living God, put them all together, this country will be equivalent unto them if it be inhabitant with good people." The Spanish controlled a vast global empire greater than the world had ever seen. Were the English, Dale wondered, about to give up an American empire that might in time rival or supplant that of Spain's?[17]

A revealing insight into the morale of the English colonists during these years is given by Don Diego de Molina, who still languished under close arrest at Jamestown; a helpless pawn in diplomatic wrangling between London and Madrid. He had come to sympathize deeply with the ordinary men of the settlement, themselves "held captives by their masters," whom he looked upon as "brothers" and whose distress he said he felt more than his own. In several letters smuggled out of the colony in 1613 and 1614 by two men in the pay of Spain (sewn between the soles of the shoes of one man and hidden in a coiled rope belonging to the other), Molina painted a bleak picture of conditions in the colony.

"Living in their midst and seeing their [the settlers'] sufferings," Molina wrote, "they look me in the face and ask: what is the king of Spain doing? Where is his mercy?" He was confident the ordinary settlers would offer no resistance to an attack because they would rather be rescued and taken away from the colony by the Spanish than continue in their present misery. Underlining the point, Molina claimed he had easily persuaded the five men who guarded him when he went out to "fish on the shore" to escape by heading for Florida. When the five men went missing and Dale discovered what had happened, he ordered the Spaniard removed from the fort and imprisoned in one of the blockhouses about a mile away, issuing strict orders that no one speak to him. According to English accounts, the five men led by one Edward Coles headed for "Ocanahowan, five daies journey . . . , where they report[ed] are Spanish inhabiting," but were cut off and slain by the Indians. Molina, however, believed Dale spread the news of their deaths merely to "terrify the people."[18]

It might not be surprising that a Spanish captive would portray the colony as being on the verge of mutiny, but Molina's testimony corroborated rumors about settlers' discontent that had been common knowledge in London for the past several years. It also provided a quite different perspective on Dale's bitter complaints to the Company about the quality of his men. In a long letter from Henrico of June 1613, the English commander explained that most of the colonists believed that by laboring as little as possible they would eventually "weary out the companye at home" and when they "see we doe not prosper here they wyll send for us hom." Without a severe hand, "thes crused [cursed] peoples" would not work at all but would rather steal from one another until the food stores were exhausted and they starved. "O sir my harte bleeds," he exclaimed, "when I thinke what men we have here."

Those who suffered under him had a different story. They cited oppressive and unjust laws "mercylessly executed, often times without tryall or Judgment" (contrary to the letter of the colony's charter), insufficient daily rations of moldy oatmeal and peas "not fytt for beasts, w[hi]ch forced many to flee for reliefe to the Savage Enemy." Many settlers, it was alleged, through want and misery, "being weery of life, digged holes in the earth and there hidd themselves till they famished." Those who survived "were Constrayned to serve the Colony, as yf they had been slaves."[19]

The Company had approved Dale's rigorous use of martial law as necessary to ensure the survival of the settlement. But Sir Thomas Smythe badly miscalculated the impact of news of the appalling conditions in the colony brought back by ships that had visited Jamestown. Don Diego Sarmiento y Acuña, Conde de Gondomar, who had been appointed ambassador in London to succeed Velasco, commented to the king after receiving Molina's letters that "even the shadow of a fleet" would drive the English out of Virginia, and echoed Molina's opinion that the great majority of settlers would surrender without a shot fired if offered the chance to return to England. Instead of wiping out the colony, the Spanish would act as liberators by rescuing the starving settlers and ending their hardships. By this means, Gondomar calculated, it might be possible to avoid a major rift between England and Spain while bringing to a close what was evidently a failure. In the capital, he reported, the colony was "in such bad repute that not a human being [could] be found to go there in any way whatever." He gave as an example a story he had heard about two "Moorish thieves" condemned to hang who had been offered the chance go to the colony. They replied at once that they "would much rather die on the gallows here, and quickly, than to die slowly so many deaths as was the case in Virginia."[20]

Sir Thomas Smythe and other Company leaders knew very well that without sufficient fresh recruits and investment the colony could not long survive. Against the backdrop of unremitting bad news, however, all they could do was pin their hopes on an end to the war with the Powhatans, which would eventually open the way to prosperity and fulfillment of the Christian mission to convert the Indians. What they desperately needed was a change of fortune.

## The Marriage

No one could have foreseen, either in Jamestown or London, that Captain Samuel Argall's trading expeditions along the Potomac River and the Eastern Shore in 1612 and 1613 would lead to a crucial breakthrough between the English and Powhatans. On previous voyages, Argall had explored the Chesapeake more extensively than anyone aside from John Smith, discovered and named the Delaware Bay, and surveyed the coast as far north as Cape Cod. Commissioned admiral of Virginia in place of Sir George Somers (who had died in the Bermudas the previous year), he was dispatched in the *Treasurer* in the summer of 1612 to trade and to serve the colony in whatever capacity he could. Arriving in mid-September, Argall and his men spent several months repairing ships and boats and joined in expeditions led by Dale against Indians "for their corn," during one of which the marshal again narrowly escaped being killed by the Nansemonds. Late in the year and in the following spring, Argall made two voyages to the Potomac where, by fair dealing, he established good relations with peoples along the river, gathered large quantities of corn, and explored inland to the headwaters of the Potomac.

But it was the kidnapping of Pocahontas—Wahunsonacock's "delight and darling"—that proved to be the most important outcome of Argall's voyages. She happened to be staying with the Patawomecks in the spring of 1613 to "exchange some of her father's commodities for theirs" and visit friends. On hearing from some Indians that Pocahontas was in the area, Argall devised a plan to hold her hostage in return for English prisoners taken by the Powhatans in recent raids.

Approaching his close friend and adopted brother, Iopassus (also an old acquaintance of John Smith's), weroance of the Pasptanzie, Argall told him his plan and offered assurances that he would not harm Pocahontas. If he did not agree to cooperate, the captain went on, they would no longer be brothers and the peace between them would be at an end. If he did help and as a consequence the Powhatans made war on the Patawomecks, then the English would join them against Wahunsonacock's warriors. Iopassus reported this to his brother, the "great King of Patawomeck," who after a lengthy council meeting agreed to Argall's plan. Shortly after, Iopassus and his wife enticed Pocahontas aboard the Englishman's ship and, after a "merry" supper, the Indians spent the night on board. The next morning, Iopassus and his wife were rewarded with a small copper kettle and "other les valuable toies" and left. Argall informed Pocahontas she would have to stay on board and return with him to Jamestown.

Sending a message to Wahunsonacock from the Potomac River, Argall demanded the return of English prisoners with all such weapons and tools stolen by the Indians, together with a "great quantitie of Corne" before his daughter was restored to him. According to Argall, the great chief was "much grieved" by the news of his daughter's capture and agreed to the captain's demands. Within a few days of Argall's arrival back in Jamestown, seven men, together with their (broken) weapons, were delivered at the fort. The prisoners, he says, were "very joyfull for that they were freed from the slavery and feare of cruell murther, which they daily before lived in." Having created the basis of peace between the English and the Powhatans, Argall claimed, he returned to fitting out the colony's ships for fishing and then went on a trading voyage to the Eastern Shore.

A different version of events written by Ralph Hamor, a settler who had arrived with Gates in 1610, is probably more accurate. According to him, although Wahunsonacock was sorely troubled by the news of Pocahontas's captivity, he did not reply to English demands for three months. Reluctant to return his prisoners, of whom "he made great use," or the weapons and tools, which "it delighted him to view, and looke upon," he was finally persuaded to give up several men and their unserviceable muskets. He sent word that he would provide five hundred bushels of corn as compensation for weapons and tools broken and stolen from him, and upon receiving his daughter he would "be for ever friends with [the English]." Dale refused, assuring the chief that his daughter was kindly treated but insisting that she would remain with the English because they could not believe that the rest of the arms held by the Indians were lost or missing. Until such time as the weapons were returned it would be his (Wahunsonacock's) choice whether "he would establish peace, or continue enemies." In Hamor's account, Dale's rejoinder was met with stony silence, and nothing more was heard from the chief for another year.[21]

Why Wahunsonacock refused to negotiate for the return of his daughter, Pocahontas, after initial exchanges in the summer is unclear. Perhaps he was unwilling to bargain further about the return of English weapons that were highly prized by the Powhatans "as Monuments and Trophies" of English "shames," or possibly he was forced to put aside his own feelings for her in view of what was at stake between his people and the murderous intruders. Much as he might have wanted his daughter back, he could not be seen as weak in his response to English demands.

Argall's voyages and subsequent negotiations over Pocahontas reveal much about the shifting relations between the English and Indians of Tsenacommacah, as well as possible implications for the great chief himself. By 1613, as messages went back and forth between Jamestown and Orapaks, Wahunsonacock's dominance over the tidewater was beginning to disintegrate. According to Argall, the Patawomecks and peoples of the Eastern Shore wished not only to trade with the English but also to enter into peace agreements. At the same time, despite fighting bravely, peoples along the James River from the Kecoughtans and Nansemonds to the Appomattocs and Powhatans had either been defeated or subjected to periodic devastating raids to which they had little answer. Wahunsonacock's stratagems had failed to dislodge the intruders from Jamestown and fresh English settlements had been entrenched in the heart of his territories. From without and within, the Powhatans' world was shrinking and so, too, was the great chief's influence among his own people.[22]

But there is another possibility—perhaps, in Wahunsonacock's mind, Pocahontas's abduction served a strategic purpose. From the ritual of "saving" Captain John Smith's life at Werowocomoco in the winter of 1607 to various other missions to Jamestown during the next years, Pocahontas had played a prominent role in relations with the English until the outbreak of open hostilities made further interventions impossible. She was probably engaged on a diplomatic mission on behalf of her father with the Patawomecks when she was abducted by Argall and taken back to Jamestown. Her intelligence, charm, youth, and close relationship to the paramount chief made her an ideal ambassador for such tasks. Although her seizure had been unforeseen, Wahunsonacock may have calculated that having his daughter close to the English commanders might turn out to be useful in gathering information about the settlers' plans.[23]

In the end, it was Dale who forced the issue with Wahunsonacock. In late March 1614, nearly a year after Pocahontas's abduction, accompanied by Argall and 150 well-armed men, Dale set out up the Pamunkey (York) River to meet the great chief and return his captive in exchange for his men, stolen weapons, tools, and a "ship full of Corne, for the wrong hee had done unto us." If the Indians agreed to the Englishmen's terms, which were the same as those delivered a year before, they would be friends; if not, then the English would "burne all." In response, the Indians informed Dale that Wahunsonacock was three days journey away but that Opechancanough could speak for him, "saying, That what hee agreed upon and did, the great King would confirme." "Opocankano," the English commander noted, "is brother to Powhatan, and is his and their chiefe Captaine: and one that can as soone (if not sooner) as Powhatan command the men."

Pushing upriver, the English encountered a hail of arrows as they went ashore. Being "justly provoked," as they saw it, they sent a strong force against their attackers, killing half a dozen warriors, burning nearby villages, and seizing the Indians' corn. The show of strength had its desired effect. As the English headed farther upriver, Indians called out asking why they had attacked them and burnt their houses, assuring the soldiers that "they would be right glad of our love, and would indeavour to helpe us to what we came for." Wahunsonacock sent a message the following day indicating that the English captives had run away because they feared being put to death by Dale, but the weapons they demanded, or as many as he had, would be returned forthwith.

The next day, however, brought no news of the swords and muskets. When Dale's soldiers disembarked near the Powhatans' "chiefest residencie" at a town called "Matchcot," the Indians mounted their own show of strength, gathering four hundred warriors armed and ready to defend themselves. As the men faced one another and traded insults, a bloodbath seemed inevitable; yet neither side was willing to make the first move. Then, two of Pocahontas's brothers came forward and demanded to see their sister. On finding her well treated and in good health "they much rejoiced" and promised to "perswade their father to redeeme her" and conclude a "firme peace forever." John Rolfe and another Englishman were sent to negotiate with the paramount chief but, unable to meet him, spoke instead to Opechancanough.

Soon after, word came (apparently) from Wahunsonacock that was sufficient to satisfy Dale and allow both sides to depart without losing face. The Englishmen's weapons and tools would be returned to Jamestown within fifteen days "with some Corne," and Pocahontas would be Dale's "child, and ever dwell" with the English, who would forthwith be the great chief's friends and live in peace. If any of Dale's men ran away to the Indians, they would be sent back; and if any of his people committed crimes against the English, they would be delivered to Dale for punishment. Being early April, the planting season, the English and Powhatans were anxious to return to their fields. Dale therefore accepted Wahunsonacock's terms on condition that if they were not fulfilled he would return after harvest and burn all the villages along the river, take their corn, "and destroy and kill as many of them" as he could.

It was an inconclusive end to hostilities. As the English commander turned his boats about and sailed back to Jamestown, he must have wondered whether the great chief had been sincere about his promises or whether he would be forced to return to carry out his threat. Perhaps to his surprise, and doubtless to his considerable relief, some of the arms were returned along with gifts of corn within the allotted time. Opechancanough, according to Dale, expressed his wish to be friends, "saying Hee [Opechancanough] was a great Captaine, and did always fight: [and] that I was also a great Captaine, and therefore he loved mee; and that my friends should bee his friends."

So "the bargaine was made" that brought to an end five years of vicious raids, sieges, massacres, and destruction of villages, livestock, and crops. Both sides could plant their corn, fish, hunt, and live in peace without the continual worry of attack. At last, the settlers would be able to subsist off their own produce and become self-sufficient, and they could continue their discovery of the country through their own explorations and information provided by the Powhatans. "Now may you judge Sir, if the God of Battailes had not a helping hand in this," Dale confided to a friend in England, "that having our Swords drawne . . . yet they [the Powhatans] tendred us peace, and strive with all alacritie to keepe us in good opinion of them; by which many benefits arise unto us."[24] A significant shift had taken place in Anglo-Powhatan relations, but it is unlikely the English commander fully understood its repercussions or appreciated the increasingly important role that Opechancanough had come to play in shaping Indian policy.

APRIL WAS A GOOD MONTH for Dale. During the expedition to the Pamunkey capital, he had been informed of John Rolfe's wish to marry Pocahontas, and she him. What lay behind her decision to marry the Englishman? Initially following her capture, Pocahontas probably assumed she would soon be released, but as the months went by she became increasingly frustrated by her father's apparent lack of effort to bring about her freedom. As she told her two brothers, she could not understand why, if her father loved her, he valued her "lesse then old Swords, Peeces, or Axes."

Sent upriver to Henrico and placed under the care of the Reverend Whitaker at Rock Hall, who was given the responsibility of teaching her the "Christian Religion," she was treated well. Gradually she learned to speak English and soon became familiar with the settlers' ways. During services held at Henrico Church, and at other religious exercises conducted by Whitaker, she regularly met the pious John Rolfe. It is likely they first got to know one another when he helped with her instruction, and then became friends. Although the depth of her feelings cannot be known, it is quite possible that she was fond of him and may have come to love him. More generally, she may have found the freedoms offered her by the English, who treated her with respect as the daughter of the Indian king, stimulating, just as the strange ways of the English would have appealed to her natural curiosity. By the time Dale made the journey to confront Wahunsonacock, it seems that Pocahontas had made up her mind to live with the English, "who loved her," to renounce her "Countrey Idolatory," and to marry Rolfe, taking the portentous name Rebecca, mother of two peoples.[25]

For his part, in an explicit letter to Dale, Rolfe revealed how he had long wrestled with his conscience about his motives for wanting to marry Pocahontas and his fears of provoking God's just anger for seeking to wed a woman whose manners were "barbarous" and whose "generacon [was] Cursed." But, he asked, why was I created "if not . . . to labour in the Lords vyneyard, there to sowe and plant, to nourishe and encrease the ffruyts thereof?" Pocahontas had shown great love toward him and desired to be "taught and instructed in the knowledge of God." Should he turn her away and "refuse to leade the blynde into the right waye," refuse to "give breade to the hungry" or "Cover the naked?" "God forbidd," he concluded, and so "for the good of the Plantacon, the honor of o[u]r Countrye, for the glorye of God, for myne owne salvacon, and for the Convertinge to the true knowledge of God and Jesus Christ an unbeleiveinge Creature, namely Pohahuntas," he requested that Dale permit him to marry her.[26]

Whatever the reasons for Rolfe and Pocahontas's decision to marry, Dale seized the opportunity to seal the peace. He was delighted to agree to the union, and when Wahunsonacock heard the news he, too, gave his consent for reasons that are less clear. Shortly after, the great chief dispatched Opachisco, Pocahontas's old uncle, and two of his sons to witness the ceremony held in Jamestown's church on April 5, 1614. To the English, the marriage symbolized the new accord with the Powhatans who now (it was hoped) would live side by side with the settlers in harmony and friendship.

Since the colony had been reorganized under Sir Thomas Smythe's leadership, a prime objective of the Company had been the conversion of the Indians to Christianity and civility, and the devout Dale had taken the responsibility seriously. My "princypall car[e] hath bin to get sum of our salvaiges to whom we maye teach both our languaige and relygyon," he wrote to Sir Thomas Smythe from Henrico the previous year, but "the elder have bin all to[o] dead setled in ther Ignorance, the chyldren are so tenderly beloved of ther paren[t]s that neyther copper nor love can drawe any from them." Now, he not only had a convert but a convert who was the daughter of the paramount chief, a high-ranking member of her people who he might reasonably expect would play a vital role in bringing over many more of her nation to the true faith.[27]

A couple of weeks after the wedding, Dale received more good news. Two messengers arrived from the Chickahominies, a "lusty and daring" people, inviting the English commander to visit them and conclude a peace. Once again, Dale set out with Captain Argall, accompanied this time with fifty men, and made his way to meet the Chickahominies' leaders, with whom Argall conducted negotiations. When the Chickahominies told Argall of their wish to be friends, Argall inquired whether

*Theodor De Bry, The Treaty with the Chickahominies.*

they would accept King James as their king and "be his men." After a brief discussion, the Indian leaders accepted, but on condition the English would fight their enemies when needed, to which Argall agreed. The English captain then gave each of the eight "great men" who collectively ruled the people a large tomahawk and a piece of copper to conclude discussions, promising to guarantee that the Chickahominies were able to move about freely on the rivers and would benefit from trade with the English.

The Chickahominies pledged not only to recognize King James as their king but also to take the "name of *Tassantasses* or Englishmen"; to provide three or four hundred bowmen to aid the English against the Spanish ("whose name [was] odious amongst them"), or any Indians who attacked them; not to kill English settlers or their cattle, or try to tear down the palisades; and each year to deliver two bushels of corn for every fighting man to the English storehouse "as tribute of their obedience to his Majestie, and to his deputy there," and in return receive "so many Iron Tomahawkes or small hatchets."

Although the Chickahominies believed they were entering the agreement as equals, there can be little doubt that the English saw them as subordinates. The Indians' "chiefe men," who had governed independently, were now described as "substitutes and Councellors under Sir Thomas Dale," and in recognition of their performance of the peace agreement they would each receive annually from James I "a red coat, or livery" and a "picture of his Majesty, ingraven in Copper, with a chaine of Copper to hange it about his necke, whereby they [would] be knowne to King JAMES [as] his noble Men." By their willingness to be called English, to render service to James, to fight in support of the colonists, and to pay an annual tribute of at least a thousand bushels of corn, the Chickahominies had become the king's vassals, symbolized by the "pseudo-feudal" ornaments of the coat of livery and copper gorgets.[28]

Understandably pleased with the rapid improvement in the colony's fortunes, Dale decided to test the limits of his new understanding with the Powhatans soon after peace negotiations with the Chickahominies were concluded. Sending Ralph Hamor with the youthful interpreter Thomas Savage (who had lived with the Powhatans for several years) to visit Wahunsonacock, Dale sought another of the great chief's daughters to marry himself, "for [the] surer pledge of peace."

Hamor left in mid-May, led by two Indian guides, and returned to "Matchcot," where Wahunsonacock met them. The chief first greeted Thomas Savage by chiding the boy for not returning after he left to visit friends in "Paspahae" (Jamestown) four years ago, reminding him that "you . . . are my child" by gift of Captain Newport. Retiring to the chief's house, Hamor delivered his message from Dale, "your Brother," saying that he had heard of the "exquisite perfection of your yongest daughter" and that if the chief would give his permission, he would gladly make the girl "his nearest companion, wife and bedfellow." His request was prompted by the fact that "now friendly and

*Theodor De Bry, Ralph Hamor visits Wahunsonacock.*

firmely united together, and made one people . . . he [Dale] would make a naturall union between [them]."[29]

Wahunsonacock was displeased by Dale's proposal. After grumbling about the gifts Hamor had brought, he told the Englishman that within the past few days his youngest daughter had already been promised to a great weroance and had departed with him. When Hamor pressed him to buy his daughter back and sell her to Dale, the old chief demurred: "[H]e loved his daughter as deere as his owne life, and though he had many Children, he delighted in none so much as in her, whom if he should not often beholde, he could not possibly live . . . [having] resolved upon no termes whatsoever to put himselfe into our hands, or come amongst us."

Wahunsonacock told Hamor that he desired no firmer assurance of Dale's friendship than the promise he had already made. From me, he said, "he hath such a pledge, one of my daughters [Pocahontas], which so long as she lives shall be sufficient," and "I holde it not a brotherly part of your King [Dale]," he continued, "to desire to bereave me of two of my children at once." And yet if the English had no such pledges at all, they need not fear injury from him or his people: "[T]oo many of his [Dale's] men and my [have been] killed, and by my occasion there shall never bee more, I which have power to performe it, have said it." Should the English become the aggressors, he knew what to do: "[M]y country is large enough," he told Hamor, "[and] I will remove my selfe farther from you. . . . I am now olde, and would gladly end my daies in peace."

That might have been the end of the matter but for a chance meeting the following day between Hamor and an Englishman, William Parker (taken from Fort Henry three years before), who had grown so like the Indians "in complexion and habite" that if it had not been for his language Hamor would not have recognized him as a fellow countryman. When he demanded that Parker must return with him, Wahunsonacock became angry and replied, "You have one of my daughters with you, and I am therewith well content, but you can no sooner see or know of any English mans being with me, but you must have him away, or else breake peace and friendship." The next morning, Hamor met the chief to discuss various gifts Dale had promised to send. Taking his leave by the riverside, Wahunsonacock told Hamor that he would gladly entertain Dale's "missives" and, if it was in his power, fulfill his "just requests"; but if he did not receive the goods from the English commander he would move three days farther away from him and "never see *English* more."[30]

Hamor's negotiations were the last held between the English and Wahunsonacock and illustrate the huge gulf in perception that continued to blight communications between the two. Although the Powhatan chief had come to accept that his warriors were incapable of dislodging the invaders from his lands for the time being, he had not capitulated and certainly did not view his people as a conquered nation. The peace of April 1614 was to Wahunsonacock's mind a truce as advantageous to the English as it was to the Powhatans, a way of halting a cycle of killing and destruction that had dragged on for five years. There is no evidence that the marriage of Pocahontas implied to him, or to Opechancanough, that the English and Powhatans were (as Dale put it) "made one people." He may have seen the marriage as merely an expedient to confirm the truce and possibly as a means of finding out more about the settlers' long-term intentions. Reluctantly, Wahunsonacock was prepared to tolerate the presence of settlers in his land, but there is little indication that he had any desire to encourage closer social or political ties. Despite his assurances, neither he nor his brother was reconciled to living alongside the English in "perpetuall friendship."

For Dale, of course, the end of the war represented a signal victory for the English. From the colonists' point of view, they had successfully fended off Powhatan attacks, consolidated their hold on the James River Valley, entered into alliances with peoples on the Potomac River and Eastern Shore, concluded articles of peace with the Chickahominies, and, by the redemption of Pocahontas, put in train the great work of converting the Indians to Christianity. Dale was eager to send home some good news after the reversals of the last few years during which he had faced not only external threats from the Indians and Spanish but also mutiny and chronic insubordination among his own men.

Now, the entire complexion of the colony had changed. With peace established between the two peoples, the natural abundance of the land could be exploited fully and God's church, a "Sanctum Sanctorum," could at last be erected. No "Country of the world afford[ed] more assured hopes of infinite riches," Dale confidently asserted; and Rolfe fervently hoped that his marriage to Pocahontas would eventually "bring to the knowledge and true worship of Jesus Christ 1000s of poor, wretched, and misbelieving people [the Powhatans], on whose faces a good Christian cannot look without sorrow, pity, and commiseration." Dale, Rolfe, and other supporters of the Company had no doubt that Virginia would soon fulfill its promise, to the "great comfort of all well affected Christians," and profit of the planters and adventurers.[31]

# 8

## For "The Good of the Plantation"

*L*EAVING THE JAMES RIVER on the ebb tide in April 1616, Captain Samuel Argall's *Treasurer* carried one of the strangest assortments of passengers ever to make the Atlantic crossing. On board were Sir Thomas Dale, returning to England now that the colony was enjoying "great prosperytye & pease"; John Rolfe and Pocahontas (the Lady Rebecca) with their infant son Thomas; Pocahontas's sister, Matachanna, and her husband, Uttamatomakkin (also called Tomakin or Tomocomo), a priest and tribal elder instructed by Wahunsonacock to keep a careful account of everything he saw in the land of the *tassantasses;* another ten or so Powhatans, mostly young women who were attending Pocahontas and who, the Virginia Company hoped, might be induced to convert to Christianity and marry suitable Englishmen; Don Diego de Molina, relieved to be boarding after five years in Jamestown; Francis Lembry, the "hispanyolated Inglishe man," captured with Molina, who had served as a pilot with the Spanish Armada of 1588, (he would be hanged from the end of Argall's yardarm as the ship approached the coast of England within sight of the land he had betrayed); and, finally, several of Dale's principals during the war, Captains Francis West, John Martin, and James Davis, who (like Dale) had decided to return home.[1]

After a relatively quick passage, the *Treasurer* docked at Plymouth in early June. Dale immediately wrote to the king's secretary of state, Sir Ralph Winwood, and informed him that he had brought back some "exceedinge good tobaco [*sic*]," sassafras, pitch, potashes, sturgeon, caviar, and "other such lyke commodytyes." But by far the most valuable cargo, unmentioned in his letter, was Pocahontas, living proof that the Powhatan Indians could be converted to Christianity and English ways. Keen to show her off at court as soon as possible, after about a week's respite Dale dispatched Pocahontas and her entourage on the long journey to the capital.

This was the first time a group of Indians had seen England's many "countries," characterized by their distinctive landscapes, communities, and agriculture. The journey took them through Devon and Somerset, where they saw fertile coastal lowlands and river valleys lined by orchards and rich pasture lands, past ancient castles and cathedral towns, across the great open expanse of Salisbury Plain with its vistas of wheat fields and sheep walks, and then through woodland and heath to the Thames Valley and London. The Powhatans were amazed "at the sight of so much Corne and Trees" during the journey, according to the Reverend Samuel Purchas, who met Pocahontas and Uttamatomakkin on several occasions in London. They thought, he wrote, that "the defect [lack] thereof" had brought the English to Virginia. After five or six days of traveling slowly along bumpy and rutted roads, they were doubtless relieved to see the city's walls stretching before them and soon after to reach their lodgings, the Belle Sauvage Inn on Ludgate Hill, chosen by the Company not for its name but for its proximity to one of the greatest churches in Christendom, St. Paul's Cathedral.[2]

As the Company hoped, news of the visitors spread rapidly throughout the city and caused a sensation. Although Indians had been seen in London before, Pocahontas's prestige as Wahunsonacock's daughter, together with the report of her marriage and conversion, were electrifying. "The most remarquable person," John Chamberlain commented, "is Pocahuntas (daughter to Powatan a Kinge or cacique of that Countrie) married to one Rolfe an Englishman." Whether fascinated by tales of an Indian princess, scandalized by the marriage of an Englishman to a "Virginian woman," or wanting to catch a glimpse of the strange company from the New World, Londoners were captivated by the Indians' arrival, and especially by Pocahontas, Lady Rebecca Rolfe.

With necessary introductions provided by Lord and Lady De La Warr and Sir Thomas Smythe, Lady Rebecca and her husband were ushered into the very highest social circles and were soon caught up in a whirl of "Plays, Balls, and other publick Entertainments." Through it all, the Reverend Purchas recalled some years later, Pocahontas "did not only accustome her selfe to civilitie, but still carried her selfe as the Daughter of a King, and was accordingly respected." The Lord Bishop of London, Purchas noted with satisfaction, afforded her "a festivall state and pompe" well beyond the usual hospitality shown to ladies.[3]

The highpoint of her stay came when the king and queen received her at the sumptuous Banqueting House shortly after Christmas for one of the highlights of the court calendar, the Twelfth Night revels. A masque, *The Vision of Delight,* written especially for the occasion by Ben Jonson, was an elaborate fabrication of song, dance, and fantasy, replete with dramatic scenic effects and illusions designed by Inigo Jones that enthralled the audience, including Pocahontas and Uttamatomakkin, who were seated prominently on the royal dais near the king. Attired in her new finery, surrounded by peers of the realm and foreign ambassadors, Pocahontas enjoyed an evening of wonderment she would never forget. Chamberlain and other cynics might have scoffed at "her tricking up with high styles and titles" when she and her husband had only a modest income, but she had won the affections of the greatest in the kingdom, including the queen, Anne of Denmark, who received her often and did her "many Honours."[4]

To publicize Pocahontas's presence in England and attract investors, the Company commissioned a young Dutch-German engraver, Simon Van de Passe, to sketch her portrait, which was then rushed into print.

The outcome was an intriguing image layered with contrasts and symbolic meanings. Her expensive clothes, the fine lace ruff, and the tall hat proclaimed her as a wealthy Englishwoman dressed in the latest fashion. Pearl earrings signified that she was from America, and more particularly from Virginia, and her fan of ostrich feathers denoted royalty. Well-dressed but not extravagantly, her attire was carefully arranged to suggest affluence without excess.

Most striking is the representation of Pocahontas herself. Van de Passe made no attempt to give her features a European cast. Instead, she has the high cheekbones and dark hair of her people. Although she was dressed as an Englishwoman, it was clear she was not English, exactly the message the Company wished to convey: It was possible to "civilize" the Indians and make them English. Less predictably, Pocahontas does not display a modest countenance, the dutiful appearance of a convert and wife, but proudly looks the viewer in the eye as if to say this is who I am, the daughter of a king. The inscription around and beneath her picture emphasized her status, "Matoaks als Rebecka daughter to the mighty Prince Powhatan Emperour of Attanoughsko-mouck als virginia," just as it confirmed that she had been "converted and baptized in the Christian faith and [was] wife to the worshipful Mr. John Rolff." Possibly, the message Pocahontas wished to convey was different from that of the Company. She had adopted English ways and converted to the English church, but had not abandoned her own culture. She remained a Powhatan, Matoaka, but was also English, Rebecca, and was both an Indian princess and an English wife.[5]

———

CAPTAIN JOHN SMITH might have been in Plymouth when the *Treasurer* docked, but if he was, he made no move to greet Pocahontas. Nor did he make any immediate effort to see her in London. Perhaps his involvement in plans for a voyage to New England explains his delay—he was traveling back and forth between Plymouth and the

*Simon Van de Passe, Matoaka als Rebecca, 1616.*

capital raising funds during much of her visit—or possibly the Virginia Company had discouraged him from approaching her. Whatever the reason, it would be many months before they met.

Smith was likely gratified by news of Pocahontas's success in London. Before she arrived in the city, he had sent Queen Anne a "little booke" that told how Pocahontas had helped save the colony and his life (the first reference to the ceremony at Werowocomoco) and described her many qualities, notably her conversion to Christianity.[6] Yet her arrival in England may have also stirred up mixed emotions in the captain. If things had worked out differently, might *he* have occupied Rolfe's position, feted by the Company and received by the king and queen? The years since his return to England had been deeply frustrating. Despite his eagerness to go back to Virginia, the Company refused to reemploy him. His *Map of Virginia, With a Description of the Country* and *Proceedings of the English Colonie in Virginia,* both published in 1612, which together provided the most detailed account of the colony, had failed to bring him any tangible mark of favor. Fairly or not, Sir Thomas Smythe and his associates held him partly to blame for the turmoil of Jamestown's first years, a consequence (they believed) of Smith's headstrong temperament.

Spurned by the Company, Smith had eventually managed to find employment in the spring of 1614 in charge of two small vessels chartered for a fishing trip to "North Virginia." Taking full advantage of the opportunity, he turned the venture into a voyage of exploration, carefully mapping the coastline and major rivers of the land he named "New England." Thereafter, he had thrown himself with all his old enthusiasm into promoting the establishment of a settlement in the north that he believed would prove more successful in the long run than the ailing colony on the Chesapeake Bay. As Smith busied himself to raise funds for a second voyage, he heard news of Pocahontas's arrival in England.[7]

In the fall, to be "out of the Smoak of the City," Pocahontas and Rolfe moved to lodgings in the village of Brentford, a few miles west of London. Here, in the company of some friends shortly before he was about to embark for New England, Smith arrived to pay his respects.

They had not seen each other for more than seven years, the last time being the night Pocahontas had run through the "irksome woods" to warn him of her father's intention to have him killed. Taken aback by seeing him again, she was initially unable to speak and only after a couple of hours alone was sufficiently composed to talk to him. A wrenchingly awkward exchange followed.

"They did tell us always you were dead," Pocahontas said, "and I knew no other till I came to Plimoth." He made no reply. He had not tried to contact her since he left Virginia, probably had not given it much thought considering that such a move would have been politically unwise and practically impossible. "You did promise Powhatan what was yours should bee his, and he the like to you," she continued forcefully, "you called him father being in his land a stranger, and by the same reason so must I doe you." At this Smith demurred, saying that he "durst not allow of that title, because she was a Kings daughter," but Pocahontas rebuked him: "Were you not afraid to come into my fathers Countrie, and caused feare in him and all his people (but [except] me) and feare you here I should call you father; I tell you then I will and you will call mee childe, and so I will bee for ever and ever your Countrieman."[8]

Smith was puzzled. Contact with Wahunsonacock had broken down completely during the spring of 1609. What, then, was the meaning of her reference to Smith's and her father's pledge to each other? Was it an echo of an agreement they had reached when the great chief released Smith from captivity, which Pocahontas thought was somehow still relevant? She assumed her relationship with Smith, which had evolved in the months following the ritual at Werowocomoco, had created a special bond that continued to unite them. For her, the intervening years—Smith's falling out with her father and departure from Virginia and her marriage to Rolfe—had not diminished that mutual commitment. But in all likelihood for him there never had been a commitment. He may have been fond of her, but that was as far as it went. What he had said and done in negotiations with her father, with Opechancanough, and even with her had been necessary expedients to stay alive or keep his men from starving. His words had been for the moment, for a specific purpose, not "for ever." It was fitting, therefore, that in her final remarks to him she mentioned that Uttamatomakkin had been sent to seek him and know the truth whether he was alive or dead, "because your Countriemen will lie much."[9]

Smith would not see her again. In March 1617, Pocahontas succumbed to an illness (possibly tuberculosis or pneumonia) at the start of the voyage back to Virginia and died shortly after at Gravesend where, as befitted the rank of a princess, she was buried in the chancel of the parish church of St. George. Her death was a grievous blow to the Company's hopes for the future. Pocahontas had represented the rarest of the rare. Having rejected "her barbarous condition," Smith wrote, she was the "first Christian of that Nation [Powhatans], the first Virginian [who] ever spake English," and the first to have "a childe in mariage by an Englishman." Years later, he commented only briefly that her visit to England had brought her "great satisfaction and content, which doubtlesse she would have deserved [requited], had she lived to arrive in Virginia."[10]

## The "deceaveable weede"

As much as Pocahontas, Uttamatomakkin, and other Powhatans had been a success in London, there was no corresponding upsurge of interest in Virginia. John Chamberlain spoke for many disgruntled investors when he commented that Dale's return brought news of a country that would be good to live in if it "were stored with people," but there was "no present profit to be expected." More than £50,000 had been invested in the venture since 1609, but at the end of the seven-year term placed on the joint stock there was little to show for it. With little immediate prospect of reaping any kind of return, the colony appeared about to fulfill the expectations of successive Spanish ambassadors and collapse from within.[11]

Chamberlain was wrong, however, to dismiss the "exceedinge good tobaco" Dale had brought back from Virginia, although he could be forgiven for his mistake. Introduced into England half a century before by mariners who had sailed to the Americas with John Hawkins and Francis Drake, tobacco became popular with fashionable gallants and the well-to-do during the 1580s and 1590s after smoking was taken up by prominent courtiers such as Sir Walter Ralegh. Depending on its quality and condition, leaf imported (legally or otherwise) from Spanish colonies might cost anywhere from £2 to £4 per pound.

Despite the expense, smoking spread rapidly from the gentry to the lower classes so that, by 1614, according to Barnaby Rich, there was not a groom so base who "commes into an Alehouse to call for his pot, but he must have his pipe of Tobacco." In London alone, he claimed, there were some 7,000 "newly erected houses" where annual sales of tobacco amounted to nearly £320,000, "All spent in smoake." In taverns and inns, during public hangings, floggings, and other spectacles, at "bull-baiting, bear-whipping, and everywhere else," the English were "constantly smoking the Nicotian weed."[12]

Among those who enjoyed a good pipe was John Rolfe. Already a confirmed smoker when he left for Virginia with the Gates fleet in 1609, not long after arriving on the James River he had the idea of raising tobacco on a commercial basis. In the summer of 1612, using seeds imported from Trinidad and Venezuela, he began experimenting with varieties of mild Spanish leaf *(Nicotiana tabacum),* anticipating that the crop would produce a leaf more suited to English tastes than the indigenous plant, *Nicotiana rustica,* smoked by Indians, which had an acrid flavor. The challenge was not only to raise a type of plant best suited to local conditions but also to determine how harvested leaf could be cured and transported to England without spoiling.

Whether he learnt the art and mystery of tobacco husbandry himself by trial and error or was taught by friendly Powhatans following his marriage to Pocahontas we don't know, but after a couple of years he met with success. "No country under the Sunne," Ralph Hamor observed "may, or doth affoord more pleasant, sweet, and strong Tobacco, then I have tasted." Hamor, like his friend Rolfe, was experimenting with his own crop and was confident that it could be cultivated by anybody who, "with the least part of his labour, tend and care will returne him both cloathes and other necessaries." Small quantities of Virginia leaf may have reached London as early as 1614, but the first substantial shipment was likely to have been in the *Treasurer* two years later. Besides acting as consort to his Powhatan bride in England, Rolfe was busily marketing his crop among merchants and tobacco sellers.[13]

No matter how popular tobacco had become in London by the time of Rolfe's visit, however, we can be sure he dared not smoke a pipe in the presence of James I. The king's vehement opposition to tobacco was well known at court and had been set out at length in his *A Counter-Blaste to Tobacco,* published in 1604, in which he attacked arguments in favor of smoking and derided claims about its medicinal qualities. He thought it deplorable that English men and women imitated "the barbarous and beastly manners of the wild, godless and slavish Indians, in so vile and stinking a custom," especially as Indian priests smoked specifically to invoke their devilish gods. Although the king welcomed revenues from tobacco duties, he was opposed to large-scale production of tobacco in Virginia.

The Company also discouraged tobacco planting on a large scale. Sir Thomas Smythe and Edwin Sandys remained committed to a mixed economy in which Virginia would supply many of the commodities currently imported into England from Europe and "divers parts of the world." Little room was afforded in this vision of the colony's future for the "smokie weed of Tobacco," which Sandys and other leaders feared would eventually fail the planters (demand being based on nothing more than a fad) and lead to the "over throw [of] the generall Plantacon." The Company's leaders in London turned their backs on the one commodity that could be produced cheaply in the colony for which there was a rapidly growing market in England.[14]

## A "Perfect Common-weale"

Shortly before setting out for England in the spring of 1616, John Rolfe, secretary of the colony, was instructed by Dale to draw up a survey of the colony. He divided Virginia into three types of men: officers, laborers, and farmers. Officers were responsible for ensuring that defenses were adequate in the settlements and that those under their charge attended to their work diligently and obeyed the martial laws. Laborers were of two kinds: Either they were employed in general work for the Company and were supported from the general store or they were skilled artisans (blacksmiths, carpenters, shoemakers, tailors, and tanners) who maintained themselves. The farmers, Rolfe thought, "live[d] at most ease." They were obliged to defend the colony "against all forraigne and domestick enemyes," and to work for the Company one month of the year; the rest of the time they were free to grow their own crops on condition each man supported himself and his family and delivered two and a half barrels of corn to the general store annually.

Six settlements were listed: (1) At Henrico, on the north side of the James River, were thirty-eight men and boys, made up of twenty-two farmers and the rest officers, together with a few laborers. (2) The most heavily populated settlement was Bermuda Nether Hundred, on the south bank five miles as the crow flies downriver from Henrico, where 119 settlers, men and women, lived (including Alexander Whitaker, who resided in the city before drowning in the spring of 1617). Incorporated as Bermuda town or "Citty," under the authority of Captain George Yeardley, deputy governor in the absence of Dale, most of the settlers were laborers who had contracted to work "for a certeyne time" (three years) producing pitch, tar, potashes, and charcoal. (3) At West and Sherley Hundred, located a few miles below Bermuda Hundred, twenty-five men were employed in cultivating tobacco. (4) On Jamestown Island, thirty-two farmers tended their crops and looked after the Company's livestock.

Jamestown had been the principal residence of Sir Thomas Gates, who fashioned the fort into "a hansome forme," including "two faire rowes of howses, all of framed Timber, two stories high, and an upper Garret, or Corne loft high, besides three large, and substantial Storehouses, joyned together . . . lately newly, and strongly impaled." (5) Near the entrance to the James River, the settlement at Kecoughtan on the Hampton River had twenty men, half of whom were farmers. (6) Finally, across the Chesapeake Bay, near Cape Charles on the Eastern Shore, was Dale's Gift, where seventeen men produced salt and fished.[15]

The colony bore the unmistakable stamp of Dale's reforms in shifting the bulk of the population upriver, described as "exceeding healthfull" (where at least 70 percent of the settlers now resided), and in the trend toward specialization of production at different settlements: corn and wheat at Henrico and Kecoughtan, cattle and swine at Jamestown, industrial commodities at Bermuda Hundred, tobacco at West and Sherley Hundred, and salted fish at Dale's Gift.

Rolfe's survey confirmed the cost of colonization in terms of English lives. From 1609 to 1616 approximately 1,500 settlers had been sent from England, but Rolfe could enumerate only 205 officers and laborers, 81 farmers, and 65 women and children, making a total of 351 for the entire colony, "a smale number," he commented, "to advaunce so great a *Worke*." The greatest need of the colony, he continued, was:

> good and sufficient men, as well of birth and quallyty to command: souldiers to march, discover and defend the Country from Invasions: as [also] artificers, Labourers and husbondmen: with whom were the *Collony* well provided; then might triall be made, what lieth hidden in the womb of the Land: the Land might yerely abound with corne and other provisions for mans sustenaunce: buildings, fortifications and shipping might be reared, wrought and framed: commodyties of divers kindes might be reaped yerely, and sought after: and many thinges . . . might come with ease to establishe a firme and perfect Common-weale.[16]

Sir Edwin Sandys could not have agreed more. The Company's precarious financial condition could no longer be tolerated. Sandys, taking a more active role in Company affairs, began developing plans to reinvigorate the colony with the support of Sir Thomas Smythe and other influential members. He continued to promote the production of a wide range of commodities in Virginia, the collection of monies pledged by investors, and public lotteries in English towns and cities to provide an income at home. But ultimately the key to the colony's prosperity, Sandys recognized, was land. Peace with the Powhatans provided an ideal opportunity to offer generous land grants to adventurers and allowed Sandys in effect, to subcontract the financing of further settlements to private investors following a precedent set in Bermuda (governed by many of the same leaders as the Virginia venture), which had proved so successful that the island colony had attracted more than 600 settlers by 1615. Together with the potential of considerable profits from Virginia's products, the guarantee of land ownership would attract sufficient investment (Sandys hoped) to transport the thousands of men and women necessary to unlock the riches of the land.[17]

Captain Samuel Argall was one of the first beneficiaries of the Company's new policy. Appointed deputy governor in the winter of 1616–1617, he and his financial backers were assigned 2,400 acres for the transportation of twenty-four settlers whom he intended to locate in an area just to the west of Jamestown at "Paspaheigh, alias Argall's towne."[18] Three other private settlements were established also: the largest of which, Smyth's Hundred (named for Sir Thomas), would eventually comprise between 80,000 and 100,000 acres on paper along the north bank of the James River from the Chickahominy to the lands of the Weyanocks about ten miles upriver. The plantation was operated as a private joint stock venture of which Smythe, Sandys, and the Earl of Southampton were among the leading investors. Altogether, about 150 to 160 settlers arrived in Virginia in 1617, including Hamor, Rolfe, and men "of good qualitie" with their families, laborers, and servants, representing the first major infusion of colonists for six years.[19]

Before Argall was able to turn his attention to the allotment of lands as instructed by the Company, however, he first had to address more urgent issues. When he arrived in mid-May, he found Jamestown's palisade and church fallen down, the wharf in pieces, and only five or six houses habitable. Elsewhere in the colony, houses lay in ruins, palisades and blockhouses had collapsed, and few of the fortifications were serviceable. Despite "a great mortality" that affected colonists and Indians alike during the summer, probably caused by diseases brought from London with new arrivals, Argall pressed ahead with repairs to Jamestown, which he preferred to locations upriver.

The deputy governor took comfort from distinct signs that the economy was improving. The settlers were well provisioned. Wheat, barley, corn, and tobacco thrived, and having distributed hemp and flax seed, Argall thought they would do well, too. Best of all, the colony was able to ship 20,000 lbs. of tobacco to London in 1618, which sold for 5s. 3d. per pound, realizing £5,250 for its investors: hardly a princely sum, but far more than the colony had managed to return before.[20] Reforms undertaken by Dale several years earlier to increase the production of foodstuffs were beginning to pay off. "When our people were fedde out of the common store and laboured jointly in the manuring of the ground, and planting corne," Ralph Hamor explained, "glad was that man that could slippe from his labour, nay the most honest of them in a generall businese, would take so much faithfull and true paines, in a weeke, as now he will doe in a day." Dale's introduction of small farms of a few acres each that allowed tenants to grow their own crops and raise livestock led to an impressive increase in food production. The problem of recurrent food shortages was solved by loosening Company control of land and by giving at least some settlers a chance to work on their own behalf.[21]

Argall arrived in the colony at an opportune moment. The country was at peace, settlers were producing enough food for their own needs, and the Company was poised to distribute large amounts of land to colonists and investors that would create growing numbers of independent planters and companies. At Jamestown, the deputy governor found "the market place, and streets, and all other spare places planted with Tobacco." Despite the Company's disapproval, tobacco cultivation had spread rapidly throughout the colony between 1615 and 1617 as increasing numbers of settlers discovered they could not only grow foodstuffs on their farms but also produce a potentially lucrative cash crop. Virginia was on the threshold of a tobacco revolution that within the space of a few years would transform the lives of everyone who lived along the James River, English and Powhatan alike.

IMPORTANT CHANGES in the way that the colony was to be governed were also introduced in these years. To "reduce the people and affaires in *Virginia* into a regular course," the colony was divided in 1618 into four cities or boroughs, named "Kiccowtan" (later Elizabeth City), James City, Charles City, and Henrico, each of which had 3,000 acres set aside for the Company's use and another 1,500 to support local administration. The Company laid out also 3,000 acres to support the governor, known as the governor's land, near Jamestown, and 10,000 acres a couple of miles from Henrico for a university and college, intended for the education of Indian youth in English religion and ways. Sandys estimated that every hundred laborers working on public lands would generate at least £1,000 annually and that there would be at least five hundred men working on Company lands within a couple of years. As their numbers increased, so would Company profits, allowing the Company to pay off its debts and begin returning regular dividends to investors, thereby attracting further investment.[22]

By the terms of "the greate Charter" of 1618, settlers who had arrived before Dale's departure two years earlier ("ancient planters") were granted 100 acres for their own adventure, and if they were investors, an additional 100 for every share. Those who arrived after April 1616 and paid their own passage would receive 50 acres for themselves and another 50 for every person they transported. The arrangement, known as the headright system, became the primary means by which laborers were recruited and sent to the colony for the rest of the century.

Concerned that the colony's severe martial code would discourage private investment and immigration, the Company instructed the governor elect, George Yeardley, in late 1618 to introduce "just Laws for the happy guiding and governing of the people." Two new councils were created: a council of state, whose members were selected by the Company in London, to assist the governor in his duties and a "generall Assemblie" that included the council and two "Burgesses" from every town, hundred, and particular plantation, "Chosen by the [free] inhabitants." The General Assembly was to be convened once a year, unless extraordinary occasions demanded more frequent meetings, and was authorized to consider all matters concerning the public "weale" of the colony and to propose such general measures for the better ordering of their affairs in conformity (or as near as may be) with laws and customs in England.

Although burgesses quickly adopted elements of parliamentary practice in developing their own procedures, the Assembly was not intended to be "a little parliament" but rather a form of local government that mirrored the weekly "Court and Assembly" and quarterly General Courts held in London, at which shareholders were able to play an active role in the administration of the Company. The thrust of Sandys' reforms was to bring symmetry to the Company's governing structure in London and Jamestown, improve the management of the colony, and thereby stimulate investment and profits. Neither he nor any other leaders of the Company wished to weaken their control over the colony or to promote greater autonomy in Virginia.

The governor retained a right of veto, and legislation passed by the Assembly could be enforced only if the Company approved. Sandys understood that if the colony was to prosper the Company had to pay attention to the demands of settlers who had adventured themselves and their purses, following the maxim that "every man will more willingly obey lawes to which he hath yielded his consent." The "libertie of a Generall Assembly being graunted them," planters would henceforth be able to participate in government through their representatives and "execute those thinges, as might best tend to their good." From the standpoint of increasingly ill-tempered relations between the Parliament at Westminster and James I, and suspicions among some parliamentarians that the king would prefer to rule without parliaments, it was a principle that Sandys may well have wished was applied in England.[23]

An impression of the scope of the burgesses' deliberations can be gained from an account of the first meeting of the General Assembly convened on July 30, 1619, in the presence of the governor and council of state. Twenty-two burgesses representing the corporations and private plantations gathered in the "Quire [choir] of the Churche" at Jamestown, and after being led in prayer by the Reverend Richard

Bucke and taking the oath of allegiance to James I, settled down to business.

They debated their own procedures and membership, considered complaints brought against settlers and requests for redress of grievances, debated recommendations for relations with the Powhatans to maintain the peace and promote "the Conversion of the Indians to Christian Religion," ordered all settlers to attend church in the morning and afternoon of the Sabbath, proposed to change the "savage name" of the corporation of Kecoughtan, set the price of tobacco and encouraged the cultivation of corn, hemp, flax, vines, and mulberry trees, regulated against idleness, gaming, drunkenness, and excess of apparel, and drew up several humble petitions addressed to the Company suggesting revisions to the charter and legislation sent by the Company, "not to the ende to correcte or controll anything therein contained, but onely in case we should finde ought not perfectly squaring with the state of this Colony." Dispersing after five days, in the sickly heat of early August, the burgesses must have been well pleased with the promising start to a new era in which they, representatives of the settlers' interests, would henceforth exert a growing influence on the running of the colony's affairs.[24]

## The Great Migration

Heartened by signs of improvement, Sandys had redoubled efforts to increase investment and recruit settlers. In the winter of 1617, he opened discussions with Pilgrim separatists, Robert Cushman and Deacon John Carver, who had been sent to London from Leiden in the Netherlands to negotiate with the Company about moving to Virginia. Led by John Robinson and William Brewster, the Pilgrims had lived in the Netherlands for a decade "as men in exile, & in a poore condition." With the twelve-year truce between the Dutch and Spanish (1609–1621) drawing to a close and the future uncertain, they had begun considering the possibility of moving to America, where they could establish their own community free from the corruption of Old World society. A heated debate followed about where they should move. Some advocated going to Guiana ("fertill places in those hott climates . . . blessed with a perpetuall spring"); others favored Virginia, where the English "had all ready made entrance, & beginning." Others still preferred New England, where fishing might provide a reliable income as well as sustenance.

Sandys played a crucial role in convincing the Pilgrims to move to Virginia. Yet, as it was to turn out, his efforts were in vain; the Pilgrims never reached the colony. Crowded aboard the *Mayflower,* they left England in mid-September 1620, ostensibly with the intention of settling at the mouth of the Hudson River at the northern extreme of Virginia. But whether they were blown far off course during a long and difficult voyage or shortly before leaving England had changed their minds and had decided to settle in New England, they ended up off the coast of Cape Cod in December and landed at Plymouth harbor, where they remained.[25]

Nevertheless, Sandys's instincts were correct in assuming that Virginia might be viewed as an attractive haven by religious dissenters. Hundreds of nonconformists embarked for the colony between 1618 and 1621 in what was the first puritan migration to America. Christopher Lawne, from Blandford, Dorset, was born about 1580; as a young man, he moved to Norwich, where he followed the trade of a buttonmaker. In or before 1610, he moved to Amsterdam and became prominent in the internal feuds that fractured the Separatist congregation (the "Ancient Church") in the city. After the breakup of the Ancient Church a few years later, he returned to England before immigrating to Virginia. He established a plantation at Warrascoyack, named Lawnes Creek, a few miles downstream from Jamestown, which became a center for puritan settlement.

Well known to Lawne was Francis Blackwell, an elder of the Ancient Church, who had also been involved in the controversies that wracked the puritans in Amsterdam. He was in London with his congregation in the summer of 1618 making preparations to leave for Virginia when he and many of his followers were arrested by Anglican authorities at a private meeting. According to the Pilgrim William Bradford, Blackwell "flatly denied the truth" of his heterodox religious convictions and "so won the Bishops' favor (but lost the Lord's)" that not only was he freed "but in open court the Archbishop [of Canterbury] gave him great applause and his solemn blessing to proceed on the voyage." Blackwell apparently justified his actions by claiming that it was important he was released so that he could continue with his preparations; after all, more and more people were going to the colony and it was known that many Separatists besides his congregation had decided to move there. A contemporary remarked in August: "[S]ome 100 or verie neere of Brownists shipped to Virginia, and shortlie there wilbe twice as many puritanes, god speede them well." Blackwell, however, would not live to see the James River. He and most of those who went with him perished in one of the most terrible crossings of the century.[26]

Besides appealing to puritans, Sandys launched a broad campaign based on recruiting colonists from all over the country, including husbandmen, skilled artisans, and tradesmen as well as destitute children on parish relief and convicted felons. In 1618, six ships embarked for the colony carrying about 400 settlers; the following year fourteen left with 1,000 settlers; and in 1620, thirteen ships carried more than 1,300. Between 1618 and 1621, fifty ships transported some 3,750 settlers to Virginia. Those "lately sent," a Company pamphlet declared, were for the most part "choise men, borne and bred up to labour and industry": for example, from Devon, about 100 men "brought up to Husbandry," out of Warwickshire and Staffordshire 110, and out of Sussex 40 "all framed to Iron-workes."

On board the *Bona Nova,* which docked at Jamestown in November 1619, were approximately 120 settlers, about 100 of whom were "tenants" (all men) sent to work on Company lands; they would serve seven years, during which they would be allowed to keep half their crop or earnings. They included husbandmen, cloth and leather workers, blacksmiths, carpenters, cooks, bakers, grocers, laborers, a couple of goldsmiths, and eight gentlemen. During 1619 and early 1620, they were joined by the recently knighted Sir George Yeardley (sent out to replace Argall), another 280 tenants for "publicke use," 90 "young maids to make wives" for planters, some 150 vagrant children sent from Bridewell Royal Hospital, London, 45 settlers brought from the Vale of Severn, Gloucestershire, to set up a plantation at Berkeley Hundred about twenty-five miles upriver from Jamestown, and a group of African captives from Angola (West Central Africa).[27]

The latter arrived in Virginia by a circuitous route. Victims of Portuguese campaigns in Angola during 1618–1619, the majority of captives were most likely Kimbundu-speaking peoples from the kingdom of Ndongo, specifically from a heavily populated region between the Lukala and Lutete Rivers that included the royal capital, Kabasa. Many would have come from urban backgrounds and may well have been introduced to at least the rudiments of Christianity because Portuguese law required all slaves to be baptized Catholics before arriving in America.

Following a trek of some 200 miles to the port of Luanda, approximately 350 slaves ended up on board the *São João Bautista,* bound for Vera Cruz, in the summer of 1619. En route, the ship was attacked in the Gulf of Campeche, off the coast of Mexico, by two privateers and robbed of some of their human cargo. The privateers, a Dutch man-of-war, the *White Lion,* and the Earl of Warwick's *Treasurer,* commanded by Daniel Elfrith, sailed to the West Indies and then on to Virginia. Some of the Angolans were traded there, including a Christian woman named "Angelo," purchased by Lieutenant William Pierce, who lived in Jamestown. Capture on the high seas and sale in Virginia resulted in lives spent laboring at the hoe on tobacco plantations rather than in the port towns, silver mines, or cane fields of Spanish America; but for most, a change of masters did not allow them to escape the fate of slavery.[28]

Africans were not the only people forcibly transported to the colony. In the fall of 1618, John Chamberlain reported that the City of London was shipping to Virginia "an hundred younge boyes and girles that [had] bin starving in the streetes which is one of the best deeds that could be don[e]." Through their numerous contacts in the capital, Sir Thomas Smythe and Sandys persuaded "divers well and godly disposed p[er]sons Charitably minded towards the Plantacon of Virginia" to contribute £500 for the transportation of destitute children supported by London parishes. The arrangement would rid the City of the children, give the Company a supply of young laborers, and rescue the children from the streets so that they could be "brought upp in some good Craftes, Trades, or Husbandry" in the colony.

Seemingly an ideal arrangement, the Company entered into a similar understanding the following year with the blessing of the Privy Council, which recorded its thanks to the City and Company "for redeeming so many poore soules from mysery and ruyne [ruin] and puttinge them in a Condicon of useful Service to the State." Many of the children did not want to go, however; in response, the Privy Council authorized the City and Company to transport the children "against their wills" if necessary and recommended that they be shipped to the colony as quickly as possible. Hundreds of destitute children were transported between 1617 and 1623, having little choice in the matter.[29]

——·—·——

RECOGNIZABLY ENGLISH, Virginia was nonetheless a peculiar variant of the parent society. In early 1620, men outnumbered women by about seven to one, and few young children or graybeards lived along the James River (the great majority of settlers were between fifteen and thirty-five years old). Alongside the English were to be found small numbers of skilled foreign artisans—French, Germans, Poles, and Italians—and thirty-two Africans (fifteen men and seventeen women) who were either enslaved or worked as servants.

Approximately 1,200 settlers occupied lands from the mouth of the James River to Falling Creek, a few miles south of the old fort abandoned by De La Warr during the war. Whereas John Rolfe had itemized only six settlements four years earlier, now there were more than two dozen. Tens of thousands of acres had been granted by the Company in the area between Jamestown and Henrico in what amounted to the colony's first land rush, much of the expansion led by private investors transporting settlers to particular plantations. At Smyth's Hundred were 105 settlers, made up of 75 men, 8 women, and 22 "younge persons"; at Flowerdieu, owned by Governor Yeardley, were 77 settlers (68 men, 5 women, and 4 children), including perhaps a dozen or more Angolans. Christopher Lawne's plantation had 110 settlers, and at Martin's Hundred, a 20,000-acre tract with its center at Wolstenholme Town, lived 72. Jamestown and its environs had grown rapidly, but the most populous areas remained upriver between the Chickahominy and Henrico, where about two-thirds of the settlers resided.

Under the impact of surging immigration, the colony had changed dramatically from the struggling outpost of a few years before. Many settlers lived in small clusters of houses within a palisaded settlement or near to a fortification, such as at Jamestown or at Flowerdieu and Wolstenholme. Others, such as the "ancient planters" who had gained their freedom after 1616, resided on their own individual smallholdings scattered along the rivers and creeks in embryonic neighborhoods, such as the eastern end of Jamestown Island or upriver on "Neck of Land" (Bermuda Hundred).[30]

Reforms introduced by Sandys had given "such incouragement to every person here," settlers later recalled, "that all of them followed their perticular labors with singular alacrity and industry, soe that through the blessinge of God . . . within the space of three yeares, our countrye flowrished with many new erected Plantations from the head of the River to Kicoughtan." It was a time of prosperity and plenty; the colony was well supplied with wheat, corn, livestock, fish, and "good provisions," and every man able to give "free entertainement both to frends and others."

During the same period, tobacco's grip on the colony tightened. "All our riches for the present," John Pory commented "doe consiste in Tobacco," so that once the "veriest beggers in the worlde," now "our Cowe-keeper here of James citty on Sundayes goes acowterd [dressed] all in freshe flaming silkes and a wife of one that in England had professed the black arte not of a scholler but of a collier of Croydon, weares her rough bever hatt w[i]th a faire perle hattband, and a silken suite." Between 40,000 and 50,000 lbs. of tobacco were exported to England in 1620; two years later, the figure had risen to 60,000. Virginia had at last found a profitable commodity, but not one that Sandys and other Company leaders had hoped for.[31]

Yet, if some settlers were getting rich quickly, most were not. Mismanagement and price gouging by colony officials and buoyant tobacco prices in England created conditions for the gross exploitation of servants, who made up the bulk of the population. "Our principall wealth (I should have said) consisteth in servants," Pory corrected himself. "[O]ne man by his owne labour hath in one yeare, raised to himselfe to the value of £200 sterling . . . another by the meanes of six servants hath cleared at one crop a thousand pound English."

The more servants a settler had the more money could be made, and profits could be substantial. Tobacco had produced estates of hundreds and even thousands of pounds per year for men who had gone to Virginia "not worth so many pence." Sir George Yeardley, who first arrived in the colony with little more than his sword, Pory recounted, when recently in London was "out of his meer gettings here, able to disburse very near three thousand pounds." No wonder the governor and his deputies, the treasurer of the colony, the marshal, and the secretary demanded that the Company send them servants, ostensibly to support the cost of their offices but in reality to provide handsome incomes. And little wonder the colony's officials soon realized that trading servants was as lucrative as selling any other goods imported from England. Most of the one hundred Company tenants who arrived on the *Bona Nova,* for example, were rented out for a year to "honest and sufficient men" instead of being put to work on Company lands as tenants "by halves" (sharecroppers) as originally intended, leading John Rolfe to remark that the practice of "buying and selling [of] men and boies" had given the colony an ugly reputation in England.[32]

As about 95 percent of those arriving during this period were tenants and servants, the experience of Richard Frethorne, a servant at Martin's Hundred, may have been more typical than that of the cow keeper of Jamestown. "I am in a most miserable and pitiful Case [state], for want of meat and want of cloathes," he wrote, "since I came out of the ship [three months before], I never at[e] anie thing but pease, and loblollie (that is water gruell)." If "you love or respect me, as yo[u]r Child release me from this bondage, and save my life," he begged his mother and father. A planter named John Jackson, sympathetic towards him, "much marvailed" his parents had sent him as a servant, saying he would have "beene better knocked on the head." The boy's parents were unable to rescue him and he died a few months after sending his last letter home.[33]

Inadequate provisions and squalid shipboard conditions so weakened passengers that mortality among servants after their arrival reached epidemic proportions, the major killers being scurvy and the bloody flux. A story circulating in Plymouth in the spring of 1620 reported that 900 men had died in the previous twelve months "and that the people [were] used w[i]th more slavery than if they were under the Turke." The Company sought to suppress the rumor, although they acknowledged that 300 had died.

Sandys was right in his assessment that to make the Company profitable the colony required a significant increase in laborers. He had not, however, accounted for the over-packing of the ships, the insufficiency and poor quality of supplies sent with servants, the lack of accommodation that forced new arrivals to live "in the woods" until dwellings were built, and the hard usage many suffered at the hands of planters. In the three years between April 1619 and March 1622, Alderman Robert Johnson (one of Sandys rivals), calculated that 3,000 people had died for "want of houses, pestring [pestilent] ships, shortness & badness of food."

Migrants who were fed stories in England of "all the Deere, Fish & Fowle" they could eat in Virginia, found only "Oatemeale and Pease and bread & water" in sickness and health. Those "lying Virginians" who put about false stories of the colony as a land of milk and honey, Thomas Nicolls complained to Sir John Wolstenholme (the major investor in Martin's Hundred), were the "chiefe causers of their [the servants'] deathes," who went to their graves "cursing them most bitterly who sent them out." Three-quarters of the servants transported died within a year, most within the first six months, to "the utter destruction of some particular *Plantations.*" As the Company's tallies of men and women sent to Virginia recorded in their court books turned into ever-longer lists of dead, Sandys' plans to reinvigorate the Company's fortunes withered on the vine.[34]

# 9

## "FATALL POSSESSION"

By "THE NATIVES LIKING AND CONSENT," a Company pamphlet confidently declared in 1616, the English were "in actuall possession of a great part of the Countrey"; a happy state of affairs confirmed by John Rolfe, who, on his return to Jamestown the following year, found the colony enjoying peace and plenty. The end of war seemed not only to usher in a new era of cooperation between the settlers and Indians but also to open the way for the rapid expansion of English settlement across the region during the next four years. Fueled by the tobacco revolution, by early 1622, thousands of acres of prime agricultural land had been taken up by settlers along both sides of the James River from Elizabeth City to the falls.[1]

The initial years of peace coincided with dramatic changes in the leadership of the Powhatans. Rumors reached the colonists before Dale left for England in 1616 that Wahunsonacock had fled his capital at Orapaks for "feare of Opochancanough [sic]." Wahunsonacock believed that Opechancanough was conspiring to oust him as paramount chief, possibly with the aid of the English. Whatever lay behind the power struggle between the two men, the following year

Wahunsonacock delegated the government of his territories to his two brothers, Opechancanough and Opitchapam. The latter, described as "decrepit and lame" by the English, nominally succeeded Wahunsonacock when he died in 1618, but effective power resided with Opechancanough.[2]

The Pamunkey chief's growing influence among his people and the English brought about an immediate improvement in relations. Wahunsonacock had been distant in his dealings with Dale, only grudgingly tolerating the presence of settlers in his lands, whereas Opechancanough openly courted English leaders. He supported the English in a violent clash with the Chickahominies in 1616 when they refused to pay tribute to the settlers as specified in the peace treaty. And he readily accepted an invitation to visit Jamestown (something Wahunsonacock had never done) to meet Argall, during which he received a gift from the Company with "great joy." Having Opechancanough as their ally, Virginia's leaders at last saw the possibility of English settlers and Powhatans living together in friendship as "one people."[3]

## The "saving of their soules"

Much as Rolfe and Dale had hoped, Pocahontas's adoption of Christianity revitalized interest in England in the godly mission of converting the Indians. Early in 1616, James I instructed the archbishops of Canterbury and York to organize charitable collections in their provinces for the establishment of churches and schools in Virginia "for the education of the children of those Barbarians." Over the next four years, the Company received a steady flow of funds for religious uses that by 1620 amounted to more than £3,000. This "most Christian, hono[ra]ble, and glorious" work, John Ferrar, deputy treasurer of the Company, declared, was of the "highest consequence unto the Plantacons . . . whereof both Church and comonwealth take their originall foundacon and happie estate."

Company and colony leaders placed their hopes in teaching Powhatan youth the "true Religion" as well as "moral virtue and Civility." The children, in turn, would be the means of converting the general population. Each "towne, citty, Burrough, and particular plantation" in the colony, the General Assembly required in 1619, was to take "a certine number" of the natives' children to be educated. The most promising boys would be "fitted for the Colledge intended for them that from thence they may be sente to that worke of conversion."

Governor Yeardley cautioned the Company, however, about unrealistic expectations of quick results. Indian parents remained reluctant to part with their children on any terms. He had reached a compromise, therefore, with Opechancanough whereby the English would build houses and set aside grounds for planting corn in their settlements so that families identified by the chief could live among them. Settlers would have an opportunity to catechize the children without having to take them from their parents, and with incentives (clothes, cattle, "and such other nessisaryes") the adults might be tempted to remain with the English and to "draw in others who shall see them live so happily."[4]

Yeardley's arrangement with Opechancanough may have been encouraged by a high-ranking (and high-minded) gentleman, George Thorpe, of Berkeley, Gloucestershire, who arrived in the colony in the spring of 1620. Formerly a member of Parliament and gentleman of the king's privy chamber, Thorpe was a major investor in Berkeley Hundred and well known to Sandys and the Virginia Company. Someone who commanded respect, besides managing the affairs of Berkeley Hundred, Thorpe was immediately put in charge of the College Lands as one of the governor's deputies and was added to the colony's council of state. He was an ideal recruit for the Company. Committed to developing a mixed economy, he made strenuous efforts to plant vines, promote silk production, and breathe new life into the colony's ailing iron works projects. Yeardley described him as a "virtuous and wyse" leader, "one upon whose shoulders the frame of this godly building the government of this whole Collony would most fittly sitt," and recommended him as the next governor.

A deeply religious man, Thorpe was convinced that lack of progress in converting the Powhatans was primarily the fault of the English. He wrote to Sandys in May 1621 and told him that few settlers could spare the Indians a good thought and most believed they had "done unto us all the wronge and injurie that the malice of the Devill or man [could] afoord." We were "not soe charitable to them as Christians ought to bee," he observed, "they beinge (espetiallye the better sort of them) of a peaceable & vertuous disposition." Yet if the Company were willing to provide gifts ("apparell & househouldestufe") to show their "love and hartie affection," the Indians would be more likely in time to respond to conversion. As they began "more and more to affect English ffassions [sic]," the Company would enjoy greater success if they first introduced the Powhatans to "the booke of the worlde as beinge nearest to theire sence." The way to bring about the Indians' redemption and win them over to English ways, in other words, lay in improving their material lives.[5]

The Company followed Thorpe's advice closely and wrote his proposals into instructions issued in July to the new governor, Sir Francis Wyatt (then still in England). Wyatt came from a distinguished Kentish family with deep roots in the county. His interest in Virginia, social prominence, and family connections to Sandys made him an ideal replacement for Yeardley. The Company requested that Wyatt take special care to see that "no injurie or oppression" be perpetrated by the English against the Indians "wherby the present peace [might] bee disturbed and ancient quarrells (now buried) might bee revived." He was instructed also to draw the "better disposed" of the Powhatans into a closer relationship with the English and to reward them accordingly. These converts would be a "great strength" to the English as allies against "the Savages [non-Christian Indians] or other Invaders whatsoever" and as missionaries for the "more gennerall Conversion of the Heathen people." Finally, earlier legislation enjoining corporations, cities, and particular plantations "to obtaine to themselves by Just meanes a Certaine number" of Indian children for religious instruction was repeated.[6]

---

THE COMPANY AND THORPE were deceived, however. Opechancanough sought friendship and reconciliation with the English for his own reasons, but he concealed them skillfully. Although appearing well disposed toward the settlers, in reality his view of the postwar period was radically different from theirs. The English had treated the Powhatans like a subjugated nation, enforcing payment of tribute in corn and reducing them to dependence on settlers' provisions in those areas where Indians had been removed from their traditional lands. The Chickahominies, Paspaheghs, and Weyanocks had all been forced off lands adjoining the growing numbers of English settlements along the James River. In the vicinity of Charles City and Henrico, the English occupied lands belonging to the Appomattocs, Arrohattocs, and Powhatans. Settlers at Elizabeth City had taken possession of the corn-rich lands of the Kecoughtan people, and colonists on the south bank of the James had begun moving into lands belonging to the Quiyoughcohannocks and Warraskoyacks. Only the Nansemonds remained relatively unscathed by the settlers' expansion.[7]

Opechancanough's experience of tactics employed by Gates and Dale during the war left him in little doubt that his warriors could not prevail against ranks of heavily armored soldiers in the field or well-armed defenders protected by palisades. Neither could the Indians defend their villages and corn lands from destructive raids by English soldiers, who were able to move up and down the rivers with impunity in their ships. He realized, perhaps as early as the summer of 1614 when he made "the bargaine" with Dale that sealed the peace, that his people could not defeat the English from without. The Indians had to discover a way of getting inside English settlements, of gaining the settlers' trust; only then could they strike to good effect, that is, before the English had time to defend themselves.

The Pamunkey chief knew he would have to wait patiently until an opportunity arose when the colonists would least expect an attack. Professions of friendship such as those extended to Dale and subsequent governors would work only if backed by actions or, sometimes, inaction. No matter what the provocation, it was vital to the success of his plan that his people appear compliant and docile. Hence, when news reached Governor Yeardley in the summer of 1621 that Opechancanough intended to use a ceremony for "the taking upp of Powhatans

[Wahunsonacock's] bones" to assemble a large force of warriors and attack English settlements, the chief "earnestly" denied the plot. Even when one of the Powhatan's greatest warriors, Nemattanew, was shot and killed by a settler in early March 1622—a bitter blow that caused Opechancanough much grief—he nevertheless sent word that the warrior's death, "beinge but one man[,] should be noe occasione of the breach of the peace, and . . . *the Skye should sooner falle then Peace be broken*" [my italics]. As further assurance of his good intentions, Opechancanough gave permission to settlers to take up land anywhere they wished along "his Rivers," except where the Indians were already seated, and entered into agreements "for reciprocall defence, mutuall transportation, [and] discovery of mines."

A measure of the success of Opechancanough's strategy can be gauged by the assurance of Governor Wyatt to the Company in January 1622 that the country was "in very great amytie and confidence w[i]th the natives." He had sent presents to Opechancanough and Opitchapam to confirm "the League" of peace (Thorpe was the messenger) between the English and Indians. Shortly after came the breakthrough the English had been waiting for: In conversations with Thorpe, Opechancanough admitted that his peoples' religion "was nott the right waye," and asked to "bee instructed" in the Christian religion because "god loved [the English] better than them."

Far more significant than Pocahontas' conversion, if Opechancanough could be persuaded to accept Christianity, and ultimately English ways of life, he would have enormous sway in winning over the Powhatans generally. Instead of the gradual conversion of individuals or families here and there, Opechancanough's apparent desire to be instructed in the Christian faith raised the prospect of converting the peoples of the entire paramount chiefdom.

So convinced were Thorpe, Wyatt, and other leaders of Opechancanough's sincerity that they entirely disregarded news that might have saved them from the disaster that was soon to befall them. Some months earlier, possibly back in the fall of 1621, Opechancanough had changed his name to Mangopeesomon; his brother, Opitchapam, took the name Sasawpen, a certain danger signal (had the English been able to read it) that the Indians were preparing an attack. Out of the misery of war and subjugation, Opechancanough forged an alliance among his peoples throughout the James and York River valleys, united by their hatred of English settlers and their determination to be rid of them.[8]

## World's End

Shortly after dawn on a crisp March morning, groups of Indians gathered in woods adjacent to English settlements before setting off to the colonists' houses carrying deer, turkeys, fish, furs, and other trade goods. There was nothing unusual about such visits, for the last couple of years they had been encouraged to frequent (and sometimes to live in) English plantations, borrow tools and provisions, and even use settlers' boats. They would have been familiar to the settlers, who knew many of them individually by name. But on this morning, the Indians had come neither to trade nor to borrow.

Taking up the settlers' own tools and weapons, a slaughter of unimaginable proportions began at first light and carried on throughout the day. Finding "our people at their [breakfast] tables," Edward Waterhouse, a Company shareholder wrote, the Indians "basely and barbarously murthered" them, "not sparing eyther age or sexe, man, woman, or childe." Many settlers were taken so completely by surprise they did not even witness the "blow that brought them to destruction." They were killed in their houses, in their yards and gardens, in the fields as they planted corn and tobacco, or as they were running errands around the plantation. Because of their familiarity with the English and their settlements, Indian warriors had a good idea where the colonists would be at the time they launched the assault and how to make the attack as deadly as possible. By this means, Waterhouse continued, on "that fatall Friday morning," March 22, 1622, "contrary to all lawes of God and men, of Nature & Nations," 347 settlers were bludgeoned, stabbed, or hacked to death.

Coordinated and organized by Opechancanough, the main force was made up of approximately 500 to 600 elite Powhatan and Pamunkey

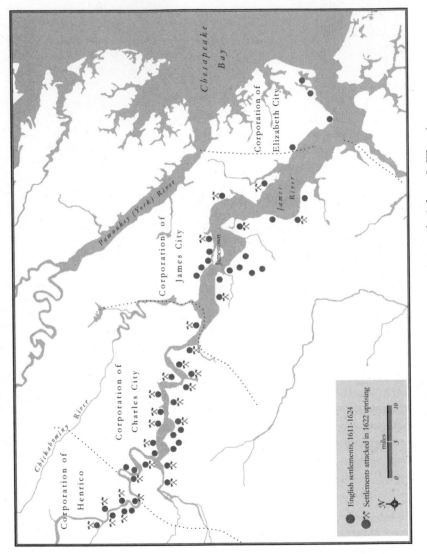

*English Settlements, 1611–1624. (Drawn by Rebecca L. Wrenn)*

warriors (strengthened by hundreds of auxiliaries), in alliance with eight or nine other peoples who formed the core of his dominions. Up-river at Henrico and beyond, the assault was led by the Powhatans, supported by the Appomattocs. At Falling Creek, the entire English population was killed (twenty-seven men, women, and children), including John Berkeley from Beverstone Castle, Gloucestershire, who had lived only a few miles from George Thorpe in England and who, like Thorpe, was a member of Virginia's council of state. Across the river, sixteen men, the majority tenants and Company laborers, were killed at the College Lands, effectively dooming the effort to build a university for the education of Indian children. At Thomas Sheffield's plantation, a couple of miles away, thirteen men, women, and children died. On Henrico Island, only five settlers died, but the Powhatans put the settlement to the torch and slaughtered all the livestock, leaving behind a smoldering ruin strewn with animal carcasses.

Along both sides of the James River from the Chickahominy River to Bermuda Hundred, the most densely populated area of the colony, nineteen settlements were attacked and 142 settlers were killed by a powerful force made up of Pamunkeys, Appomattocs, Weyanocks, Chickahominies, and Quiyoughcohannocks. On small, isolated plantations in the vicinity of Charles City, near the Curls and "Neck of Land," few English escaped. At Lieutenant Gibbs's property, twelve died; at William Ferrar's house, ten; at Richard Owens's, six; at Captain Roger Smith's, five; and at a nearby plantation, another eight. In a few instances, settlers were able to grab weapons and fight back. Nathaniel Causey, one "of the old company of Captaine Smith," although seriously wounded managed to "cleave one of their [warrior's] heads," with an ax "whereby the rest fled." Near Henrico, John Proctor's wife, described as "a proper, civill, modest Gentlewoman," was able to organize men working on the plantation to defend themselves and drive off attacking Powhatans.

Downriver, George Thorpe was not so lucky. He was at Berkeley Hundred when news came of the attack but refused to heed the alarm and went out to greet the Indians who had entered the fortified enclosure, "so void of all suspition, and so full of confidence," Waterhouse wrote, that the Indians "had sooner killed him, then hee could or would believe they meant any ill against him." Thorpe died alongside ten others at the plantation that morning, never knowing why Opechancanough had turned against him.

Elsewhere, colonists experienced mixed fortunes. Sir George Yeardley's plantation at Weyanock, attacked by Pamunkeys, Weyanocks, and Chickahominies, lost twenty-one people, while his well-fortified plantation across the river, Flowerdieu, lost six men and women. Jamestown escaped unscathed. The evening before the uprising, an Indian boy who had been converted to Christianity and lived on the plantation of Richard Pace across the river from Jamestown, was visited by his "Brother" who told him to kill Pace, "being so commanded from their King," saying further "that by such an houre in the morning a number [of warriors] would come from divers places to finish the Execution." Later that evening or during the night, possibly after his brother had left, the boy informed his master of the plot and, after securing his own house, Pace rowed across to Jamestown Island to alert Governor Wyatt.

It was too late to send out a general warning, however, and all the governor could do was prepare a defense of the town and give warning to a few nearby settlements. Four boats full of warriors assaulted Jamestown from the river but were quickly driven off by musket fire. Martin's Hundred, only seven miles away, was attacked by a large group of Pamunkeys and Kiskiacks and suffered the heaviest losses of any one site. Of "sevenscore, there were but 22 lefte alive," Richard Frethorne reported. Wolstenholme Town, the principal settlement, was burned to the ground, and neighboring plantations were totally destroyed, leaving only two houses and "a peece of a Church" standing. "Our master doth saye that £3000 pounds will not make good our Plantacon againe," Frethorne wrote, and added that merchants would get "little or nothinge" that year.

Over the river, in and around Edward Bennett's plantation, fifty-three men and women died in desperate hand-to-hand fighting against Warrascoyacks and Nansemonds. At Ralph Hamor's half-built house on Hog Island, he and his men fought a group of Warrascoyacks with

*Theodor De Bry, The Indian Uprising of 1622.*

"spades, axes, and brickbats," until half a dozen musketeers sent by ship to aid the Englishmen finally beat off the warriors. A few miles away, "Master Baldwin" saved himself and his badly wounded wife by blasting away repeatedly with his musket. When a neighbor's house was set on fire, Thomas Hamor (Ralph's brother) brought eighteen women and children to Baldwin's and helped defend them until the Indians left. By contrast, farther down the peninsula no fighting was reported at either Newport News or Kecoughtan (Elizabeth City). Possibly the Kecoughtans and Nansemonds failed to coordinate an attack or the main Powhatan/Pamunkey strike force chose not to risk an assault against two strongly defended positions.[9]

Throughout the day, Indian warriors moved quickly from one plantation to another and then disappeared back into the woods.

Opechancanough knew that to retain the critically important element of surprise, his men had to proceed rapidly, not affording the English opportunities to warn each other or to regroup into effective fighting units. Local Indians made the initial attacks and were followed by large groups of warriors (anywhere from fifty to several hundred), who joined the fighting, finished off survivors, and torched settlements. Reflecting the English tactics of indiscriminate killing employed by Gates and Dale, the Indians' intention was to kill as many men, women, and children as possible, destroy their houses, equipment, livestock, and property. Any English who escaped would starve or be dispatched later.

The attack was a massive and decisive blow designed to sweep the intruders from their lands, a repudiation of English occupation and everything the English stood for. To show their utter contempt for settlers, some corpses (such as Thorpe's) were mutilated beyond recognition or beheaded. Few prisoners were taken, but a group of male captives from Martin's Hundred were never seen again and were assumed to have been put to death. If the day's events had not ended in complete success for the Indians—Jamestown and many other settlements remained intact—nevertheless by nightfall at least a quarter of the settlers were dead and the colony devastated.

Opechancanough probably did not expected that a single day's attack would succeed in expelling the English entirely from Tsenacommacah; but by destroying settlers' plantations, forcing them to take refuge in confined locations, and so cutting off food supplies, he hoped the English would eventually become so debilitated that they would either fall victim to his warriors or decide enough was enough and abandon the colony, as nearly happened during the "starving time" of 1609–1610. Several months after the uprising, the chief predicted that "before the end of two Moones there should not be an Englishman in all their Countries."[10]

Panic gripped the colonists in the wake of the uprising. Sporadic Indian attacks continued over the next month, forcing settlers to quit their "dispersed and stragling Plantacions" and find safety in larger, fortified settlements. To better protect themselves, Wyatt ordered colonists to abandon outlying and "petty" plantations and withdraw to Kecoughtan, Newport News, Jamestown, Smyth's (Southampton's Hundred), Flowerdieu, West and Shirley Hundred, and Jordan's Journey, near Charles City. As the English evacuated, so Opechancanough's warriors, now "the Lords of those Lands," moved in and continued the destruction of settlers' property.

"The land is ruinated and spoyled," Frethorne lamented: "[W]ee live in feare of the Enimy everie hower [hour]. . . for o[u]r Plantacon is very weake, by reason of the dearth, and sicknes." At Martin's Hundred, only 32 men were left to fight against hundreds of Indians should they return: "[T]he nighest helpe that Wee have is ten miles of us," Frethorne wrote, "and when the rogues [Indians] overcame this place last, they slew 80 Persons, how then shall wee doe for wee lye even in their teeth." John Pountis, vice admiral of the colony, complained to the governor in June that Southampton Hundred had been so "often infested" with Indians that the settlers had been unable to plant tobacco and had no "corne for . . . to maintain life." An old planter, William Capps, spoke for many settlers who survived the attack: "God forgive me I think the last massacre killed all our Countrie, besides them they killed, they burst the heart of all the rest."[11]

The brilliance of Opechancanough's strategy was that it depended above all on the English settlers' unquestioning belief in their own superiority and their fatal underestimation of Indian tactical and fighting ability. It was incomprehensible to Yeardley, Wyatt, and Thorpe, or to Company leaders in London, that the Indian chief was capable of conceiving and mounting such an audacious attack after lulling "the English asleep" by pursuing years of peace and feigned friendship. Not only had the colony sustained great losses of life and property, the English had been completely fooled by the Powhatans and their allies. Reflecting on the uprising, Governor Wyatt's father, George, a man who had seen action in the Netherlands and was something of a military theorist, wrote, "Neither did this their enterprise [the Powhatan uprising] . . . want [lack] politie or corage [courage]." The Indians had planned the attack meticulously; they ensured that the fighting would take the form of hand-to-hand combat that suited them best, and executed the attack with great skill. It was "hurtful" to overestimate an enemy, George cautioned his son, but just as dangerous to underestimate him.

The similarities of the uprising to the fate that befell the Spanish Jesuit missionaries of Ajacán fifty years earlier are uncanny. Father Juan de Segura had been convinced that Paquiquineo (Don Luís) was genuine in his desire to bring the Catholic faith to his people and, like George Thorpe, went to his grave bewildered by the Indian betrayal. During the nine years he lived with the Spanish, Paquiquineo, in portraying himself as a convert, duped Philip II, his ministers, the high-ranking churchmen, and the able governor of Florida, Pedro Menéndez, as well as numerous Dominican and Jesuit fathers. Paquiquineo exercised astonishing patience while waiting for the opportunity to return to his country and rid himself of the Jesuits who accompanied him. Opechancanough waited six bitter years for the right moment to strike against the English. If he and Paquiquineo were not the same man, Opechancanough must surely have learned from Paquiquineo that the Europeans' greatest vulnerability was their arrogance.[12]

## "Perpetuall Warre"

News of the uprising reached the Company's leaders in London in the summer of 1622 and was greeted with disbelief and outrage, which was aimed at the colony's leaders as well as the Powhatans. "Wee have to o[u]r extreame grief und[e]rstood of the great Massacre executed on o[u]r people in Virginia," the Company wrote to Governor Wyatt on August 1:

> and that in such a maner as is more miserable than death it self; to fall by the hands of men so contemptible; to be surprised by treacherie in a time of known danger; to be deaf to so plaine a warning (as we now to[o] late und[e]rstand) was last yeare given; . . . not to p[er]ceive any thing in so open and generall conspiracie; but to be made in parte instruments of contriving it, and almost guiltie of the destruccon by

blindfold and stupid entertaininge it . . . are circumstances, that do add much to o[u]r sorrow.

Settlers' neglect of divine worship, their drunkenness and excessive ways, already notorious among any who had "but heard the name Virginia," were sins that cried out to heaven and had inevitably brought down the "heavie hand of Allmightie God" upon them in retribution. The Company enjoined colonists to reconcile themselves humbly with "the devine Ma[jes]tie" and conform to "his most just and holie lawes." Only with God's protection and blessing could the settlers secure themselves from the hands of their enemies and those "that hate you."[13]

Of more practical help, the Company requested permission from the government to ship to the colony "certaine old cast Armes remaining in the Tower [of London] . . . altogether unfit, and of no use for moderne Service, [which] might nevertheles be serviceable against the naked people." The king was pleased to grant the request and in September the Company took possession of 1,000 "browne bills," or halberds; 700 calivers (a light form of musket); 300 "short pistols w[i]th fire locks"; 300 harquebuses; 500 coats and shirts of mail; 2,000 "skulls," or iron helmets; 400 bows; and 800 sheaves of arrows. His majesty's royal gift, Wyatt informed the Company, would be employed "to the honor of our Countrey and revenge of his subjects blood."[14]

The Company adopted a defiant tone in their instructions to the colony's leaders. Any thoughts of quitting the colony or the James River area in favor of another location (across the bay on the Eastern Shore) were to be dismissed, since it would be "a Sinne against the dead, to abandon the enterprise, till we have fully settled the possession, for w[hi]ch so many of o[u]r Brethren have lost theire lives," the governor was told. The uprising might even work to the Company's advantage—private investors appeared to be renewing their support for the colony and were sending over large numbers of settlers to replace those killed. Projects long advocated by the Company—the iron works, viticulture, silk manufacture, and production of crops and other commodities—were to be restarted as soon as possible.

Sending out more settlers was the basis for reviving the colony, Company leaders believed, "for, in the multitude of people is the strength of a Kingdome," and hundreds of servants were dispatched despite difficulties in recruiting as news of the "great Massacre" spread in England. Although the Company could not afford to transport its own tenants, the governor and council in Virginia were encouraged to provide as much assistance as possible to new arrivals sent by private interests. Settlements were to be established in "compact and orderly villages," considered by the Company as the "most proper, and succesfull maner of proceedinge in new Plantacons." Resettling Charles City, Henrico, Martin's Hundred, the Iron Works, and College Lands, abandoned after the uprising, were "of absolute necessitie; lest the best fire that maintain[ed] the accon [action] [t]here alive be putt out," the Company emphasized. The uprising had been a grave setback, but Sandys and the Earl of Southampton (who had taken over as treasurer in 1620) were determined that there should be no change of course.[15]

Yet in one crucial respect, Company policy changed significantly. Ending all efforts to proselytize the Powhatans, Company leaders outlawed them as a cursed nation and condemned them as no "longer a people upon the face of the Earth." Citing the sixteenth-century Spanish historian Gonzalo Fernández de Oviedo as his authority, Edward Waterhouse described Indians as "by nature sloathfull and idle, vitious . . . [and] of all people the most lying and most inconstant in the world." Trust had proved *"the mother of Deceipt,"* and now the English knew the Indians could never be trusted.

Wyatt was ordered to root them out by "surprisinge them in their habitations, intercepting them in their hunting, burninge their Townes, demolishing theire Temples, destroyinge theire Canoes, plucking upp theire weares [fish weirs], carrying away theire Corne, and depriving them of whatsoever may yeeld them succor or relief." Waterhouse advocated adopting Spanish methods in chasing them down, using "horses, and blood-Hounds to draw after them, and Mastives to [seaze] them." Only children were to be spared, "whose bodies may, by labor and service become profitable." A "false-hearted people, that know not God nor faith," the Powhatans were to be killed, driven out of the region, or enslaved.[16]

Company officials were also quick to point out how the disaster might benefit English ambitions in Virginia. Waterhouse wrote: "[We] hitherto have had possession of no more ground then their [the Indians'] waste, and our purchase at a valuable consideration." Now "by right of Warre, and law of Nations," the English could "invade the Country, and destroy them that sought to destroy us." Besides taking the Indians' agricultural lands and villages, the English would be free to exploit the natural resources of former hunting grounds and fishing waters, both of which would increase provisions. And it would be far easier, Waterhouse observed, to conquer them than to civilize them by fair means; "for they are a rude, barbarous, and naked people."

Vehement expressions of anti-Indian sentiment interpreted the uprising as a struggle between murderous, unregenerate heathens and godly English seeking only to bring true religion, prosperity, and peace to the Indians. Christopher Brooke contrasted the Powhatans, described as "Errors of Nature, of inhumane Birthe" quaffing "the life-blood of deare Christian Soules," with the saintly George Thorpe:

> Who didst attempt to make those *Indians* know
> Th'Eternall God; their Sinewy necks to bow
> To his obedience; and on that ground
> To make them apt to what thou didst propound
> For our Commerce with them; their good, our peace,
> And both to helpe with mutual increase.

The Reverend Samuel Purchas, who years before had been so admiring of Pocahontas, summed up arguments of a generation of theorists in one of the most influential tracts of the period to justify England's right to take possession of the land. Prior to 1622, he wrote, "Temperance and Justice had before kissed each other, and seemed to blesse the cohabitations of English and Indians in Virginia." But by "this last butchery" the Powhatans had revealed themselves "more brutish than the beasts they hunt, more wild and unmanly then that

unmanned [under-populated] wild Countrey, which they range rather
then inhabite." They were unworthy of the "name of a Nation," he asserted, and were rather "Borderers and Out-lawes of Humanity" who,
forfeiting their rights by their actions in the uprising, had made "their
Country wholly English."[17]

Proposals were made to the Company by experienced (or former)
settlers about the best way to counter the Indian threat. Captain John
Smith was still living in London trying to drum up support for his
New England schemes when he heard news of the uprising. He had
tried unsuccessfully to involve himself in the *Mayflower* Pilgrims' plans
to settle in northern Virginia, and with equal lack of success had
sought to interest city merchants in a plan to create a colony in New
England that would serve as a base for English fishing fleets. Charac-
teristically, Smith had an opinion of what had gone wrong in Virginia
and a solution (that included a key role for him). Lucrative returns
from tobacco had corrupted the settlers, he remarked, leading them to
indulge themselves like the "curious, costly, and consuming Gallants
here in England." Settlers had become complacent about the
Powhatans. Those who lived far apart from one another did not exercise in the use of arms, and had neither forts nor cannon to protect
them from the "Salvages." Yet while colonists rooted "in the ground
about Tobacco like Swine," he wrote, the Indians who lived among
them continually practiced with their bows and arrows. Even more extraordinary, supposedly friendly Indians had been taught the use of
firearms by settlers themselves, so that they could be employed in
hunting and fowling.

To restore the country and escape the "labyrinth of melancholy" in
which the colony and Company languished, Smith proposed he be
given command of 100 soldiers, whom he would fashion into a running army to harass the Indians until they were driven out of English
lands or brought "to that feare and subjection that every [English] man
should follow their businesse securely." In addition, he suggested constructing a palisade fortified with block houses between the James and
Pamunkey rivers to create a safe haven "much bigger then the Summer
Isles [the Bermudas]," sufficient to support 10,000 settlers.

Company leaders showed little interest in Smith's plan, explaining that "the charge would be too great" and hinting (with some justification) that the settlers were quite capable of putting into effect Smith's ideas themselves without any help from him. In fact, the captain's old rival John Martin had a more realistic proposal that included a force of 200 men "Contynuallie harrowinge and burneinge all their Townes in wynter, and spoileinge their weares [weirs]," backed by ten shallops that would patrol the river and bay and prevent Indians from acquiring corn or other provisions from elsewhere. In this way, the Powhatans would soon be starved into submission. Unlike Company leaders in England, Martin did not advocate a policy of extermination, which he believed would be contrary to "holy writt" and destructive of a valuable source of labor (the Indians being "apter for worke then yet [the] English"), but rather favored employing them in the cultivation of silk, hemp, and flax, as guides for expeditions into neighboring "Countries," and to "rowe in Gallies & friggetts."[18]

WYATT AND THE COLONY'S LEADERS needed little advice from the Company or anyone else about how to respond to the Indians, however. "Our first worke is expulsion of the Salvages to gaine free range of the countrey," the governor declared, "for it is infinitely better to have no heathen among us, who at best were but as thornes in our sides, then to be at peace and league with them." During the summer and fall, raiding parties were sent against the Powhatans, Pamunkeys, Weyanocks, Chickahominies, Quiyoughcohannocks, Warrascoyacks, Nansemonds, and Rappahannocks to "reveng their cruell deeds."

In these raids, the English once again applied the tactics of Dale and Gates: They sailed freely up and down the rivers, along the way destroying Indian villages and burning Indian fields after taking corn and other crops. For their part, employing a hit-and-run approach also developed in the previous war, the Powhatans continued picking off settlers whenever the opportunity arose. In combat, casualties on both sides were relatively light. Indian warriors avoided pitched battles in open country, while English soldiers were protected from Powhatan bowmen by their armor. On one occasion, however, some of the men in a raiding party commanded by Yeardley were wounded when they were fired upon by a group of Pamunkeys "in ambuscado" who had "English peeces" (muskets). The incident was a strong indication that if Opechancanough's warriors had secured more firearms they would have been able to blunt English raids and wait for disease and starvation to reduce the settlers until such time as another large-scale Indian assault could finish them off.[19]

During the winter of 1622–1623, the colony's second "starving time," Opechancanough's strategy appeared to have a chance of success. So many English died that it was described as the "fearefullest age that ever christians lyved in." Provisions were in such short supply that one settler reported paying £12 for a hogshead of meal (partly "in good silver plate"), adding that the "poorer sort" were not able to live. As Edward Hill wrote to his brother in London: "We are all like to have the greatest famine in the land that ever was"; as soon as he could, he continued, he intended to leave the country, "god willing." In the same letter, he mentioned another "Massacre" in which the Indians had "cutt off" a pinnace, a shallop, and a small boat with twenty-six men all in "compleat Armour."

The incident occurred on the Potomac River at the end of March 1623 when several hundred Patawomecks attacked Captain Henry Spelman (who had once lived with them) and two dozen men who had gone to the region to trade for corn. Formerly well disposed towards the English, the Patawomecks had been angered by an unprovoked attack the previous year by Captain Isaac Maddison, who had also gone to the region to trade and, suspecting treachery by the Indians, had taken the weroance and his son prisoner and slaughtered thirty or forty men, women, and children. In retaliation, Spelman and most of his men were slain or captured by the Patawomecks and his shallop captured along with muskets and armor; the accompanying pinnace, *Tiger,* only just managed to escape after five crewmen fought off attacking warriors and set sail, pursued by about sixty canoes. News of the loss was bad enough—Indians had never before attacked a ship—but settlers realized also that the Indians had acquired a large cache of arms and might soon renew their assaults on English settlements using the colonists' own weapons against them. Owing to Maddison's blunder, settlers could no longer rely on supplies from the Patawomecks as in previous years of scarcity.[20]

In early April, however, the governor received a surprise visit from two Indians, Chanco and Comahum, who came as messengers from Opitchapam with an offer of peace. The "greate Kinge," they said, believed "blud inough had already been shedd one [on] both sides." Many of his people were starving as a result of the English taking away their corn and burning their fields and villages. Opitchapam asked that they might be allowed "to plante at Pomunkie [Pamunkey], and theire former Seates." In exchange, English prisoners taken during the uprising would be returned. To show their good faith, some days later Mrs. Alice Boyse, dressed like an Indian queen (the Indians wanted the English to take note that she had been well treated), arrived back at the fort. A few weeks later in May, Opitchapam sent word that if the governor would dispatch ten or twelve soldiers, he would deliver the rest of the captives and also "his Brother Opachankano who was the Author of the Massacre into the hands of the English either alive or dead."[21]

Was the offer genuine? Did it indicate that Opechancanough, who had not been seen or heard of by the English for nearly a year, had fallen out of favor with his people because they blamed him for the attacks and devastation that had befallen them? Or was it merely a ploy to lure English soldiers into a trap? The latter is more likely. Opechancanough and Opitchapam were aware of the disastrous winter suffered by the colonists and would have heard also from the Patawomecks of the death of Spelman and his men. The invitation to send a dozen soldiers to the Indians was suspicious and reminiscent of a similar invitation a few years before made by Nettattanew for "8 or tenn Engleshe w[i]th ther Armes" to join a war party of Powhatan warriors against a people called the "Massituppamohtnock," who lived a day's journey beyond the falls. The English had consented and, although it is unclear whether the expedition ever took place, there are suggestions that the men sent by the English were never seen again. Needing

firearms, Opitchapam dangled his brother Opechancanough and captive colonists as bait before Wyatt to draw the Englishmen into his
reach.²²

The governor and his council had no intention of accepting
Opitchapam's offer, but they did see an opportunity to take advantage
of the opening. Captain William Tucker was sent to the Pamunkey
River with a dozen men ostensibly to retrieve the settlers and conclude
a peace with Opitchapam, both sides pretending friendship in their
mutual hostility to Opechancanough. After many "fayned [feigned]
speeches," Tucker handed bottles of sack to the assembled chiefs and
their men to drink to their health and the new accord. Before the Indians would drink, however, Tucker and his interpreter tasted the sack to
show that no treachery was intended. They drank from a different bot-
tle, however, while the Indians, including Opitchapam, the chief of
the Kiskiacks, their sons, and "great men" drank poisoned wine.

How many died is unknown, but approximately 200 fell sick and,
in the confusion that followed, Tucker had his men fire a volley that
killed "som 50 more," including two kings. As proof of success, Tucker
"brought hom parte of ther [the Indians'] heades." No criticism of the
nature of the attack was voiced in Virginia, from where Robert Bennett wrote that it would be "a great desmayinge to the blodye
infidelles." The governor and council argued: "[W]ee hold nothinge
injuste, that may tende to theire [the Indians'] ruine." Neither did
Company officials in London express misgivings. The Earl of
Southampton reported in November that by a "successful Stratagem"
the colonists had not only regained the English captives but had also
"cutt of[f] divers Indian Kinges and great Comaunders: Amongst
whome they [were] confident that Opachankano was one[,] it [having
been] impossible for him to escape."²³

Although it later became apparent that neither Opitchapam nor
Opechancanough was killed, the attack was nonetheless a major setback
for the Pamunkeys, not least because the English discovered where the
Indians were residing and growing their corn and would soon move
against them to deliver "a blowe that [would] neare or altogether ruinate
them." From summer through fall, the governor launched another wave

of assaults against Indian peoples of the James River, principally the Powhatans, Weyanocks, Appomattocs, Quiyoughcohannocks, Warrascoyacks, and Nansemonds that once again targeted villages and cornfields; at the same time, the Powhatans continued to harass English settlements.

The decisive battle of the war took place the following year. In July 1624, Wyatt, with sixty men in armor, sailed up the Pamunkey River into the heartland of Opitchapam's territory, where they were confronted by approximately 800 bowmen and an unspecified number of allies "that cam[e] to assiste them." Encouraged by their own numbers, or the "paucytie of ours," as Wyatt commented, on this occasion Pamunkey warriors took on the English "in open fielde" and fought with great determination to defend their villages and a great quantity of corn. They fought also to defend their reputation as the elite of Powhatan warriors, the "Pomunkeys having made greate braggs, of what they would doe, Amonge the Northerne nationes." The battle continued for two days but, despite their valor, which even Wyatt acknowledged, the Pamunkeys were beaten back by the firepower of soldiers armed with snaphaunce muskets, an early form of flintlock that was far more effective than the old matchlock. Eventually, after sustaining heavy losses, the Indians "gave over fightinge and dismayedly, stood most ruthfully [ruefully] looking on while theire Corne was Cutt downe." The English, protected by their armor, suffered only light casualties.[24]

Whether or not Opechancanough was present at the defeat of his men is uncertain. In the past he had avoided exposing his warriors to the murderous fire of English muskets in frontal assaults, and yet on this occasion the opportunity to inflict a major defeat on the colonists and obtain their weapons may have been too tempting to resist. From this point of view, it is even possible that he planned the confrontation as an elaborate ambush. Anticipating that the English would sooner or later invade their territories to carry off their corn, the Pamunkeys gathered a huge force to meet them, confident as their "greate braggs" revealed that they would emerge the victors. Either way, the crushing defeat of the flower of Pamunkey warriors was a major turning point in the conflict. Sporadic hostilities continued for the next eight years, but Opechancanough must have realized there was little hope of expelling the colonists from his lands. The defeat of the Pamunkeys was the beginning of the end of the Powhatan empire.[25]

## A "Plantacon of Sorrowes"

George Sandys, younger brother of Sir Edwin, traveled widely before arriving in Virginia in 1621. Middle-aged and restless, he had decided to make a extended journey through France and Italy, along the east coast of the Adriatic Sea and into the Aegean en route to Constantinople (Istanbul), where he spent four months before moving on to Cairo, Egypt, and the Holy Land. Throughout his two years abroad, he carefully recorded his observations. He paid particular attention to the customs of ordinary people, to which he added insights gleaned from the classics, church fathers, geographers, historians, and recent accounts in learned quotations and commentary that embellished his narrative.

After his return to England, the success of his account of his travels, published in 1615, and translation of several books of Ovid's *Metamorphoses* into English confirmed his growing reputation as a writer and poet. On the fringes of the Virginia Company for seven or eight years, he rose to prominence shortly after Sir Edwin assumed leadership of the Company. George was respected for his loyalty to his brother and his administrative abilities, and his experiences overseas demonstrated a keen analytical mind as well as a practical capacity to take care of himself in dangerous situations. So when the Company created the office of a resident treasurer in Virginia to supervise the collection of annual rents and implement the Company's instructions, he was considered a natural choice and was elected without opposition.

He took ship on the *George,* along with his kinsman Sir Francis Wyatt and arrived at Jamestown in October 1621. His first impressions have not survived, but he was optimistic when he wrote to England in the early spring to report that he had taken steps to limit the planting of tobacco and was encouraging the planting of corn, English grains, vines, mulberry trees, fig trees, and fruits. Having surveyed both banks of the James River, he was confident the colony would be able to support a profitable ironworks and glassworks within the year.

Sandys's plans were thrown into utter disarray shortly after, however, by Opechancanough's uprising. He played an active role in the counter offensive during the summer and fall, twice leading troops against the Quiyoughcohannocks; but, suffering from the effects of illness and overwork, he might have experienced a physical breakdown in the winter. By the spring of 1623, he appears to have recovered his health and, in a series of detailed letters, provided the most valuable testimony of the final collapse of the Company's and (more poignantly) his brother's hopes for Virginia.[26]

"In this generall decay," Sandys wrote in March, describing the state of the colony, "if you blame us, you must blame the hand of God." He proceeded to account for the failure to establish shipbuilding in the colony following the deaths of the master shipwright and six or seven of his men. He discussed the many setbacks attending the construction of the glassworks, which had been blown down in "a tempest," temporarily abandoned after the uprising, destroyed in an accident, and sabotaged by one of the Italian glassworkers hired by the Company. A "more damned crew hell never vomited," he wrote of the Italians, but the "desperate fellowes" could not be punished without further jeopardizing the project. They would gladly make the work appear impractical so they could break their contracts and return to England. Tenants (sharecroppers), "sent on that so absurd Condition of halves," could not support themselves let alone return half their crop to the Company. They were so dejected "that most [gave] themselves over, and die[d] of Melancholye" or fell far into debt. Mulberry trees planted the previous year had come to nothing because "of the trouble of the times," and little tobacco remained for the Company after the merchants and mariners had taken their share of a disappointing crop.

Without question, the most serious problem faced by the colonists as they tried to recover from the uprising was the heavy loss of new arrivals and planters through disease, sickness, and malnutrition. "Extreame hath beene the mortalitie of this yeare," Sandys wrote. "I am afraid [it] hath do[u]bled the Number of those w[hi]ch were massacred." Sir William Nuce, the colony's marshal, arrived in Virginia at the same time as Sandys with a group of Company laborers described as "weake and unserviceable." Nuce died shortly after, leaving eleven laborers whom Sandys was forced to "sell" because he could not provide for them. Of these, two were dead before they could be delivered to their masters and two ran away to the Indians. So many had come over with inadequate provisions, Sandys complained, which was "a maine Cause of their debts and deathes and of . . . small retournes."

Hundreds of new arrivals sent by the Company to replace those killed in the attack died of scurvy, the bloody flux, and other diseases brought by ships crowded with "infected people." Following the arrival of the *Abigail* (which brought Lady Margaret Wyatt, the governor's wife, to Virginia), a virulent pestilence swept the colony, which Sandys blamed on the ship's having been provisioned with "stinking beere" that "poisoned most of the Passengers, and spread the Infection all over the Collony," carrying off so many that *"the lyving"* were *"hardlie able to bury the dead."* A visitor described men and women "dyinge under hedges and in the woods," and corpses lying "for many dayes unregarded and unburied." Between the spring of 1622 and 1623, the worst year the English had endured in Virginia, at least a thousand settlers perished, leaving survivors fearful and traumatized.

Sandys was particularly concerned about the consequences of permitting settlers to live on plantations at vast distances from one another. The only benefit of the uprising had been to draw planters together for their better protection, but the Company had ordered that the governor and council allow them to return to their settlements. "[L]ike quicksilver throwne into the fire," they had immediately dispersed and were now scattered throughout the colony. Living closer together would have encouraged comfort and security, the advancement of manufactures and husbandry, the building of houses and towns; in general, "strength, beautie pleasure, riches and reputacon added forthwith to the Collonie." But in its present state, Sandys asked, "how is it possible to governe a people so dispersed; especially such as for the most part are sent over? how can they repaire to divine service, except every plantation have a Minister? how can we raise soldiers to goe uppon the enimy or workemen for publique imployments, w[i]thout weakeninge them to[o] much, or undoinge them by drawinge the[m] fro[m] their labors?"

For Sandys, tolerating the settlers' dispersed manner of living was the biggest mistake the Company had made, and from it stemmed the ills outlined in his letters. All the calamities that had befallen the English in Virginia, sent by God "to scourge a disobedient people," could have brought about a "reformacon" if the colony's leaders had been able to make "true use of it" by bringing the people together. Sandys censured Company officials in London who "glorie[d] in their wisdomes" though knowing nothing of Virginia, and who would rather persist with unrealistic schemes than "acknowledge their Errors."

George Sandys sought to encourage a common approach by investors in London and settlers in Virginia alike to challenges faced by the colony. He shared Sir Edwin's dislike of tobacco and his brother's enthusiasm for a mixed economy based on the precepts that had guided colonial projects since the days of Richard Hakluyt. Unflinching in his assessment of what had gone wrong, he did not give up hope that the colony would one day prosper. He was even inclined to occasional flights of fancy, such as when he mentioned the likelihood "of the vicinity of the South sea," which lay beyond the mountains only four days journey from the falls of the James River. But for the most part, he offered sound, practical advice. "Be not offended that I speake the truth," he wrote to John Ferrar, and, in words that surely must have come back to haunt him: "[Y]ou know little, & wee not much more."

Sandys was determined to provide a realistic assessment of Virginia's condition for his brother, Sir Edwin, and trusted supporters in England, convinced that if the Company's leaders better understood the gravity of the problems facing the colony they would be able to collaborate more effectively with the governor and council in Jamestown to bring about necessary remedies. It is ironic, therefore, that his correspondence should fall into the hands of political rivals when some two

dozen letters sent to England in 1623 were seized by royal commissioners recently established to investigate the Company's alleged
mismanagement of Virginia.[27]

—•—

EVER SINCE SIR EDWIN SANDYS's election to the position of treasurer of the Company in April 1619 in place of Sir Thomas Smythe
(who had been in charge during the previous decade), divisions had
grown within the ranks of the Company's leadership. Sir Edwin first
fell out with Smythe and then with a powerful faction led by Sir
Robert Rich, Earl of Warwick. Divisions deepened in the early 1620s
during a protracted dispute about whether the Company should enter
into an agreement with the government relating to terms for the sole
right to import Virginia tobacco into England, which led to the Warwick party joining forces with Smythe to bring about a decisive defeat
of Sandys's recommended acceptance.[28]

Against the background of bitter internal feuding within the Company, news arrived in London in the spring of 1623 of the terrible loss
of life in the colony during the winter. Especially damaging was an account authored by Captain Nathaniel Butler entitled "The Unmasked
face of o[u]r Colony in Virginia as it was in the Winter of the yeare
1622," which he submitted to the Privy Council. Butler had been governor of Bermuda between 1619 and 1622 and was a loyal follower of
Warwick's. No friend of the leadership in Virginia, he visited the
colony in the winter of 1622–1623 and, upon returning to England, reported that conditions were far worse than the Company was letting
on. Painted in lurid colors, his account was a thorough exposé of earlier descriptions of Virginia published by the Company that portrayed
the colony as thriving. By contrast, according to Butler, the colony was
in complete disarray, "so that in steed of a Plantacon itt [would]
shortly gett the name of a slaughter house and soe justly become both
odious to our selves and contemptible to all the world."

On the basis of Butler's report and corroborating information submitted by Alderman Robert Johnson, the Smythe and Warwick
factions' petition to the king for a formal investigation was granted. A

crown commission was established in May 1623 headed by Sir Richard Jones, justice of the Court of Common Pleas, followed five months later by a special commission of four men sent to Virginia to assess conditions in the colony. Both commissions drew upon an enormous amount of evidence, including official Company records, the testimony of former planters and merchants, eyewitness accounts and letters from the colony (including those of George Sandys), and voluminous submissions by the contesting parties.[29]

The allegations of Company mismanagement presented by Sir Edwin's enemies were frequently exaggerated, but there could be little doubt that cumulatively they added up to a crushing indictment of Company policy. In the four years that Sandys and Southampton had been in control, thousands of poorly provisioned settlers had been sent to their deaths, the Company had become bankrupt, and efforts to create a diversified economy had failed completely. The colony was defenseless, public works set up in Sir Thomas Smythe's time of government were "either ruined or demolished," Indians continued to threaten, and colonists lived "for the most parte in great want and miserye."

By the summer of 1623, the Jones commission concluded that the colony was in a most "weak and miserable" condition and declared (echoing Butler) that if action were not taken to remedy the situation the entire plantation was in danger of collapse. In response, the king instructed Attorney General Sir Thomas Coventry to sue for recovery of the Company's charter. In early November, a writ of *quo warranto* was filed in the Court of the King's Bench that required the Company to provide reasons why it should not surrender its rights to the colony. Legal proceedings dragged on for six months, but the outcome was never in question. On May 24, 1624, the Company's charter was revoked. Responsibility for Virginia reverted to the Crown, and the Company era was at an end.[30]

---

ON THE OTHER SIDE OF THE OCEAN, George Sandys had been well aware of the growing threat faced by Sir Edwin and his supporters in London. Throughout 1623 and early 1624, he continued to persevere in trying to keep his brother's dream of a prosperous Virginia alive. He labored tirelessly to develop profitable commodities, traveled up and down the James River collecting Company revenues, and traded across the Bay to the Eastern Shore and as far as the Potomac River exchanging English goods for provisions with Indians hostile to the Powhatans. With Wyatt, he played a prominent role in shaping the General Assembly's response to attacks on the Company by the Smythe and Warwick factions, helped draft a point-by-point rebuttal of Butler's account, drew up a "humble Petition" to James I, and wrote letter after letter to the king's commissioners.

But in the end none of his efforts were sufficient to save the Company. Opechancanough's uprising had triggered a series of events that fully exposed the failure of Sir Edwin's schemes, and there was little that either George or his brother could have done to prevent the Company's demise once the facts about Virginia's troubles came out into the open. Despite being reappointed to the colony's council in late 1624, Sandys made up his mind to return to England after learning of the Company's dissolution. Believing his office of treasurer defunct and his duties done, he left Virginia the following summer. He took with him his translation of the last eight books of *Metamorphoses*, completed in spare moments over the previous four years, and resumed his literary career under the patronage of the new king, Charles I, becoming in the 1630s one of the best-known poets of his day.[31]

# Epilogue

## *After the Fall*

THE VIRGINIA COMPANY HAD COLLAPSED, not the colony, and when James I died suddenly in late March 1625, it was left to his son, Charles I, to determine Virginia's fate. Would the colony be handed back to Sir Thomas Smythe or to some other mercantile group, or would the Crown take over formal responsibility? Anxious colonists and investors did not have to wait long to find out. On May 13, eighteen years to the day after the settlement of Jamestown, the king affirmed that he would "protect, maintain, and support [the plantation]," in the same measure as any other part of his dominions. Henceforth, Virginia's government, he declared, would "immediately depend upon Our Selfe, and not be committed to any Company or Corporation, to whom it may be proper to trust matters of Trade and Commerce, but cannot bee fit or safe to communicate the ordering of State-affaires, be they of never so meane consequence."

Company land grants would be honored and the king pledged to maintain all "publique Officers and Ministers" at the crown's charge. The proclamation put to rest lingering doubts about Virginia's future, clarified its status as a royal colony, and confirmed that Charles did not intend to use Virginia as a pawn in diplomatic negotiations with the Spanish king, Philip IV.[1]

By 1625, "the skarrs of the massacre" were fading. The tobacco trade was thriving and the colony's population had largely recovered to its pre-uprising level. A muster taken in January and February listed 1,218 men, women, and children living in 21 English settlements along the James River and on the Eastern Shore. Jamestown was described as having 125 settlers, and an additional 212 lived on the island and nearby. "New Towne," immediately to the east of the fort, which had been laid out in the early 1620s, was growing rapidly as a cluster of private dwellings, storehouses, and workshops where wealthy merchants, artisans, and public officials lived and worked. Although the capital was a far cry from the great cities and bustling market towns that English and European settlers (as well as some enslaved Angolans) would have known, it was at least beginning to take on the semblance of an urban community; as was Elizabeth City at the mouth of the James River, where planters were said to "enjoy their healths and live as plentifully as in any parte of England."[2]

Tobacco was Virginia's salvation. Company efforts to produce a wide variety of goods for European markets had failed miserably. But tobacco promised high returns, particularly as new trade restrictions imposed by the government banned domestic production in England, as well as imports of foreign leaf, and lowered duties payable to the crown. For those men able to acquire sufficient laborers—merchants, such as Abraham Piersey and Samuel Mathews, and officials such as Governor Wyatt and Sir George Yeardley—prospects were especially bright. The tobacco barons of America's first boom might clear from £500 to £1,000 annually from leaf, and in addition amassed fortunes from importing English goods, trading servants and corn, acquiring land, and taking advantage of the perks of public office. Little wonder that Wyatt reported to the king's commissioners in June 1625 that Virginia was "in a hopefull waye" and "as good a Conditione as ever."[3]

There remained no place in the colony for the Powhatans, however. "The termes betwixt us and them [the Indians] are irreconcilable," the General Assembly bluntly declared. "Extirpating of the Salvages" and the "winning of the Forrest," Governor Wyatt was convinced, were vital steps necessary to ensure the success of Virginia. Both for defense and "future increase of plenty," the Assembly recommended erecting a six-mile-long palisade across the peninsula from Jamestown to Kiskiack, which would create a safe haven for further settlement, an enormous range for livestock, and lands for planting crops. A physical barrier was built to keep the Indians out of 300,000 acres of English land.[4]

Lost to the English once and for all on that "fatall Friday," March 22, 1622, was the vision of a Christian empire in the New World that would unite English and Indian in a Protestant commonwealth, spreading the true faith across the continent and creating a religious bulwark against Catholic Spain. Preaching to the Virginia Company in 1615, Thomas Cooper informed his audience that the gospel had been restored to the English so they could take the word to their "posterity and brethren, the nations far and near," and lay the foundations of a Protestant international. The divine work of the English was to bring to the "rude and savage nations" of Ireland and Virginia "this blessed light," and thereby make "an inviolable league between those nations and [their] colonies." Following the opening of the Thirty Years' War in 1618, which pitched Protestants against Catholics in a series of ruinous conflicts that laid waste entire regions of Europe, that godly mission seemed all the more imperative. This "little island," Cooper wrote of England, had become the "sanctuary of all the Christian world."

After the uprising, Virginia would remain a symbol of resistance to Spain, of an English America in the Spanish Atlantic, but the colony would no longer be the ground of a Protestant crusade, nor would it offer a gentler alternative (as the English saw it) to Spanish brutality towards the Indians. From 1622, the Powhatans were excluded from English Virginia other than as drudges and slaves.[5]

## Time's Trial

Captain John Smith knew that the Virginia Company's collapse offered an opportunity to memorialize the founding of English America and his own role in it. He had been thinking about a new literary project since completing two small books about New England in 1622. When news of the uprising reached London, he saw the possibility of a larger work that would bring together his previous publications and which might earn some money. *The Generall Historie of Virginia, New-England, and the Summer Isles,* published in 1624, was his masterwork. Divided into six books, four were devoted to Virginia and one book apiece to Bermuda and New England. (There was no room for a description of English activities in Guiana or the West Indies). The *Generall Historie* was not intended to be a compendium of English exploration and colonization along the lines of Richard Hakluyt's massive *Principal Navigations of the English Nation*. Rather, it was a personal history based on his own experiences and those of other adventurers and settlers. It revealed the depth of his devotion to Virginia and New England, which he described as "my children . . . my Wife, my Hawks, Hounds, my Cards, my Dice, and in totall, my best content."[6]

Considering that Smith's claim to be the father of New England was somewhat tenuous (he had made only one voyage to the region a decade before), Virginia was bound to loom large in his narrative.[7] Unsurprisingly, Smith contrasted what he saw as his own pragmatic efforts to place Virginia on a secure footing with the incompetent, incoherent, and unrealistic schemes of the colony's leaders at Jamestown and in London that eventually led to bankruptcy and the disasters of the uprising and its aftermath. If only the Company had followed his advice, he believed, they could have avoided the "miracles of misery" that had brought the colony to its knees as well as "those contentions and divisions which [would] hazard [jeopardize] if not ruine the prosperitie of Virginia, if present remedy bee not found."

The remedy, according to Smith, was trade. He pointed to the Dutch, whose financial success of the previous thirty years was based on their fishing fleets and worldwide commerce. Dutch commerce had increased to such a degree that "no state but Venice of twice their magnitude [was] so well furnished, with so many faire Cities, goodly Townes, strong Fortresses, and that abundance of shipping, and all sorts of Merchandize." If Virginia, unlike the Spanish Indies, offered no gold or silver mines, nonetheless England's colonies would prosper through trade and industry, which in his judgment were a surer route to wealth.[8]

Smith's *Generall Historie* was written at a moment when the entire English colonizing effort hung in the balance. New England was in its infancy. Virginia's future continued to be uncertain, and Bermuda, which had enjoyed modest success during its first fifteen years, might be lost if the Spanish chose to mount a determined attack. At the time of the *Generall Historie*'s publication, it was not clear whether Smith was writing at the dawn of a new age of colonial expansion or was composing English America's epitaph.

As it turned out, Smith was right. Over the next half century, transatlantic commerce fueled an enormous growth in population and wealth in English colonies; although he would probably have been surprised by the major sources of prosperity, not New England's fisheries but the two great staples of colonial trade: West Indian sugar and Chesapeake tobacco. By the 1680s, hundreds of ships left London and the outports annually for American waters carrying manufactured goods and foodstuffs to be exchanged for colonial commodities worth hundreds of thousands of pounds sterling, of which the "king of sweets," sugar, and leaf from Virginia and Maryland made up more than 80 percent in value. Tobacco was the first of the major American staples to emerge. Imports into England rose dramatically from 300,000 lbs. in 1630 to more than 1 million in 1640, 15 million in 1670, and 28 million in 1700.

Shifting consumer patterns across England and Europe stimulated this enormous increase over the course of the century. Demand for to-bacco and sugar was soon followed by the emergence of coffee, chocolate, and tea, all of which would develop mass markets. At the end of the century, a commentator remarked, it was "beyond all Con-troversie, that it [was] the Interest of All Nations to Increase their Trade," the "Increase of which begetteth Wealth, and Riches." He added: "*Trade* is a richer and more dureable *Mine* than any in *Mexico* or *Peru*." Governments were responsible for policies that promoted commerce and overseas expansion to ensure the security of the state and well-being of subjects.[9]

European populations in North America experienced explosive growth. Fewer than 5,000 settlers inhabited English America in Smith's day, most of them in Virginia and Bermuda; by 1680, about 150,000 Europeans (the majority English) and 7,000 enslaved Africans lived in settlements stretching some 1,200 miles along the North American coast from Maine to the Carolinas. To the south, another 42,000 whites and 76,000 blacks lived in the West Indies in a great arc from Jamaica to Barbados.

Across the seventeenth century, some 350,000 English and Irish set-tlers crossed the Atlantic, of which approximately 175,000 went to the Caribbean, 125,000 to the Chesapeake, 24,000 to the middle colonies (Delaware, Pennsylvania, New Jersey, and New York) and a similar number to New England. Sectionalism in the Americas emerged early. Nearly 250,000 enslaved Africans, predominantly from West Africa and West Central Africa, were transported to English colonies during the century, of which 95 percent ended up in the Caribbean. Most of the remainder went to the Chesapeake, and a couple of thousand ended up in the middle and northern colonies. Measured in immi-grants, black or white, the middle and northern colonies were backwaters compared to the Chesapeake and the West Indies, where planters imported huge numbers of poor white laborers and African slaves to work in the tobacco and cane fields.[10]

Jamestown was the first English colony to endure in America. It was England's first sustained experiment in establishing profitable commercial enterprises and stable political and social forms in the New World. In Virginia, the three key requirements for successful colonization were first put into practice: private property in land, a representative assembly for ordering local affairs, and civilian control of the military.[11] The colony was not intended as a model for some kind of idealized version of English society, a "Citty upon a Hill," or as a religious refuge for "God's chosen people." Nor was it meant to be a temporary privateering base, mining camp, or trading post. Jamestown was to be a permanent settlement that signaled England's claim to those vast lands between Spanish Florida in the south and French territories in the far north that were yet uninhabited by Europeans.

Virginia was founded on the fundamental principles of English colonial policy formulated during Elizabeth I's reign, notably in the writings of Richard Hakluyt the younger. Hakluyt's theories underpinned the rationale for colonial trade for the next two centuries: Colonies would produce goods in demand in England that hitherto had to be imported from Europe and Asia, and English merchants would provide colonists with necessary credit, laborers, and supplies. It was a harmonious vision in which settlers benefited from exploiting the natural wealth of the New World and Indians were converted to Christianity. The mother country profited from the importation of a wide range of valuable products, was able to put its poor and unemployed to work in the colonies, and prospered from the growth of domestic industries and overseas trade.[12]

England's empire was an "empire of goods." Tobacco, and later sugar and other staples, unlocked the wealth of America for Europeans. Virginia, like other colonies, created bright new opportunities for tens of thousands of merchants, retailers, and younger sons of gentry families who, with a bit of luck, might move into the ranks of middling or even large planters "and live like . . . Gentlem[e]n," attaining a social position they could have never achieved at home. Sir George Yeardley and the "collier of Croydon" would not be the first to arrive with little in their pockets and in a short time grow rich. For hundreds of thousands of poor men and women who arrived as indentured servants (contracted to serve as field laborers for between four and seven years), the Chesapeake offered them the possibility of setting up households on their own land and acquiring a modest sufficiency. Many died young or simply exchanged one kind of poverty in England for a different kind in Virginia; but faced with limited prospects in the mother country compared to at least a chance of becoming an independent smallholder in America, most who emigrated in the great movement after 1625 probably believed the gamble was worth it.[13]

Yet whatever the opportunities for Europeans, the creation of new societies in America unleashed powerful destructive forces. Wahunsonacock had told John Smith that the English had come "not for trade, but to invade my people and possesse my Country." With the steady spread of English settlements throughout the James and York River valleys during the second half of the 1620s and 1630s, some Indian peoples moved out beyond the reach of settlers, while others sought an accommodation as best they could. Opechancanough launched another attack in 1644 that claimed the lives of about 400 settlers, but by then any attempt to expel the English from Virginia was futile. Old, feeble, and near a hundred years old, he died a prisoner in a squalid Jamestown jail two years later, shot in the back by one of the guards.

For Indians, the rapid growth of settler populations and the spread of English settlement in North America was disastrous. Sporadic wars and European diseases dramatically reduced their numbers by the end of the century. Hostilities between the English and Powhatans were merely the first in a vicious cycle of war, plunder, and exploitation by which Europeans took possession of the land and dispossessed its peoples, the carnage and theft repeated over and over again across North America during the next two and a half centuries.[14]

Land was half the equation, labor the other. To maximize profits and increase production, planters needed a regular supply of laborers who could be forcibly controlled. The arrival of the first Africans (Angolans) at Jamestown in 1619 has been highlighted by historians seeking the origins of slavery and racism in North America. But the "20. and Odd Negroes" brought into Virginia were not the first slaves to arrive in English colonies—several were recorded in Bermuda a few years before—and planters did not have to look far for examples of full-blown slave regimes elsewhere in the Atlantic world, notably in Spanish and Portuguese colonies. The West Indies, not the Chesapeake, emerged as the epicenter of slavery in British America by the mid-seventeenth century, and the islands exerted an increasingly important influence on the development of slavery on the mainland. By 1660, the enslaved population of the British West Indies approached 33,000, compared to less than 1,700 in Virginia and Maryland, where white servants made up the main source of field labor until the final quarter of the century.

Down to the 1650s, when the number of slaves in Virginia was small and Africans worked alongside servants and masters to bring in the crop, relations between the two races may have been relatively relaxed. Occasionally, slaves were freed or were able to purchase their liberty. Some formerly enslaved people eventually acquired property and slaves of their own and proceeded to live peaceably alongside their white neighbors. But the limited opportunities for blacks should not be overstated. As early as the 1630s, the General Assembly began enacting measures that denied blacks the same civil protections enjoyed by English settlers and buttressed planters' disciplinary powers over their enslaved workers. With the rising volume of coerced African immigration after 1670, conditions of blacks in the colony, free and enslaved, deteriorated further, culminating in the comprehensive slave legislation of 1705 that gave formal sanction to an increasingly stark racial system.[15]

The decision of planters to switch from servants to slaves was motivated primarily by economics, a desire to reduce labor costs, because in the long run, enslaved Africans were considered a better investment. Few could have foreseen the momentous consequences of this shift. By 1750, Virginia's enslaved population stood at 107,000 (46 percent of the colony's total population), and in many tidewater counties north of the James River slaves made up a growing majority. The entire social terrain of Virginia had been transformed, slavery had become entrenched throughout the colony, and the lives of hundreds of thousands of African Americans and their descendants would continue to be blighted for more than a century to come. Virginia was by no means unique in its wholesale adoption of slavery in this period (South Carolina was another example), but it was the most populous and wealthiest of the mainland colonies, it had by far the largest enslaved population, and it would play a major role in defending the institution down to the Civil War. Surrender at Appomattox Courthouse in April 1865 was a long way from Jamestown in August 1619, but Virginia's history across nearly two and half centuries illustrates many of the salient features of plantation slavery in North America.[16]

## Beyond Jamestown

Captain John Smith still gazes across the James River. His statue, erected on Jamestown Island in 1909, portrays him in a resolute pose: hand on sword scanning the horizon for Spanish warships or much-needed provisions from England. Possibly it is how he would have liked to be remembered—vigilant, self-reliant, and resourceful—more so perhaps than by the overblown mythology of his relationship with Pocahontas. (She, too, has a statue on the Island, less than a hundred yards from Smith's). What would he have thought of a recent poll that indicates the great majority of Americans know little about what occurred at Jamestown 400 years ago or even where Jamestown is? Although he was an advocate for New England as well, he might well have been surprised to learn that many Americans today believe the Pilgrims founded America in 1620 at Plymouth, where (it is said) the first Thanksgiving took place. Why was Jamestown forgotten?

Part of the explanation lies in the rivalry that emerged between New England and the South in the years following the American Revolution. Each section developed its own foundation myth—the hardy, God-fearing, independent Pilgrims of Plymouth, who in an earlier age had separated themselves from Britain—contrasted to John Smith's salvation by Pocahontas and her subsequent conversion to Christianity. Smith's rescue was viewed as a crucial "generative moment" in which "each of the founders of a specifically southern culture was at the height of his or her powers. Smith is courageous and stoic, Pocahontas is courageous and generous, and Powhatan tempers justice for the deaths of his warriors with the mercy inspired by the love of his daughter." Smith and Pocahontas's story symbolized not only the origins of a distinctive southern character (emphasizing chivalry, honor, paternalism, and natural virtue), but also came to be seen as symbolic of the supposed acquiescence of Indians and Africans in the ways and ethos of white society.[17]

Following the Civil War, the cultural ascendancy of the North led to New England's foundation myth, almost completely eclipsing that of the South and becoming synonymous with America's founding. For a century after 1865, the South lagged behind the North in economic, urban, and cultural development and, according to Jack P. Greene, "seemed destined to remain on the peripheries of American society." Successive generations of professional historians, mostly trained in northern universities, constructed a national history (memory) that emphasized the centrality of New England puritanism to the nation's cultural roots while depicting the history of the South as largely irrelevant to modern America. New England was represented as forward-looking, progressive, and modern, the South as a social and cultural backwater haunted by the ghosts of a discredited past.[18]

No single foundation myth could possibly encompass the diverse origins of modern American society, of course, and historians today no more elevate the Pilgrims to the role of English America's first founders than they do Smith and Pocahontas. Nevertheless, the survival of Jamestown mattered for the future of America.

Had Jamestown failed, as seemed probable on any number of occasions in its first fifteen years, English attempts to establish settlements in the Chesapeake might have been delayed for several decades, or even abandoned. Possibly other European powers, such as the French or Dutch, might have colonized the mid-Atlantic region, which in turn could have discouraged the establishment of English settlements in New England. The Pilgrims might have ended up in Guiana (an alternative discussed at the time) instead of Plymouth, and the Massachusetts puritans might have joined puritan groups moving to

Providence Island, off the coast of Central America, and other islands in the West Indies.[19] The English might never have established themselves as the major colonial power on the mainland and might have confined their activities to the Caribbean instead. It is even possible that England would have turned away from colonizing projects in America altogether, apart from establishing small-scale trading posts, and concentrated on the carrying trade much as the Dutch did after losing New Netherland (New York) to the English in 1664.

Early America was littered with European failures—the Spanish in Florida, the French at Fort Caroline and Port Royal, and the English at Baffin Island, Roanoke, and Sagadahoc. But against all odds, Jamestown survived and, by surviving, became the first transatlantic site of an empire that would eventually carry the English language, laws, and institutions across North America. This is not to celebrate an English version of manifest destiny but rather to underline the point that if Virginia had collapsed, the history of North America and consequently the origins of modern American society would have been quite different. Representative government, first established at Jamestown in 1619, would in time blossom into a vibrant political culture throughout the British colonies and contribute to a new republican credo expressed in the founding of the United States, which itself would become an inspiration to peoples around the world seeking, in Thomas Jefferson's words, the "blessings and security of self-government."[20]

None of the foregoing should obscure the appalling consequences of European colonization for Indian peoples and enslaved Africans. Yet in the history of the founding of Jamestown can be glimpsed lines of development that have continued to influence American society ever since. At Jamestown, the peoples of America, Europe, and Africa first encountered one another, lived and worked alongside each other, traded with and fought one another, survived and persisted, and in so doing began the long process—often contentious, sometimes tragic, but ultimately successful—by which together they shaped a new world and forged a new people.

# Illustration Credits

12    The Powhatans. Drawn by Rebecca L. Wrenn.

18    John White/Theodor De Bry, Secota (1585). Courtesy of the John D. Rockefeller, Jr. Library, Colonial Williamsburg Foundation.

21    Okeus, from John Smith's *The Generall Historie of Virginia, New-England, and the Summer Isles*, (1632 edition). Courtesy of the John D. Rockefeller, Jr. Library, Colonial Williamsburg Foundation.

28    John White/Theodor De Bry, Americae pars, Nunc Virginia dicta, 1590. Courtesy of the John D. Rockefeller, Jr. Library, Colonial Williamsburg Foundation.

36    John Smith, from Smith's *Generall Historie*, (1632 edition). Courtesy of the John D. Rockefeller, Jr. Library, Colonial Williamsburg Foundation.

61    John Smith is captured by the Pamunkeys, from Smith's *Generall Historie*, (1632 edition). Courtesy of the John D. Rockefeller Jr. Library, Colonial Williamsburg Foundation.

63    The "triumph" of the Pamunkeys over John Smith, from Smith's *Generall Historie*, (1632 edition). Courtesy of the John D. Rockefeller, Jr. Library, Colonial Williamsburg Foundation.

69    John Smith saved by Pocahontas, from Smith's *Generall Historie*, (1632 edition). Courtesy of the John D. Rockefeller, Jr. Library, Colonial Williamsburg Foundation.

85    John Smith, Map of Virginia, 1624 (detail). Courtesy of the John D. Rockefeller, Jr. Library, Colonial Williamsburg Foundation.

101   Detail from John Smith's sketch map of 1608. Drawn by Rebecca L. Wrenn.

116   John Smith, Map of Virginia, 1624. Courtesy of the John D. Rockefeller, Jr. Library, Colonial Williamsburg Foundation.

126   John Smith in combat with Opechancanough, from Smith's *Generall Historie* (1632 edition). Courtesy of the John D. Rockefeller, Jr. Library, Colonial Williamsburg Foundation.

166   Principal Powhatan and English Settlements, 1607–1611. Drawn by Rebecca L. Wrenn.

194   Sir Thomas Dale. Artist unknown, Virginia Museum of Fine Arts, Richmond, Virginia. The Adolph D. and Wilkins C. Williams Fund.

219   Theodor De Bry, The Treaty with the Chickahominies. Courtesy of the John Carter Brown Library.

221   Theodor De Bry, Ralph Hamor visits Wahunsonacock. Courtesy of the John Carter Brown Library.

229   Simon Van de Passe, Matoaka als Rebecca, 1616 (engraving), from Smith's *Generall Historie*, (1624). Courtesy of the John Carter Brown Library.

256   English Settlements 1611–1624. Drawn by Rebecca L. Wrenn.

259   Theodor De Bry, The Indian Uprising of 1622. Courtesy of the John D. Rockefeller, Jr. Library, Colonial Williamsburg Foundation.

# Notes

## Prologue: Before Jamestown

1. Paul E. Hoffman, *A New Andalucia and a Way to the Orient: The American Southeast During the Sixteenth Century* (Baton Rouge, 1990), 57, 181–183. Velazquez had sailed with the expedition of Tristan de Luna to the Gulf of Mexico two years before. At the time of the storm, his ship, the *Santa Catalina,* was taking supplies to a Spanish colony that was being established at Santa Elena.

2. J. H. Elliott, *Imperial Spain, 1469–1716,* (Harmondsworth, England, 1970, Pelican edition), 181–189, 249–258; J. H. Elliott, *Spain and Its World, 1500–1700: Selected Essays* (New Haven, 1989), 7–24; Geoffrey Parker, *The Grand Strategy of Philip II* (New Haven, 1998).

3. Hoffman, *New Andalucia,* 183–187. Different accounts of where the Indians were initially taken vary, in some to Spain and in others to Havana and Mexico, see David B. Quinn, *North America from Earliest Discovery to First Settlements: The Norse Voyages to 1612* (New York, 1975), 239, and Clifford M. Lewis and Albert J. Loomie, *The Spanish Jesuit Mission in Virginia, 1570–1572* (Chapel Hill, N.C., 1953), 156. For the Powhatans and Spanish, see Charlotte M. Gradie, "The Powhatans in the Context of the Spanish Empire," in Helen C. Rountree, ed., *Powhatan Foreign Relations, 1500–1722* (Charlottesville, Va., 1993), 154–172.

4. Lewis and Loomie, *Spanish Jesuit Mission in Virginia, 1570–1572,* 19, 131, 156.

5. Spanish interest in establishing a colony on the North American mainland dates from Juan Ponce de León's discovery of Florida in 1513. David J. Weber, *The*

*Spanish Frontier in North America* (New Haven and London, 1992), 30–75; Hoffman, *A New Andalucia,* 3–102; Charles Hudson, *Knights of Spain, Warriors of the Sun: Hernando de Soto and the South's Ancient Chiefdoms* (Athens and London, 1997); Gradie, "The Powhatans," 155–165.

6. David B. Quinn, ed., *New American World: A Documentary History of North America to 1612,* 5 vols. (New York, 1979), 2:400–401, 415, 457–458, 535; Hoffman, *New Andalucia.*

7. Eugene Lyon, *The Enterprise of Florida: Pedro Menéndez de Avilés and the Spanish Conquest of 1565–1568* (Gainesville, Fla., 1976).

8. Lewis and Loomie, *Spanish Jesuit Mission in Virginia,* 89–92, 158.

9. It is clear from the accounts of Juan Rogel and Juan de la Carrera that the village where Don Luís stayed was a considerable distance from the Jesuits' settlement, described variously as "a day and a half away," and "10 leagues" from the Spanish, Lewis and Loomie, *Spanish Jesuit Mission in Virginia,* 109, 119, 134.

10. Ibid., 109–111, 134–139, 159, 180–185.

11. Ibid., 161, 195.

12. Quinn, *North America,* 240–261, 296–298; Woodbury Lowry, *The Spanish Settlements Within the Present Limits of the United States: Florida, 1562–1574* (New York, 1959), 155–207; John T. McGrath, *The French in Early Florida: In the Eye of the Hurricane* (Gainesville, Fla., 2000), 133–155; Lyon, *Enterprise of Florida,* 100–130.

## Chapter One: Two Worlds

1. Other influences on the rise of the Powhatan chiefdom may have been news of English attempts to establish a colony at Roanoke Island in the late 1580s, and fear of incursions by powerful Iroquoian-speaking peoples from the north, such as the Massawomecks, Helen C. Rountree, *Pocahontas's People: The Powhatan Indians of Virginia Through Four Centuries* (Norman, Okla., 1990), 24–25.

2. William Strachey, *The Historie of Travell into Virginia Britania* (1612), ed. Louis B. Wright and Virginia Freud, (London, 1953), 57; Frederick J. Fausz, "Patterns of Anglo-Indian Aggression and Accommodation Along the Mid-Atlantic Coast, 1584–1634," in William W. Fitzhugh, ed., *Cultures in Contact: The European Impact on Native Cultural Institutions in Eastern North America, A. D. 1000–1800* (Washington D.C., 1985), 226–236; Helen C. Rountree, *The Powhatan Indians of Virginia: Their Traditional Culture* (Lincoln, Neb., 1989), 7–15; Frederic W. Gleach, *Powhatan's World and Colonial Virginia: A Conflict of Cultures* (Lincoln, Neb., 1997), 22–28. The tidewater is the coastal region below the fall line where the rivers are tidal. In Virginia, the region extended about a hundred miles from the coast into the interior. The piedmont is the term used to describe the gently sloping plateau that runs up to the Blue Ridge Mountains, the eastern chain of the Appalachians.

3. Strachey, *Virginia Britania,* 43–44, 56–58, 104–105.

4. Philip L. Barbour, ed., *The Complete Works of Captain John Smith,* 3 vols. (Chapel Hill, N.C., 1986), 1:174–175. Following the defeat of the Kecoughtans,

which may have occurred in 1596 or 1597, the remnants of the people were transported over the York River and settled "amongest his owne people." Loyal supporters were moved into the Kecoughtans' former lands, under the rule of the paramount chief's son. Rountree, *Powhatan Indians*, 118–119; Gleach, *Powhatan's World*, 32–34.

5. Fausz, "Patterns of Anglo-Indian Aggression," 227–229.

6. Barbour, ed., *Complete Works*, 1:55.

7. Rountree, *Powhatan Indians*, 109–111.

8. The term commonly used to described the Powhatan political structure is "paramount chiefdom." The Chickahomines did not recognize themselves as Powhatans and were governed not by a single weroance but by a council of eight elders, Rountree, *Powhatan Indians*, 8–9.

9. Robert Beverley, *The History and Present State of Virginia*, ed. Louis B. Wright (Chapel Hill, N.C., 1947), 45, 61; J. Frederick Fausz, "Opechancanough: Indian Resistance Leader," in David G. Sweet and Gary B. Nash, eds., *Struggle and Survival in Colonial America* (Berkeley and Los Angeles, 1981), 23; Philip L. Barbour, ed., *The Jamestown Voyages Under the First Charter, 1606–1609*, 2 vols. (Cambridge, 1969), 1:93; Barbour, ed., *Complete Works*, 1:147; 2:97–99.

10. Ralph Hamor, A True Discourse of the Present State of Virginia (London, 1615), 13; Beverley, *History and Present State*, 61. Most modern historians dismiss the theory that Paquiquineo and Opechancanough were the same person; see, for example, Rountree, *Pocahontas's People*, 18–20. Frederic W. Gleach speculates that Paquiquineo (Don Luís) was Opechancanough's father, and that Opechancanough and Powhatan were cousins rather than brothers, *Powhatan's World*, 142–143. Opechancanough took a great deal of interest in John Smith's description of the Englishmen's "ships, and sayling the seas, the earth and skies," and was said to have "some knowledge of many of the fixed starrs, and had observed the north Starr and the course of the Constellatione about it, and called the greate beare Manguahaian, which in their language signifies the same," Barbour, ed., *Complete Works*, 1:49.

11. Estimates are derived from Christian F. Feest, in Bruce G. Trigger, ed., *Northeast* (Washington D.C., 1978), 241–242, 255–256, vol. 15 of William C. Sturtevant, ed., *Handbook of North American Indians*; E. Randolph Turner, "Socio-Political Organization Within the Powhatan Chiefdom and the Effects of European Contact, A.D. 1607–1646," in Fitzhugh, ed., *Cultures in Contact, 193.*

12. Helen C. Rountree, "The Powhatans and Other Woodland Indians as Travelers," in Rountree, ed., *Powhatan Foreign Relations, 29–36, 44–49.*

13. Strachey, *Virginia Britania*, 77–78; Barbour, ed., *Complete Works*, 1:161–162.

14. David B. Quinn, ed., *The Roanoke Voyages, 1584–1590*, 2 vols. (London, 1955), 1:420–423; Strachey, *Virginia Britania*, 79–80.

15. Strachey, *Virginia Britania*, 109–110; Barbour, ed., *Complete Works*, 1:166–167; Rountree, *Powhatan Indians*, 122–124.

16. Rountree, *Powhatan Indians,*79–87.

17. Barbour, ed., *Complete Works*, 1:165; Rountree, *Powhatan Indians*, 100–101, 117–120; John Frederick Fausz, "The Powhatan Uprising of 1622: A Historical Study

of Ethnocentrism and Cultural Conflict" (PhD diss., College of William and Mary, 1977), 84–90.

18. Beverley, *History and Present State,* 201; Strachey, *Virginia Britania,* 89; Edward Wright Haile, ed., *Jamestown Narratives: Eyewitness Accounts of the Virginia Colony, the First Decade: 1607–1617* (Champlain, Va., 1998), 486–487.

19. Barbour, ed., *Complete Works,* 1:55, 246–247.

20. Kenneth R. Andrews, *Trade, Plunder and Settlement: Maritime Enterprise and the Genesis of the British Empire, 1480–1630* (Cambridge, 1984), 41–63; David B. Quinn, *England and the Discovery of America, 1481–1620* (New York, 1974), 160–194.

21. Quinn, ed. *New American World, A Documentary History of North America to 1612,* 5 vols. (New York, 1979), 3:34–59; Andrews, *Trade, Plunder and Settlement,* 64–69, 139–141, 167–179, 183–199; David B. Quinn, *Explorers and Colonies: America, 1500–1625* (London, 1990), 207–223; Peter J. French, *John Dee: The World of an Elizabethan Magus* (London, 1972), 178–199; David Armitage, *The Ideological Origins of the British Empire* (Cambridge, 2000), 105–108; Benjamin Woolley, *The Queen's Conjuror: The Science and Magic of Dr. John Dee, Adviser to Queen Elizabeth I* (New York, 2001).

22. The Reverend Richard Hakluyt (known as the younger to distinguish him from his older cousin, the lawyer, of the same name), *Divers voyages touching the discovery of America . . .* (London, 1582), 8; Quinn, ed., *New American World,* 3:85, 89. E.G.R. Taylor, ed., *The Original Writings and Correspondence of the Two Richard Hakluyts,* 2 vols. (London, 1935), 2:211–326, 347; Jack P. Greene, *The Intellectual Construction of America: Exceptionalism and Identity from 1492 to 1800* (Chapel Hill, N.C., 1993), 36–46.

23. Susan Brigden, *New Worlds, Lost Worlds: The Rule of the Tudors, 1485–1603* (New York, 2000), 213–221, 245–248, 263–282; J. H. Elliott, *Spain and Its World,1500–1700: Selected Essays* (New Haven and London, 1989), 8–10; Geoffrey Parker, *The Grand Strategy of Philip II* (New Haven, 1998).

24. Ireland, not America, was the site of England's first important experiment in planting colonies. See Brigden, *New Worlds, Lost Worlds,* 155–162, 227–231, 254–263; David B. Quinn, *Raleigh and the British Empire* (London, 1947), 129–161; Nicholas Canny, "The Ideology of English Colonization: From Ireland to America," *William and Mary Quarterly* 30, (1973), 575–598; and ibid., *Making Ireland British, 1580–1650* (Oxford, 2001), 59–164.

25. James McDermott, *Martin Frobisher: Elizabethan Privateer* (New Haven, 2001), 28–256; Andrews, *Trade, Plunder and Settlement,* 167–178, 183–185. The standard biography of Gilbert is by David B. Quinn, ed., *The Voyages and Colonizing Enterprises of Sir Humphrey Gilbert,* 2 vols. (London, 1940), but see also David B. Quinn and N. M. Cheshire, *The New Found Land of Stephen Parmenius* (Toronto, 1972) for supplementary material.

26. Andrews, *Trade, Plunder and Settlement,* 116–166; John Sugden, *Sir Francis Drake* (London, 1990), 17–144; Samuel Bawlf, *The Secret Voyage of Sir Francis Drake* (New York, 2003).

27. Quinn, ed., *Roanoke Voyages:* 2:514.

28. David B. Quinn, *North America from Earliest Discovery to First Settlements: The Norse Voyages to 1612* (New York, 1975), 328–332.

29. Karen Ordahl Kupperman, *Roanoke: The Abandoned Colony* (Totowa, N.J., 1984), 15–44; Quinn, ed., *Roanoke Voyages*, 1:208–210.

30. David B. Quinn, *Set Fair for Roanoke: Voyages and Colonists, 1584–1606* (Chapel Hill, N.C., 1985), 106–108; ibid., ed., *Roanoke Voyages*, 1:257–258.

31. Quinn, ed., *Roanoke Voyages*, 1:258–261, 263–264, 268–270.

32. Kupperman, *Roanoke*, 84–87.

33. Quinn, *Set Fair for Roanoke*, 248–264. Little is known of the settlers' origins but it is likely most were recruited by John White from London and Essex with additions from the Portsmouth area. Besides White and Fernandes, two settlers, John Wright and James Lacie, can be identified with the 1585 expedition, Quinn, ed., *Roanoke Voyages*, 1:196.

34. Quinn, ed., *Roanoke Voyages*, 2:517–536, 608–622; Kupperman, *Roanoke*, 105–133. The fate of the lost colonists is discussed further in chapter 5 below.

35. Quinn, *England and the Discovery of America*, 291–302; Andrews, *Trade, Plunder, and Settlement*, 223–255; Parker, *Grand Strategy*, 179–268; Penryn Williams, *The Later Tudors: England, 1547–1603* (Oxford, 1995), 320–324. Similarly, the maritime war influenced Spanish plans to secure North America and led to the abandonment of a proposal to establish a garrison of three hundred men in the Chesapeake Bay.

36. There was no place at the king's court for Ralegh. The king disliked him personally for his opinions and influence, and Ralegh was quickly stripped of his privileges, ejected from his quarters at Durham House, and by the summer confined to the Tower of London charged with high treason. Raleigh Trevelyan, *Sir Walter Raleigh* (New York, 2002), 348–369; Quinn, ed., *New American World*, 5:168; Charles M. Andrews, *The Colonial Period of American History*, 4 vols. (1934; reprint, New Haven, 1964), 1:73–75, 84.

37. Philip L. Barbour, *The Three Worlds of Captain John Smith* (London, 1964), 3–108; Barbour, ed., *Complete Works*, 1:lvi–lvii; 3:377–384.

38. Among other things, Popham was interested in using Virginia as a place to send cashiered soldiers, poor artisans, and vagrants. Barbour, ed., *Complete Works*, 2:137.

39. Wesley Frank Craven, *The Southern Colonies in the Seventeenth Century, 1607–1689* (Baton Rouge, La., 1970), 61–63; Barbour, ed., *Jamestown Voyages*, 1:13–21, 24–34. An exploratory expedition sent by the Plymouth group in August 1606 to select a site for the northern settlement was captured by the Spanish off Florida. At the end of May the following year, two ships, the *Mary and John* and *Gift of God*, left Plymouth carrying more than 100 colonists and arrived off the coast of Maine in August. A settlement, Fort St. George, was established at the mouth of the Sagadahoc (present day Kennebec) River, which lasted a little over a year before being abandoned, Andrews, *Colonial Period*, 1:90–95.

## Chapter Two: The "Pearl and the Gold"

1. Kenneth Andrews, "Christopher Newport of Limehouse, Mariner," *William and Mary Quarterly* 11, 3d ser. (1954): 28–41.

2. John Ratcliffe's real name was Sicklemore. He may have been wealthy because he subscribed £50 to the Virginia Company, a relatively large sum. The term "pinnace" is used generally to describe a small vessel with a sail sometimes combined with oars.

3. Two incomplete lists survive from the period, each published in Smith's writings, which combined give the names and occupations of eighty-five men and boys. Other sources have revealed the names of an additional six planters and twenty-one of the forty sailors who remained in Virginia for a couple of months before returning to England. Philip L. Barbour, *The Three Worlds of Captain John Smith* (London, 1964), 3–63; Philip L. Barbour, ed., *The Complete Works of Captain John Smith*, 3 vols. (Chapel Hill, N.C., 1986) 1:208–209, 2:140–142; Philip L. Barbour, ed., *The Jamestown Voyages Under the First Charter, 1606–1609*, 2 vols. (Cambridge, 1969), 1:81–82, 143–145; William M. Kelso, with Beverly Straube, *Jamestown Rediscovery, 1994–2004* (Association for the Preservation of Virginia Antiquities, 2004): 19–23; Susan E. Sutton, "The First Virginia Colonists" (unpublished report, Jamestown-Yorktown Foundation, 1988).

4. David B. Quinn, ed., *The Roanoke Voyages, 1584–1590*, 2 vols. (London, 1955), 1:223.

5. See the "Instructions" issued by the London Council "by way of Advice" shortly before the expedition set out, Barbour, ed., *Jamestown Voyages*, 1:49–54.

6. Barbour, *Three Worlds of Captain John Smith*, 112–113.

7. Barbour, ed., *Complete Works*, 1:204–207; Barbour, ed., *Jamestown Voyages*, 1:129.

8. Barbour, ed., *Jamestown Voyages*, 1:133; Barbour, ed., *Complete Works*, 1:205.

9. Barbour, ed., *Jamestown Voyages*, 1:133–134; Barbour, ed., *Complete Works*, 1:205. According to Smith, only five Indians took part in the attack.

10. Barbour, *Three Worlds of Captain John Smith*, 102–105.

11. Barbour, ed., *Jamestown Voyages*, 1:88, 134–135. Patricia Seed, *Ceremonies of Possession in Europe's Conquest of the New World, 1492–1640* (Cambridge, 1995), 1–15, 41–63, 69–73, 179–193.

12. Barbour, ed., *Jamestown Voyages*, 1:69–71, 136–138.

13. Such was the Virginia Council's fear of the colonists suffering the same fate as the French at Fort Caroline that in their instructions "by way of advice" drawn up in December 1606, just before the expedition left England, they recommended establishing a settlement as far as a hundred miles inland. Ibid., 1:50.

14. Barbour, ed., *Complete Works*, 1:205–206; Barbour, ed., *Jamestown Voyages*, 1:138–140.

15. Barbour, ed., *Jamestown Voyages*, 1:80–81. The "Laake mentyoned by others," and "Mountaynes Apalatsi" (Appalachian Mountains) derive from Jacques Le

Moyne's *Floridae Americae Provinciae* (1591) and Theodore De Bry's *Collectiones Peregrinationum in Indiam Orientales . . .* , part 2 (Frankfurt, 1591).

16. Barbour, ed., *Jamestown Voyages,* 1:80–95, 98–102, 141.

17. Ibid., 1:95.

18. There were any number of precedents for such a design in Europe, derived from Renaissance concepts of town planning that allowed orderly growth along the main thoroughfares while providing formal space for the town's public activities; but the major influence may well have been Spanish America, where the central square and grid pattern was commonplace after being introduced in Lima in 1535. The central square and grid plan was also adopted in British settlements in Ulster during the early seventeenth century, notably at Londonderry. Ibid., 1:52, 95–98, 142. See for example, *Discovering the Americas: The Archive of the Indies* (New York, 1997), 164.

19. John W. Reps, *Tidewater Towns: City Planning in Colonial Virginia and Maryland* (Williamsburg, Va., 1972), 11–12, 33–37.

20. In fact, Don Pedro de Zúñiga, the Spanish ambassador in London, had written to Philip III about the Virginia expedition in January 1607 and informed him of the plan to occupy "the country above the Cape of Santa Elena." Barbour, ed., *Jamestown Voyages,* 1:69–71, 78–80, 98, 101–103, 107.

21. Cope thought the culprit was Captain John Martin, son of Sir Richard Martin, master of the mint.

22. Barbour, ed., *Jamestown Voyages,* 1:111–119.

23. Barbour, ed., *Complete Works,* 1:29.

24. A man in his middle-to-late thirties, buried with a captain's staff in a gabled-lidded coffin just outside the west palisade of the fort, has been recently unearthed by William Kelso and his team of archaeologists at Jamestown. This find may be the remains of Gosnold, who was thirty-six when he died, Kelso, with Straube, *Jamestown Rediscovery,* 120–125.

25. Carville V. Earle, "Environment, Disease, and Mortality in Early Virginia," in Thad W. Tate and David L. Ammerman, eds., *The Chesapeake in the Seventeenth Century: Essays on Anglo-American Society* (Chapel Hill, N.C., 1979), 96–125; Barbour, ed., *Jamestown Voyages,* 1:143–145; Barbour, ed., *Complete Works,* 1:33, 210.

26. Barbour, ed., *Jamestown Voyages,* 1:213–234. The prime mover in Wingfield's downfall, according to his account, was not Ratcliffe, Smith, or Martin, but Gabriel Archer, a man he accused of "allwayes hatching of some mutany."

27. Ibid., 1:145, 214–216; Barbour, ed., *Complete Works,* 1:210.

28. Barbour, ed., *Complete Works,* 1:35–37, 2:144–145.

29. Ibid., 1:45–47, 2:146–147.

30. Ibid., 1:39–53, 2:145–149. The ship that carried off several Toppahannocks may have been commanded by Samuel Mace in 1603.

31. Ibid., 1:59, 2:149–150. Frederic W. Gleach argues that the ceremony was not for the purpose of divining Smith's intentions; rather, it was part of an elaborate process (that included the extended marches of previous weeks) to absorb the English settlement ritually into the Powhatan's world, see Frederic W. Gleach, *Powhatan's World and Colonial Virginia: A Conflict of Cultures* (Lincoln, Neb., 1997), 112–116.

32. The site has recently been discovered and is being investigated by archaeologists.

33. Barbour, ed., *Complete Works*, 1:53–57, 2:150–151.

34. Ibid., 1:136–139; J. Leo Lemay, *Did Pocahontas Save Captain John Smith?* (Athens, Ga., 1992); Peter Hulme, *Colonial Encounters: Europe and the Native Caribbean, 1492–1797* (London, 1986), 140–152. I owe the point about Pocahontas's instructing Smith in Algonquian to Camilla Townsend, *Pocahontas and the Powhatan Dilemma* (New York, 2004), 73–74.

35. Barbour, ed., *Complete Works*, 2:151. On the role of Pocahontas as a "Beloved Woman" in the ritual, see Paula Gunn Allen, *Pocahontas: Medicine Woman, Spy, Entrepreneur, Diplomat* (New York, 2003), 31, 39–52.

## Chapter Three: Smith's Epic

1. Philip L. Barbour, ed., *The Complete Works of Captain John Smith*, 3 vols. (Chapel Hill, N.C., 1986), 1:61, 213–214, 2:151–153; Philip L. Barbour, ed., *The Jamestown Voyages Under the First Charter, 1606–1609*, 2 vols. (Cambridge, 1969), 1:227.

2. Barbour, ed., *Jamestown Voyages*, 1:159–161. Back in London, winter's grip was equally intense. The Thames froze to such a thickness that shopkeepers and hawkers were able to set up stalls and hold markets (frost fairs) on the river, see David B. Quinn, *Explorers and Colonies: America, 1500–1625* (London, 1990), 416–417.

3. Barbour, ed., *Complete Works*, 1:61, 214, 217–218, 222–223, 2:153–154, 157, 160–163; Barbour, ed., *Jamestown Voyages*, 1:227–228.

4. Barbour, ed., *Complete Works*, 1:61–63.

5. Ibid., 63–67.

6. Ibid., 69–71, 2:156.

7. Ibid., 1:73–79, 216–217, 2:156–158.

8. Ibid., 1:79–81, 2:158. In fact, Smith was no more than ten miles from the Blackwater River, one of the Chowan's major tributaries.

9. Ibid., 2:153–154, 157–158.

10. Smith's opposition to an expedition to the lands of the Monacans was reported by Anas Todkill in the *Proceedings* (published in 1612), but no mention of his reluctance is found in his own earlier account, *A True Relation*. Given his appetite for exploration it is unlikely he would have dragged his feet when given the opportunity to lead a company of sixty men into the interior. Ibid., 1:85–87, 220.

11. Kiptopeke was the brother of Debbedeavon (Tapatiaton), the "laughing king" of the Accomacs. Ibid., 1:224–225, 2:163.

12. Ibid., 1:226–229, 2:162–169; Philip L. Barbour, *The Three Worlds of Captain John Smith* (London, 1964), 200–211.

13. Smith was familiar with the account of Sir Francis Drake's voyage "into the South Sea, and there hence about the whole Globe of the Earth, begun in the yeere of our Lord 1577," which has a description of Indians on the coast of California pleading with Drake to become their king and they his subjects. Drake accepted in

the name of Queen Elizabeth, "wishing that the riches & treasure thereof might so conveniently be transported to the inriching of her kingdome at home." Henry R. Wagner, *Sir Francis Drake's Voyage Around the World: Its Aims and Achievements* (San Francisco, 1926), 274–277.

14. Barbour, ed., *Complete Works*, 1:232, 2:172.

15. Ibid., 2:170–180.

16. Ibid., 1:226–227, 2:207. The "Spanish Decades" refers to Richard Eden's translation of *The Decades of the newe worlde or west India* by Pietro Martire d'Anghiera (London, 1555), and "the Relations of Master Hackluit" to Richard Hakluyt's *The Principal Navigations, Voyages, Traffiques and Discoveries of the English Nation*, 3 vols. (London, 1598–1600).

17. Barbour, ed., *Complete Works*, 2:129, 168, 176–178.

18. Ibid., 206–207.

## Chapter Four: Innocence Lost

1. Philip L. Barbour, ed., *The Complete Works of Captain John Smith*, 3 vols. (Chapel Hill, N.C., 1986), 1:233–234.

2. Philip L. Barbour, ed., *The Jamestown Voyages Under the First Charter, 1606–1609*, 2 vols. (Cambridge, 1969), 1:236–240; Barbour, ed., *Complete* Works, 1:49, 55, 63.

3. David B. Quinn, *England and the Discovery of America, 1481–1620* (New York, 1974), 450–452.

4. Barbour, ed., *Complete Works*, 1:234.

5. Ibid., 1:233–235.

6. For an interpretation of the Powhatan meaning of this ritual see Paula Gunn Allen, *Pocahontas: Medicine Woman, Spy, Entrepreneur, Diplomat* (New York, 2003), 87–89.

7. Barbour, ed., *Complete Works*, 1:236–237. The cloak, "Powhatan's mantle," is in the Ashmolean Museum, Oxford, England.

8. David B. Quinn, ed., *The Roanoke Voyages, 1584–1590*, 2 vols. (London, 1955), 1:279, 2:531. John White reported: "[O]ur Savage Manteo, by the commandement of Sir Walter Ralegh, was christened in Roanoak, and called Lord thereof, and of Dasamongueponke, in reward of his faithfull service." Evidently, conversion to Christianity was not considered a necessary precondition for Wahunsonacock's coronation.

9. Edward Wright Haile, ed., *Jamestown Narratives: Eyewitness Accounts of the Virginia Colony, the First Decade: 1607–1617* (Champlain, Va., 1998), 486, 492.

10. Cecil Papers, Hatfield House, Hertfordshire, England, Class Cecil, 1605–1612, 78, 80–81, 112, 170–171, 177–179, 184–186, 193–195; Virginia Colonial Records Project, Survey Report 08495.

11. William Strachey gives a more optimistic account of Newport's expedition and the possibility of discovering valuable minerals in the "Mountaynes," in *The Historie*

*of Travell into Virginia Britania* (1612), ed. Louis B. Wright and Virginia Freud (London, 1953), 33–34.

12. Barbour, ed., *Complete Works,* 1:238–239; 2:185–187.

13. Ibid., 1:140–141, 144, 150–151; 2:187–190.

14. Ibid., 1:143–177.

15. Ibid., 240–245.

16. Ibid., 246–250, 2:199.

17. Captain Peter Wynne was left in charge of the fort in Smith's absence. He arrived with the second supply, was immediately appointed to the council, accompanied Newport on his expedition, and wrote enthusiastically about Virginia to Sir John Egerton in a letter of 26 November 1608 (see Barbour, ed., *Jamestown Voyages,* 1:245–246). He died the following spring.

18. Barbour, ed., *Complete Works,* 1:250–256, 2:199–205.

19. Ibid., 1:254–262.

20. Ibid., 263–268, 2:213–214.

## Chapter Five: Virginea Britannia

1. Emmanuel Le Roy Lauderie, *Times of Feast, Times of Famine: A History of Climate Since the Year 1000* (New York, 1971), 378.

2. Charles M. Andrews, *The Colonial Period of American History,* 4 vols. (1934; reprint, New Haven, 1964), 1:104–105; Alexander Brown, *The Genesis of the United States,* 2 vols. (New York, 1980), 2:1012–1013.

3. Brown, *Genesis,* 2:894.

4. Philip L. Barbour, ed., *The Jamestown Voyages Under the First Charter, 1606–1609,* 2 vols. (Cambridge, 1969), 1:163.

5. Alexander Brown, *The First Republic in America* (Boston and New York, 1898), 73–74, 83; Brown, *Genesis,* 1:341–342.

6. Andrews, *Colonial Period,* 1:102–103; Brown, *Genesis,* 2:992; Theodore K. Rabb, *Jacobean Gentleman: Sir Edwin Sandys, 1561–1629* (Princeton, 1998).

7. For the sake of clarity and consistency, unless there is a specific reason for referring to the Virginia Council (the ruling body of the Company) I use the terms "Virginia Company" or "London Company" instead.

8. Samuel M. Bemiss, *The Three Charters of the Virginia Company of London . . . 1606–1621* (Williamsburg, Virginia, 1957), 42, 47–48; Wesley Frank Craven, *Dissolution of the Virginia Company: The Failure of a Colonial Experiment* (New York, 1932), 29–33. A sure sign of the Company's concerns about Captain John Smith's leadership was the express command that the president and council "nowe resident" in Virginia resign their offices and render obedience to the new governor as soon as he arrived.

9. Bemiss, *Three Charters,* 42–43.

10. Brown, *Genesis,* 1:248–253; Brown, *First Republic,* 101–104; David B. Quinn, ed., *New American World: A Documentary History of North America to 1612,* 5 vols. (New York, 1979), 5:206.

11. Quinn, ed., *New American World,* 5:238–248.

12. Earlier promotional literature of the 1570s and 1580s had also invoked spreading the gospel as one of the "manifold" benefits that would follow from the enlargement of the "Realme of Englande" by founding colonies in America, but the evangelical impulse was very much a secondary theme. John Parker, "Religion and the Virginia Colony, 1609–10," in K. R. Andrews, N. P. Canny, and P. E. H. Hair, eds., *The Westward Enterprise: English activities in Ireland, the Atlantic and America, 1480–1650* (Liverpool, U.K., 1978), 247–248; E. G. R. Taylor, ed., *The Original Writings and Correspondence of the Two Richard Hakluyts,* 2 vols. (London, 1935), 2:211–216; Jack P. Greene, *The Intellectual Construction of America: Exceptionalism and Identity from 1492 to 1800* (Chapel Hill, N.C., 1993), 36–37.

13. Parker, "Religion and the Virginia Colony," 257–260; Edward L. Bond, *Damned Souls in a Tobacco Colony: Religion in Seventeenth-Century Virginia* (Macon, Ga., 2000), 1–29; Andrew Fitzmaurice emphasizes ideals of honor and glory as promoted by humanists in colonization literature of the period, see *Humanism and America: An Intellectual History of English Colonization* (Cambridge, 2003), 71–78, 85–87.

14. Quinn, ed., *New American World,* 5:239–240; Brown, *Genesis,* 1:256, 298–299, 314, 369, 374–375; Robert Gray, *A Good Speed to Virginia* (London, 1609), n.p.

15. Patrick Collinson, *The Birthpangs of Protestant England: Religious and Cultural Change in the Sixteenth and Seventeenth Centuries* (London, 1988), 1–27; James Ellison, *George Sandys: Travel, Colonialism, and Tolerance in the Seventeenth Century* (Cambridge, 2002), 90–98; David Cressy, *Bonfires and Bells: National Memory and the Protestant Calendar in Elizabethan and Stuart England* (Los Angeles, 1989); Bond, *Damned Souls,* 11–15, 19; Brown, *Genesis,* 1:289–290. For a providential account of England's victory over the Spanish Armada, see Samuel Purchas, *Hakluytus Posthumus or Purchas His Pilgrimes . . . ,* 20 vols. (Glasgow, 1906–1908), 19:466–510.

16. Barbour, ed., *Jamestown Voyages,* 2:254–260.

17. Bemiss, *Three Charters,* 66–67; Quinn, ed., *New American World,* 5:214.

18. Edward D. Neill, *History of the Virginia Company of London* (1869; reprint, New York, 1968), 26–27.

19. Alden T. Vaughan, "Powhatans Abroad: Virginia Indians in England," in Robert Appelbaum and John Wood Sweet, eds., *Envisioning an English Empire: Jamestown and the Making of the North Atlantic World* (Philadelphia, 2005), 51–54.

20. William Strachey, *The Historie of Travell into Virginia Britania* (1612), ed. Louis B. Wright and Virginia Freud (London, 1953), 34, 91.

21. The standard interpretation of the fate of the lost colonists is derived from the works of David Beers Quinn, especially *England and the Discovery of America,* 453–480, and *Set Fair for Roanoke,* 345–353. It is worth noting that Strachey himself made no connection between the destruction of the Chesapeakes and the killing of the lost colonists. Strachey, *Virginia Britania,* 104–105; Helen C. Rountree, *Pocahontas's People: The Powhatan Indians of Virginia Through Four Centuries* (Norman, Okla., 1990), 21–28.

22. Lee Miller argues the lost colonists were attacked along the Chowan River shortly after leaving Roanoke Island in 1587 or 1588, and dispersed throughout the Carolina piedmont by the Mangoags and Occaneechees, *Roanoke: Solving the Mystery of the Lost Colony* (New York, 2001), 227–260. There is no evidence, however, that such an attack took place.

23. For Strachey's comments on the southern and western limits of the Powhatans' influence, see *Virginia Britania*, 36, 56, 106. Strachey is explicit that the lost colonists were killed *outside* Wahunsonacock's dominions. The Powhatan chief, he wrote, had ordered the slaughter "of so many of our Nation without offence given, and such as were seated far from him, and in the Territory of those Weroances which did in no sort depend on him, or acknowledge him." Either as a result of the chief's influence over neighboring peoples to the south or by direct involvement of his warriors, scattered English survivors were tracked down and murdered about the time of Newport's expedition to the falls. Edward Bland and five other Englishmen who explored the Virginia interior from Fort Henry on the Appomattox River to the falls of the Roanoke River in 1650 heard a story from their Indian guides that "many years since" the "late great Emperour Appachancano [Opechancanough]" had led an expedition southwards to "make a War upon the Tuskarood [Tuscaroras]." Another story told by the Indians described the murder of the king of the Chowanocs by the "King of Pawhatan," possibly Wahunsonacock himself or one of his sons. At the falls of the Roanoke River, Bland and his party discovered several "great heapes of bones"; when they inquired how the bones came to be there, the Indians recounted that "Appachancano one morning with four hundred men treacherously slew two hundred and forty" Indians who lived by the river. The Englishmen named the place "Golgotha." They learnt also that "there were other English amongst the Indians" further in the interior, but were unable to make contact, Clarence Walworth Alvord and Lee Bidgood, *The First Explorations of the Trans-Allegheny Region by the Virginians, 1650–1674* (Cleveland, Ohio, 1912), 122–123, 125, 128.

24. Strachey, *Virginia Britania*, 106–107.

25. A fuller account of the argument can be found in James Horn, *Slaughter at Roanoak: Finding the Lost Colonists* (in progress).

26. For a recent account that argues allegations about the killing of the lost colonists by Powhatan warriors were fabricated by the Virginia Company to justify its increasingly bellicose posture towards the Indians, see Miller, *Roanoke*, 218–222; Strachey, *Virginia Britania*, 89, 91.

27. Strachey, *Virginia Britania*, 91–93; Quinn, ed., *New American World*, 5:215–216.

28. Strachey, *Virginia Britania*, 34; Edward Wright Haile, ed., *Jamestown Narratives: Eyewitness Accounts of the Virginia Colony, the First Decade: 1607–1617* (Champlain, Va., 1998), 367; Bemiss, *Three Charters*, 59–61. Jamestown would be reduced to a small garrison and port.

29. Philip L. Barbour, ed., *The Complete Works of Captain John Smith,* 3 vols. (Chapel Hill, N.C., 1986), 1:265–266. In fact, a passage from *A True and Sincere Declaration,* published the following year, suggests that one of the expeditions sent by

John Smith to search the lands of the Mangoags did in fact find evidence of the lost colonists alive in the North Carolina interior but were prevented by the Indians from making contact with them, Haile, ed., *Jamestown Narratives,* 367.

30. Barbour, ed., *Complete Works,* 1:266–267, 2:216–217.

31. Ibid., 1:267, 2:217; Haile, ed., *Jamestown Narratives,* 363; Barbour, ed., *Jamestown Voyages,* 2:276.

32. Barbour, ed., *Jamestown Voyages,* 2:282, 291–301. The Indians' account reveals how information about Jamestown had spread to peoples some three hundred miles away.

33. Ibid., 2:301–319. On the return journey, Captain Écija learned from Guale Indians that the English settlement "had many people" and "Negroes with them." There is a good deal more to this account than is presented here, especially in regard to Écija's influence among the Indian peoples of the coastal regions of Georgia and South Carolina, who he had visited four years before on a scouting expedition to the Outer Banks, see Irene A. Wright, "Spanish Policy Toward Virginia, 1606–1612: Jamestown, Écija, and John Clark of the Mayflower," *American Historical Review* 25 (1920), 450–452, 463–465.

34. Barbour, ed., *Complete Works,* 1:266.

## Chapter Six: War and Retribution

1. A fleet of six ships and a ketch (a small vessel with two masts) sailed from Blackwall, London, in mid-May and was joined at Plymouth by the *Blessing* and the pinnace, *Virginia.* The pinnace was built at Sagadahoc in 1607 and was the first English ship constructed in America. She returned to England after only a week at sea, presumably having sprung a leak. Besides other passengers, the *Blessing* carried twenty women and children.

2. David B. Quinn, *Explorers and Colonies: America, 1500–1625* (London, 1990), 418; Alexander Brown, *The Genesis of the United States,* 2 vols. (New York, 1980), 1:289, 297–298.

3. Samuel Purchas, *Hakluytus Posthumus or Purchas His Pilgrimes . . . ,* 20 vols. (Glasgow, 1906–1908), 19:5. The Company had expected the three principals to sail on different ships, each carrying a copy of the governor's commission, ensuring that should any mishap befall Gates during the voyage the next in command would take over. Possibly because Somers and Newport could not agree on who should take precedence and sail in which ship, or for some other reason, both men (with their copies of the commission) ended up on the *Sea Venture.* Somers was knighted in 1603 and during the early years of James I's reign represented the Dorset port of Lyme Regis in Parliament, David F. Raine, *Sir George Somers: A Man and His Times* (Newell, Iowa, 1984), 23–91.

4. Purchas, *Hakluytus Posthumus,* 19:1–2, 5–8.

5. Ibid., 8–15; *A True Declaration of the estate of the Colonie in Virginia* (London, 1610), 10 (published by the Virginia Company); Nathaniel Butler, *Historye of the*

*Bermudaes or Summer Islands*, ed. Sir Henry J. Lefroy, Hakluyt Society, no. 65 (London, 1882), 11–12.

6. Purchas, *Hakluytus Posthumus*, 19:25–27; Butler, *Historye of the Bermudaes or Summer Islands*, 13–14. Butler's account mentions fourteen "of their most resolute men" attempted the voyage to Virginia.

7. Purchas, *Hakluytus Posthumus*, 19:27–34; Butler, *Historye of the Bermudaes*, 14. Gates's council was made up of Sir George Somers, Capt. John Smith, Capt. John Ratcliffe, Capt. John Martin, Capt. Peter Wynne, Capt. Richard Waldo, Master Matthew Scrivener, Capt. Thomas Woode, and a "Master Fleetewoode," three of whom (Wynne, Waldo, and Scrivener) were already dead by the time Gates received his instructions from the London Company in mid-May 1609.

8. Purchas, *Hakluytus Posthumus*, 19:2–4; Philip L. Barbour, ed., *The Complete Works of Captain John Smith*, 3 vols. (Chapel Hill, N.C., 1986), 1:268–269, 2:219–220; George Percy, "A Trewe Relacyon of the Procedeinges and Occurrentes of Moment which have hapned in Virginia" [1609–1612], in *Tylers Quarterly Magazine* 3 (1922): 262; Philip L. Barbour, ed., *The Jamestown Voyages Under the First Charter, 1606–1609*, 2 vols. (Cambridge, 1969), 2:283–284, 287.

9. In Smith's *Proceedings* and *Generall Historie*, the number of men sent to Nansemond with Capt. Martin is given as "neare as many" as went to the falls (120), Barbour, ed., *Complete Works*, 1:269, 2:220. George Percy states that Francis West went to he falls with 140 men, "Trewe Relacyon," 262–263. The creation of two new settlements may have been an echo of Gates' instructions (probably relayed to other leaders) that required him to abandon Jamestown as the colony's principal seat and establish settlements to the south in the North Carolina interior and at the falls. Edward Wright Haile, ed., *Jamestown Narratives: Eyewitness Accounts of the Virginia Colony, the First Decade: 1607–1617* (Champlain, Va., 1998), 895.

10. Percy, "Trewe Relacyon," 262–263; William Strachey, *The Historie of Travell into Virginia Britania* (1612), ed. Louis B. Wright and Virginia Freud (London, 1953), 66. Smith described the Nansemonds' territory as a "1000. Acres of most excellent fertill ground, so sweete, so pleasant, so beautifull, and so strong a prospect, for an invincible strong Citty, with so many commodities, that [he] kn[e]w as yet [he had] not seene," Barbour, ed., *Complete Works*, 1:81.

11. J. Frederick Fausz, "'An Abundance of Blood Shed on Both Sides': England's First Indian War, 1609–1614," *Virginia Magazine of History and Biography* 98 (1990): 22–24. My interpretation of Smith's negotiations with Parahunt for the village of Powhatan is different from that of Fausz.

12. Barbour, ed., *Complete Works*, 1:270–271; Haile, ed., *Jamestown Narratives*, 482–483; Percy, "Trewe Relacyon," 262–264.

13. Barbour, ed., *Complete Works*, 1:272–275; Percy, "Trewe Relacyon," 264; Barbour, ed., *Jamestown Voyages*, 2:283–284.

14. Barbour, ed., *Jamestown Voyages*, 2:285–287. Five ships left Virginia at the beginning of October but two were lost in a storm off the coast of France on the last leg of the voyage.

15. Haile, ed., *Jamestown Narratives*, 356–369; Brown, *Genesis*, 1:354.

16. Percy, "Trewe Relacyon," 264–265. Fort Algernon had about fifty men and was commanded by John Ratcliffe.

17. Percy, "Trewe Relacyon," 265–266; Haile, ed., *Jamestown Narratives,* 483–484; Purchas, *Hakluytus Posthumus,* 19:68–69. Captain James Davis had arrived in October with 16 men on the pinnace *Virginia* and was placed in charge of Fort Algernon when Ratcliffe was killed. He was an experienced mariner who had sailed with George Popham to the Sagadahoc River, Maine, in 1607.

18. Percy, "Trewe Relacyon," 266–267; Barbour, ed., *Complete Works,* 2:232–233. Examples of cannibalism practiced by Europeans in this period are rare but see Percy, "Trewe Relacyon," 261; Jean de Léry, *History of a Voyage to the Land of Brazil, Otherwise Called America,* trans. Janet Whatley (Berkeley, 1992), xxvii-xxix, 132–133, 212–213. See also Michel Eyquem de Montaigne's famous essay, "Of the Cannibales" (1580), in which he argued the wars of religion in Europe precipitated far greater barbarity on the part of Europeans than any behavior exhibited by New World Indians, in Andrew Hadfield, ed., *Amazons, Savages, and Machiavels. Travel and Colonial Writing in English, 1550–1630: An Anthology* (Oxford, 2001), 286–295. Archaeological evidence supports Percy's description of settlers eating their horses, dogs, cats, snakes, rats, and other vermin, but no conclusive proof exists of cannibalism, see Joanne Bowen and Susan Trevarthen Andrews, "The Starving Time at Jamestown . . . " (unpublished report submitted to Jamestown Rediscovery, 2000); William M. Kelso, with Beverly Straube, *Jamestown Rediscovery, 1994–2004* (Association for the Preservation of Virginia Antiquities, 2004), 62–63. I am grateful to Bowen and Andrews for allowing me to read their report. For the Virginia Company's version of the allegation about the husband who butchered and ate his wife, see Haile, ed., *Jamestown Narratives,* 473–474.

19. Fausz, "An 'Abundance of Blood Shed on Both Sides,'" 55.

20. Percy, "Trewe Relacyon," 268; Haile, ed., *Jamestown Narratives,* 457, 895–896.

21. Purchas, *Hakluytus Posthumus,* 19:32–42. Strachey described the larger of the two pinnaces, *Deliverance,* as being forty feet long at the keel and nineteen feet at the beam. About 130 settlers made the voyage to Virginia, 2 were left behind on Bermuda, and another 14 to 20 had died or been lost at sea.

22. Percy, "Trewe Relacyon," 268–269; Purchas, *Hakluytus Posthumus,* 19:44–45; *A True Declaration of the estate of the Colonie in Virginia* (London, 1610), 12; Haile, ed., *Jamestown Narratives,* 456–457.

23. Percy, "Trewe Relacyon," 269; Purchas, *Hakluytus Posthusmus,* 19:44–46, 52–54; Brown, *Genesis,* 1:363; Haile, ed., *Jamestown Narratives,* 702. In fact, Gates intended to wait at Point Comfort for ten days in case De La Warr's fleet arrived before setting off for Newfoundland.

24. Barbour, ed., *Complete Works,* 2:234; Purchas, *Hakluytus Posthumus,* 19:54, 59–60; Haile, ed., *Jamestown Narratives,* 466–467. By a strange coincidence, De La Warr and Zúñiga left England on the same day, April 11, one heading west into the Atlantic and the other southeast to return to Spain.

25. Darrett B. Rutman, "The Virginia Company and Its Military Regime," in Darrett B. Rutman, ed., *The Old Dominion: Essays for Thomas Perkins Abernethy* (Charlottesville, Va., 1964), 10–11.

26. Lord De La Warr was thirty-three when he arrived in Virginia, had distinguished himself in the wars in the Netherlands and Ireland, served in Parliament, and was a member of the king's Privy Council. Purchas, *Hakluytus Posthumus,* 19:60–61; Haile, ed., *Jamestown Narratives,* 458–459; Samuel M. Bemiss, *The Three Charters of the Virginia Company of London . . . 1606–1621* (Williamsburg, Va., 1957), 72; David H. Flaherty, ed., *Lawes Divine, Morall and Martiall, etc.* (Charlottesville, Va., 1969), x-xxxv, 10–17. For a general discussion of the laws see Rutman, "The Virginia Company" and David Thomas Konig, "'Dale's Laws' and the Non-Common Law Origins of Criminal Justice in Virginia," *The American Journal of Legal History* 26 (1982): 354–375.

27. Purchas, *Hakluytus Posthumus,* 19:61–62.

28. Haile, ed., *Jamestown Narratives,* 466; Purchas, *Hakluytus Posthumus,* 19:56–58; Kelso with Straube, *Jamestown Rediscovery, 1994–2004,* 47–52.

29. Bemiss, *Three Charters,* 73; *Hakluytus Posthumus,* 19:63–65.

30. Generally on the war, see Fausz, "An 'Abundance of Blood Shed on Both Sides,'" 3–56, and Ivor Noël Hume, *The Virginia Adventure. Roanoke to James Towne: An Archaeological and Historical Odyssey* (New York, 1994), 284–295. Percy, "Trewe Relacyon," 268, 270; Strachey, *Virginia Britania,* 67–68; Haile, ed., *Jamestown Narratives,* 897–898.

31. Percy, "Trewe Relacyon," 271–273.

32. *Hakluytus Posthumus,* 19:66–67; Strachey, *Virginia Britania,* 65–66; Percy, "Trewe Relacyon," 273.

33. Bemiss, *Three Charters,* 66; Strachey, *Virginia Britania,* 64; Percy, "Trewe Relacyon," 273–274.

34. Strachey, *Virginia Britania,* 85–86; Percy, "Trewe Relacyon," 274–275; Haile, ed., *Jamestown Narratives,* 527–530, 898; *The Relation of the Right Honourable the Lord De-La-Warre . . .* (London, 1611), 1–2.

35. Haile, ed., *Jamestown Narratives,* 530–532; *The Relation of the Right Honourable the Lord De-La-Warre . . . ,* 2–3.

36. Barbour, ed., *Complete Works,* 2:234–235; *A True Declaration.* See also Richard (or Robert) Rich, "News from Virginia," in Haile, ed., *Jamestown Narratives,* 372–379.

37. *A True Declaration;* Alexander Brown, *The First Republic in America* (Boston and New York, 1898), 140–141.

# Chapter Seven: Redeeming Pocahontas

1. Alexander Brown, *The Genesis of the United States,* 2 vols. (New York, 1980), 1:463; Philip L. Barbour, ed., *The Complete Works of Captain John Smith,* 3 vols. (Chapel Hill, N.C., 1986), 2:239; Darrett B. Rutman, "The Historian and the Mar-

shal: A Note on the Background of Sir Thomas Dale," *Virginia Magazine of History and Biography* 68 (1960): 284–294.

2. Bodleian Library, Ashmole 1005, ff. 209–210 (VCRP X.12); George Percy, "A Trewe Relacyon of the Procedeinges and Occurrentes of Moment which have hapned in Virginia" [1609–1612], in *Tylers Quarterly Magazine* 3 (1922): 275–276.

3. Barbour, ed., *Complete Works*, 2:239; Dale to Salisbury, 17 August, 1611, Public Record Office, CO1/1, f. 95 (VCRP 622); David H. Flaherty, ed., *Lawes Divine, Morall and Martiall, etc.* (Charlottesville, Va., 1969), 26–101; Edward Wright Haile, ed., *Jamestown Narratives: Eyewitness Accounts of the Virginia Colony, the First Decade: 1607–1617* (Champlain, Va., 1998), 899–900; Darrett B. Rutman, "The Virginia Company and Its Military Regime," in Darrett B. Rutman, ed., *The Old Dominion: Essays for Thomas Perkins Abernethy* (Charlottesville, Va., 1964), 18–19; Percy, "Trewe Relacyon," 276; [Robert Johnson], *The New Life of Virginea . . . Being the Second part of Nova Britannia* (London, 1612), 13; Susan Myra Kingsbury, ed., *The Records of the Virginia Company*, 4 vols. (Washington, D.C., 1906–1935), 3:32; Ralph Hamor, *A True Discourse of the Present State of Virginia* (London, 1615).

4. Bodleian Library, Ashmole 1005, ff. 208–210 (VCRP X.12).

5. Dale to Salisbury, 17 August 1611, Public Record Office, CO1/1, ff. 94–95 (VCRP 622); Percy, "Trewe Relacyon," 276–277.

6. Alexander Whitaker to the Reverend William Crashaw, 9 August 1611, Bodleian Library, Ashmole 1147, ff. 219–221 (VCRP X.13); Percy, "Trewe Relacyon," 277–278; *New Life of Virginea*, 9, 18.

7. Irene A. Wright, "Spanish Policy Toward Virginia, 1606–1612: Jamestown, Écija, and John Clark of the Mayflower," *American Historical Review* 25 (1920): 452–454; Philip L. Barbour, ed., *The Jamestown Voyages Under the First Charter, 1606–1609*, 2 vols. (Cambridge, 1969), 1:151–157. Whatever the fanciful embellishments of Magnel's account, it may have raised echoes in the king's mind of Spain's own ambitions in the Chesapeake region as set out by Pedro Menéndez de Avilés some forty years earlier.

8. Barbour, ed., *Jamestown Voyages*, 2:293–319; Wright, "Spanish Policy," 452–454, 463–467.

9. Brown, *Genesis*, 1:455–457.

10. For Philip's strategy of "Pax Hispanica" see Paul C. Allen, *Philip III and the Pax Hispanica, 1598–1621: The Failure of Grand Strategy* (New Haven and London, 2000); Brown, *Genesis*, 1:476. The twelve-year truce also had far-reaching implications for the English and Dutch in America. Despite strenuous efforts by Spanish negotiators, the Dutch had refused to give up their commerce with the Indies (east and west) although they agreed not to trade with regions already occupied by Spain. Henry Hudson's voyage along the east coast of America in the summer of 1609 led a few years later to the establishment of Dutch settlements at Fort Orange (Albany) and on Manhattan Island at the entrance to the Hudson River, from where a profitable trade in furs with the Iroquois developed. For the Virginia Company, peace in Europe released English soldiers who had been serving in the Netherlands from

active duty and opened up possibilities of recruiting veterans and possibly some Dutch settlers for the English colony.

11. Brown, *Genesis*, 1:515–518.

12. Wright, "Spanish Policy," 467–473; Percy, "Trewe Relacyon," 278–279; Hamor, *True Discourse*, 27–28.

13. Hamor, *True Discourse*, 27–29.27–29; Percy, "Trewe Relacyon," 278–280; Lyon Gardiner Tyler, ed., *Narratives of Early Virginia, 1606–1625* (1907; reprint, New York, 1966), 221.

14. Hamor, *True Discourse*, 31–32; Charles E. Hatch, *The First Seventeen Years: Virginia, 1607–1624* (Charlottesville, Va., 1957), 12–16, 47–53, 60–65.

15. Dale to Salisbury, 17 August 1611, Public Record Office, CO1/1, f. 95 (VCRP 622); Irene Hecht, "The Virginia Colony, 1607–1640: A Study in Frontier Growth" (PhD diss., University of Washington, 1969), 68–74; *New Life of Virginea*, 4; Wesley Frank Craven, *The Southern Colonies in the Seventeenth Century, 1607–1689* (Baton Rouge, 1949), 110–115; Alexander Brown, *The First Republic in America* (Boston and New York, 1898), 179.

16. Brown, *Genesis*, 2:569–570, 572–573, 575, 588–590, 592–594, 646–654, 656–657; John Sanford in Madrid to William Trumbull in Brussells, October, 18, 1612, Berkshire Record Office, Trumbull Manuscripts (VRCP 07129), nos. 60–61.

17. Brown, *Genesis*, 2:639–640. To protect English claims to northern Virginia (New England), south of 45 degrees north latitude, Argall destroyed small French settlements at Mount Desert Island, on the coast of Maine, and St. Croix and Port Royal in the Bay of Fundy, Nova Scotia, in two expeditions during the summer and fall of 1613.

18. Brown, *Genesis*, 2:738–745; Barbour, ed., *Complete Works*, 2:240.

19. Lyon Gardiner Tyler, ed., *Narratives of Early Virginia, 1606–1625* (New York, 1966), 422–423.

20. Haile, ed., *Jamestown Narratives*, 767, 775; Percy, "Trewe Relacyon," 280; Brown, *Genesis*, 2:738–740.

21. Hamor, *True Discourse*, 4–5; Samuel Purchas, *Hakluytus Posthumus or Purchas His Pilgrimes . . .* , 20 vols. (Glasgow, 1906–08), 19:90–93. In London, the court gossip and correspondent John Chamberlain wrote to his friend Sir Dudley Carleton at the Hague in August 1613 about the capture of Pocahontas, which had breathed life into Virginia at a time when the venture was at a last gasp. The Indian king, "theyre greatest enemie," had promised to do whatever in his power to retrieve his daughter and to bring the English "where they shall meet with gold mines." Yet, Chamberlain added dryly, the ship that carried the news "brought . . . no commodities from thence but only these fayre tales and hopes." Letter of August 1, 1613, quoted in Frances Mossiker, *Pocahontas: The Life and the Legend* (New York, 1996), 162–163.

22. J. Frederick Fausz, "'An Abundance of Blood Shed on Both Sides': England's First Indian War, 1609–1614," *Virginia Magazine of History and Biography* 98 (1990): 44–45.

23. Purchas, *Hakluytus Posthumus*, 19:104–106. Paula Gunn Allen argues that Pocahontas, whose personal name was Matoaka and sacred name was Amonute, was a

powerful shaman ("Beloved Woman") and "negotiator" between the worlds of the English and Powhatans, *Pocahontas: Medicine Woman, Spy, Entrepreneur, Diplomat* (New York, 2003).

24. Hamor, *True Discourse*, 6–11; Purchas, *Hakluytus Posthumus*, 1:104–106.

25. Mossiker, *Pocahontas*, 174–176; Camilla Townsend, *Pocahontas and the Powhatan Dilemma* (New York, 2004), 118–121; Purchas, *Hakluytus Posthumus*, 19:104, 106. Rebecca's story is told in Genesis 24:10–67; 25:20–26, 28; 26:6–11, and 27:5–11. The Lord told Rebecca: "Two nations are in your womb. Two peoples shall be separated from your body. One people shall be stronger than the other," Genesis 25:23.

26. Hamor, *True Discourse*, 61–68; Mossiker, *Pocahontas*, 344–348. The marriage of Pocahontas and Rolfe may have been the first to reflect English aspirations to convert the Powhatans to Christianity and Englishness but it was not the first union between English and Indian. The Spanish ambassador, Zúñiga, reported to Philip III in 1612 that between forty and fifty Englishmen and some of the women had "married" or run away to the Powhatans, an account that was probably exaggerated but nevertheless suggests that for those who could no longer bear the harsh conditions at English settlements joining the Powhatans was an attractive (or possibly only) option, see Brown, *Genesis*, 2:572.

27. Haile, ed., *Jamestown Narratives*, 761.

28. No one who read the account of the event by Ralph Hamor could have possibly come to any other conclusion than what the author intended: a powerful neighboring Indian people had of their own volition submitted to Dale and placed themselves under the protection of the English; Hamor, *True Discourse*, 11–16; Purchas, *Hakluytus Posthumus*, 19:106–107; Nicholas Canny, "England's New World and the Old, 1480s–1630s," in Nicholas Canny, ed., *The Origins of Empire: British Overseas Enterprise to the Close of the Seventeenth Century* (Oxford, 1998), 156–159.

29. Dale was married already and his wife, Elizabeth Throckmorton, resided in England.

30. Hamor, *True Discourse*, 37–46.

31. Purchas, *Hakluytus Posthumus*, 19:108; Haile, ed., *Jamestown Narratives*, 875–876; Hamor, *True Discourse*, sig. A4$^r$, 68.

## Chapter Eight: For "The Good of the Plantation"

1. Frances Mossiker, *Pocahontas: The Life and the Legend* (New York, 1996), 210. From at least the time of her baptism, if not before, Pocahontas would have been known by her English name Rebecca, but for the sake of clarity the name Pocahontas is retained in the following sections. Whether or not a specific incident during the voyage led to Lembry being executed is uncertain. Perhaps his part in piloting Spanish ships during the Armada invasion attempt of 1588 became known and Dale and Argall chose to wait until they sighted England before hanging him.

2. Alexander Brown, *The Genesis of the United States*, 2 vols. (New York, 1980), 2:783; Samuel Purchas, *Hakluytus Posthumus or Purchas His Pilgrimes . . .*, 20 vols. (Glasgow, 1906–1908), 19:119. It is likely Dale, accompanied by his captains, continued onto London by ship, carrying the prisoner Molina and cargo from Virginia. Besides emphasizing conversion, the Cathedral was associated with more practical matters in that St. Paul's Churchyard was the location of the forthcoming Virginia lottery, which the Company hoped would be a principal means of raising money for the colony.

3. Camilla Townsend, *Pocahontas and the Powhatan Dilemma* (New York, 2004), 139–158; Mossiker, *Pocahontas*, 219–245; Robert Beverley, *The History and Present State of Virginia*, ed. Louis B. Wright (Chapel Hill, N.C., 1947), 43; Purchas, *Hakluytus Posthumus*, 19:118.

4. Mossiker, *Pocahontas*, 246–253, 277–283.

5. Townsend, *Pocahontas*, 152–154; Karen Ordahl Kupperman, *Indians and English Facing Off in Early America* (Ithaca and London, 2000), 199–201.

6. Philip L. Barbour, ed., *The Complete Works of Captain John Smith*, 3 vols. (Chapel Hill, N.C., 1986), 2:258–259.

7. Mossiker, *Pocahontas*, 271–275; Philip L. Barbour, *The Three Worlds of Captain John Smith* (London, 1964), 298–328. About the time Pocahontas arrived in London Smith's *Description of New England* was published, which described in detail the great natural bounty of the region.

8. Barbour, ed., *Complete Works*, 2:260–261.

9. Ibid., 198–199, 261–262. In a sense both Smith and Pocahontas experienced conversion, although Smith did not have the remotest intention of becoming a Powhatan weroance. Peter Hulme remarks: "'Civility'—European civility—can only guarantee the stability of its own foundations by denying the substantiality of other worlds, other words, other narratives," *Colonial Encounters: Europe and the Native Caribbean, 1492–1797* (London, 1986), 156.

10. Mossiker, *Pocahontas*, 246–253, 277–283; Barbour, ed., *Complete Works*, 2:259–262 Three Indians died whilst staying at Sir Thomas Smythe's residence in Philpot Lane, and a maid who lived with Mr. Gough (probably the Reverend William, cousin of Alexander Whitaker) at Blackfriars, London, was reported very weak of "Consumpcon" in May 1620. Two other "maydes" were shipped off to the Bermudas as wives for planters, Susan Myra Kingsbury, ed., *The Records of the Virginia Company*, 4 vols. (Washington, D.C., 1906–1935), 1:338, 496; Virginia Bernhard, *Slaves and Slaveholders in Bermuda, 1616–1782* (Columbia, 1999), 10–11.

11. Wesley Frank Craven, *The Southern Colonies in the Seventeenth Century, 1607–1689* (Baton Rouge, 1949), 116–118; Brown, *Genesis*, 2:740, 774, 776; Charles M. Andrews, *The Colonial Period of American History*, 4 vols. (1934; reprint, New Haven, 1964), 1:126; *A Briefe Declaration of the Present State of Things in Virginia* (London, 1616), 5–6 (pamphlet published by the Virginia Company).

12. C. M. MacInnes, *The Early English Tobacco Trade* (London, 1926), 27–36, 47–48; Jeffrey Knapp, "Elizabethan Tobacco," in Stephen Greenblatt, ed., *New World Encounters* (Berkeley, 1993), 272–312.

13. Mossiker, *Pocahontas,* 198–201; Hamor, *True Discourse,* 24, 34. Small shipments of tobacco from Bermuda began in 1613–1614.

14. MacInnes, *Early English Tobacco Trade,* 42, 46, 51–53; Kingsbury, ed., *Records of the Virginia Company,* 1:329, 480, 3:309–315.

15. John Rolfe, *A True Relation of the State of Virginia lefte by Sir Thomas Dale Knight in May Last 1616* (Charlottesville, Va., 1971), 7–10; Ralph Hamor, *A True Discourse of the Present State of Virginia* (London, 1615), 33. William Kelso and his team of archaeologists have recently excavated a large structure inside the western palisade of the fort (structure 172), 167 feet by 18 feet, which might be one of the "faire rowes of howses" built by Gates in this period.

16. Samuel Purchas, *Purchas his Pilgrimage, or Relations of the World, and the Religions Observed in All Ages and Places Discovered from the Creation unto this present* (London, 1614), 761; Rolfe, *A True Relation,* 3, 11, 14–15. In contrast to favorable assessments of the colony circulated by Rolfe and Hamor, the Spanish ambassador, Gondomar, wrote to Philip III that although matters had improved in Virginia since peace with the Indians, the English "complain very much of the misery endured there," Alexander Brown, *The First Republic in America* (Boston and New York, 1898), 243.

17. A Briefe Declaration, 5; Craven, *Southern Colonies,* 117–120. Letters from Daniel Skynner to William Trumbull, July 27, 1616, Berkshire Record Office, Trumbull manuscripts, VRCP, 07129, no. 108; Robert C. Johnson, "The 'Running Lotteries' of the Virginia Company," *Virginia Magazine of History and Biography* 68 (1960): 156–165. Gondomar commented to Philip III in the fall of 1614 that compared to Virginia the "Colony of Bermuda has a very different and creditable reputation; and thus is assisted in both men and in money," Brown, *Genesis,* 2:740.

18. A map of the James River of c.1617 shows the location of Argall's Town, see Michael Jarvis and Jeroen van Driel, "The Vingaboons Chart of the James River, Virginia, circa 1617," *William and Mary Quarterly* 54, 3d ser. (1997): 386.

19. Kingsbury, ed., *Records of the Virginia Company,* 3:68–69; Brown, *First Republic,* 235, 248–250; Charles E. Hatch, *The First Seventeen Years: Virginia, 1607–1624* (Charlottesville, Va., 1957), 18, 35–39, 75, 104; Irene Hecht, "The Virginia Colony, 1607–1640: A Study in Frontier Growth" (PhD diss., University of Washington, 1969), 79. Martins Brandon across the river from Smyth's Hundred originated in an extraordinary grant to Captain John Martin, a survivor from the colony's first days. He was given ten shares of land (comprising several thousand acres) to "hold and enjoy in as large & ample manner and to all intents and purposes as any Lord of Mannor here in England." Martin was also granted the right of free trade in the Chesapeake Bay and its rivers and to hold "convenient markets" on his land.

20. Barbour, ed., *Complete Works,* 2:262–263; Kingsbury, ed., *Records of the Virginia Company,* 3:71, 73–74, 92; Brown, *First Republic,* 268.

21. Hamor, True Discourse, 16–20; Edward Wright Haile, ed., *Jamestown Narratives: Eyewitness Accounts of the Virginia Colony, The First Decade: 1607–1617* (Champlain, Va., 1998), 763–765; Barbour, ed., *Complete Works,* 2;247. Hamor exaggerated by stating that

Dale had allocated "every man" in the colony a farm of three acres, it is clear the deputy governor did not include common laborers or soldiers.

22. Kingsbury, ed., *Records of the Virginia Company,* 1:256, 262, 268, 3:309–310; Hatch, *First Seventeen Years,* 37, 53–54; Peter Walne, "The Collections for Henrico College, 1616–1618," *Virginia Magazine of History and Biography* 80 (1972): 258.

23. Kingsbury, ed., *Records of the Virginia Company,* 3:98–102, 310–311, 482–484, 4:523; Wesley Frank Craven, *Dissolution of the Virginia Company: The Failure of a Colonial Experiment* (New York, 1932), 67–79; Craven, *Southern Colonies,* 126–136; Warren M. Billings, *A Little Parliament: The Virginia General Assembly in the Seventeenth Century* (Richmond, 2004), 5–10. The General Assembly, particularly the House of Burgesses, was a means of restraining the power of the governor, a consideration of some urgency given the example of Argall's period of office during which he brazenly pursued his own self-interests and embezzled the Company. For Sir Edwin Sandys' liberalism, see James Ellison, *George Sandys: Travel, Colonialism, and Tolerance in the 17ᵗʰ Century* (Cambridge, 2002), 30–48.

24. Kingsbury, ed., *Records of the Virginia Company,* 3:153–177; Billings, *Little Parliament,* 10.

25. Theodore K. Rabb, *Jacobean Gentleman: Sir Edwin Sandys, 1561–1629* (Princeton, 1998), 320–321; Edmund S. Morgan, *Visible Saints: The History of a Puritan Idea* (Ithaca, 1963), 16–18; Andrews, *Colonial Period,* 1:247–264; William Bradford, *Of Plymouth Plantation,* ed. Harvey Wish (New York, 1962), 34–45; Neal Salisbury doubts the Pilgrims had any intention of settling on the Hudson River, *Manitou and Providence: Indians, Europeans, and the Making of New England, 1500–1643* (Oxford, 1982), 109. John Clark, the pilot captured when the Spanish caravel commanded by Don Diego de Molina entered the James River in 1611, was mate on board the *Mayflower.*

26. John Bennett Boddie, *Seventeenth-Century Isle of Wight County, Virginia* (Chicago, 1938), 14–26; letter from Thomas Locke to William Trumbull, August 28, 1618, Berkshire Record Office, Trumbull manuscripts, VRCP, 07127, no. 101. Robert Cushman reported to the Leiden Pilgrims that 130 out of 180 passengers died on board the *William and Thomas,* many from the bloody flux and lack of fresh water. The ship had been driven far to the south and did not arrive in the colony until March 1619 following a crossing of more than six months. Given the terrible shipboard conditions, Cushman was surprised as many as fifty survived.

27. Kingsbury, ed., *Records of the Virginia Company,* 3:115–116, 309, 536–537; Hecht, "Virginia Colony," 79, 108–116; David R. Ransome, "Wives for Virginia," *William and Mary Quarterly* 43, 3d ser. (1991): 3–18; William Thorndale, "A Passenger List of the 1619 *Bona Nova,*" *Virginia Genealogical Society* 33 (1995): 3–11; Barbour, ed., *Complete Works,* 2:266; Robert Hume, *Early Child Immigrants to Virginia, 1618–1642* (Baltimore, 1986), 8–17; Engel Sluiter, "New Light on the '20. and Odd Negroes' Arriving in Virginia, August 1619," *William and Mary Quarterly* 54, 3d ser. (1997): 395–398; John Thornton, "The African Experience of the 20. and Odd Negroes' Arriving in Virginia in 1619," *William and Mary Quarterly* 55, 3d ser. (1998): 421–434.

28. Thornton, "African Experience," 421–434; Virginia M. Meyer and John Frederick Dorman, eds., *Adventurers of Purse and Person, Virginia, 1607–1624/5* (Richmond, Va., 1987), 31. Whether or not the first Africans continued to be slaves in Virginia is a controversial topic, see Alden T. Vaughan in "Blacks in Virginia: A Note on the First Decade," *William and Mary Quarterly* 29, 3d ser. (1973): 469–478. Thornton and Linda Heywood are completing a detailed study of the origins of the first Africans in Virginia. Daniel Elfrith left twenty-nine Angolans on Bermuda, who were seized by the Earl of Warwick and enslaved, Michael Jarvis, "'In the Eye of All Trade': Maritime Revolution and the Transformation of Bermudian Society, 1612–1800" (PhD diss., College of William and Mary, 1998), 103.

29. PRO, SP14/103, Letter from John Chamberlain, October 14, 1618, no. 33; Kingsbury, ed., *Records of the Virginia Company,* 1:270–271, 304–306; PRO, PC2/30, January 28, 1620, 400–401; Peter Wilson Coldham, *Emigrants in Chains: A Social History of Forced Emigration to the Americas . . .* (Baltimore, Md., 1992), 41–47. More than 300 children and vagrants were sent from the Bridewell Royal Hospital, Blackfriars, London, in an eighteen-month period between August 1618 and February 1620. Smaller numbers of felons were also transported, see Abbot Emerson Smith, *Colonists in Bondage: White Servitude and Convict Labor in America, 1607–1776* (Chapel Hill, N.C., 1947), 92–93.

30. William Thorndale argues the muster dates from March 1619 but internal evidence (as well as other sources) proves conclusively that it derives from a year later, "The Virginia Census of 1619," *Virginia Genealogical Society* 33 (1995), 155–170; William M. Kelso, Nicholas M. Luccketti, and Beverly A. Straube, *Jamestown Rediscovery, 1994–2004* (Association for the Preservation of Virginia Antiquities, 1999), 21–33; *Jamestown Archaeological Assessment* (National Park Service, 2001), 46–47; David R. Ransome, "Village Tensions in Early Virginia: Sex, Land, and Status at the Neck of Land in the 1620s," *The Historical Journal,* 43 (2000), 365–381.

31. PRO, CO1/3, f. 85; Kingsbury, ed., *Records of the Virginia Company,* 3:220–221; Hecht, "Virginia Colony," 176.

32. Kingsbury, ed., *Records of the Virginia Company,* 3:220–221, 226–227, 246, 489; Barbour, ed., *Complete Works,* 2:268, 284.

33. Kingsbury, ed., *Records of the Virginia Company,* 4:41, 58–59, 62; Emily Rose, "The Politics of Pathos: Richard Frethorne's Letters Home," in Robert Appelbaum and John Wood Sweet, eds., *Envisioning an English Empire,* 92–108.

34. Kingsbury, ed., *Records of the Virginia Company,* 1:319–329; 334–335; 3:220, 246, 275, 536–537, 4:175, 231–232.

# Chapter Nine: "Fatall Possession"

1. John Rolfe, *A True Relation of the State of Virginia lefte by Sir Thomas Dale Knight in May Last 1616* (Charlottesville, Va., 1971), 4–5 (pamphlet published by the Virginia Company).

2. Quoted in Helen C. Rountree, *Pocahontas's People: The Powhatan Indians of Virginia Through Four Centuries* (Norman, Okla., 1990), 62; Helen C. Rountree, *The Powhatan Indians of Virginia: Their Traditional Culture* (Lincoln, Neb., 1989), 118; Susan Myra Kingsbury, ed., *The Records of the Virginia Company,* 4 vols. (Washington, D.C., 1906–1935), 3:71–72.

3. Kingsbury, ed., *Records of the Virginia Company,* 1:320, 3:71, 73–74, 92; Philip L. Barbour, ed., *The Complete Works of Captain John Smith,* 3 vols. (Chapel Hill, N.C., 1986), 2:256–257, 261.

4. Peter Walne, "The Collections for Henrico College," *Virginia Magazine of History and Biography* 80 (1972): 259–261; Kingsbury, ed., *Records of the Virginia Company,* 1:537, 539, 3:102, 128–129, 147, 165–166.

5. Kingsbury, ed., *Records of the Virginia Company,* 1:379, 3:123–124, 446–448; John Frederick Fausz, "The Powhatan Uprising of 1622: A Historical Study of Ethnocentrism and Cultural Conflict," (PhD diss., College of William and Mary, 1977), 330–339.

6. Kingsbury, ed., *Records of the Virginia Company,* 3:220, 243–244, 447, 469–470; Warren M. Billings, *A Little Parliament: The Virginia General Assembly in the Seventeenth Century* (Richmond, 2004), 69. Captain John Smith commented a few years later that whereas in years past settlers had treated Opechancanough and the Indians only with suspicion, now the English were so confident about the peace that "there [was] now no more feare nor danger either of their [Indians'] power or trechery, so that every man plante[d] himself where he please[d]," Barbour, ed., *Complete Works,* 2:284.

7. Rountree, *Pocahontas's People,* 66–67; Fausz, "Powhatan Uprising," 310–311.

8. Fausz, "Powhatan Uprising," 340–357; Samuel Purchas, *Hakluytus Posthumus or Purchas His Pilgrimes . . . ,* 20 vols. (Glasgow, 1906–08), 19:153; Kingsbury, ed., *Records of the Virginia Company,* 3:583–584, 4:10–11; Rountree, *Pocahontas's People,* 72–73. Thirty-six years before, Wingina took the name Permisapan before plotting the destruction of Ralph Lane's colonists on Roanoke Island.

9. Frethorne exaggerated the losses at Martin's Hundred, which historians have estimated were about seventy-four killed and twenty captured. Kingsbury, ed., *Records of the Virginia Company,* 3:541–571, 612, 4:41; Barbour, ed., *Complete Works,* 2, 293–302. I am indebted to Fausz, who provides the most detailed account of the uprising, "Powhatan Uprising," 363–403. Robert C. Johnson, "The Indians Massacre of 1622: Some Correspondence of the Reverend Joseph Mead," *Virginia Magazine of History and Biography* 71 (1963): 408–410; "Two Tragic Events," *William and Mary Quarterly* 9, 1st ser. (1901), 213. Rountree argues that the Kecoughtans had been dispersed since the English raids of 1610.

10. Barbour, ed., *Complete Works,* 2:308.

11. Ibid., 302; Kingsbury, ed., *Records of the Virginia Company,* 2:520, 3:612, 652, 656, 678–679, 4:38, 41, 58.

12. No evidence suggests that the English knew about the destruction of the Jesuit mission and killing of the priests. Kingsbury, ed., *Records of the Virginia Company,*

2:395; J. Frederick Fausz and Jon Kukla, "A Letter of Advice to the Governor of Virginia, 1624," *William and Mary Quarterly* 34, 3d ser. (1977): 116–118.

13. Kingsbury, ed., *Records of the Virginia Company,* 3:666–667. Thomas Locke wrote to William Trumbull in Brussels on July 26, 1622: "There hath bin a great slaughter of the English lately in Virginia by the salvages, almost 400 of them have bin massacred," Berkshire Record Office, Trumbull manuscripts, VRCP, 07127, no. 135. See the Reverend Mead's letter of July 13, 1622, in Johnson, "The Indians Massacre of 1622," 408.

14. William S. Powell, "Aftermath of the Massacre: The First Indian War, 1622–1632," *Virginia Magazine of History and Biography* 66 (1958), 49; Kingsbury, ed., *Records of the Virginia Company,* 3:665, 676, 683; 4:9.

15. Kingsbury, ed., *Records of the Virginia Company,* 3:544–545, 669–670, 683, my emphasis; Alexander Brown, *The First Republic in America* (Boston and New York, 1898), 488–489. Sandys has been criticized by historians for being hopelessly out of touch with realities in post-uprising Virginia, Wesley Frank Craven, *Dissolution of the Virginia Company: The Failure of a Colonial Experiment* (New York, 1932), 204–220.

16. Kingsbury, ed., *Records of the Virginia Company,* 3:542, 553, 557–559, 561–562, 671–673, 683; Fausz, "Powhatan Uprising," 415–426; Alden T. Vaughan, "'Expulsion of the Savages': English Policy and the Virginia Massacre of 1622," *William and Mary Quarterly* 35, 3d ser. (1978): 76–80.

17. Kingsbury, ed., *Records of the Virginia Company,* 3:556–559; Robert C. Johnson, "A Poem on the Late Massacre in Virginia," *Virginia Magazine of History and Biography* 72 (1964): 282–285; Purchas, *Hakluytus Posthumus,* 19:224, 228–231, 246, 266; Fausz, "Powhatan Uprising," 431–434.

18. Barbour, ed., *Complete Works,* 2:285, 303–307; Kingsbury, ed., *Records of the Virginia Company,* 3:558–559, 705–707; Ian K. Steele, *Warpaths: Invasions of North America* (Oxford, 1994), 46–47.

19. Kingsbury, ed., *Records of the Virginia Company,* 3:678–679, 4:9; Barbour, ed., *Complete Works,* 2:315; "Letter of Sir Francis Wyatt, Governor of Virginia, 1621–1626," *William and Mary Quarterly* 6, 2d ser. (1926), 118; Frederic W. Gleach, *Powhatan's World and Colonial Virginia: A Conflict of Cultures* (Lincoln, Neb., 1997), 160–169. The following paragraphs rely on Fausz, "Powhatan Uprising," 447–468, 471–472, 486–515.

20. Kingsbury, ed., *Records of the Virginia Company,* 4:61, 89, 108, 147, 231, 234–235; Barbour, ed., *Complete Works,* 2:320–321.

21. Kingsbury, ed., *Records of the Virginia Company,* 2:483, 4:98.

22. Ibid., 3:228; Fausz, "Powhatan Uprising," 326–327.

23. Kingsbury, ed., *Records of the Virginia Company,* 2:482, 486, 4:221–222, 451.

24. Ibid., 2:482, 4:507–508; Fausz, "Powhatan Uprising," 493, 509–511; Rountree, *Pocahontas's People,* 78.

25. Kingsbury, ed., *Records of the Virginia Company,* 4:508; Rountree, *Pocahontas's People,* 78–81; Edmund S. Morgan, *American Slavery, American Freedom: The Ordeal of Colonial Virginia* (New York, 1975), 404.

26. Richard Beale Davis, *George Sandys: Poet Adventurer* (London, 1955), 44–125; James Ellison, *George Sandys: Travel, Colonialism, and Tolerance in the Seventeenth Century* (Cambridge, 2002), 49–89. His brother, the Reverend David Sandys, had arrived the previous year and in 1625 lived across the river from Jamestown on the plantation belonging to Samuel Mathews. George Sandys acquired a plantation of 200 acres, possibly on the south side of the James River, but he also resided in Jamestown at the house of Captain William Pierce ("the fairest in Virginia") on "Back Street" in New Town then being laid out near the fort.

27. Kingsbury, ed., *Records of the Virginia Company*, 2:375, 4:22–26, 64–68, 70–75, 104–111, 228–229, 232–234; Davis, *George Sandys*, 132–162; Craven, *Dissolution*, 206–220.

28. Details of the factionalism that plagued the Company and controversy over the tobacco contract can be found in Charles M. Andrews, *The Colonial Period of American History*, 4 vols. (1934; reprint, New Haven, 1964), 1:150–179; Craven, *Dissolution*, 105–147, 221–250; and Rabb, *Jacobean Gentleman*, 337–339, 344–381.

29. Kingsbury, ed., *Records of the Virginia Company*, 2:374–376, 381–387 (for the Company's immediate response).

30. Ibid., 4:130–151; Barbour, ed., *Complete Works*, 2:328–329; Andrews, *Colonial Period*, 1:176–179; Craven, *Dissolution*, 251–328.

31. Kingsbury, ed., *Records of the Virginia Company*, 4:450–455, 476, 501, 519–551; Henry R. McIlwaine, ed., *Journals of the House of Burgesses, 1619–1658/59* (Richmond, Va., 1915), 21–37; Davis, *George Sandys*, 153, 193–200.

# Epilogue: After the Fall

1. Warren M. Billings, *A Little Parliament: The Virginia General Assembly in the Seventeenth Century* (Richmond, Va., 2004), 12; Thomas Cary Johnson, Jr., ed., *A Proclamation for setling the Plantation of Virginia, 1625* (Charlottesville, Va., 1946). Despite Charles I's remarks concerning commercial companies and their fitness to undertake "State-affaires," he continued to grant charters to private companies, as for example to the New England Company in 1628 and the Massachusetts Bay Company the following year, Andrews *Colonial Period*, Charles M. Andrews, *The Colonial Period of American History*, 4 vols. (1934; reprint, New Haven, 1964), 1:353–374. Philip IV ascended the Spanish throne in April 1621.

2. Susan Myra Kingsbury, ed., *The Records of the Virginia Company*, 4 vols. (Washington, D.C., 1906–1935), 2:381, 4:508; Virginia M. Meyer and John Frederick Dorman, eds., *Adventurers of Purse and Person, Virginia, 1607–1624/5* (Richmond, Va., 1987), 7–71; Irene Hecht, "The Virginia Muster of 1624/25 as a Source for Demographic History," *William and Mary Quarterly* 30, 3d ser. (1973): 70–77. Elizabeth City was listed as having 348 settlers and the area around Charles City 235. Beyond Charles City, as a consequence of the war and continuing anxieties about exposure to Indian attacks, English settlements thinned out. Of the 1,218 inhabitants about three-quarters were male and a similar proportion younger than thirty years old.

Apart from twenty-three "Negroes" and one Indian, all were European, and the vast majority English. Edmund Morgan estimates the colony's population in 1625 was nearer 1300, *American Slavery, American Freedom: The Ordeal of Colonial Virginia* (New York, 1975), 404.

3. Edmund S. Morgan, *American Slavery, American Freedom,* 108–130, 404; Kingsbury, ed., *Records of the Virginia Company,* 4:562

4. Henry R. McIlwaine, ed., *Journals of the House of Burgesses, 1619–1658/59* (Richmond, Va., 1915), 37, 38; "Letter of Sir Francis Wyatt," 118–119; Ian K. Steele, *Warpaths: Invasions of North America* (Oxford, 1994), 47.

5. Samuel Purchas, *Hakluytus Posthumus or Purchas His Pilgrimes . . . ,* 20 vols. (Glasgow, 1906–1908), 19:224, 228–231, 246, 266–267; Patrick Collison, *The Birthplace of Protestant England: Religious and Cultural Change in the Sixteenth and Seventeenth Centuries* (London, 1988), 1–27, especially 5, 17; John Carey, ed., *John Donne: The Major Works* (Oxford, 2000), 321; Kingsbury, ed., *Records of the Virginia Company,* 3:672.

6. The idea of a history of Virginia had been raised in April 1621 by a member of the Company, John Smythe of North Nibley, Gloucestershire, steward of the Lords Berkeley and prime mover of Berkeley plantation on the James River. Philip L. Barbour, ed., *The Complete Works of Captain John Smith,* 3 vols. (Chapel Hill, N.C., 1986), 2:61–475, quote, 462; J. A. Leo Lemay, *The American Dream of Captain John Smith* (Charlottesville, Va., 1991), 47–54, 203–212.

7. Charles M. Andrews, *The Colonial Period of American History,* 4 vols. (1934; reprint, New Haven, 1964), 1:269–270. Although Smith made the most of the 1614 voyage, which was the basis of his published descriptions and map of New England, for one reason or another he was never able to return. Much to his frustration, the *Mayflower* Pilgrims chose Miles Standish to help guide them in America.

8. Barbour, ed., *Complete Works,* 2:326, 409, 436, 462; Lemay, *American Dream,* 84–88. Smith placed particular emphasis on fishing because he continued to hope to be involved in New England schemes.

9. Nuala Zahedieh, "Overseas Expansion and Trade in the Seventeenth Century," in Nicholas Canny, ed., *The Origins of Empire: British Overseas Enterprise to the Close of the Seventeenth Century* (Oxford, 1998), 410–411; Hecht, "Virginia Colony," 191–199; Russell R. Menard, "The Tobacco Industry in the Chesapeake Colonies, 1617–1730: An Interpretation," *Research in Economic History* 5 (1980): 157–161; Carole Shammas, "The Revolutionary Impact of European Demand for Tropical Goods," in John J. McCusker and Kenneth Morgan, eds., *The Early Modern Atlantic Economy* (Cambridge, 2000), 169–170; David Armitage, *The Ideological Origins of the British Empire* (Cambridge, 2000), 148, 159. For a broad overview see Nuala Zahedieh, "Economy," in David Armitage and Michael J. Braddick, eds., *The British Atlantic World, 1500–1800* (New York, 2002), 51–68.

10. Population figures are derived from John J. McCusker and Russell R. Menard, *The Economy of British America* (Chapel Hill, N.C., 1985), 103, 136, 154, 172, 203. Estimates for English and Irish migration are based on Nicholas Canny, "English Migration into and Across the Atlantic During the Seventeenth and Eighteenth

Centuries" and L. M. Cullen, "The Irish Diaspora of the Seventeenth and Eighteenth Centuries," in Nicholas Canny, ed., *Europeans on the Move: Studies on European Migration, 1500–1800* (Oxford, 1994), 64, 76–90, 139; Henry A. Gemery, "Markets for Migrants: English Indentured Servitude and Emigration in the Seventeenth and Eighteenth Centuries," in P. C. Emmer, ed., *Colonialism and Migration: Indentured Labour before and after Slavery* (Dordrecht, 1986), 38–40; David Eltis, "The Volume and Structure of the Atlantic Slave Trade: A Reassessment," *William and Mary Quarterly* 58, 3d ser. (2001), 45. More generally, see David Eltis, *The Rise of African Slavery in the Americas* (New York, 2000).

11. I owe this point to Karen Ordahl Kupperman, *Providence Island, 1630–1641: The Other Puritan Colony* (Cambridge, 1993), 19.

12. Jack P. Greene, *The Intellectual Construction of America: Exceptionalism and Identity from 1492 to 1800* (Chapel Hill, N.C., 1993), 36–46.

13. William Bullock, *Virginia Impartially Examined* (London, 1649), 44; Lois Green Carr, "Emigration and the Standard of Living: The Seventeenth-Century Chesapeake," *Journal of Economic History*, 52 (1991): 271–291.

14. Thomas Glover, "An Account of Virginia," Royal Society Archives, London; Robert Beverley, *The History and Present State of Virginia*, ed. Louis B. Wright (Chapel Hill, N.C., 1947), 62, 232; Barbour, ed., *Complete Works*, 2:245; Helen C. Rountree, *Pocahontas's People: The Powhatan Indians of Virginia Through Four Centuries* (Norman, Okla., 1990), 82–218; Francis Jennings, *Founders of America: From the Earliest Migrations to the Present* (New York, 1994), 233–411.

15. Winthrop D. Jordan, *White Over Black: American Attitudes Toward the Negro, 1550–1812* (Chapel Hill, N.C., 1969), pt. 1; Alden T. Vaughan, "The Origins Debate: Slavery and Racism in Seventeenth-Century Virginia," *VMHB* 97 (1989): 311–354; Ira Berlin, *Many Thousands Gone: The First Two Centuries of Slavery in North America* (Cambridge, Mass., 1998), 17–46, 109–111; Robin Blackburn, *The Making of New World Slavery: From the Baroque to the Modern, 1492–1800* (London and New York, 1997), 219–276; April Lee Hatfield, *Atlantic Virginia: Intercolonial Relations in the Seventeenth Century* (Chapel Hill, N.C., 2004), 137–168; Philip D. Morgan, "British Encounters with Africans and African-Americans, circa 1600–1780," in Bernard Bailyn and Philip D. Morgan, eds., *Strangers within the Realm: Cultural Margins of the First British Empire* (Chapel Hill, N.C., 1991), 159–161, 171–172; T. H. Breen and Stephen Innes, *"Myne Owne Ground:" Race and Freedom on Virginia's Eastern Shore, 1640–1676* (New York, 1980); Anthony S. Parent, Jr., *Foul Means: The Formation of a Slave Society in Virginia, 1660–1740* (Chapel Hill, N.C., 2003), 55–134.

16. Philip D. Morgan, *Slave Counterpoint: Black Culture in the Eighteenth-Century Chesapeake and Lowcountry* (Chapel Hill, N.C., 1998), 61, 98; Morgan, *American Slavery, American Freedom*, 375–387; Drew Gilpin Faust, ed., *The Ideology of Slavery: Proslavery Thought in the Antebellum South, 1830–1860* (Baton Rouge, La., 1981); Ira Berlin, *Many Thousands Gone: The First Two Centuries of Slavery in North America*, pts. 2–3 (Cambridge, Mass., 1998).

17. Robert S. Tilton, *Pocahontas: The Evolution of an American Narrative* (Cambridge, 1994), 173.

18. Jack P. Greene, *Pursuits of Happiness: The Social Development of Early Modern British Colonies and the Formation of American Culture* (Chapel Hill, N.C., 1988), 1–5. See also Ann Uhry Abrams, *The Pilgrims and Pocahontas: Rival Myths of American Origins* (Boulder, Co., 1999); John Seelye, *Memory's Nation: The Place of Plymouth Rock* (Chapel Hill, N.C., 1998); and Tilton, *Pocahontas,* 145–175.

19. Kupperman, *Providence Island.*

20. Billings, *Little Parliament;* J. R. Pole, *Political Representation in England and the Origins of the American Republic* (London, 1966); Bernard Bailyn, *The Ideological Origins of the American Revolution* (Cambridge, Mass., 1967); Linda Colley, *Britons: Forging the Nation, 1707–1837* (London, 1992), 132–135; Eliga H. Gould, *The Persistence of Empire: British Political Culture in the Age of the American Revolution* (Chapel Hill, N.C., 2000); Merrill D. Peterson, ed., *Thomas Jefferson, Writings* (New York, 1984), 1517.

# Index

Ahone (Powhatan god), 20–21
Algonquians, the, 13, 22
Alonso, 154
Alonso de Olmos, 5, 8–9
Amoroleck, 93, 96
Anne (Queen of Denmark), 227, 230
Appomattocs, the
    attacks against, 189, 207, 271
    attacks by, 52, 189, 257
    initial contact with the colonists, 49
Archer, Gabriel
    abandonment of the colony, plans
        for, 74
    departure of, 81
    exclusion from council membership,
        47
    expedition of 1609, 158
    exploration upriver, 50
    leadership, squabbling among the,
        111–112, 163–164
    recruitment of, 40
    returns of the colony, calculation of
        likely, 55
    Smith, opposition to, 74, 169–170

Argall, Samuel
    arrival at Jamestown, 152–153,
        155–156
    Bermuda, provisions sought at, 182
    as deputy governor, 237–238
    leadership position under De La
        Warr, 181
    offensives against the Indians,
        187–188
    Opechancanough, meeting with at
        Jamestown, 250
    passage to the Chesapeake,
        employment to find a shorter, 134
    peace agreement with the
        Chickahominies, negotiation of,
        218–219
    Pocahontas, kidnapping of, 212–214
    return to England, 225
    Smythe's meetings with after the
        expedition of 1609, 171
    trade with the Indians, 191, 211–212
Aylmer, John, 140

Bagnall, Anthony, 89, 92
Bahîa Santa Marîa. *See* Chesapeake Bay
Baldwin, "Master," 259
Beaulieu, John, 171
Bennett, Edward, 258
Bennett, Robert, 270
Benson, George, 139
Berkeley, John, 257
Bermuda, 160–163, 177–178, 237, 287
Beverly, Robert, 15
Blackwell, Francis, 242–243
Blunt, Humphrey, 185
Box, William, 164
Boyse, Mrs. Alice, 269
Bradford, William, 242–243
Brewster, Edward, 187–188, 189, 206
Brewster, William, 40, 55, 241
Brinton, Edward, 105
Brooke, Christopher, 265
Bucke, Reverend Richard, 158, 181, 240–241
Buckler, Andrew, 105
Burrowes, Anna, 118
Butler, Nathaniel, 276

Calicut, William, 109
Capps, William, 261
Carlton, Dudley, 56
Carrera, Brother Juan de la, 7
Carver, John, 241
Causey, Nathaniel, 257
Cecil, Robert. *See* Salisbury, Earl of
Chamberlain, John, 56, 227, 232, 244
Chanco, 269
Charles I (King of England), 278–280
Chesapeake Bay
    the English in, initial explorations of, 30–31, 38
    the Jamestown colony. *See* Jamestown colony
    Jesuit missionaries in, 5–8, 262
    Ralegh's abortive colonial attempt on the, 31–32
    the Spanish in, 1–9

Chesapeakes, the, 13, 145
Chickahominies, the
    attacks against, 186–188, 250, 267
    attacks by, 257–258
    peace agreement with, 218–220
    plot to attack the settlement, 82
    Powhatans, relative independence of the, 15
    trade with, 60
Children, transport to Virginia of destitute, 244–245
Choapock, 49, 59
Chowanocs, the, 145–146, 151
Christianity, conversion of the Indians to, 138–141, 218, 250–252, 254, 281
Clark, John, 204
Clinton, Henry, 132
Coles, Edward, 209
Collier, Samuel, 105, 119
Comahum, 269
Cooper, Thomas, 281
Cope, Sir Walter, 55
Cornwallis, Sir Charles, 109
Coventry, Sir Thomas, 277
Crakanthorpe, Reverend Richard, 139
Crashaw, William, 139, 179, 199–200
Crofts, Richard, 40
Cushman, Robert, 241
Cuttatawomen, the, 92

Dale, Sir Thomas
    background of, 193, 195
    conversion of the Indians to Christianity, goal of, 218
    departure from England, 193
    encounter with the Spanish, 204–205
    Gates and, 133
    indiscriminate killing tactics, Indian emulation of, 260
    leadership of, 195–200
    marriage proposal of, 220–221

peace agreement with the
Chickahominies, negotiation of,
218, 220
Pocahontas, actions following the
kidnapping of, 213–216
Pocahontas and Rolfe, marriage of,
217–218
portrait of, 194
on the prospects of the post-peace
agreement colony, 223
reforms instituted by, impact of, 238
reports from in 1611 and 1613,
208–210
return to England, 225–226
survey of the colony ordered by, 234
tobacco, bringing to England of,
232
upriver base, establishment of,
205–207
Davis, James
encounter with the Spanish, 204
execution of and attacks against the
Indians, 187
at Fort Algernon, 175, 177
leadership position under Dale, 196
return to England, 226
Dee, John, 23, 27
Delaware Bay, discovery and naming of,
211
De La Warr, twelfth Baron
appointment as governor, 136
expedition of 1610, 180
ill health and departure of, 190, 195
leadership of and war against the
Indians, 180–190
planned expedition of, 172–173
Pocahontas and husband,
introduction of in England, 227
report to the Virginia Company,
190–191
Wahunsonacock, relations with,
184–185
Don Luís de Velasco, 2–9, 15–16, 38,
65, 262

Dowse, Thomas, 189
Drake, Sir Francis, 26, 31, 133, 233

*Eastward Hoe,* 102–103
Écija, Francisco Fernández de, 153–155,
201
Elfrith, Daniel, 244
Elizabeth I (Queen of England), 23,
25–26, 34
Ellesmere, Earl of, 142
Emry, Thomas, 61
England
ceremony of possession of Virginia,
48
colonization, arguments favoring, 10,
22–26, 33
commerce and trade, colonial empire
based on, 283–286
the Jamestown venture. *See*
Jamestown colony
peace treaty with Spain, 34
Pocahontas in, 225–232
providential favoring of, 139–141
Roanoke and early efforts to establish
colonies, 26–33
Spanish threat to, 25–26, 32
Esmy Shichans, 84

Fernandes, Simon, 27, 32
Ferrar, John, 250
Ferrar, William, 257
Fetherstone, Richard, 92
Frethorne, Richard, 247, 258, 261
Frobisher, Martin, 26, 55

Gates, Sir Thomas
abandon the colony, decision to,
179–180
appointment as lieutenant governor,
136
background of, 132–133
confidential instructions issued to,
142–143, 146–147, 149, 181
Dale, friendship with, 195

Gates, Sir Thomas *(continued)*
  De La Warr, arrival of and leadership
    position under, 180–181
  expedition of 1609, 157, 159,
    161–163, 177–178
  expedition of 1611, 205–206
  Indians, conflict with, 185–187
  indiscriminate killing tactic, Indian
    emulation of, 260
  Jamestown as principal residence of,
    235
  return to London and report of, 191
*Generall Historie of Virginia, New-
    England, and the Summer Isles, The*
    (Smith), 282–283
Gibbs, Lieutenant, 257
Gilbert, Sir Humphrey, 26–27, 132
Gondomar, Don Diego Sarmiento y
    Acuña, Conde de, 210–211
Gonzáles, Vicente, 9
Gorges, Sir Ferdinando, 34
Gosnold, Anthony, 40, 127
Gosnold, Anthony, Jr., 40
Gosnold, Bartholomew
  death of, 57
  initial voyage to Jamestown, 39
  landfall and leadership of the council,
    45–46
  New England, expedition to, 38
  origins of the colony, role in, 34–35
  recruiting the personnel, 40
  selection of a site, opinion regarding,
    49
  Smith, saving from the gallows, 44
  Somers, discussions with, 158
Gray, Robert, 140
Greene, Jack P., 289

Hakluyt, Richard, the younger
  the Atlantic as a highway for English
    commerce, vision of, 41
  colonization, rationale for, 23–25, 33
  future of the colony, discussions
    regarding, 134, 144

mixed economy and trade,
    promotion of colonies based on,
    24–25, 32, 98, 285
  *Principal Navigations of the English
    Nation,* 282
Hamor, Ralph
  agricultural reforms, comments on,
    238
  arrival in 1617, 237
  Dale's marriage proposal, negotiation
    with Wahunsonacock regarding,
    220–222
  Indian attack, fending off, 258–259
  kidnapping of Pocahontas, account of
    Wahunsonacock's reaction to, 213
  Opechancanough, on possible origins
    of, 15
  on Virginia tobacco, 233
Hamor, Thomas, 259
Hariot, Thomas
  the Atlantic as a highway for English
    commerce, vision of, 41
  *Brief and True Report of the New
    Found Land of Virginia,* 33
  Chesapeake Bay region, initial
    explorations of, 38
  exploration upriver, 50
  future of the colony, discussions
    regarding, 134, 143–144
  the Roanoke settlement, 27, 30
Hawkins, John, 26, 233
Headright system, 239
Hill, Edward, 268
Holcroft, Thomas, 181, 186, 189
Hopkins, Stephen, 162
Hudson, Henry, 100
Hunt, Reverend Robert, 42, 44, 74

Ibarra, Pedro de, 153–154
Indians, conflict with the
  Appomattocs, attacks against, 189,
    207, 271
  Appomattocs, attacks by, 52, 189,
    257

Chickahominies, attacks against, 186–188, 250, 267
Chickahominies, attacks by, 257–258
De La Warr's war, 183–190
English settlements, attacks of 1622, 255–262
English settlements, attacks of 1644, 286
English settlements, response to attacks of 1622, 267–272
Jamestown settlers, initial attacks against, 45, 52–53, 81–82
Kecoughtans, attacks against, 13, 185–186, 188
Kecoughtans, attacks by, 259
Kiskiacks, attacks against, 258
Kiskiacks, attacks by, 52
Mannahoacs, attacks by, 92–93
Massawomecks, attacks by, 88
Nansemonds, attacks against, 165, 167, 198–199, 267, 271
Nansemonds, attacks by, 94–95, 175, 258–259
Pamunkeys. *See* Opechancanough; Pamunkeys, the
Paspaheghs, attacks against, 128, 186–188
Paspaheghs, attacks by, 52, 195
Patawomecks, antagonizing of, 175
Powhatans. *See* Powhatans, the; Wahunsonacock
Quiyoughcohannocks, attacks against, 267, 271
Quiyoughcohannocks, attacks by, 52, 257
Rappahannocks, attacks by, 91–92
Roanoke settlers, hostilities between the Secotans and, 31–32
Roanoke settlers, Wahunsonacock's attacks against, 145–147
Spanish and, 7–9
Warraskoyacks, attacks against, 187–188, 267, 271
Warraskoyacks, attacks by, 258–259

Weyanocks, attacks against, 267, 271
Weyanocks, attacks by, 52, 257–258
Indians, the
dispossession of by Europeans, 286
exclusion of from English Virginia, 281–282
expansion of settlements and increase in settlers, impact of, 253
peace agreements with, 215–216, 218–220
Powhatans, dominance of, 11–17, 19–20. *See also* Powhatans, the
religious conversion of, 138–141, 218, 250–252, 254, 281
the Spanish and, 1–9
trade with, 60, 76, 79–80, 88, 94, 110, 118–119, 191, 212
travel systems of, 16–17
Virginia Company policy regarding, 147–150
warfare, mode of, 17, 19–20
*See also* names of peoples/tribes
Iopassus, 212
Iroquoian peoples, 14, 22

Jackson, John, 247–248
James I (King of England)
ascension to the throne, 34, 135
Catholic plot to blow up Parliament, saving from, 140
Company charter, revocation of, 277
death of, 279
education and religious conversion of the Indians, instructions regarding, 250
Roanoke settlers, response to slaughter of, 147
Spain, peace treaty negotiations with, 102
tobacco, opposition to, 234
Jamestown colony, initial version (1606–1609)
Argall's arrival at, 152–153, 155–156

Jamestown colony, initial version
(1606–1609) *(continued)*
betrayal of by the Germans,
123–124, 128–130, 151
the ceremony of possession, 48
crossing the Atlantic, 42–44
fire at, 76
first expedition, departure of, 39–40
first supply, arrival of, 74–83
fort construction, 53–54
gold fever at, 80–81
landfall and organizing the local
council, 45–47
leadership, squabbling among the,
42–44, 47, 57–59, 74, 83, 87,
103–105, 110–113
Newport's ship, corruption aboard,
110–111
origin and organization of the
venture, 33–38
personnel of, 40–42, 75
second supply, arrival of, 103–104
site selection, 49–50, 56
Smith in charge, 99–100, 104,
109–110, 118, 127–130,
151–153, 155–156
Smith's explorations, 83–98
tribulations and explorations of the
first year, 47–60
Wahunsonacock, Smith's
confrontation with, 118–123
Jamestown colony, reformed version
(1609–1614)
administrative reforms and creation
of "governor" position, 135–136
code of laws for, 181–182, 196–197,
210
Dale, arrival and leadership of,
195–200
De La Warr, arrival and leadership of,
180–183
deteriorating conditions and the
decision to abandon, 171–180

difficult conditions, 1611–1613,
208–211
the expedition of 1609, 157–163
Gates, arrival of, 177–178, 205–206
leadership, squabbling among the,
163–165, 168–170
ownership and direction of. *See*
Virginia Company
peace agreement with the Indians,
215–216
principal settlements of, 166
recruitment of settlers and investors,
136–138
reduced role in plans for a new and
reformed settlement, 142–143
report of De La Warr and the
company's continued commitment
to, 190–192
Smith, downfall of, 164–171
Somers, arrival of, 177–178
Spanish reconnaissance mission to,
200–205
upriver base, establishment of,
205–207
war against the Indians, 183–190
Jamestown colony, post-peace
agreement (1614–1625)
attacks of 1622, attempts to recover
from, 272–276
deaths of new arrivals, 1622–1623,
274
development, apportionment, and
reinvigoration of, 236–238
Indian attacks of 1622, 255–262
Indian attacks of 1622, response to,
267–272
marriage of Pocahontas, 217–218
political institutions and laws,
redesign of, 239–241
prosperity and peace in, 249
religious conversion of the Indians,
renewed interest in, 250–252
as royal colony beginning in 1625,
279–281

servants and laborers, squalid
conditions and death among,
247–248
settlements of 1611–1624, map of,
256
settlers, influx of, 241–248
starvation during the winter of
1622–1623, 268
survey of in 1616, 234–236
Jamestown colony, memory and lasting
significance of, 288–290
Jefferson, Thomas, 290
Jesuits, the, 5–8, 262
Johnson, Robert, 138–140, 197, 200,
248, 276
Jones, Inigo, 227
Jones, Sir Richard, 277
Jonson, Ben, 227

Kecoughtans, the
attacks against, 13, 185–186, 188
attacks by, 259
Blunt, killing of, 185–186
hosting of Smith and his men, 119,
186
initial contact with the colonists, 48
trade with, 60
Kekataugh, 15
Kemps, 129
Kendall, George, 40, 46, 54
Kiskiack, Jesuit settlement at, 5–8
Kiskiacks, the, 52, 258

Land grants, attracting settlers through,
237
Lane, Ralph, 27, 30–32, 86, 133, 145
Lawne, Christopher, 242, 246
Lawson, Thomas, 181
Laxon, William, 129
Laydon, John, 118
Lembry, Francis, 203–204, 225–226
London, winter of 1608–1609, 131–132
London Company
chartering of, 37

initial reports of colonists, 54–56
letter and report from Smith,
111–115
the lost colony of Roanoke,
102–104
plans of and fears of the Spanish,
108–109
Wingfield, allegations against and by,
58–59
*See also* Virginia Company

Macanoe, 82
Mace, Samuel, 38
Machumps, 144
Maddison, Isaac, 268
Magnel, Francis, 200–201
Mangoags, the, 14, 30, 151
Mangopeesomon, 254. *See also*
Opechancanough
Mannahoacs, the, 14, 17, 65, 71,
93–94
Manteo, 27, 38, 145
*Map of Virginia, A* (Smith), 69–70, 97,
230
Martin, George, 40, 46
Martin, John
departure of, 83
leadership, squabbling among the,
57–58
leadership of, 46, 59–60, 163, 165,
167, 174
recruitment of, 40
response to the Indian attacks of
1622, proposal for, 267
return to England, 226
Smith, finishing off, 169–170
wounding of, 198
Martin, John, Jr., 46
Martinez, Bartolomé, 9
Massawomecks, the, 14, 17, 85–86, 88,
93
Matachanna, 225
Mathews, Samuel, 280
Mease, Reverend William, 171

Menatonon, 30–31
Menéndez de Avilés, Pedro, 3–5, 8–9, 38, 262
Mexico City, 3
Molina, Don Diego de, 203–204, 209–210, 225
Monacans, the, 14, 17, 50, 93, 106–107
Monson, Sir William, 201–202
Moraughtacunds, the, 91–92, 94
Mosco, 91, 92, 94

Namontack, 79, 81, 105–107
Nansemonds, the
  attacks against, 165, 167, 198–199, 267, 271
  attacks by, 94–95, 175, 258–259
  trade with, 118
Nantaughtacunds, the, 92
Nelson, Francis, 75, 82–83
Nemattanew, 206, 254
Newport, Christopher
  coronation of Wahunsonacock, 105–108
  departure for England and report on the colony's progress, 54–56, 133
  expedition of 1609, 157–158, 163
  explorations of, 47–52, 104–105, 108–109
  "first supply" for the colony, 74–76
  initial voyage to Jamestown, 39, 42–44
  landfall and leadership of the council, 45–47
  leadership, squabbling among the, 42–44, 103–105, 110, 112–113
  leadership position under De La Warr, 181
  second departure of, 81
  "second supply" for the colony, 103–104
  Smith's complaints regarding, 112–113

  third departure of, 115, 118
  Wahunsonacock, meeting with, 77–80
Nicholls, Thomas, 248
*Nova Britannia* (Johnson), 138
Nuce, Sir William, 274

Ocanahowan, 67, 101–102, 143, 148–149, 150, 209
Okeus (Powhatan god), 20–22
Opachisco, 218
Opechancanough
  allies in war, ability to call upon, 19–20
  attacks of 1622, 255, 260–262, 278
  attacks of 1644, 286
  attacks subsequent to the 1622 uprising, 268–272
  attempted poisoning of, 270
  "chain of pearl" worn by, 51
  death of, 286
  the English, negotiations/relations with, 215–216, 250–251
  the English, strategy against, 252–255
  English ships, concerns regarding, 59
  lost colony of Roanoke, mention of, 102
  marriage of Pocahontas, meaning of, 223
  power and origins of, 15–16
  Smith and, 61–65, 123–127, 169
  the Spanish and, 11
  Wahunsonacock, power struggle with and succession of, 249–250
Opitchapam, 15, 66, 250, 254, 269–270
Opossunoquonuske, 189
Oviedo, Gonzalo Fernández de, 264
Owens, Richard, 257

Pace, Richard, 258
Paine, Henry, 177

Pamunkeys, the
attacks of 1622, 255, 257–259
attacks of 1622, English response to,
267–272
initial contact with the colonists, 51
Powhatan control of, 15
Smith, capture and captivity of,
61–66
Smith's conflict with
Opechancanough, 123–127
warriors of, 15, 19
*See also* Opechancanough
Paquiquineo. *See* Don Luís de Velasco
Parahunt, 15, 52, 167–169
Parker, William, 222
Paspaheghs, the
attacks against, 128, 186–188
attacks by, 52, 195
initial contact with the colonists, 48
the Jamestown site and, 56
plot to attack the settlement, 82
Wahunsonacock's referral to, 78
Patawomecks, the, 87, 175, 212, 214,
268–269
Peckham, Sir George, 23
Percy, George
the area and the native peoples,
observations regarding, 45, 47, 49,
51
attacks against the Nansemonds,
description of, 165, 199
on the ceremony of possession, 48
on the colonists' willingness to fight,
183, 205
crossing the Atlantic, description of,
42–43
disease and death among the
colonists, description of, 176,
178
exclusion from council membership,
47
exploration upriver, 50
Indians, offensives against, 186–187,
189

on the laws of Jamestown, 197
leadership, squabbling among,
164–165
leadership of, 174–177, 181, 190
Opechancanough, conflict with,
124–125
Point Comfort, effort to live at, 129
rebels from Martin's settlement,
comments on, 174
recruitment of, 40
report to Dale on the condition of
the colony, 195
Smith, allegations against, 168–169
trading trip to the Chickahominies,
110
on Wingfield, 58
Peréda, Don Gaspar de, 201
Perez, Marco Antonio, 203–204
Philip II (King of Spain), 2, 9, 25–26,
32, 262
Philip III (King of Spain), 141–142,
153, 200–203, 208
Piankatanks, the, 13
Pierce, William, 244
Piersey, Abraham, 280
Pilgrims, the, 241–242, 289
Piracy. *See* Privateers and piracy
Pissasecks, the, 92
Plymouth Company, 35, 37
Pocahontas
death of, 232
England, trip to, 225–232
kidnapping and captivity of,
212–215
marriage of, 217–218
portrait of, 228–229
Smith and, 68–70, 122–123,
230–232, 288–289
Pochins, 15
Popham, Sir John, 34–35
Pory, John, 246–247
Potts, Richard, 164
Pountis, John, 261
Powell, Nathaniel, 89, 151, 173

Powhatans, the
  attacks of 1622, 255–259
  attacks of 1622, English response to, 267–272
  De La Warr's war against, 183–190
  the English, initial contact with, 52–53
  Europeans, experience and knowledge of prior to Jamestown, 38
  European weapons, desire to obtain, 70–71
  exclusion of from English Virginia, 281–282
  Indian policy of the Virginia Company and, 147–149
  kidnapping of Pocahontas, confrontation regarding, 211–215
  leadership, change in, 249–250
  lost colony of Roanoke, slaughter of, 144–147
  peace with the English, establishment of, 215–216
  power shift in conflict with the English, 127
  principal settlements of, 1607–1611, 166
  proclamation of the English as, 78
  religion among, 20–22
  rise of, 11–16
  settlements and customs of, 16–22
  Smith, capture and captivity of, 61–71
  trip to England by a group of, 225–227
  upriver settlement, attacks against, 206–207
  West's settlement and, 167–169
  *See also* Wahunsonacock
Powle, Sir Stephen, 157
Price, Hugh, 178
Priests (Indian), 20–22, 65–66, 147
Privateers and piracy
  Dutch, 244

English, 24, 26, 33, 244
  English interest in Virginia and, 133
*Proceedings of the English Colonie in Virginia* (Smith), 230
Proctor, Mrs. John, 257
Purchas, Reverend Samuel, 226–227, 265–266

Quejo, Pedro de, 2
Quirós, Father Luís de, 5–7
Quiyoughcohannocks, the
  attacks against, 267, 271
  attacks by, 52, 257
  initial contact with the colonists, 48–49
  lost colonists, assistance in searching for, 173

Ralegh, Walter
  Chesapeake Bay region, initial exploration of, 38
  desire for riches as a motivator, observations regarding, 41
  the lost colony of Roanoke, 101, 103
  the Roanoke settlement, 26–27, 31–33
  tobacco, smoking of, 233
Rappahannocks, the, 91–92, 94, 267
Rastell, John, 23
Ratcliffe, John
  abandonment of the venture, plans for, 44, 74
  death of, 175
  discussions with Smythe, 133
  imprisonment of, 99
  initial voyage to Jamestown, 39–40
  leadership, squabbling among the, 57–58, 83, 87, 110–112, 163–165
  leadership of, 46, 59–60, 74, 83, 87–88
  Smith, finishing off, 169–170
Read, James, 58

Religion
  Christianity, conversion of the
    Indians to, 138–141, 200, 218,
    250–252, 254, 281
  dissenters, recruitment as settlers,
    241–243
  English colonization and, 24
  Jesuit missionary efforts, 5–8
  and magic, use of against the English,
    198–200
  Powhatan practices regarding, 20–22
  Spanish missionary efforts, 3–8
Ribault, Jean, 205
Rich, Barnaby, 233
Rich, Sir Robert, 276
Roanoke
  lost colonists of, 64, 101–104,
    143–147, 172–173
  settlement at, 26–33
Robinson, John, 241
Robinson, John (Jehu), 57, 61–62
Rolfe, John
  arrival in Virginia in 1617, 237, 249
  on the buying and selling of men and
    boys, 247
  expedition of 1609, departure of, 158
  marriage to Pocahontas, 217–218,
    223
  negotiations with Opechancanough,
    215
  return to England, 225, 230
  survey of the colony in 1616,
    234–236, 245
  tobacco, smoking and growing of,
    233–234
Rolfe, Lady Rebecca. *See* Pocahontas
Russell, John, 124

Salisbury, Earl of
  Dale, early recognition of the abilities
    of, 195
  Kendall, connections with, 46
  origins of the colony, role in, 35
  recruiting personnel, 40

settlers, Dale's complaints regarding
  the quality of, 196
Smith, letter making allegations
  against, 111–112
Sandys, George, 272–275, 277–278
Sandys, Sir Edwin
  attacks of 1622, response to, 264
  factional disputes in the Company,
    276–277
  failure of, 278
  Jamestown colony, supporter of, 46
  new charter for the colony, drafting
    of, 134–136
  recruitment of settlers, 241–244,
    248
  reinvigorate the colony, efforts to,
    236–237, 239–240, 246
  tobacco, opposition to, 234
Sasawpen, 254. *See also* Opitchapam
Sasenticum, 187
Savage, Richard, 118
Savage, Thomas, 79, 220
Scrivener, Matthew, 81, 88, 118, 127
Secota, 17–18
Secotans, the, 31–32
Segura, Father Juan de, 5, 7–8, 262
Sheffield, Thomas, 257
Sicklemore, Michael, 118, 151, 165,
  174
Siouan peoples, 14, 22
Slavery, 244–245, 284, 286–288
Smith, John
  on the aborted abandonment of the
    colony, 180
  background of, 35
  captivity, charges against after return
    from, 73–75
  captivity of, 61–71
  coronation of Wahunsonacock,
    105–108
  downfall of, 167–171
  in England, 230
  exploration of the Chesapeake Bay
    area, 50, 81, 83–98

Smith, John *(continued)*
  fortune, seeking of in America, 41
  *The Generall Historie of Virginia,
    New-England, and the Summer
    Isles,* 282–283
  gold fever and rivalries with other
    leaders, 80–81
  on Gosnold, 34
  Indians, allegations regarding
    treatment of, 105, 110
  Indians, loss of influence with, 127
  initial voyage to Jamestown, 42–44
  Kecoughtans, spending of Christmas
    with the, 186
  leadership, squabbling among the,
    42–44, 57–58, 74, 83, 103–105,
    110–113, 163–165
  leadership of, 46–47, 60, 81–82,
    99–100, 104, 109–110, 118,
    127–130, 136, 151–153, 155–156
  London Company, frustrations
    with/expressed to, 104–105,
    111–115, 133–134
  the lost colonists and, 173
  *Map of Virginia, A,* 69–70, 97, 230
  observations: the colony, 50, 56,
    59–60
  observations: the Indians, 19–20, 59
  Opechancanough, conflict with,
    123–127, 169
  Pocahontas and, 68–70, 122–123,
    228, 230–232, 288–289
  portrait of, 36
  *Proceedings of the English Colonie in
    Virginia, The,* 97
  response to the Indian attacks of
    1622, proposal for, 266–267
  self-memorializing of, 95–97
  Somers, discussions with, 158
  statue of, 288
  Virginia, map of, 69–70, 85,
    100–104, 114–117, 143
  Virginia Company plans, probable
    reaction to, 150–151

    Wahunsonacock and, 13, 22, 62,
      65–71, 73, 76–78, 83–84, 89,
      105–108, 118–123, 127, 169
Smith, Roger, 257
Smythe, Sir Thomas
  background and connections of, 132
  colonial activity in North America,
    support for, 34
  conditions at Jamestown,
    miscalculation and concerns
    regarding, 210–211
  conversion of the Indians to
    Christianity, goal of, 139, 218
  Dale, letter from in 1613, 208–209
  destitute children, transport of to
    Virginia, 244
  expedition of 1609, 157, 171, 174
  factional disputes in the Company,
    276–277
  laws of Jamestown, criticism based
    on, 197
  new colony in Virginia, plans for,
    142–144, 146–147
  on Newport's ore samples, 56
  Pocahontas and husband,
    introduction of in England, 227
  recruiting personnel, 40
  reform of the colony, 133, 135–137
  reinvigorate the colony, efforts to,
    236–237
  Smith, blame placed on, 230
  tobacco, opposition to, 234
Somers, Sir George
  Bermuda, provisions sought at, 182,
    195
  death of, 211
  expedition of 1609, 157–163,
    177–178
  leadership position under De La
    Warr, 181
Spain
  early activities in the Chesapeake Bay,
    1–9

Jamestown, reconnaissance
expeditions to, 153–155, 200–205
peace treaty with England, 34
rumored attack on Virginia by, 109,
208
threat posed to England by, 25–26,
32
Spelman, Henry, 168, 268
Strachey, William
agriculture, potential for, 149
expedition of 1609, 158–162, 178
Gates, policy toward the Indians of,
185
houses in Jamestown, description of,
183
Indian policy of the Virginia
Company, 147–148
Indians, observations regarding, 17,
20
the Kecoughtans as farmers, abilities
of, 186
laws of Jamestown, compilation of,
197
leadership position under De La
Warr, 181
lost colony of Roanoke, information
regarding, 144, 146
on the miserable state of the colony,
179
Wahunsonacock, description of, 13
West's deserters, description of, 175
Sugar, 283–284
Susquehannocks, the, 14, 17, 89–91
Symonds, Reverend William, 139–141

Tackonekintaco, 188
Tassore, 129
Thorpe, George, 251–252, 254,
257–258, 261
Tindall, Robert, 182
Tobacco
increasing cultivation and trade of,
238, 246–247, 280, 283–284

mixed reception of in England,
232–234
Tockwoughs, the, 88–89
Todkill, Anas, 89, 91–92, 151, 173
Trumbull, William, 171
Tucker, William, 270

Uttamatomakkin, 20, 225–227, 232

Van de Passe, Simon, 228
Velasco, Don Luís de, 201–203, 208
Velazquez, Antonio, 2–3
Virginia
the Chesapeake Bay. *See* Chesapeake
Bay
commerce and trade, significance of,
283–286
English ceremony of possession, 48
Jamestown colony. *See* Jamestown
colony
migrants to, wave of, 241–248
plans for a new and reformed
settlement in, 142–150
Protestant crusade, anticipation of,
138–141
Roanoke settlement, 26–33
slavery in, 244–245, 284, 286–288
Smith's map of, 69–70, 85, 97,
100–104, 114–117, 143, 230
tobacco growing in, 232–234, 238,
246–247, 280, 283–284
Virginia Company
attacks of 1622, attempts to recover
from, 272–276
attacks of 1622, response to,
262–267, 270
demise of, 276–278
expedition of 1609, response to the
disaster of, 171–174
factional disputes in, 276–277
financial difficulties of, 208
Indian policy of, 147–149,
183–184

Virginia Company *(continued)*
the lost colony of Roanoke and, 143–147, 172–173
maintaining control in Virginia, 240
plans for a new and reformed settlement, 142–150
plans for a new and reformed settlement, Smith's probable reaction to, 150–151
Pocahontas and additional Indians, bringing to England of, 225–230, 232
Protestantism, conversion of the Indians to, 138–139, 250–252, 281
recruitment of settlers, 241–245, 248
reform of the colony in 1609, 132–138
reinvigoration of the colony, efforts lead by Sandys toward, 236–241
reports of De La Warr and Gates, 190–192
significance of the activities of, 193
sincerity of the Indians regarding peace, belief in, 261
Smith and, 136, 152–153, 170–171, 230
tobacco, opposition to and profit from, 234, 246–247
*See also* London Company
Virginia Council
creation of, 37
creation of new version in 1609, 135
instructions of, 50, 52–53
leadership of the colony, arrangements regarding, 43, 46–47
Sandys as member of, 135

Wahunsonacock
ambush set by, 175
attacks commanded by, 86–87
"coronation" of, 105–108
Dale's marriage proposal, response to, 220–222
Dale's plan to subdue, 198
De La Warr, relations with, 184–185
departure and death of, 249–250
dominance of, challenges to, 214
the English, initial description of to, 31, 50
the English, perceptions of, 286
the English, testing of, 52–53
the Germans, winning over and usage of, 123–124
gods, satan, and magic, use of against the English, 199
lost colony of Roanoke and, 102, 144–147, 173
Newport, meeting with, 77–80
peace agreement with the English, perception of, 222–223
Pocahontas, consent to the marriage of, 218
Pocahontas, response to the kidnapping of, 212–216
rise of the chiefdom of, 12–15
Smith and, 13, 22, 62, 65–71, 73–74, 83–84, 89, 105–108, 118–123, 127, 151–152, 169
the Spanish and, 11
upriver base of the English, attempts to thwart, 206–207
Virginia Company policy regarding, 147–149
warfare of, 17, 19–20
Wainman, Sir Ferdinando, 181
Waldo, Richard, 105, 127
Wanchese, 27, 38
Want, John, 161–162
Warraskoyacks, the, 118–119, 187–188, 258–259, 267, 271
Warwick, Earl of, 276
Waterhouse, Edward, 255, 257–258, 264–265
Weld, Hugh, 137
West, Francis
antagonizing the Indians, 175
fort at the falls left by, 189
leadership, squabbling among, 164–165
leadership of, 167–169

Opechancanough, conflict with,
124–125
return to England, 226
Smith, finishing off, 169
upriver, effort to live, 129
wounding of, 198
West, Sir Thomas. *See* De La Warr,
twelfth Baron
West, William, 190
Weyanocks, the, 52, 257–258, 267, 271
Whitaker, Alexander, 199–200, 217,
235
White, John
Chesapeake Bay region, initial
explorations of, 38
Chesapeake Bay settlement, abortive
attempt at, 31–32
maps drawn by, 115
the Roanoke colony, 27, 30, 103, 145
Winganuske, 144
Wingfield, Edward Maria
departure of, 81
landfall and leadership of the council,
45–47
leadership, squabbling among the,
57–59, 74
origins of the colony, role in, 34
recruiting the personnel, 40
selection of a site, opinion regarding,
49
Smith, dislike of, 43–44, 58
Somers, discussions with, 158
Wingina, 31
Winwood, Sir Ralph, 226
Wolstenholme, Sir John, 248
Wotton, Thomas, 74
Wowinchopunck, 64, 102, 104, 128,
190
Wyatt, George, 261–262
Wyatt, Lady Margaret, 274
Wyatt, Sir Francis
arrival at Jamestown in 1621,
272
attacks of 1622, response to, 258,
261, 263–264, 267, 271, 278

bright prospects of, 280
King's commissioners, report to, 281
relations with the Indians,
instructions regarding, 252
sincerity of the Indians regarding
peace, belief in, 254, 261
Wynne, Peter, 163

Yeardley, Sir George
arrival in Virginia in 1619, 243
attacks of 1622, 258
attacks of 1622, response to, 268
Bermuda Nether Hundred,
leadership at, 235
bright prospects of, 280
enrichment of in Virginia, 247, 285
Fort Charles, abandonment of, 189
Kecoughtan territory, temporary
overseeing of, 186
leadership position under De La
Warr, 181
new laws, instructions to introduce,
239
plantation owned by, 245
religious conversion of the Indians,
cautions regarding, 251
sincerity of the Indians regarding
peace, belief in, 253–254, 261
on Thorpe, 251

Zúñiga, Don Pedro de
De La Warr's expedition, report on,
180
deteriorating conditions at
Jamestown, report of, 171
English preparations for a new
expedition, concerns regarding,
141–142
Smith's "map of Virginia," 90
Virginia, report on English interest
in, 56, 133